"Accomplished, sophisticated…this biography is splendid in every way."

— WASHINGTON POST

"Lambert brings the perspective of a Hollywood insider and family intimate."

— DAILY NEWS

"His ability to spin a yarn makes this a bio that's revealing and rewarding without slinging mud."

— PEOPLE

"[A] scrupulously written and highly insightful book….a page-turner of a biography."

— THE ADVOCATE

"Gavin Lambert has found an almost perfect subject….She was a movie star, from probably the last period when stars were still icons and not like other people, and she made all of stardom's stops – multiple lovers, marriages, substance abuse, suicide attempts…Lambert's special gift is to understand perfectly both the star and the complicated child woman…Robert Wagner gave him unconditional access and freedom from having to dissimulate [that] give the book its power and grace."

— THE NEW YORK REVIEW OF BOOKS

"Engrossing."

— SAN FRANCISCO CHRONICLE

"Gavin Lambert's riveting biography of Natalie Wood is sure to surprise and enlighten even veteran industry insiders as well as neophytes, film buffs and social anthropologists. It's an honest, meticulously researched work."

— VARIETY

"Gavin Lambert does nearly everything right with his straightforward account of the late actress Natalie Wood…never dull, always confident, and sometimes quite lively."

— THE SANTA FE NEW MEXICAN

"Wagner gave Lambert full cooperation for the book, telling his friends to share their memories as well."
— CNN.COM

"Where Lambert really scores is in his appreciation of Natalie Wood as an actress. He accurately and elegantly rates her talents, which were, ironically, in full bloom at the time of her death."
— LIZ SMITH, NEW YORK POST

"While there is plenty of frothy gossip here, the author's relationship with his subject gives this biography a special poignancy."
— FORT WORTH STAR TELEGRAM

"Lambert deconstructs Wood's multifaceted character and supplies an insider's look at her life."
— OMAHA WORLD-HERALD

"This affectionate new bio gets straight to the heart of the matter, illuminating the particular appeal of the angst-ridden deb of *Rebel Without a Cause* and *Splendor in the Grass.*"
— SEATTLE WEEKLY

"Lambert has written something unique in biographical literature: a book that regards its subject with objectivity, yet is unsparingly personal when it comes to dealing with the details of an inner life that only a close friend would know. And this is ideal for Natalie Wood – an actress whose singular power was an ability to evoke intimacy."
— LA WEEKLY

"[A] very good book."
— MERCURY NEWS

"A splendid recounting of an actress's life."
— ATLANTA JOURNAL-CONSTITUTION

"A fully researched book that sheds much new light on the career and tragic end at age 43 of one of film's most beautiful stars."
— RICHMOND TIMES

# NATALIE WOOD

# NATALIE WOOD

— *A Life* —

# GAVIN LAMBERT

BACK STAGE BOOKS / NEW YORK

Senior Editor: Mark Glubke
Project Editor: Katherine Happ
Cover Design: Carol Devine Carson
Interior Design: Virginia Tam
Production Manager: Hector Campbell

Paperback edition first published in 2005 by Back Stage Books, an imprint of Watson-Guptill Publications, a division of VNU Business Media, Inc., 770 Broadway, New York, NY 10003
www.wgpub.com

Published by arrangement with Alfred A. Knopf, a division of Random House, Inc.

Library of Congress Control Number: 2005920414

ISBN: 0-8230-8829-4

Cover photograph: Photofest

Manufactured in the United States of America

First printing 2005

1 2 3 4 5 6 7 8 9 / 12 11 10 09 08 07 06 05

This book was set in Adobe Garamond.
Composed by North Market Street Graphics,
Lancaseter, Pennsylvania

*To Leslie Caron*

Everyone who has studied the matter in depth says it is not necessary to die, ever, but one by one everybody has died, including the specialists who had said that it was really not necessary, but they probably left messages saying that yes, it is not necessary, they simply decided they wanted to, and did, and thus became the same as the rest of us, the living who die, but one thing is certain and painful: it is not fun at all when somebody dies prematurely.

—William Saroyan, *Obituaries*

# CONTENTS

# ILLUSTRATIONS

# NATALIE
# WOOD

# I

# Out of Russia

*Everything Russian is feeling. Everything in the Russian landscape is full of the melody of the inside. That is Russia. It is not America. We are agitated, but we are not emotionally free people. We don't cry when the snow falls. The English are not like that either, neither are the French. There is only Russia left, with that extreme sensibility of reacting, caring, feeling.*

—STELLA ADLER

SHORTLY AFTER ELEVEN P.M. on November 6, 1917 (New Style calendar), the Bolsheviks seized power by storming government buildings and the Winter Palace in Petrograd (now St. Petersburg). After months of violent disorders throughout Russia, the revolution was under way; and as the majority members (*Bolsheviki*) of the Socialist Party believed in "dictatorship of the proletariat and the peasants," thousands of wealthy landowners and businessmen realized their lands and businesses would be confiscated, and fled the country with all the money and possessions they could take with them. Supporters and/or relatives of Tsar Nicholas II (government ministers, army officers, princes and grand dukes with their wives and children) also took flight, and when fighting between Bolshevik and anti-Bolshevik forces erupted across the country, thousands more fled their homes to become refugees from a savage and devastating civil war.

Among the refugees were two families, one rich, one poor, living three thousand miles apart. A daughter of the rich family and a son of the poor family eventually emigrated to California, met in San Francisco, and were married on February 8, 1938. The Russian Orthodox ceremony took place at the Russian church on Fulton Street, when the bride was almost five months pregnant, and the following July a future star was born.

IN 1917, Stepan Zudilov was forty-two years old, a portly, prosperous middle-class businessman who owned soap and candle factories in Barnaul, southern Siberia, and an estate in the outlying countryside. By then he had fathered a large family: two sons and two daughters by his first wife, who died in 1905 after giving birth to their younger daughter; and by his second wife, whom he married a year later, two more daughters followed by two more sons.

His youngest daughter, Maria Stepanovna, born in 1912, claimed years later in California that her mother came from an aristocratic family with Romanov connections, and had "married beneath her." But this was Maria the fabulist speaking, with her dreams of nobility, and Zudilov the outspoken tsarist and land-and-factory owner had no need of Romanov connections to qualify for the Bolshevik hit list. The Zudilovs were known as "gentry," and to the Bolsheviks all landowning gentry were suspect, like the family of the great Russian writer Ivan Bunin (who won the Nobel Prize for literature in 1933). "Any of us who had the slightest chance to escape did so," Bunin wrote after he fled from his estate in central Russia to France by way of Romania.

But the armies of the new government headed by Lenin were slow to gain control of an enormous country, and for almost a year the Zudilovs, like their tsarist neighbors, were in no imminent danger by remaining in Barnaul. It was not until the summer of 1918, six months after the civil war broke out, that the Bolsheviks managed to gain control of all southern and central Russia. On the night of July 16, Tsar Nicholas II, his entire family, their doctor and servants, were executed by a squad of Red Guards at Ekaterinburg, the western terminus of the Trans-Siberian Railway. When the news reached Barnaul, it sent tremors of fear throughout the neighboring gentry; and by late November, Red Guard units were only a hundred miles from the town, after executing suspected tsarists en route.

Zudilov had arranged to be warned of their approach in advance, and when the alert came, the family hurried to a prepared hiding place on the estate, stuffing as much money and jewelry as they could inside loose-fitting peasant clothes. Forgotten in the panic of the moment was eighteen-year-old Mikhail, Zudilov's eldest son, who happened to be out of the house.

After the soldiers moved on, the family left their hiding place. Just outside the house, they were confronted by Mikhail hanging from a tree. The sight of her dead half-brother sent six-year-old Maria into convulsions.

KNOWING THE SOLDIERS were bound to return, the Zudilovs quickly made plans to leave Russia, and in the dead of winter they set out for Harbin in Manchuria, the northeastern province of China. Maria claimed later that they traveled by private train, with a retinue of servants as well as stacks of rubles and the family jewels stowed in their luggage. Although there's no doubt they escaped with enough assets to live very comfortably in exile, the private train is almost certainly another example of Maria the fabulist.

Red Guards were still searching the area for potential enemies of the new Soviet Russia, and a private train would have aroused immediate suspicion. But as Barnaul was a stop on the Trans-Siberian Railway, only four hundred miles from the Manchurian frontier, and Harbin the last stop before Vladivostok for eastbound trains, it seems far more likely that the Zudilovs decided to keep a low profile and traveled by the regular route.

When the child from a secluded country estate looked out the train window during that journey of almost three thousand miles, she would have glimpsed the same frighteningly alien world as the Anglo-Russian novelist William Gerhardie, who traveled by the Trans-Siberian that same year. He saw a "stricken land of misery," with ravenous and spectral refugees huddled on the platform when the train slowed down past a wayside station; dismal tracts of frozen steppe, occasionally swept by a violent gale that caused the coaches to rattle, squeal and shudder; and near the Chinese frontier, where civil war had been especially ferocious, a wake of gutted villages and more desperate refugees, some dying or dead.

*Ivan Bunin: No one who did not actually witness it can com-
prehend what the Russian Revolution quickly turned into.
The spectacle was sheer terror for anyone who had not utterly
lost sight of God.*

Like thousands of other refugees, Zudilov chose Harbin because it
was a Chinese city with a strong Russian presence. The Byzantine dome
of the Russian cathedral dominated its skyline, and there was an extensive Russian quarter, part business, part residential, with street signs in
Russian, droshkies instead of rickshaws, restaurants that served borsch
and beef Stroganoff. Japan had also moved in, with trading concessions
at the port on the Songhua River, investments in the city's grain mills,
and a chain of "Happiness Mansions," brothels that featured very young
boys as well as girls; and Britain, with the British Export Company,
which employed ruthlessly underpaid Chinese to slaughter thousands of
pigs, fowl and sheep every year, then freeze them for export to the homeland and the United States.

Business as usual, of course, meant politics as usual, colonial expan-
sion in a country weakened by years of internal rebellions led by rival
warlords. By the spring of 1918, Russian nationals formed almost a third
of Harbin's population of three hundred thousand, and the Chinese
quarter was just a suburb, like a picturesque Chinatown set in a Hollywood silent movie; while the much larger central downtown area, with
its handsome beaux-arts railroad station and Hotel Moderne, looked
solidly Western. Under the agreement between Russia and China, the
stretch of the Trans-Siberian that crossed Manchuria was officially
known as the Chinese Eastern Railway; but it was Russian-financed,
maintained by Russian workers, and guarded by regiments of Russian
soldiers headquartered in Harbin.

And in the wake of the revolution, the Zudilovs escaped one political
upheaval only to find themselves in the middle of another. Not long
before they arrived, fighting had broken out between Red and White
Russian workers and guards on the railway. The Soviet government had
sent in militiamen to rout the anti-Bolsheviks; and in case a full-scale
civil war developed, the Japanese made ready to invade Manchuria and
seize control of the Chinese Eastern. At the end of December, when the
Zudilovs reached Harbin, the Chinese government intervened by send-

ing in an army to disarm and deport the Soviet militia; and for the moment at least, the situation was defused.

A few weeks later, on February 8, 1919, the Zudilovs celebrated Maria's seventh birthday. Although she was too young, of course, to understand the ways of the great world, the flight from Barnaul had stamped images of warning and terror on her mind. Like most Russian refugees, the Zudilovs stayed within their own community of exiles, ignoring China and the Chinese; but as she grew up, Maria couldn't fail to notice—beyond the house in the Russian quarter where Zudilov established his family with a Chinese cook and a German nanny for the girls, and the Russian school where she occasionally took ballet lessons as well as regular classes—more warning signs that the great world was a disturbingly insecure place.

Throughout the 1920s, the city witnessed several outbreaks of fighting between Red and White Russians, parades of underpaid Chinese workers on strike against foreign companies, and street demonstrations by the growing nationalist movement. In 1920 one of these demonstrations led to violence, and smoke covered the city when the storage plant of the British Export Company was burned to the ground. Occasional Soviet threats to invade Manchuria and restore order sent shivers of alarm through the exiles; and an increasingly familiar experience for Maria was the sight of Russians who had arrived in style, like her own family, reduced to begging in the streets when their money ran out.

The sight of her half-brother hanging from a tree had produced Maria's first convulsion. It soon led to others, when something frightened her or when she didn't get her own way. As a result she was considered delicate, pampered and spoiled by her parents and nanny. As a further result, Maria learned that she could get her own way by throwing a fit. She grew cunning, but at the same time incurably superstitious, and most of her superstitions were based on fear. At first they were the conventional ones: the bad luck caused by breaking a mirror, leaving a hat on your bed, or touching a peacock feather. But they grew quite bizarre with time, like her more extreme fantasies. Years later, in California, she told her daughters that she was a foundling, born into a Gypsy family that taught her fortune-telling, explained the dangers lurking in everyday signs, and later abandoned her on a Siberian steppe.

AMONG THE MULTITUDE of poor Russians, peasants and laborers, some had never heard the word "revolution" before, and thought it meant a woman chosen to replace the tsar. The poor, in fact, simply fled the chaos of civil war: famine, butchery, looting, skyrocketing inflation. In Vladivostok, a subzero city on a bleak peninsula in Far Eastern Siberia, almost half the population had been reduced to near-starvation, and some died of cold on the wooden sidewalks rotting under heavy snow.

Hundreds more died in the street fighting that broke out in November 1918 between Red and White Russian soldiers. Among the dead was Stepan Zacharenko, who worked in a chocolate factory and joined the anti-Bolshevik civilian forces who fought side by side with the Whites. His widow escaped by train to Shanghai with her three young sons, and wrote to ask for help from her brother, who had emigrated to Canada. With the money he sent, she bought steerage tickets on a boat that left Shanghai for Vancouver, but it's unclear whether she traveled with her sons or remained behind.

In August 2000, the youngest Zacharenko son, Dmitri, was living in Palm Springs. At first he insisted that his mother remarried in Shanghai, and her new husband, a Russian engineer, brought her to Canada, where the family was reunited. But at eighty-five Dmitri's memory was erratic, and he later contradicted himself by insisting that he and his brothers were sent to live with their uncle and aunt in Montreal.

Although Dmitri wasn't always sure what he remembered, it's certain that he and his brothers, Nikolai and Vladimir, attended school in Montreal, learned to speak serviceable English, and soon heard the call to go west. As a young boy, Nikolai had acquired a passion for reading and learned to play the balalaika. As a young man, he became a migrant worker, took any job that would bring him nearer California, and developed into an expert carpenter along the way. But in San Francisco he had to take the only job on offer at first, as a janitor at the Standard Oil Building.

Vladimir, the oldest brother, played violin; Dmitri played mandolin; and when the three Zacharenkos met up in San Francisco, they formed a trio with Nikolai on balalaika to earn extra money at local dance halls. Although Vladimir eventually became a nuclear engineer, and Dmitri worked as chief accountant to an automobile tire company after joining the U.S. Army and being awarded a Purple Heart in World War II, Nikolai appeared to place his future on indefinite hold. In 1934, the year he met Maria, he was working at the docks, loading and unloading the sugarcane boats that plied the coastal ports between San Francisco and San Diego.

A PHOTOGRAPH of Maria in Harbin with her mother, sister, two half-sisters and German nanny shows a dark-haired girl with strikingly intense eyes. She faces the camera confidently, directly, as if daring it not to find her more attractive than her siblings. She looks around sixteen, so the photograph was probably taken in 1928, the year she met and fell in love with a Russian-Armenian regimental officer from one of the military units stationed in Harbin.

"When I was young," Maria said many years later in California, "I was ruled by my heart, not my head." So was her own mother, she added, who was forced to break off her affair with an impoverished aristocrat to marry Zudilov, a merger arranged by the heads of their respective families. And Maria claimed to have married Captain Alexei Tatulov in secret, because she feared her father would consider him "unsuitable."

For "heart that ruled the head," read "sexual drive." Maria probably inherited it from her mother, and there's no doubt the same gene recurred even more strongly in her famous daughter.

IN MARIA'S sometimes conflicting accounts of her early life, she never discussed her parents' reaction to her secret marriage to Tatulov. But in 1929, after the birth of their daughter, Olga, it was clearly no longer a secret. At Tatulov's insistence, Olga was baptized in the Armenian Orthodox Church; and when Zudilov learned that he had a grand-daughter, he accepted the situation on condition that a Russian Orthodox priest rebaptize her.

Maria also claimed that her father started to run short of funds soon after Olga was born, and as he could no longer afford to make her an allowance, she earned money by joining a ballet company. But her daughter Olga Viripaeff, who lives today in the Richmond district of San Francisco, where so many early Russian immigrants settled, says she

*Harbin, 1927. Left to right: seated, Maria and her mother; standing, Zoya, Lilia, German nanny, Kalia*

never heard that the Zudilovs had financial problems, and in any case Maria never had enough training to be accepted by a ballet company. Olga knew for certain, however, that one of her father's Russian friends emigrated to San Francisco, found employment there with an upholstery company and encouraged Tatulov to follow his example.

Toward the end of 1929, Tatulov left by boat to San Francisco, promising to arrange for wife and daughter to join him soon as he found a job. For an immigrant seeking his fortune in the United States, the timing was bad. The stock market had crashed a few weeks earlier, and the Great Depression soon followed. Although Tatulov managed to find work in the shipyards, he also found true love; and as he wrote Maria in the summer of 1930, he was living with another woman but wanted to bring his wife and daughter to safety in the U.S.A.

In November 1930 the American consul in Harbin granted Maria a visa. Many years later, in the course of an interview as a "Star Mother," she claimed that her voyage to California with eighteen-month-old Olga began as a long overland trip to Pusan in Korea, continued by ferry to the Japanese mainland, then by another train to Yokohama, where they boarded a Japanese ship. Bound for San Francisco by way of Hawaii, it arrived there the first week of January 1931.

The Japanese ship is the only reality here. But they boarded it from Shanghai, reached far more easily and quickly by direct train from Harbin. Maria, whose flair for dramatic fabrication coexisted with a very practical talent for camouflage, no doubt invented the more arduous route partly to underscore her disillusion at journey's end and partly to cover her tracks. In the same interview, Maria never mentioned that she met another exiled Russian on board the *Tatuta Maru*. Nicholas Lepko had been working for an American newsreel company based in Shanghai, where the pay (known locally as "rice money") was very low; and he accepted at once when a former colleague, who had emigrated to Los Angeles, offered to arrange an apprentice job with a film company there. Lepko's wife, Tamara, was a dancer who had studied with Olga Preobrajenskaya, a prima ballerina at the Maryinsky Theater in St. Petersburg. Like so many Russian dancers, they went into exile after the revolution, Preobrajenskaya to Paris and Tamara to Shanghai, where she proved extraordinarily resourceful. From chorus girl in elaborate floor shows at the city's nightclubs, she graduated to choreographing routines; and as she earned better money than her husband, she decided to remain in Shanghai until his future in California appeared settled.

Maria and Lepko: a shipboard romance or just good friends? In view of Maria's later history, romance is a possibility; but she certainly became more than good friends with Lepko fourteen years later in California.

Also in the same interview, Maria created a more dramatic version of her arrival in San Francisco and the reunion with her husband, who now spelled his name Tatuloff, following the example of most Russian immigrants with a last name ending in -ov. She claimed that he'd never written to tell her about the woman he was living with, but broke the news on the quayside. ("We Armenians," he explained, "are very passionate, we can't stay a whole year without. . . .") Then he insisted that he still loved Maria as well as his other love ("He was very nice man") and proposed a ménage à trois. Although she refused, Maria, Olga, Tatuloff and his other love lived together for a while in one room at a wretched boardinghouse. And although Tatuloff was very passionate, "I wouldn't let him touch me."

After the trauma of escaping from Russia, Maria also said, she at least had the consolation of loving parents and a comfortable home in

*Harbin, 1928. Just married: Maria and Alexei Tatuloff*

Harbin; but her second exile began in near-poverty, she had lost her husband to another woman, she spoke and understood hardly any English—and furthermore she hated Coca-Cola.

Maria undoubtedly fell on material and emotional hard times for a while, but Olga's account of their first months in San Francisco differs in a few significant details and is generally more credible. She agreed that her father was waiting on the quayside, but as he'd already written the "Dear Maria" letter, he simply took them both to the rooming house where he and several other immigrant shipyard workers lived. To Maria, the place seemed horribly unrefined, and she demanded that Tatuloff find an apartment for the three of them. Over the next few months, Olga recalled, they kept moving from one small apartment to another, and as Maria's addiction to American movies soon became as intense as her dislike of Coca-Cola, she embarked on the impossible search for an affordable home with a touch of Hollywood class.

Olga also remembered that while Tatuloff spent most evenings with his other love, Maria began to lead a fairly active and romantic social life. In fact, after the shock of a second displacement, from husband as well as family, she was obliged to fall back almost entirely on herself.

And if the Maria of the 1930s is remembered as witty, charming, generous and pleasure-loving, strikingly at variance with the later, demonic Maria, it's because her demons were still (sometimes uneasily) asleep.

By one of the many recurring coincidences in Maria's life, Alexei Tatuloff had become friends with a fellow worker at the docks whose real name was Nikolai Zacharenko but now called himself Nicholas Gurdin (easier to pronounce and spell, he thought, especially for prospective employers; more American, yet not totally un-Russian). And after changing Maria's life by bringing her to California, Tatuloff did the same for Nick Gurdin by introducing him to his future wife.

Nick's handsome, sensitive face, with its small, dark, narrow eyes, seemed at odds with his stocky build and powerful hands, but it was only after they married that Maria discovered a man at odds with himself. When they first met, she was charmed by the way he played and sang ineffably sad Russian folksongs on his balalaika; and their mutual love of music and dancing, as well as nostalgia for tsarist Russia, brought the couple together. In April 1936 Maria left Tatuloff and moved into Nick's one-room apartment with Olga. A year later she secured her divorce, and in October 1937 Nick asked her to marry him. Did he wait until he'd earned enough to support a wife and stepdaughter, was it simply another example of his habit of postponing the future or had he noticed signs of the temperamental differences that would erupt later?

All of the above, most likely. Nick had certainly fallen in love with Maria, and Maria certainly found him very attractive. But when she hesitated before agreeing to become Nick's wife, she had two very urgent reasons that he knew nothing about.

Of the several Russian immigrants who took the China route to California, hoped to create new lives for themselves, and in the process became major prenatal influences on the life of an unborn star, Tatuloff was the first. Maria followed, then Nick Gurdin; and last but far from least came the remarkable George Zepaloff, the "great romantic love" of Maria's life and the main cause of her hesitation over Nick's proposal.

Zepaloff's father had worked for the Trans-Siberian Railway and was transferred to Harbin around 1920. George never met Maria or any of

the Zudilovs there, and when his parents separated, he and his sister
went to live with their mother, who found work in Shanghai as governess in a Chinese family. Until 1929 or 1930, when he emigrated to
California, there's a gap in Zepaloff's life, and although he talked very
little about his past, including his life in Shanghai, growing up in that
city at that time surely helped him acquire a taste for the fancy-free existence he managed to lead later as a sailor.

Shanghai was Harbin on a larger, wealthier and more sophisticated
scale. Once again Western and Japanese corporations dominated ship-
ping, manufacturing and transportation; and the Chinese quarter, where
the poor lived, formed less than a tenth of the area occupied by the International Settlement and the French Concession. When Zepaloff lived
there, Shanghai was a city of rival opium gangs and raffish dockside
cafes, where sailors from all over the world picked up White Russian
prostitutes, and of more upscale dance palaces with Chinese taxi dancers
and White Russian "hostesses." The Hungarian wife of an English broker was another kind of hostess. Bernardine Fritz (later a colorful resident of Hollywood in the 1960s) gave lavish parties for the international
set, mixing European diplomats and bankers with Chinese opera singers
and an elegant madam from San Francisco, who ran the most expensive
whorehouse in town, stocked exclusively with American girls.

Wallis Warfield Simpson, waiting out her divorce from a wealthy
husband, divided her time between Bernardine's soirées and the garden
courtyard of the Majestic Hotel, where moonlight, jasmine and a Fil-
ipino orchestra playing "Tea for Two" made her feel that Shanghai was
"very good, almost too good for a woman." In 1927, in that same courtyard, the same orchestra played "Here Comes the Bride" at the wedding
of Chiang Kai-shek and Mei-ling Soong. Their marriage sealed an
alliance between the commander-in-chief of the Nationalist Army and
the wealthiest family in China, most of whom believed that Chiang was
the only man capable of uniting the country against the warlords and an
emergent Communist Party. A year later, when Chiang became head of
the Nationalist government as well as its army, it was a sign that the old
days would soon be over in Shanghai as well.

For George Zepaloff (who at first spelled his last name with the Russian -ov), the new days began when he joined the Mercury Athletic Club
in San Francisco. He played for its soccer team and quickly developed
into a versatile gymnast and athlete. In 1932 he competed in the Los

Angeles Summer Olympics and was awarded a gold cup inscribed "All Around Gymnastic Trophy, First Place Won by George Zepalov."

Back in San Francisco he became George Zepaloff, studied navigation, then got a job as second mate on a Matson Line cruise ship that made the San Francisco–Los Angeles–Honolulu round trip. And by the time he met Maria, she was a popular figure at dances and charity balls.

THERE WERE TWO social clubs for Russian exiles in San Francisco, the Russian Center and Kolobok. Both held regular dances, staged occasional plays and ballets. Like many Russians, Maria was captivated by the glamour of ballet, and although she had never seen Diaghilev's Ballets Russes, she had heard about their great success in Europe; and at the Russian Center she met another ballerina from the Maryinsky. Nadjeda Ermolova, now a ballet teacher, had seen Nijinsky and Karsavina perform. Several times a year she presented excerpts from *Les Sylphides* and *Swan Lake* danced by her students, and Maria quickly became part of her circle.

At the Center Maria also met Nina Kiyaschenko, whose father had been a well-known tsarist general. Nina was only a year old when she escaped with her parents in the winter of 1918–19 and, like Maria, made the Trans-Siberian journey to Harbin. After moving on to Shanghai, the Kiyaschenkos eventually emigrated to San Francisco; and when Nina's father appeared at the Center, he always wore a two-headed eagle pin in his lapel and, from shoulders to hip, a tsarist ribbon in white, blue and red.

But nostalgia for the old days wasn't confined to the older generation. When they fled Russia, the parents of Maria and Nina, the Lepkos, Ermolova and many others were convinced the revolution would fail and they'd be able to return. They passed on this belief to their children and the children of their friends; and like Kiyaschenko with his tsarist ribbon and pin, Maria persisted in the fantasy of her mother's connection to the Romanovs, lowering her voice to a reverent hush when she mentioned their name. But after Stalin became the absolute ruler of Soviet Russia, parents and children alike had to face the reality of permanent exile.

For Maria, the Center's two most important charity balls, held once a year in aid of the White Russian Veterans and the Russian Invalids, were invitations to nostalgia. Whoever collected the most money for these causes became Queen of the Ball; and Maria worked her way up from one of four Princesses in 1935 to Queen of the Invalids in 1936, then Queen of the Veterans in 1937. Photographs of her royal triumphs show her posed in a Romanov dream, wearing a ballgown and a pasteboard crown studded with costume jewelry.

At Kolobok, according to Nina Kiyaschenko, the atmosphere was "more bohemian." Although Saturday nights were reserved for "old-timers who wore evening clothes and danced the waltz," on other nights the young fox-trotted to an American-style dance band, played pool, appeared in plays or performed solos. Olga recalled that her mother liked to sing, "and although she couldn't carry a tune, she'd get up on the Kolobok stage and interpret the words of Russian folksongs so vividly that she always got a round of applause." Maria also entertained by consulting tarot cards to tell fortunes, and took small parts in a few plays.

But the star performer at Kolobok was the dance band's young man with a trumpet, George Zepaloff. "He charmed all the girls," Nina remembered. "He would open and close his trumpet stops and make naughty, suggestive noises. Everyone laughed and asked for more." Although not strikingly handsome, and of medium height, Zepaloff had "a very good physique, perfectly proportioned body, slim waist, fine muscles." Initially attracted to Maria, he later married Nina for a while, and he became "the great romantic love" of both their lives. And the affair with Maria, which began before she met Nick Gurdin and was still living together with but apart from Alexei Tatuloff, would last on and off for more than thirty years.

Years later, Maria claimed that she became pregnant in the mid-1930s by a man she refused to name, hemorrhaged in childbirth, was pronounced dead at the hospital, then woke up in the embalming room and screamed for help. It sounds like a fantasy, but Olga said it actually happened. No doubt Zepaloff was the father, as Tatuloff discovered Maria in bed with him soon after their affair began. Not that he minded. By then he'd left the other love for another love, and after hearing that Maria's life was in danger, he brought a priest to the hospital, then accompanied her supposedly dead body to the embalming room.

*Nina (Kiyaschenko) Jaure: I think some of those young lives were wilder then than the lives of the young today. But they*

*San Francisco, 1935. Maria, a "Princess"*
*at the White Russian Veterans Ball*

*had so little money, their future was so uncertain, they needed*
*adventure and were often reckless in searching for it.*

Five feet tall, with a sharp chin and eyes that Olga described as "changeable gray-blue" and others recalled as "almost black" and "ice-blue," Maria never struck anyone as a great beauty, just as Zepaloff (who Maria later said looked like George Murphy, the actor-dancer she'd admired in *Broadway Melody of 1938*) was not conventionally handsome. But they both had vitality, charm and (at least in the early days) an alluring erotic energy.

There was also a temperamental affinity. Zepaloff "lived two lives, one out at sea, and one in port," according to Richard Benson, the companion of his daughter by Nina. "He often talked about 'life in different ports of call,' where he spent much more time than at home. And he was charismatic. He drew you in." And Maria, as she began to live two lives like Zepaloff, could draw people into her fantasies as persuasively as she drew them into the truth when she decided to tell it.

Zepaloff, who was presumably at sea when Maria almost died, graduated to first mate in January 1937 and shortly afterward proposed marriage. Maria said she needed time to think it over, and this time her head overruled her heart. The marriage would never work, she decided, because her lover spent weeks and sometimes months at sea, they met only when his ship put in at San Francisco, and during a long separation Maria grew afraid that the Captain (as she always referred to him after his promotion some years later) would fall in love with someone else.

Did Maria have the example of Tatuloff in mind, even though she herself had taken Nick Gurdin as a lover during one of those long separations from her Captain? In any case, contradictions never seemed to bother her. When Nick proposed in October that year, she'd been living with him for eighteen months while remaining secretly "faithful" to the Captain each time he returned to port.

But Maria's fear of a precarious life as Mrs. Zepaloff was not her only reason for becoming Mrs. Gurdin. She was pregnant; and having juggled assignations with two lovers all the while, she remembered her last loving farewell to the Captain before he went to sea again and concluded (a belief she held for the rest of her life) that he was the father. She also probably knew that Zepaloff was not interested in fatherhood, something he later made very clear to Nina and their daughter.

Although marriage to Nicholas Gurdin didn't make Maria a faithful wife, and the Captain's marriage to Nina Kiyaschenko didn't make him a faithful husband, the shared excitement of secrecy, deceit, mischief and a life on the edge kept the lovers faithful to each other. Because it was a Russian custom for the second given name of a child to acknowledge his or her father's first name, Stepan Zudilov's daughter had been baptized Maria Stepanovna. Was Maria sending a secret, mischievous signal (she later sent many others) when the birth certificate dated July 20, 1938, recorded the name of Maria and Nicholas Gurdin's daughter as, simply, Natalie Zacharenko?

*San Francisco, 1941. Just married: Nina Kiyaschenko*
*and "the Captain," George Zepaloff*

WHEN I FIRST spoke with Nina Kiyaschenko Jaure, the Captain (whom she'd married in 1941 and divorced six years later) was in an advanced state of senile dementia at a sanitarium in northern California. "My daughter and I never talked of this before," she said, "because we didn't think it right. For someone as famous as Natalie Wood, it could have been very harmful." Nina continued to keep silent after Natalie died, she explained, because she read "the cheap, horrible book that Lana Wood wrote about her sister, and didn't wish to be known as that kind of person." Then, "George and I named our daughter Natalie, but we always called her Natasha, just as Natalie Wood's parents always called her Natasha. A coincidence, of course. The two Natashas met as children, and people commented how much they looked alike. But you must ask my daughter to tell you the rest of the story."

About Zepaloff as a husband, Nina said that "his looks were wonderful but his disposition wasn't so good. He was very secretive, and never said a word about Natalie Wood. He could also be mean and nasty, and at times I was frightened of him." After the divorce, Nina married "a man who worshiped me, was wonderful to me until the day he died. I was in love with George Zepaloff, but I really *loved* my late husband, George Jaure."


LIKE HER MOTHER, Natasha Zepaloff also kept silent, although after a few meetings with Natalie Wood "I felt a strong connection, but was too young to understand why." Later, both Maria and the Captain began dropping hints, respectively teasing and cryptic; but even when Maria unburdened herself after Natalie died, Natasha remained silent. "I never wanted people to think I was after money, and would make a claim on her estate," she said. "You read so many stories like that."


THERE WERE TWO REASONS why Nick never suspected that he might not be Natasha Gurdin's father: he didn't yet know his wife well enough, and Tatuloff had never told him about the Captain. When Maria gave birth to Natasha in Franklin Hospital, the Gurdins were renting the upper floor of a house in the Panhandle, on the edge of the Richmond district.

Page was not then a fashionable street, although the house at 1690 was (and still is) a modest example of classic late-nineteenth-century San Francisco domestic architecture, with a gabled roof and attic window. The other houses on Page are considerably larger and more ornate, and like 1690 they have been discreetly gentrified with coats of fresh paint. One block away is the Panhandle end of Golden Gate Park, drab and neglected-looking today, where Maria used to wheel Natasha for an airing in her baby carriage.

By then Maria had learned to find her way around material hard times. In Harbin, when Olga was born, Tatuloff could afford to employ a nanny. But when Olga became sick on board the *Tatuta Maru*, Maria passed her first test. With no nanny and no medical knowledge, she used

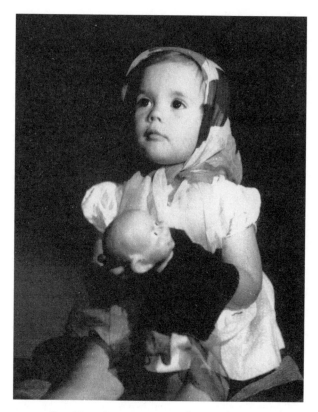

*San Francisco, 1941. Natalie Gurdin, age 3*

her charm to get permission to carry her sick child up to the first-class deck, where she persuaded the ship's doctor to examine Olga and prescribe medication for free. In San Francisco, her sharp eye soon discovered a brand of soda that often contained a nickel under the bottle cap; and when she found work in a factory after Natasha was born, she used her charm again to persuade the supervisor of the children's playground in Golden Gate Park to look after her baby during the day—for free, of course.

In the fall of 1938, Maria's half-sister Kalia, her husband, Sergei Liuzunie, and their young son, Constantin, arrived by boat from Shanghai. Maria had helped them obtain visas through a connection at the Russian Center and invited them to stay at 1690 Page until they found work. The families slept respectively four and three to a room, and although the Liuzunies knew no English, "they learned fairly quickly," according to Constantin. Within a few weeks, Kalia got a job as a waitress, Sergei as a furniture refinisher, and the last of Maria's family to leave China moved to a place of their own.

After the Liuzunies departed, the Gurdins didn't stay long at 1690 Page. During the early years of their marriage, as Olga recalled, they were nomadic. They moved "all over San Francisco" and rented a series of small houses or apartments, some cramped and mediocre, all cold and damp in winter, warmed only by a single kerosene heater. On weekends the couple often left Olga to baby-sit Natasha while they went out to one of the dance halls where Nick and his brothers used to earn extra money as a musical trio. In 1941 the family settled (again not for long) in their first house with two bedrooms, part of a low-income housing project called Sunnyvale.

Why did they move so often? Partly because Nick took work where and when he could find it, and partly because Maria was dissatisfied and restless. Shopping for a new place to live had boosted her spirits during those first anxious years in San Francisco, and after only a few months as Mrs. Gurdin she needed the same fix. By the time they moved to Sunnyvale, where Nick found work in the naval shipyard, the couple had lived up to Abraham Lincoln's definition of marriage: not heaven or hell, but purgatory.

As Maria's complaints about her husband's lack of ambition grew more insistent, Nick began to drink heavily. Instead of taking his wife to a dance hall, he left the house at night to tour the bars with Tatuloff, who once saved his life by taking Nick to hospital after he'd been badly beaten up in a street fight and left for dead. "Very nice when sober," as Olga remembered, her stepfather managed to save enough money to send her to ballet school and take piano lessons (Maria's wish). Under the influence, though, he became "abusive and violent." When Olga was in the room during a row with Maria, his rage exploded at the two of them; and when he picked up whatever object came to hand, they ran for cover just in time for the chair or lamp to miss its target and hit the wall.

Meanwhile, for a while, Natasha slept through the turbulence, at first in her crib, then in the bedroom she shared with Olga after they moved to Sunnyvale.

IT WAS NOT ONLY Maria's accusations of failure that drove Nick to alcohol and violence. The morning after the street fighting in Vladivostok, according to William Gerhardie, who witnessed it, "revealed a frozen landscape of massacred bodies. The square, the streets, the yards, the rails, and sundry ditches betrayed them lying in horrid postures, dead or dying." Did ten-year-old Nikolai Zacharenko see his father's body among them—or among the dying whom the Bolsheviks finished off with bayonets and "unspeakable" battle cries? Although he never spoke of the civil war in detail, he often referred to it as a time of horror that "destroyed" his family; and for the rest of his life, outbursts of fanatical hatred for Soviet Russia alternated with passionate admiration for Tsar Nicholas II, whose portrait he packed in his suitcase when the Zacharenkos fled to Shanghai, and later hung in the bedroom he shared with Maria.

The other side of Nick Gurdin emerged during the evenings he sat alone in a chair, quietly singing a folksong and accompanying himself on the balalaika, or rereading the novels of Tolstoy and Turgenev, in private remembrance of a past that the revolution had shattered forever. But Maria, who had endured her own baptism of horror, reacted by searching for compensation in the present. Like many Russian exiles, she needed to make up for everything she'd lost—country, family, security and the sense of "being someone"—by becoming "someone" again.

A fatal difference in temperament disrupted the Gurdins' marriage; and Maria's decision to regain her sense of self through her daughter disrupted Natalie Wood's life.

ONE RESTLESS DAY in the late summer of 1942, a Sunnyvale neighbor took Maria and her daughters for a drive to Santa Rosa, a small inland town forty miles north of San Francisco. Always shopping for a new place to live, Maria saw a small house under repair at 2168 Humboldt Street. She went inside, found a contractor at work and learned that the owner was desperate to sell because his wife had just left him. "Among other things," according to Olga, "my mother was a very good con artist." By the end of the day Maria had contacted the owner and persuaded him to accept a down payment of $100 on the $5,400 asking price, most of the furniture included.

The price was way beyond Nick Gurdin's means, of course, and Olga had no idea exactly how her mother managed to raise money for a loan, "but she conned somebody into that as well." Less surprisingly, she persuaded Nick to accept the situation, even though he'd have to commute forty miles to work in the shipyard or find a new job. Although it was only a whim that caused Maria to uproot the family to Santa Rosa, it became another of those coincidences that played a major part in her life and that she always seemed to take for granted.

EARLIER THAT SUMMER, Alfred Hitchcock had shot the location scenes for *Shadow of a Doubt* in Santa Rosa. Less than a year later, Irving Pichel remembered their classic small-town look when he needed a similar location not too far from Los Angeles for *Happy Land*. Originally a stage actor, Pichel moved to Hollywood in the early 1930s, played a few character roles (the prosecutor in Sternberg's version of *An American Tragedy*, Fagin in a cut-rate production of *Oliver Twist*), and directed a few routine B movies. In 1940, a contract with 20th Century–Fox promoted him to A movies, and he became the house specialist in anti-Nazi and/or homefront World War II stories. After *The Pied Piper* and *The Moon Is Down*, the next in line was *Happy Land*, from the best-seller by MacKinlay Kantor (*The Best Years of Our Lives*). A "typical" American father, devastated when his son is killed in the Pacific, receives an unexpected visitor from the "Happy Land." It's Gramp, his own grandfather, a Civil War veteran, who persuades him to rise above grief and take pride in the boy who sacrificed himself so nobly for his country.

Olga, a student at Santa Rosa High in 1943, came out of school one day, saw the *Happy Land* company (Don Ameche, Frances Dee, Ann Rutherford) at work a few blocks down the street. When she got home, she told Maria about it. But her mother gave no sign that she found the news exciting, or even particularly interesting. A few days later, Olga and a school friend were walking along the main street of nearby Healdsburg. Further ahead, they saw trailers and trucks, a camera crew, a crowd of extras. Irving Pichel was rehearsing a Fourth of July parade scene for *Happy Land,* and when he called for more extras, Olga was among the passersby rounded up. She found herself sharing a trailer with Ann Rutherford, then shown her place in a crowd shot. A few takes later, while the camera crew prepared the next setup, Pichel waited in his director's chair.

As if on cue, Maria appeared with five-year-old Natasha in tow. Without telling Olga or Nick, she had made inquiries, learned that

Pichel would be shooting the parade scene that day, and planned for her daughter to be "discovered," like her favorite actress, Lana Turner, whom a talent scout had supposedly swept to stardom from the counter of Schwab's drugstore. When she saw that Pichel was alone, Maria whispered something to her daughter and thrust her into the startled director's lap. Years later, Natalie Wood told me that her mother had said, "Make Mr. Pichel love you," or something very like it. Then she stuck her finger in her mouth and made a gagging sound. She also recalled "talking to him," although not what she said, and "singing a little song."

It could, of course, have been repellent—the precocious, innocently corrupted moppet coached by a stage mother to be adorable. Hollywood history is full of them, too many with nothing to fall back on as adults except a manufactured childhood. But as her movies make clear, there was nothing manufactured or corrupted about Natalie Wood the child actress. And like the child in the movies, the child *of* the movies was no different offscreen. Against heavy odds, she managed to be almost unnaturally happy for much of the time, and especially on a movie set.

Although there was no camera to record it, Maria had pitched Natasha into her first screen test; and Pichel was so captivated that he created a brief moment for her in the parade scene. But it's not *A Star Is Born* yet. She has only to drop her ice-cream cone on the sidewalk, then start to cry, and in the final version of *Happy Land* her reaction is cut. You glimpse Natasha for a few seconds as she drops her cone, while Olga gets more screen time in the passing parade. But something about the performance (and the performance on his lap) made a strong impression on Pichel.

Fan magazines of the 1940s and -50s contain various accounts of what happened next. Pichel immediately promised her a part in his next movie. He advised Maria against pursuing a movie career for her daughter, because child actors nearly always suffered the consequences of an unnatural childhood. He was so charmed by Natalie that he offered to adopt her. But like all fan-magazine "inside stories," they can be discounted as ghosted inventions of studio publicists.

Fortunately, Natalie once told me that she remembered Pichel coming to the house on Humboldt Street to say goodbye before the *Happy Land* company returned to Los Angeles. Before leaving, he took Maria aside. She also remembered Maria's account of the conversation, "which was probably true." Natasha, he said, had talent; there might be a part for her in a film he hoped to make the following year, and he promised to get in touch when it was definitely scheduled for production.

Subsequent events confirm Maria's account, and it's not surprising that Pichel recognized an instinctive performer in the little girl who burst into tears for the scene that landed on the cutting-room floor. Many directors and actors who worked with Natalie Wood in her earliest movies had the same reaction. As for the scene on Pichel's lap, others before him had found Natasha an exceptionally bright and appealing child. First photographed as a naked two-month-old baby, she laughs and points delightedly at something or someone off-camera. At two and a half, she sits on Maria's lap, an eager smile on her round, open face. Living in a bilingual household where her parents speak English with a marked Russian accent, Natasha sounds all-American, but she also speaks basic Russian with an American accent. And by the age of four, Natasha Gurdin is creating her own imaginary world. Dancing around in a slip like a miniature Isadora Duncan, she improvises steps and hums or sings music to accompany them. When Maria takes her out for a walk, she displays the first sign of a sense of humor that will later act as a shield against the world. She mimics passing strangers—performances sometimes so wickedly accurate that they tell Maria her little girl could be another Shirley Temple.

Music to Maria's ears, but the conversation with Pichel was more than that. She translated a conditional promise into a firm guarantee that Natasha was on the brink of a great career in movies. The memory of that initial bitterness and sense of isolation as an exile would no longer haunt her; the drabness and disappointment of her life with Nick would soon be over, and Maria herself transformed from nobody to somebody, the mother of a star. "She decided to take a chance and move to Hollywood," in Olga's words; and after confronting Nick with a fait accompli by taking their daughter to the set of *Happy Land* without his knowledge, Maria confronted him with more of the same. She'd placed their house on the market, and as soon as it sold, the family was moving to Hollywood.

If Nick had been drunk, he would certainly have retaliated with violence. Sober, he was easily reduced to submission when Maria held the winning cards. God and Irving Pichel had offered Natasha what the inadequate family breadwinner had failed to provide: a ticket to the future.

By the end of May 1944, the house on Humboldt Street had been sold. Two weeks later Natasha said goodbye to the small-town life she'd led for less than two years. Her few memories of it soon faded: the back-yard swing that Nick had made; the Protection of the Holy Virgin Russian Orthodox Church, which she attended with her family; her kindergarten friend and neighbor Ed Canevari, whose father owned the delicatessen that Ed manages today.

The Gurdins spent the first night of their 450-mile journey to Los Angeles in the car, parked off the highway at midpoint along the coast. Next night they arrived at 1716 North Alexandria Avenue, a house in the Hollywood foothills. It belonged to Nadjeda Ermolova, the ballet teacher Maria had met in San Francisco. Her "Dancing Studio" for chil-dren, and her own private apartment, occupied the first floor of the property that Ermolova bought when she moved to Los Angeles, and she supplemented her income by renting out the second-floor apart-ment. It was unoccupied when Maria contacted her, and Ermolova offered to let the Gurdins stay there temporarily; and as it remained untenanted, they stayed for the rest of the year.

They lived very frugally, as Nick found only occasional work as a laborer, and there was just enough money for fourteen-year-old Olga to exchange Santa Rosa High for Hollywood High, where Maria enrolled her in drama class. (Maybe both her daughters would become famous actresses?) Maria tried to contact Pichel, but he was no longer working at Fox. As for Natasha, the only reliable witness is Olga, who remembers only that Maria enrolled her sister at Ermolova's studio.

The studio's brochure advertised courses for children in "Ballet, Toe, Character and Step Dances." But its photos suggest that Ermolova's heart belonged to Diaghilev. In the cover portrait she wears an elaborate headdress studded with pearls that might have come from the last scene of *The Firebird;* and among the snapshots of kiddie students with mainly Russian names is one of Natasha Gurdina in ethnic costume, striking a folk-dance pose like a Polovtsian maiden from *Prince Igor.*

Natasha had started kindergarten before the Gurdins left Santa Rosa, but Olga was vague about her sister's education during the rest of 1944—and about her life beyond Ermolova's studio. "Perhaps," she suggested,

*Hollywood, 1944.
"Natasha Gurdina" at
Ermolova's "Dancing Studio"*

"our mother got Natasha to try out for different parts." This seems more than unlikely. Long gone were the days when a stage mother (especially if she spoke with a Russian accent) could occasionally sneak into a studio and persuade someone to audition the daughter she insisted was a child prodigy. With the coming of sound, a guard was posted at every studio entrance, and no one could gain admittance without a pass.

On Maria's life, Olga was more specific. She remembered that when her mother went off for a day or two "to visit the Liuzunies," Nick gave no sign that he suspected anything. In fact, she had kept in touch with the Captain, and whenever his ship came in, Maria went off to meet her great romantic love. On those occasions, Olga also remembered, she helped her mother choose a dress, and watched the special care she took with her appearance.

But Maria's secret assignations didn't prevent her from keeping a sharp eye on the main chance. She had discovered the existence of *Variety* and the *Hollywood Reporter,* and in December 1944 she learned that Irving Pichel's next movie would be *Tomorrow Is Forever* for International Pictures, a subsidiary of RKO, and that he planned to conduct a search for a child to play the orphaned ward of Orson Welles.

Now that she knew how to contact Pichel, Maria called RKO. The "con artist" had no trouble getting through directly to his office, and when he agreed to test Natasha for the part, it was a turning point for both mother and daughter.

PICHEL HAD BEEN approached to direct *Tomorrow Is Forever* while he was shooting *Happy Land,* but it took more than a year of story conferences and script revisions to adapt a preposterous novel, and meanwhile he made another movie. Claudette Colbert's reluctance to play the mother of a draft-age son was a further reason for the delay in production of *Tomorrow Is Forever,* and she finally committed when Welles, "deeply ashamed but in need of money," accepted the role of her supposedly dead husband. In fact, after being wounded and disfigured in World War I, he's undergone plastic surgery, assumed German identity, and become a successful industrial scientist. After World War II, he gets a job with an American company and finds himself working for Colbert's second husband. It takes a great many puzzled stares before Colbert suspects that he's really husband number 1, but for the sake of her marriage to husband number 2, and the orphaned ward he wants her to adopt, he refuses to admit it and dies that same night.

In current studio slang, *Tomorrow Is Forever* was a weeper, and Pichel told Maria that the test scene would require Natasha's tears to flow as spontaneously as they had when she dropped her ice-cream cone in *Happy Land.* Maria assured him yet again that her little girl was a born actress; but the surest way to stop the born actress in her tracks was to remind her, as Maria repeatedly did, that the future depended on her ability to cry on demand.

When the very small child entered a huge, dim, cavernous studio soundstage for the first time in February 1945, five months before her seventh birthday, she was not only still feeling the effect of sudden displacement from home and kindergarten in Santa Rosa to a ballet class in Hollywood where she posed for photographs in Polovtsian costume. She was tense on account of her mother's tension. And when the test began, Natasha was so overwhelmed by the battery of studio lights, the camera's eye confronting her, and Maria's eyes fixed on her from the sidelines that the scene went dead and her own eyes remained dry.

When Pichel called next day with the news that Natasha had failed the test, it didn't stop Maria in *her* tracks. She gave Natasha a tongue-lashing, then called Pichel back, saying her little girl had burst into tears at the news and begging him to give her another chance. (It was Maria's anger, of course, that had provoked her little girl's tears.) The fact that Pichel agreed to another test tells as much about his intuition as about Maria's persistence. He shot the first test because of the impression that Natasha had made on him in Santa Rosa; and the former actor had seen enough of Maria to guess what went wrong in the studio.

Meanwhile, Olga had acquired some basic Stanislavsky in drama class, and when Natasha asked her to suggest a way of crying on demand, she advised her "to think of something very sad," then reminded Natasha of a day not long before they left Santa Rosa, when they took her German shepherd puppy for a walk. It suddenly dashed across the street, and they saw it run over by a truck. No doubt Pichel prepared Natasha for the second test with his usual kindness and patience, and kept Maria in the background (as far as such a thing was possible); but Natasha had only to think of her dead puppy to weep copious tears. And once she started thinking about it, she couldn't stop. As a result, she rose to a pitch of emotional intensity that astonished Pichel, producer David Lewis and the president of International Pictures, William Goetz, when they ran the test.

As well as the part, Natasha acquired a new name. Lewis and Goetz decided that Natasha should revert to her baptismal Natalie (more American), and they changed her last name to Wood as a "good-luck gesture" to their mutual friend Sam Wood, director of the recent box-office hit *Kings Row*. And until Warner Bros. signed her to a long-term contract ten years later, Natalie Wood was effectively under contract to her mother, who personally negotiated the deal ($100 a week) with International, then went house shopping, and moved the family to a rented bungalow on Harland Avenue in West Hollywood.

Maria also accepted an offer from Famous Artists to represent Natalie, and on her behalf signed a three-year contract, to be renewed every three years by mutual consent. But she insisted on the right to approve or veto every offer that Natalie received, and when she disagreed with the first Famous Artists agent assigned to handle Natalie, she refused to deal with him anymore and moved on to the next. Over the years, six Famous Artists heads rolled; and after a merger transformed the agency to Ashley-Famous, Maria had a new batch of surrogates to fire if anyone stepped out of line. Meanwhile, several major talent agencies balanced Maria's reputation against her daughter's growing desirability, and the scales didn't tilt in Natalie's favor until 1957.

By then Maria had become "someone" again. In her powerful new identity as a Star Mother, she had authorized Natalie Wood to appear in twenty-one movies, twelve TV shows, one TV series that ran for a year, and one radio show, and approved her seven-year contract with Warners. Soon after *Tomorrow Is Forever* made Natalie famous, Maria also bought herself a car, even though she hadn't learned to drive. She took lessons from an instructor, but failed the test no less than seven times. For her eighth test, the "con artist" arrived at the Department of Motor Vehicles with a handful of signed photographs of Natalie Wood and presented them to various employees, including her examiner. "I'm her mother!" she told everyone. The examiner passed her.

Maria remained "a fairly crazy driver," according to Olga, who remembered that she once drove straight over a street divider when she wanted to make a left turn. As well as taking the jolt and the honk of indignant horns in her stride, Maria did no serious damage to the car. But unlike Nick, who eventually lost his license after a third drunken-driving offense, she never had a citation or an accident during all the years that she covered thousands of miles to meet her Captain and to take Natalie to studios from Burbank to Beverly Hills almost every working day.

At the studio, Lon McCallister, who acted with Natalie in *Scudda Hoo! Scudda Hay!* (1947), remembered, "Maria remained a watchful silent presence, always on the set." Later she became more vocal, especially to visiting journalists; but even when silent she could make everyone aware of her.

> *Natalie Wood: I went to work early in the morning so often that it seemed a normal thing for a child my age to do.*

Because the mind of a child is usually open, it's receptive to any kind of rubbish thrown into it. Although this particular child's mind received more than its fair share, the rubbish was disguised with a layer of enticing perfume; and it was only once in a while, after the perfume wore off, that Natalie sniffed something rotten in its place. At seven she had woken up to find herself famous, but at fifteen she woke up to compute the price of fame. Until then the Wonder Child had never found the time to look back on her life since the first day she entered a studio soundstage and to question what she had always been told to take for granted. At fifteen her feeling of confinement was acute enough, and her mind sharp enough, to make her think and feel for herself, instead of what others had always tried to make her think and feel. And after confronting things in her life that she didn't know that she knew, or hadn't wanted to admit, she felt the ground, along with her own identity, give way under her feet.

# 2

# Lost Childhood

*I raised my daughter to be a movie star.*

——MARIA GURDIN

*Her mother was genuinely, fanatically obsessed with Natalie's talent and possibilities. It became the focus of her life, and sometimes made her as close to certifiable as you can get.*

——ROBERT WAGNER

LITTLE STAR BIG FUTURE" was the title of a publicity brochure that International Pictures circulated in February 1946, when *Tomorrow Is Forever* went into general release. It included a fanciful account (courtesy Maria Gurdin) of Natalie's family background; quoted reviews from newspapers across the country ("A new child star emerges," "Brilliant child discovery," "Natalie steals the picture in every scene in which she appears"); mentioned the "honor award" from Louella Parsons in *Cosmopolitan* ("Natalie Wood eats your heart out"); and featured a series of carefully posed portraits by Madame Valeska, famous for her "candid camera."

Five years earlier, Roddy McDowall had received the same kind of publicity after his first American movie, *How Green Was My Valley.* By the time they became good friends, both he and Natalie had successfully negotiated the difficult passage to adult acting careers; and McDowall once commented that for children, acting in front of a camera became an expanded version of "Let's Pretend," the imaginative games they played at home. "We *believed* in our roles," he said. "We never had to question a motivation, and ask, 'Why do I have to do that?' But as adults, we had to begin all over again, to ask questions before we could play a scene convincingly, and acquire the technique to make an audience believe it."

Among the child stars of that era, in fact, there were performing moppets as well as genuinely talented actors, and the performers usually found it impossible to begin all over again. Shirley Temple was a phenomenal little darling who sang and tap-danced and winked her way through the 1930s. But by the mid-1940s she had lost her identity as the antidepressant mascot of the Depression years, and seemed unable to find another in "grown-up" roles. Offscreen she became a tough, shrewd little adult, whose mother had taught her two important lessons: the difference between Shirley "acting" and Shirley "just being herself," and between "fact and fantasy." As a result, the performing moppet was able to leave fantasy behind at twenty-one and move on to marriage, motherhood and Republican politics.

But Natalie's mother never taught her child to separate fact from fantasy, because she often blurred the line herself. This would create pain and confusion in Natalie's adult life, although it encouraged the child in her game of "Let's Pretend" in front of the camera. Far from "just being herself" in her first movie role, she had to imagine and portray an Austrian World War II orphan whose parents were killed in an air raid. Haphazard schooling meant that she was barely able to read and had to memorize her lines in each scene with the aid of a dialogue coach provided by the studio. The coach also taught her, by speaking the words aloud and asking Natalie to repeat them, how to say some of her lines in German and the rest in English with a German accent.

Hair blonded and braided in the style of an infant fräulein, she was basically as disguised as Orson Welles, with *his* German accent, dark wig and beard streaked with white, limp and cane. Six foot three to her three foot ten, he brought his bravura presence and theatrical skills to a role desperately in need of them. But although the novice could only follow her instincts and Pichel's patient instructions, she managed to get under the skin of her character, stubborn yet helpless, self-contained yet lonely; she also cried without hesitation on (frequent) demand, reacted hysterically to the sound of a popgun that reminded her of World War II and listened with uncanny intentness to the other actors in her scenes. By contrast, Colbert and George Brent (as husband number 2) seemed no

*Hollywood, 1946. Natalie Wood and Orson Welles
in* Tomorrow Is Forever

more than smoothly efficient; as *Look* magazine noted in its review of
the movie, Welles's "only acting rival is his tiny bilingual screen ward."

Welles agreed, finding Natalie's performance "almost terrifyingly
professional." But as he told his friend Henry Jaglom many years later,
he also found "something very sad and lonely about this compelling
child." One day, during a break between takes, she seemed so in need of
comfort that he sat her on his knee. She was surprised at first, then
pleased, and snuggled closer—until Maria suddenly appeared, snatched
her daughter away, and darted a look of such ferocious anger at Welles
that he "felt terrible, as if he'd done something wrong."

No doubt Maria also made the compelling child feel she'd done
something wrong. Like her tongue-lashing of Natalie after she failed the

first test, it was a sign that Maria could suddenly turn from loving mother into emotional terrorist.

WELLES LATER described Irving Pichel as "a perfectly competent man," a fair verdict on a style of filmmaking as deliberate and theatrically trained as Pichel's own voice. (He had been the offscreen narrator of *How Green Was My Valley*.) But Pichel was more than competent in his interplay with actors, especially children. (He had previously directed Roddy McDowall and Peggy Ann Garner in *The Pied Piper*.) On August 10, 1979, at the American Film Institute Film and Humanities Seminar with Natalie Wood, Natalie remarked that directors who start out as actors always have an "extra understanding of an actor's problems." Pichel had it, she said, and was a wonderful mentor on her first movie. He also gave her mother some excellent advice. Untrained children respond more naturally to imaginary situations, he explained, and warned Maria "not to send me to any acting coaches or schools." Fortunately, Maria listened. Just as Welles realized that Natalie needed no training, she was aware of her daughter's intrinsically strong imagination. Did she also guess where it came from?

*TOMORROW IS FOREVER* completed ten weeks of shooting in June 1945, and as California law obliged child actors to go to school for three hours a day, Natalie had begun to catch up on her education at the studio schoolhouse. Two weeks after the last day of shooting, Pichel sent her one of the dresses she wore in the movie "as a memento of the nice days when you were making it"; and in January 1946 *Tomorrow Is Forever* had a gala opening at the Carthay Circle Theater.

Guests at the premiere included Gary Cooper, Edward G. Robinson, Ronald Reagan and his current wife, Jane Wyman, but a "women's picture" demanded a cluster of female stars to swell the list. Olivia de Havilland, Greer Garson, Merle Oberon, Ann Sothern, Barbara Stanwyck and Gene Tierney were also corraled for the occasion, and they all attended the private party hosted by Colbert and Pichel afterward. And when *Variety* correctly prophesied "good biz in class houses," this meant very good biz indeed, as there were hundreds more class houses then than now.

LESS FORTUNATELY, Maria had also listened to Pichel when he offered to cast Natalie in his next picture. *The Bride Wore Boots,* a sagebrush comedy about a wife (Barbara Stanwyck) who loves horses and the wide-open spaces and a husband (Robert Cummings) who doesn't, defeated even the great Stanwyck, whose daughter Natalie played. And there were fewer "nice days" on this movie for Paramount, which Pichel began shooting in mid-July, a month after he completed *Tomorrow Is Forever.* During the eight weeks of production, Stanwyck grew very impatient with Pichel's insistence on retakes that she considered unnecessary, and one afternoon she threatened to walk off the picture if he demanded take 6. Pichel also directed Natalie to play standard cute; but he probably had no choice, as Paramount had remodeled her to look like Shirley Temple. Hair tightly ringleted and garnished with ribbons, she was again far from "just being herself," but for the wrong reasons.

*The Bride Wore Boots* was a critical and commercial flop when it opened in June 1946, but in Natalie's case the success of *Tomorrow Is Forever* overshadowed it. Six months later she posed for photographers when she accepted an award from *Parents* magazine as "The Most Talented Juvenile Picture Star of 1946," and again when she received a Blue Ribbon citation from *Box Office* for a notable debut in one of the box-office hits of the year.

BY THIS TIME Maria had given birth to another daughter, at St. John's Hospital in Santa Monica. Born March 1, 1946, the baby's given name was Svetlana, but Maria soon shortened it to Lana, in homage to her favorite movie star, and with an eye on the possibility of a second child actress in the family.

A few weeks earlier, Olga had come home from school to find a drunken Nick pointing a knife at his pregnant wife's belly. Her arrival defused the situation; and as she was now "suffering from bad nerves" on account of the violent scenes between her mother and stepfather, Olga reacted to this one as simply another sign that she must make up her mind to leave the Gurdin household and go to live with her father in San Francisco.

But she didn't know that Nick had recently learned about Maria's

*Natalie with Richard Long (playing Claudette Colbert's son)*
*on the set of* Tomorrow Is Forever

continuing affair with George Zepaloff. Inevitably, he suspected that she'd always loved the Captain more than she loved him. (He was right. Stricken with Alzheimer's disease in her last years, Maria spoke her Captain's name more often than Nick's.) Inevitably, too, Nick had to recognize his failure as a husband. But the humiliation also aggravated his sense of failure as a man whose lack of will sentenced him to a life of dependency.

Part of the bond between Maria and the Captain was the excitement of living on the edge; and the excitement of provoking her husband to violence, or the threat of it, was one reason why Maria never left Nick. "My mother knew how to taunt him," Olga recalled, and when Nick aimed a knife at Maria's belly that day, had she taunted him by suggesting that someone else might be the child's father? We don't know; but Olga remembers that Maria confided the name of her third child's biological father a few days after Lana was born.

Ironically, rumors about Lana's paternity had begun to circulate while Maria was still pregnant, and several years later Natalie heard that the Captain was a prime suspect. Did she confront her mother about this? Again, we don't know; but Olga remembers that "when Natalie was around sixteen," Maria told her the truth, and the three of them agreed it should be kept from Lana.

NICHOLAS LEPKO, whom Maria had first met in 1931 on board the *Tatuta Maru*, eventually became a technician at the laboratory owned by the Los Angeles film company that first employed him as an apprentice. Around 1936 it was sold to a Japanese company, which offered him a new and better-paid contract in Japan. Lepko decided to accept, and arranged for Tamara and their ten-year-old daughter, Irene, to join him in Kyoto.

Meanwhile, Tamara not only had continued to dance and choreograph floor shows, but had worked as assistant to a leading producer of cabaret in Shanghai. Irene couldn't recall his name, but most likely he was Austrian-born Joe Farren, who once managed a circus in Vienna and eventually settled in Shanghai, where he opened a casino with nightclub attached. The club was famous for its chorus line, known as the Paramount Peaches; and as Shanghai favored blondes, all the Peaches were White Russian blondes, like Tamara herself.

Apart from missionaries, the Lepkos were the only foreigners in Kyoto in the 1930s. But they soon learned serviceable Japanese, and the resourceful Tamara danced in musical shows that toured Korea and Shanghai, as well as opened a ballet studio where she taught missionary children. The Lepkos remained in Japan after the outbreak of World War II in Europe, but in December 1940, a year before the attack on Pearl Harbor, the Japanese company abruptly terminated Lepko's contract. The family was rescued from a precarious situation by the bishop in charge of the Episcopal Church's missionary work in Kyoto. His children were among Tamara's ballet students, and he offered to sponsor the Lepkos as immigrants to the United States.

> *Irene (Lepko) Agnew: In the early 1940s, Maria and Nick Gurdin with their daughters Olga and Natasha first came to visit us in our small apartment in Hollywood. Since we were all Russian immigrants, and my father had met Maria on the boat from Shanghai, there was immediate camaraderie and friendship.*

The Lepkos had arrived in Los Angeles in February 1941, a few weeks before the Gurdins moved to the house in Sunnyvale. "We had no belongings except our clothes," Irene recalled; but with the extraordinary resilience of so many Russian immigrants, Nicholas and Tamara soon found employment. Nick's qualifications landed him a job as laboratory technician at Pathé, and later at Columbia Pictures. "That was the extent of his career," according to Irene, and he never earned more than a modest salary.

Tamara worked as a hospital orderly, then in a factory that bottled bath salts, until a Russian neighbor recommended her to the Geller Theater Workshop. She was engaged to teach ballet there and continued to do so until she started her own studio in 1950. Olga places that first visit to the Lepkos around December 1944, just before Irving Pichel had agreed to test Natalie for *Tomorrow Is Forever,* and Irene remembers that Nick Gurdin talked a great deal of the horrors of the revolution, while Maria recalled her triumphs at the Russian Center as Queen of the White Russian Veterans and Invalids. On subsequent evenings, nostalgia for the old days usually prevailed: "Nick [Gurdin] played Russian songs to my mother and they sang along together and shed a few tears for days gone by. And when Nick felt blue he would phone my mother and play Russian records, and she'd sing to them, or they'd recite poetry and tell Russian jokes."

To his daughter, Nicholas Lepko always seemed like "a background figure," not only during those evenings but throughout his life; and Nick Gurdin made the same impression on everyone who met him. Lepko's professional career was stable but undistinguished, Gurdin's a failure, and they both married women exceptionally strong in different ways. Was this one reason for the episode between Lepko and Maria that occurred within a few months of that first visit? Another, according to Olga, was that her mother became "very competitive" with Tamara. She sometimes cooked Russian dishes for the Lepkos, and Tamara found them so delicious that she asked for the recipes. Maria obligingly wrote them out for her, "but with one ingredient changed or missing. And when Tamara wondered why the same dishes were never as good when she made them, my mother laughed about it to me."

Olga also suspected that Lepko made the opening move to her mother, because "he once put his hand over mine and pressed it," and Maria confided that her "relations" with Nick had grown "very bad" at the time: "When she told me about Lepko, she said, 'It just happened.' She didn't go into details, and I had the impression it wasn't a real affair, maybe 'just happened' only once, and probably after one of the parties the Lepkos used to give, where all their Russian friends got very sad and merry and excited."

Although Olga was almost seventeen by then, pretty but "rather

*Harland Avenue, 1946*

prudish," and "shocked" by Lepko appearing "to make advances to her," she knew her mother well enough to recognize the line between the fabulist and the woman of her word. Hindsight draws the line even more clearly. The key to Maria the fabulist is her craving for self-esteem. She began by romanticizing her past in Russia (the Romanov connection, the private train to Harbin); after *Tomorrow Is Forever* she exaggerated her role, important though it was, in Natalie's career as a movie star, and invented new details about her past. She also enjoyed demonstrating her own fabulist powers. One evening when they were alone together in the Harland Avenue bungalow, she convinced Olga that a burglar was trying to break in through a rear window. Then she saw the look of fear on her daughter's face, laughed and said it wasn't true.

But it would not have suited Maria's craving for self-esteem to fantasize that she was pregnant with Zepaloff's child when she married Nick Gurdin; and to reveal that the child in question was Natalie Wood would have seriously damaged her movie-star daughter's career. (Today, of course, it would enhance it.) Instead, she made a point of advertising her belief in "respectability" throughout Natalie's life—a necessary precaution for both their sakes in Maria's view—and for once she resisted the temptation to confide in Olga, her daughter confessor.

After Lana was born, Maria went house shopping again, and in the fall of 1946 she moved the family to Burbank, where real estate was less expensive than in West Hollywood, and she could rent a house with an extra bedroom for the same price. Nicholas Lepko occasionally dropped by for a visit, and when Olga noticed that "he would sit and *just stare* at baby Lana," she felt doubly certain that her mother had spoken the truth.

In the eyes of the world, if not in his own, Nick Gurdin accepted Lana as his daughter. Without adding to his humiliation, what else could he do?

NATALIE, OF COURSE, knew nothing of this when she began work on her third and fourth movies in November 1946. Each proved a more agreeable experience and a more successful movie than *The Bride Wore Boots,* although her role in *The Ghost and Mrs. Muir,* a compound of period romance and the supernatural, was scarcely more rewarding. In early 1900s England, a young widow (Gene Tierney) buys a house by the sea that turns out to be haunted by the ghost of a sea captain (Rex Harrison). The English setting was also a compound, of studio interiors on the 20th Century–Fox lot, exterior scenes shot near Palos Verdes down the coast, and a house near Big Sur up the coast, used for back-projection plates for the house by the sea. The story takes place over thirty years, and while Tierney ages discreetly in a series of elegant grayish, pearl-gray, and silver-gray wigs, Natalie as her daughter soon grows up into Vanessa Brown.

The picture was one of several that Joseph L. Mankiewicz made early in his career as a contract director at Fox, to prove himself commercially and be allowed to write and direct his own material for the studio. Famous Artists had sent Natalie on an interview for the role, and Mankiewicz (like Pichel) was immediately charmed. He was also impressed by her reaction when he asked if she'd read "the whole script or just your part." She looked very surprised, then told him: "The whole script."

Maria, of course, was on the set every day that Natalie worked, and beginning to assert herself. One day, when shooting ran slightly behind schedule, she asked Mankiewicz how much longer her daughter would be kept waiting. Years later, Mankiewicz related the sequel to his screenwriter son, Tom:

> Disguising his irritation with a joke, my father told Maria he'd be ready for Natalie in the morning if she could spell his name correctly. Next morning, when put to the test, Natalie seemed uncharacteristically nervous, and my father feared that Maria had been tutoring her half the night. She spelt his name correctly until she faltered at the last letter, which became T instead of Z. My father thought Maria was going to hit her. But shortly afterward Natalie came up to him with a charming smile and spelt it right.

In the early 1960s, Mankiewicz told his son, the sequel had a sequel. As he walked down a corridor at Cedars-Sinai Hospital on his way to visit his agent, who was recovering from surgery, Mankiewicz heard a crisp, amused voice behind him call out his name, letter by letter: "M-A-N-K-I-E-W-I-C-Z!" He turned around and saw Natalie Wood, near the peak of her stardom, with the same charming smile.

A WEEK AFTER she reported for work on *The Ghost and Mrs. Muir,* Natalie was interviewed by George Seaton, another writer-director under contract to Fox. Like Mankiewicz, he was charmed, and cast her in one of the key roles of her screen childhood: the girl in *Miracle on 34th Street* who doesn't believe in Santa Claus. Although the movie was set in New York, its stars performed against back-projection plates for most of the exteriors, but Natalie was flown to the city during the week before Christmas for interior scenes in Macy's.

Back in California, she was shuttled for a few days between two sound stages, sometimes playing Tierney's daughter in the morning, breaking for lunch and three hours of school, then playing Maureen O'Hara's daughter for the rest of the afternoon. Changing from period to contemporary costume, like changing characters and screen mothers, also became part of "the normal thing" for an eight-year-old child to do. And like her schedule, the title of Seaton's movie was constantly switching, from *My Heart Tells Me* to *The Big Heart,* then to *It's Only Human,* and finally to *Miracle on 34th Street.* More important, the movie gave Natalie her first chance to display a talent for comedy.

Although not an orphan, Susan's the child of divorced parents who lives with her mother (Maureen O'Hara); and from the vantage point of this movie, an overview reveals how *Tomorrow Is Forever* set the pattern of Natalie's early career. Aside from minor roles in a handful of domestic comedies and dramas where she comes from a relatively "normal" background, she plays an emotionally displaced child whose problems are resolved by understanding adults (thanks, of course, to the understanding filmmakers who contrive a happy ending). In *Driftwood* and *One Desire,* she's an orphan again; in *The Star,* another child of divorced parents; in *The Blue Veil* and *Just for You,* a neglected daughter. In *The Green Promise* she rebels against her father, and in *No Sad Songs for Me* her mother dies of cancer.

Not all these movies are weepers, although they all share an underlying sentimentality, and reflect the formulaic unreal world that Natalie was schooled to believe in from the age of seven. The benign old gentleman (Edmund Gwenn) hired to play Santa Claus for Macy's Thanksgiving Parade and Christmas shopping season in *Miracle on 34th Street*—is he the genuine article or just pretending? Susan, whose mother has brought her up to distrust make-believe, accuses him of being a fraud and gives him a look of wonderfully comic disbelief when he insists that he's as real as his beard. But the movie knows better than to commit itself. Instead, it hinges on Susan's "conversion," when her heart tells her that the old gentleman is "so kind and nice and jolly, he *must* be Santa Claus."

It's the signal, of course, that a kind and nice and jolly ending for everyone will follow. An unhappy marriage has caused Susan's mother, Doris, to reject a number of illusions, including love; but now she's enabled to see Fred (John Payne), her devoted neighbor, as a man to trust. And by accepting his love, she cues the audience to accept the human need for belief.

In a memo to Seaton about the movie's first-draft script, the vice-president in charge of production at Fox, Darryl F. Zanuck, complained that Doris was too "cold" and "heartless." But in their anxiety to make the movie's heart as big as possible, and remove anything that might disturb, Seaton and his writing partner, Valentine Davies, did more than trim a few of Doris's "cold" (read "realistic") lines. By eliminating the character of her alcoholic ex-husband, who's only referred to in the final version, they made her insistence on "life's harsh realities" less understandable.

Early in the movie, Fred tells Doris that "faith is believing in something when common sense tells you not to." She doesn't buy it and retorts, "You don't get ahead that way." But by the end she understands Fred's answer: "It all depends what you mean by getting ahead." This is not the only hollow echo of Capra's *It's a Wonderful Life*. Like the guardian angel in that picture, Macy's Kris Kringle performs a "miracle" by guiding Doris, Fred and Susan herself to the suburban house of their dreams. Loss of belief in Santa Claus, in fact, is equated with loss of belief, period; and when the consequences of no more Santa are pointed out, material interests and spiritual values hold hands at the thought of toy business and Christmas business in general falling off, and workers being laid off.

There's also a hint of Capra-esque whimsy when a friend of old Kringle's remarks that even if he's only pretending to be Santa, "he's only a little crazy, like composers, painters, and some of those people in Washington." Not so whimsical is the portrait of a psychiatrist who tries to account for the "illusion" of belief in Santa in Freudian terms. He's

Miracle on 34th Street. *Monkey business: Natalie,*
*John Payne, Edmund Gwenn*

put down with the comment that "there's a lot of 'isms' floating around today"—a clear reference to the warming climate of anticommunism.

It had grown even warmer when *Miracle on 34th Street* opened in July 1947, and while the movie was still in general release, on October 20, the House Un-American Activities Committee opened its hearings in Washington. Ironically, the most ferocious witness for the prosecution was Sam Wood, the director who had supplied Natalie with her new last name, and a few months later had founded the Motion Picture Alliance for the Preservation of American Ideals. His friend Ayn Rand, equally obsessed with the Red Menace, had written the Alliance's book of rules, which included a list of "don'ts" that "patriotic" American filmmakers were morally bound to observe: *Don't* Glorify Failure; *Don't* Deify the Common Man; *Don't* Smear the Free Enterprise System, Success and Industrialists.

In a further irony, Irving Pichel was one of the Hollywood Nineteen that Wood accused of Communist sympathies. The committee investigated him as a case of "premature antifascism," which it equated with communism, because he'd made an anti-Nazi film (*The Man I Married,* 1940) before America entered World War II, and had once played Joseph Stalin. Unlike many of the committee's victims, who went to jail, were blacklisted or struck humiliating plea bargains and identified various colleagues as Party members, Pichel was cleared. But he developed a chronic heart condition soon afterward and was on medication until he died in 1954.

Like Maria in China, Natalie was too young to understand the ways of the great world. Although she couldn't fail to appreciate the blatant celebration of "family values" in several of her movies from the late 1940s to the late 1950s, the occasional subtext of anticommunism (and/or the Preservation of American Ideals) passed her by. But Maria had taught her the importance of flattering two powerful, implacably right-wing columnists. Both Hedda Hopper and Louella Parsons kept a hawkish eye on private and public lives. Hopper was the more dangerous, as she controlled a more efficient network of spies (doormen, waiters, chauffeurs, hairdressers, personal maids), and the FBI used her to leak names of suspected Communists due for investigation. During 1947, enraged by *Monsieur Verdoux,* she spearheaded a campaign against Charlie Chaplin's personal, political and fiscal life that would end in his expulsion from the country. But she was also highly susceptible to cozying up, and on December 18, 1947, she wrote Natalie, on notepaper headed HEDDA HOPPER'S HOLLYWOOD: "What a darling you are, sending me that beautiful box of candy. But don't you ever do it again. You added at least an inch to my waistline."

Hedda Hopper's Hollywood, of course, was also Maria Gurdin's Hollywood, as well as the Hollywood of literally hundreds of actors, directors, producers and agents who regularly sent the columnist a Christmas gift. And as a Star Mother, Maria not only had taken charge of supervising Natalie's public relations; she reinvented herself in the process. The "Little Star Big Future" brochure noted that she was born Maria Kuleff, "a former ballerina of Franco-Russian descent," and had taught her daughter "spiritual values." (This information was accompanied by a "candid camera" shot by Madame Valeska of the Wonder Child at prayer.) In fact the most important "spiritual value" that Maria would teach her daughter was to mistrust anyone, especially a contemporary, who wanted to be her friend. Afraid that a true friend of Natalie's could become her mother's enemy, Maria insisted that neighborhood children were "no good," and any child actor with a role in one of Natalie's movies was "jealous" and trying "to do her in."

*Miracle on 34th Street* earned Natalie another Blue Ribbon citation from *Box Office;* honorary membership in the Polly Pigtails Club; a trip to New York, where she appeared with Maureen O'Hara in Macy's Thanksgiving Parade; and an offer of two more pictures from Fox. As Nick Gurdin was out of work at the time, with the usual consequences, the former-ballerina-turned-developing-businesswoman created another successful persona for herself. She instructed Natalie's currently-in-favor agent to make the two-picture deal conditional on Fox adding Nick to its payroll as a studio carpenter and appointing her "in charge of Natalie Wood's fan mail" at $100 a week.

Although the developing businesswoman Star Mother seemed firmly grounded in reality, she was projecting some dangerous new fantasies on her daughter. When she took Natalie to the movies, they often saw the RKO-Pathé newsreels that ended with a close shot of the camera lens aimed directly at the audience. It became the cue for Maria to whisper urgently: "Smile! You're being photographed!" And when Natalie wondered why they always sat in back-row seats, she received a stern warning: "If you move any closer to the screen, Jack the Jabber will get you!" The Jabber, according to Maria, was a serial killer who crept up behind young girls sitting in movie theaters and knifed them in the back.

Maria also told Natalie a story that sounds like a fantasy, but according to Olga it actually happened. Out walking one day in Harbin with her half-sister Kalia, she encountered a Gypsy fortune-teller. "Beware of dark water," the Gypsy warned Maria, and predicted she would drown in it.

The woman of her word implanted a lifelong fear of dark water in Natalie by relating the Gypsy's warning; and the fabulist (who didn't always know when to stop) also claimed that the Gypsy had predicted that Maria's second daughter would become "a world-famous beauty."

AFTER APPROVING the $800-a-week deal with Fox, Maria moved the family to a house in Northridge, fifteen miles west of Burbank in the San Fernando Valley. A year later, for reasons that Natalie never understood, she moved the family again, ten miles back east to Sherman Oaks. Each move sent Natalie to a different school, Burbank Public Elementary, Robert Fulton Junior, Van Nuys High. And each time she made a movie, her education was dislocated yet again by attending studio school at Fox, Columbia or RKO.

MEANWHILE, in June 1947, Olga had graduated from Hollywood High. With her mother totally fixated on Natalie's career, and a studio job failing to prevent Nick from hurling insults and chairs around in one of his drunken rages, she decided to live with her father in San Francisco. By then he had a regular job with an upholstery company, and Olga returned to the city where she's lived ever since.

The increasingly tense situation between her mother and Nick was another reason that impelled Olga to leave. Maria had recently confided that Nick "was having an affair with a Mexican woman," which explained something that had puzzled Olga when the family was at supper one evening. The phone rang, Nick hurried to answer it, and she heard him tell the caller never to phone at that hour. Then he hung up abruptly.

On both sides, the saddest farewells were between Olga and Natalie. They had grown very close since the early days in San Francisco, when Olga used to baby-sit Natalie and change her diapers on the nights Maria and Nick went dancing. "I had taken a few baby-sitting jobs for pocket money and didn't feel anything special," she remembered. "But with Natalie it became something very special." They grew even closer after Olga's advice helped Natalie succeed in her second test for *Tomorrow Is Forever*, and when she drove Natalie to and from Paramount for *The Bride Wore Boots* during the final weeks of Maria's pregnancy.

> *Olga Viripaeff: I felt really bad about abandoning Natalie when things were so bad between my mother and Nick, but I was in such a state of nerves that my hands were literally shaking, and I was in no condition to help or protect her.*

With phone calls and visits to each other, the half-sisters remained close for the rest of Natalie's life, unlike Maria and Nick with their respective families. The 1917 revolution, of course, had already splintered

Zacharenkos and Zudilovs. Unlike their brother, Vladimir and Dmitri retained the family name, and visited each other more often than they visited Nick. Dmitri, increasingly reclusive in old age, reacted with a long silence when I mentioned Nick and Maria and was hardly more communicative about Natalie: "I knew her just to say hello and goodbye."

Of the Zudilovs, Maria's mother had died in the early 1940s, in the Russian church at Harbin. After making her confession, she knelt down to pray and suffered a fatal heart attack. Maria's father died shortly afterward. The last news of her sister Zoya was that she'd married a Russian businessman and moved with him to Shanghai. After Japan invaded China and occupied the city, the rest was silence. The same ominous silence overtook her half-sister Lilia, who had remained in Harbin and was deported to Soviet Russia. Kalia, the only other Zudilov to leave China, settled in San Francisco with her husband; and their son Constantin remembered that the Gurdins and Liuzunies visited each other "maybe half a dozen times" in thirty years.

In the early San Francisco days, when Natasha was a baby, Olga became a target of Nick Gurdin's drunken violence if she happened to be in the same room as Maria. Now, with Lana a baby and Olga gone, Natalie hid under her bed to avoid his outbursts. As well as fearing and dreading her father when drunk, she was confused by the Jekyll-and-Hyde contrast with his sober self. (When visitors were expected, he was always quietly charming. Constantin Liuzunie recalled that he never saw Nick drunk, and found it hard to reconcile the man he met on family visits with the stories about him.) Later, Natalie came to understand that Nick was a defeated man, humiliated by Maria's taunts that he failed to support his family while she made Natalie Wood a star, and by the suspicion that he was not Lana's father.


MARIA HAD ONCE hoped that Olga might become an opera singer or a pianist, and after her departure she decided that Natalie should resume the piano lessons she'd begun at the age of four and continued until she was cast in *Tomorrow Is Forever*. Playing the piano, her mother explained, could be even more important to an actress's career than ballet dancing: yet another item of received wisdom in the "normal" childhood of the little trouper, who enjoyed the lessons but never found them as challenging as ballet or, most of all, acting.

Box Office *editors (at left) present Natalie with the Blue Ribbon Award.*
*Beside her, Maria, Nick and little Lana*

As Natalie couldn't fit the man she believed to be her father into the pattern of what she supposed was normality, and also couldn't help being afraid of Nick, acting became more and more a way of escape. The studio soundstage was her surest emotional refuge, where she pleased her mother (so warm and loving when pleased), was surrounded by affection and approval, and acquired the sense of pride so important to a child. And as an actress, Hollywood's Blue Ribboned juvenile found herself living in a world where sorrows and dangers eventually dissolved, and tears were always fondly wiped away.

Between 1947 and 1949 Natalie appeared in six Fox productions, each a family picture except for the supernatural romance of *The Ghost and Mrs. Muir.* At Fox, she also found someone whose affection and approval had nothing to do with her career. Among her teachers at the studio schoolhouse was Frances Klampt, small and trim, fortyish and

God-fearing, unemotional but not unfeeling, who ten years earlier had taught Shirley Temple. As well as degrees from UCLA and USC in history, geography, math and education, Klampt had a sense of mission. She believed in the natural creativity of children, and encouraged her pupils to develop talents and interests beyond the world of the soundstage. Klampt's extracurricular talent was for designing ceramics, some of which she kept on display in the schoolroom. When her sharp eye registered Natalie's fascination with them, she not only encouraged her to design her own ceramics, but offered after-hours support.

Natalie gave several of her ceramics to the screen mother she called Mama Maureen. "They were small and really quite beautiful," O'Hara remembered. "I kept them all, and took them to my house in the Caribbean, where they were blown away along with almost everything else by Hurricane Hugo." But Klampt had aroused an interest that continued to develop after Natalie left the schoolroom.

SCUDDA HOO! SCUDDA HAY! was the first of two negligible movies Natalie made for Fox under the contract authorized by Maria. Filming began on February 24, two days after *Miracle on 34th Street* completed production, and the leading players in this down-on-the-farm "comedy romance" had names supposedly parodying *Tobacco Road.* Lon McCallister played Snug; June Haver, his girlfriend, Rad; and Natalie, his kid sister, Bean. The movie also featured Walter Brennan, two mules, and in the unlikely role of a stablehand's girlfriend, the walk-on screen debut of Marilyn Monroe. But when the picture was released in October 1947, she'd walked off again in a twinkle.

McCallister remembered Natalie as "completely unaffected on the set, very bright but the opposite of a precocious child show-off. In a word, adorable." In four more words, Maureen O'Hara (mother to Natalie in the 1949 *Father Was a Fullback* as well as *Miracle on 34th Street*) remembered her as "wonderful, very polite and serious." Child actress Gigi Perreau, who worked with her twice, "liked her very much." And Andrew J. Paris, who called himself the Bubble Gum King of America and first met Natalie on December 27, 1947, wrote her a letter that same day: "Thanks for the luncheon date that revealed to me the remarkable depth of character of a charming little girl."

Maria, of course, was also at the luncheon, whose purpose was to make a deal for Natalie to star in a radio version of *Alice in Wonderland,* sponsored by the Paris Gum Corporation. It aired in late February 1948, on Mutual Broadcasting System's *Family Theatre,* and President Paris expressed his appreciation by sending Alice in Radioland a case of bubble gum.

Fox hadn't chosen Natalie's second contract picture by the time she finished *Scudda Hoo!,* so Maria approved a deal to ship her to Republic Studios for a leading role in a B movie of mysterious provenance. It was her introduction to high-speed eighteen-day shooting schedules and penurious sets, and although the movie in question was homespun Americana, it had originated with two of the less fortunate emigré producers and directors from Europe, who never gained a foothold in the A world of 1940s Hollywood.

Arnold Pressburger, an emigré from Hungary by way of Britain, had managed to produce *The Shanghai Gesture* in 1941 for Josef von Sternberg and *Hangmen Also Die* in 1943 for Fritz Lang, masterly visual stylists who knew how to make the kind of picture that *Variety* labeled "definitely a budgeter" look relatively expensive. In 1945, *Liberty* magazine published *Heaven for Jenny,* a story set in the American heartland by Mary Loos (niece of Anita). Pressburger optioned it and commissioned a screenplay from Loos and Richard Sale, her writing partner and future husband. Did he pick such unlikely material in the hope of "Americanizing" his reputation? If so, he turned for help to the most unlikely director. Léonide Moguy (formerly Maguilevsky) was a Russian who fled to France soon after the 1917 revolution and made several films there before fleeing to America after Hitler's army entered Paris. His work in Hollywood showed that he was no von Sternberg or Lang; its highest (or least low) point was *Whistle Stop,* a toothless and obviously frugal gangster movie with George Raft and Ava Gardner in her first starring role.

After unsuccessfully shopping *Heaven for Jenny* around for more than a year, Pressburger managed to unload it, although not himself or Moguy, on Republic. Among the directors under contract to the studio was Allan Dwan, a silent-movie veteran and a favorite of Republic's owner, Herbert Yates. (He had directed Vera Hruba Ralston, Yates's girlfriend and a former Ice Capades skater, in a couple of pictures that came reasonably close to turning a sow's ear into a silk purse.) Dwan, who had also worked very amicably on a movie written by Loos and Sale the previous year, liked *Heaven for Jenny* well enough to accept Yates's proposal that he direct it. It's not known who decided to change the title to *Drift-wood*, and no producer is listed on the credits, although studio work-sheets name Dwan as associate producer as well as director.

Dwan shot the picture between May 15 and June 2, 1947, and Repub-lic's chronic need for quick returns actually bundled it into general release a month before *Scudda Hoo!* All the same, it allowed Natalie to reveal more depth of character than in most of her major studio produc-tions. Fiercely independent-minded, but at the same time eager to trust other people and consequently very vulnerable, Jenny was the childhood role closest to Natalie's childhood self. But she didn't realize it until she was an adolescent and had learned how to make the leap from "Let's Pre-tend" to Stanislavsky during *Rebel Without a Cause*.

Working with Moguy, a refugee from the Russian Revolution like Natalie's parents, would have been a strange coincidence with dire results. Luckily, another kind of coincidence preempted it. B-movie eco-nomics, combined with the good working relationships between Yates and Dwan, and Mary Loos and Dwan, placed Natalie in the hands of a shrewd and inventive craftsman. Dwan had been Gloria Swanson's favorite director and, more significantly, had given thirteen-year-old Jane Peters (later Carole Lombard) and fourteen-year-old Ida Lupino their first screen roles. "Mary Loos discovered some information about a virus carried by squirrels that hits people . . . and that intrigued her," he said twenty years later, discussing *Driftwood* in an interview with Peter Bogdanovich. "What intrigued me . . . was the ability of the child we found—little Natalie Wood. She had a real talent for acting, an ability to characterize and interpret, and . . . she was a natural."

Orphaned again, from the backwoods instead of post–World War II Europe, Natalie's Jenny is brought up by her grandfather, a hellfire preacher. But he soon dies, and she's left on her own with her beloved collie (shades of *Lassie*), until they're both adopted by an idealistic small-town doctor. A Little Miss Fix-It in the Shirley Temple mold, Jenny has acquired from her grandfather a repertory of judgmental biblical quotes for every situation. At first she finds almost everyone in the town insin-cere and hypocritical, but changes her mind after she almost dies from the squirrel virus. A wonder drug discovered by the doctor and the townsfolk's all-night prayer vigil outside her window combine to save her. As a result, she fervently endorses small-town life: "It's not Sodom and Gomorrah. It's heaven. That's what it is. It's just heaven!" *Miracle on*

*34th Street* did good business by coupling faith with good business, and *Driftwood* did the same by giving its seal of approval to a merger of faith and pharmacology.

"Like all of us," Mary Loos remembered, "Dwan fell in love with Natalie." Under his direction she also gave Jenny a sharp edge of reality. When she quotes the Bible, she really means it; when the virus strikes, she looks genuinely sick and frightened; and with the "ability to characterize" that Dwan noted, she dominates a cast of strangely assorted professionals, among them two friends of the veteran director: H. B. Warner (Christ in DeMille's 1927 *King of Kings*) plays the preacher, and Francis Ford (brother of John) replays his familiar role of town drunk locked up for the night in the town jail. Margaret Hamilton (wicked witch of *The Wizard of Oz*) appears as a vinegary spinster, and Charlotte Greenwood (eccentric cartwheeling dancer of *Down Argentine Way*) as an amiable one; Dean Jagger (*Brigham Young*) plays the doctor, and Ruth Warrick (first wife of *Citizen Kane*) the schoolteacher he's in love with; Walter Brennan is the town's cantankerous old bachelor, and Jerome Cowan (Bogart's partner, shot by Mary Astor, in *The Maltese Falcon*) its mayor.

> *Mary (Loos) Sale: When any of those actors forgot a line, Natalie knew it and prompted them right away. Nobody took offense because they knew she wasn't trying to be clever, she was just genuinely enthusiastic and professional. At that time Natalie was tremendously happy being an actress.*

And at that time, when she was only nine, Natalie's salary averaged $3,000 a movie, slightly less or more according to the number of weeks she was employed. Ten percent of her earnings went to the developing businesswoman, another 10 percent to Famous Artists, and 5 percent to Natalie herself; the rest was invested in government bonds, to remain in a trust fund until her twenty-first birthday.

In spite of her personal success in *Driftwood*, Natalie didn't work for a year after its release. Maria, who refused to accept temporary unemployment as a fact of any actor's life, bristled with disappointment and displeasure. Natalie couldn't fail to notice this, but the idea that Maria's love depended on her daughter going almost immediately from one movie to the next was too painful to admit. Although she banished it to

*As Jenny in* Driftwood

the limbo of denial, like other painful realities of her family life, Robert Wagner feels sure it created "Natalie's drive to work." But her agent kept Little Star in the public eye. As well as becoming a poster child for the American Cancer Society, she attended several movie premieres with Maria in proud attendance. Famous enough to have autograph books thrust in her face, Natalie was photographed arriving at Grauman's Chinese and the Carthay Circle, pigtailed and pinafored among Joan Crawford and Ava Gardner.

Although fame itself became yet another part of "normal" childhood, Natalie was still too young to realize that she was now being marketed as a valuable asset in the celebrity business. She simply found it natural for people to recognize you in person after they'd seen you many times larger than life on a movie screen.

UNTIL FOX SHUTTLED Natalie back to the world of George Seaton for her second contract picture, she attended school at Burbank Public Elementary, and ballet class at Michael Panaieff's studio on La Brea Avenue in Hollywood.

Since 1940, Panaieff had been the reigning exiled Russian ballet teacher in Hollywood, successor to Theodore Kosloff in the 1920s, who was equally in demand by show business. Kosloff, a former member of Diaghilev's Ballets Russes, had choreographed dance sequences for several Cecil B. DeMille movies. Panaieff, a former member of the Ballet Russe de Monte Carlo, partnered the British ice skater and dancer Belita (Belita Jepson-Turner in her pre-Hollywood days) in an evening of ballet at the Hollywood Bowl; played the ballet master in *Hans Christian Andersen;* and appeared in several other movies as a sinister or volatile Russian. The Hollywood connection was catnip to Maria, and also to the mothers of Jill St. John and Stefanie Powers; and it's one of the many ironies of Natalie's life that her ballet classmates should have included the third Mrs. Robert Wagner and his TV wife in *Hart to Hart.*

Panaieff was an exceptionally handsome and accomplished dancer, whose classes attracted Alexandra Danilova whenever the Ballet Russe de Monte Carlo performed in Los Angeles, and Leslie Caron after MGM signed her for *An American in Paris.* At his studio Natalie became friends with Robert Banas, who remembered Maria as "a watchdog" there. He danced with Natalie in several student shows as well as a local TV program, *Backstage with NTG,* and at Natalie's invitation joined her on a TV game show, where "the prize went to the guest who invented the best tongue-twister. As the winning twister was fixed in advance, and Natalie knew it, I won. The prize was a pair of skates, which I didn't want. When I told Natalie I'd rather have a camera, she persuaded the show's MC to make an exchange."

The San Fernando Valley was still partly ranchland when the Gurdins moved to Northridge, where Natalie first learned to ride on a palomino. She quickly became an expert horsewoman, as Banas discovered when they went riding together in Griffith Park. He also admired her skill at leaping like a kangaroo on a pogo stick: as Nick Gurdin was not athletic, perhaps Natalie had inherited a Zepaloff gene.

"After high school," Banas recalled, "our paths diverged," but he visited Natalie a year later on the set of *Never a Dull Moment,* and they met again on the set of *West Side Story.* By then he'd worked as a professional dancer with Jerome Robbins, who created the role of Joyboy (one of the Jets) for him in the movie version.

When Panaieff was working on a movie, Tamara Lepko replaced him, until she joined the Buckley School in 1950. Banas described her as

*Michael Panaieff's ballet class. Center, Natalie*
*on point. Bob Banas is on her right.*

"a wonderful woman and teacher"; Jill St. John Wagner remembered "a rather stern-looking woman with blond hair parted in the middle and pulled back into a bun." Evidently Maria kept her secret well, and Irene Lepko, in high school at the time, heard not even the whisper of a rumor, then or later. The Gurdins and the Lepkos continued to spend "family" evenings together, and Maria moved Natalie to the Buckley School when Tamara began teaching there.

This was typical of Maria, compulsive giver as well as taker of risks. "She loved giving presents," Olga remembered, "even to the extent of giving away my ballet-class tutus before I finished ballet school." And no one could have been so reckless so often, in her personal life or at the wheel of a car, without getting a rush of adrenaline to the head.

IN LATE AUGUST 1948 Natalie reported for work on *Chicken Every Sunday,* adapted from a Broadway play adapted from a best-selling novel. To play the father of a large family whose addiction to disastrous investment schemes kept him on the edge of bankruptcy, and the mother whose need for security led her to the brink of divorce, George Seaton had wanted Henry Fonda and Maureen O'Hara. When they proved unavailable, he settled for an unlikely pair of second-string contract players at Fox, Dan Dailey and Celeste Holm. In box-office terms, it seems to have made no difference. Although set in the early 1900s, the movie's fortune-cookie wisdom about togetherness 1940s-style ensured a popular success. But while Mom and Dad realize they have all the security they need in "loving each other," Natalie as their youngest daughter is less well provided for. The role was sketchy; for once reviewers found little or nothing to say about her, and in later life she couldn't remember if she ever saw it.

Although Natalie was always grateful to Seaton for *Miracle on 34th Street,* she was personally fonder of Mama Maureen and Edmund Gwenn, the ideal grandfather figure. She visited the wily actor in 1958 when he was stricken with cancer; and after he died, she often told a story about his almost-last words to Seaton. The director saw his pain and said very quietly, "I know it must be difficult." "It is," Gwenn answered. "Dying is very difficult. But not quite as difficult as playing comedy."

A NEAR-DEATH EXPERIENCE may not be quite as difficult as playing comedy, but you remember it for the rest of your life; and it was Natalie's very specific and fearful memory of the movie she made immediately after *Chicken Every Sunday.* The provenance of *The Green Promise,* like the movie itself, was bizarre. "A Glenn McCarthy Production," it was financed by the Texas oil tycoon of that name, whose worth in 1948 was estimated at between $200 million and $400 million. As well as oil and hotels, he promoted family values and the 4-H Clubs, youth organizations that educated children of farmers in the latest agricultural skills and encouraged them to develop a code of truth telling and self-reliance. The screenplay of *The Green Promise* was brought to McCarthy by Robert Paige, an undistinguished leading man of undistinguished pictures (*Shady Lady, Son of Dracula*), and Monty Collins, former gag man for two-reel comedies in the silent era. This odd couple had presumably heard through McCarthy's friend Howard Hughes of his interest in producing a dramatic movie that would combine family and 4-H values. In any case, they struck a deal for themselves as co-producers, and Hughes agreed to distribute the picture through RKO, in which he'd recently acquired controlling stock. To complete the first eccentric circle, William D. Russell, director of a few routine comedies, was signed at the suggestion of his friend Collins.

Casting completed the second circle. As the pigheaded farmer who ignores a 4-H warning that if he cuts down a hillside forest, erosion and dangerous slides will occur when the next storm breaks: Walter Brennan. As the nineteen-year-old daughter of the family he tyrannizes: former child actress Diana Lynn, age twenty. (But she broke her arm ten days into shooting and was replaced by Marguerite Chapman, at thirty-two a veteran of more than twenty B movies.) As the two younger daughters: Natalie and a child actress soon to disappear from movies, Connie Marshall. As the son: child actor Ted Donaldson (*A Tree Grows in Brooklyn*), by then fifteen, whose career also had not much longer to run. And as the 4-H representative, whose romance with the eldest daughter is vetoed by her father: co-producer Paige, age thirty-nine and starting to put on weight.

A hard man with a buck, McCarthy was determined to advertise his convictions as cheaply as possible. *The Green Promise* required a small cast, minimal sets, simple exteriors, and a very modest splurge on the climactic storm scene. Interiors were shot on the edge of Poverty Row at Monogram Pictures, home of *The Wolf Man*, *The Ape Man*, and *Night Monster;* but inexperienced producers, and the delay caused by replacing Diana Lynn, meant that the picture was twice as long in production as the usual cut-rate enterprise. It began shooting on August 23, 1948, and finished six weeks later, on October 2.

What was Natalie doing in such grungy company? In spite of Maria's later protestations ("I didn't want her money, I came from family with money"), she expected the offers to keep rolling in. And Natalie's agent was shrewd enough to realize that her role was the best in the picture. As the only member of the family courageous enough to stand up to her father, she would stand out from everyone else.

Although her agent proved right, the personal cost to Natalie was unforeseeably high. The climactic scene of *The Green Promise* occurs after Susan is told at a 4-H meeting, "The thing you do for yourself always gives you the most satisfaction." It's too late for anyone to save the hillside when a violent storm breaks, but not too late for Susan to rescue her two pet lambs. Darkness has fallen by the time she reaches a wooden footbridge over a formerly dry creek that's now a torrent, surging with the debris of uprooted trees and scrub. The screenplay describes what happens next:

EXT. BANK OF CREEK—NIGHT
SUSAN faces the bridge, then, plunging blindly, runs across the
trembling waters. She has scarcely reached the far bank when,
with a crack of fracturing wood, the bridge gives way and is torn
out of the scene by the rushing waters.

Like the director, crew and special-effects team, Maria knew that the footbridge was timed to collapse; and she agreed that Natalie mustn't be told, because it might frighten her. On Russell's call of "Action!" Natalie started running, but the bridge broke in half too soon. She couldn't turn back, as the first half had disintegrated. But immediately ahead of her, a plank was suspended from the remaining half, and by clinging to it she managed to stop herself falling into the torrent below and being swept to almost certain death. Fortunately the plank held firm while she clambered to safety in driving rain and wind, and so did the rest of the bridge until she reached the opposite bank.

Russell ordered the camera to keep turning, and the shot remains in the movie. It records an expression of terror on Natalie's face that is clearly not acted, but a naked moment of "just being herself." Physically, her only injury was a distended wristbone. When Maria learned that surgery might not succeed in resetting the bone, she wanted to sue the production company for negligence, but was advised it could harm Natalie's career. And for the rest of her life, Natalie concealed the protruding bone on her left wrist with a bracelet, a leather band, a long sleeve, or (when wearing a swimsuit) a flesh-colored Band-Aid.

Psychologically, she suffered more than one permanent injury, and in retrospect 1948 was Natalie's year of ironies. The fear of dark water created by Maria widened to any expanse of water apart from a swimming pool—a bitter legacy in view of the terrible circumstances of her actual death. And when she learned that her mother had known the bridge would collapse, it added to the feelings she wasn't yet ready to confront: anxiety and confusion about the life she'd led, or been led into, from the

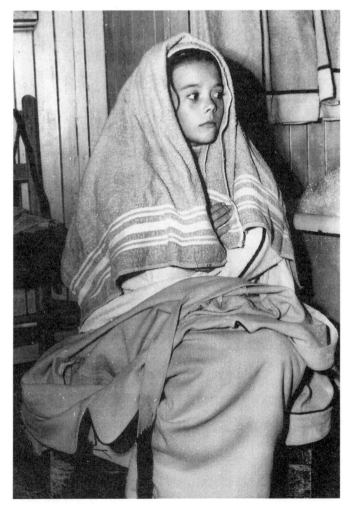

The Green Promise, *after the near-death experience*

day she thought of her dead puppy and won the part in *Tomorrow Is Forever.*

A SIX-MONTH DELAY occurred in distributing *The Green Promise* after it completed production, as Glenn McCarthy wanted the premiere to coincide with the opening of his new Shamrock Hotel in Houston. The hotel wasn't ready until late March 1949, when a not-quite-A list of star guests (including Sonja Henie, Robert Stack, Pat O'Brien, Dorothy

Lamour, Robert Ryan, Van Heflin and Joan Caulfield) boarded the Shamrock Special from Union Station and were treated to dinner and an overnight stay after the movie. Two weeks later, *The Green Promise* was coolly received by the press, although Natalie's performance drew the usual accolades of "natural" and "exceptionally clever." But the movie made good money in the heartland; and by taking the moral high ground, as well as adding useful tips on farming to yet another story of family problems resolved and true love finding a way, it gained public endorsements from the Daughters of the American Revolution, the General Federation of Women's Clubs, the Girl Scouts, the Southern California Council of Church Women—and of course the 4-H Clubs.

ALTHOUGH MARY PICKFORD was twenty-nine when she played *Little Lord Fauntleroy,* the usual cutoff age for a child star is around fourteen, so Natalie had four years left after *The Green Promise.* During that time she made nine movies, all except one produced or released by major studios. Her new screen mothers included Irene Dunne, Margaret Sullavan, Joan Blondell, and Bette Davis. Among her screen fathers were Fred MacMurray, James Stewart, and Bing Crosby—actors with considerably more star power than the previous trio (Robert Cummings, John Payne, Walter Brennan). One screen father and one screen mother neglected her at first but made up for it later. Two screen mothers were divorced career women. A third died and was replaced by a (loving, not wicked) stepmother.

But only one of the nine movies allowed Natalie to display more than uncomplaining professionalism; and while she spent most of her screen life in a familiar unreal world, she had time offscreen for almost another year of regular school, as well as two trips to San Francisco. A photograph taken during the late fall of 1948, when the Gurdins visited Olga and the Liuzunie family, shows Natalie looking more like the lonely orphan of *Tomorrow Is Forever* than the girl joyfully converted to belief in Santa Claus in *Miracle on 34th Street.* But on February 20, 1949, the Gurdins attended Olga's wedding to Alexei Viripaeff, an insurance broker, at the same Russian church on Fulton Street where Maria had married Nicholas Gurdin eleven years earlier; and this time, photographed in her bridesmaid's gown, Natalie looks as genuinely happy as she's supposed to be at the end of her next movie.

Her contract with Fox entitled the studio to an option for two more pictures, and it was exercised after the success of *Chicken Every Sunday.* The first, *Father Was a Fullback,* began shooting a month after Olga's wedding, and starred Fred MacMurray as the coach of a successful university football team. When it hits a losing streak, the situation creates problems with his wife (Maureen O'Hara) and family; and the script, written mainly by Mary Loos and Richard Sale, reworks *Chicken Every Sunday.* (Mary [Loos] Sale: "When you're under contract, sometimes you have to do as you're told.") Although both movies are equally insignificant, the later one has more attractive leading players and gives Natalie, in her first "brat" role, a few more opportunities. As well as a black eye for defending her father, she received favorable notices in the reviews that noticed her.

The very mild commercial success of *Father Was a Fullback* was probably due to a director less at ease with sitcom than George Seaton. John M. Stahl, a silent-movie veteran, had reached his peak in the 1930s and early 1940s with a series of pre–Douglas Sirk emotional melodramas that culminated in *Leave Her to Heaven.* But George Marshall, who directed Natalie's next movie, was a more commonplace silent-movie veteran who had reached only one peak (*Destry Rides Again,* 1939); and *Never a Dull Moment,* which began shooting in May 1949, was one of his deeper valleys.

In a sagebrush comedy that reversed the situation of *The Bride Wore Boots,* a city sophisticate tries to adjust to life in Wyoming with her rancher husband. Screen-mothered by Irene Dunne (after Myrna Loy turned the part down) and screen-fathered once again by Fred MacMurray, Natalie had two key scenes with her screen sister, eight-year-old Gigi Perreau. Offscreen, as Perreau remembered, they had a few more during their obligatory hours at the studio schoolhouse: "I liked Natalie very much, but was very perplexed by the notes she kept slipping me in class. I don't recall the exact words, only the meaning, which was the same every time—'*I'm* going to be a star, but *you're* not.' Then my first encounter with Natalie's incredibly pushy mother, who was furious that the studio had decided to bill my name above Natalie's, made me realize that some of her ambition had rubbed off on her daughter." It was "a whole new concept" for Perreau, whose parents were not ambitious for her, and who had never experienced "this kind of relentless drive before. In those days we worked for the fun of it, and the recognition. Prestige was as important as money, unlike today, when it's all a question of how much you can earn how quickly." But Maria (incorrectly) believed that Perreau planned to upstage her daughter, and as Natalie had never before been jealous of other child actors, there's no doubt who originated the idea of those notes. All the same, Natalie's role of accomplice suggests that her mother's ambition had begun to rub off, and Little Star had begun to believe that she was somehow special. As if to confirm it, the Children's Day Council voted her Child Star of the Year at the end of 1950.

Not coincidentally, the adult Natalie Wood took stardom very seriously, but also made fun of herself for being so serious about it.


DURING THE FILMING of *Never a Dull Moment,* another episode occurred that underscores the appalling emotional divide between Natalie's own family and the families she belonged to in movies. When a piece of furniture on the set needed repairing one day, a studio carpenter was summoned to fix it. Minutes later, Nick Gurdin appeared. "Hi, Dad!" his excited daughter called out, and a pall of silence descended over the entire stage. Director and cast stared from child star to carpenter and back again, and Natalie would have run to greet her father if Maria hadn't held her back.

Later, her mother told Natalie that she'd seriously embarrassed her co-workers. A carpenter, like a grip or an electrician, was a social inferior who never fraternized with directors or actors, least of all with a star or, of course, a star's mother. And Maria warned Natalie never to acknowledge her father if she encountered him at the studio again.


SOME TIME AFTER *Never a Dull Moment* completed production, Maria drove Natalie to visit Olga and her husband at their vacation cottage in Camp Rose, north of San Francisco. (Miraculously, Maria negotiated the round trip on Pacific Coast Highway, and others she made later, without incident or accident.) A few miles before Camp Rose, she parked the car outside a beauty shop in Healdsburg, only a few blocks from the scene of Natalie's movie debut in *Happy Land.* The shop was run by Maria's old friend Nina Kiyaschenko, who had divorced George Zepaloff after a marriage that lasted less than six years.

*Natalie as a bridesmaid at*
*Olga Viripaeff's wedding*

In 1946 the Captain had told Nina, "I'm going away again, and this time I'm not coming back." A year later Nina heard that her husband had returned to San Francisco, and managed to track him down: "I told him he should at least meet our daughter, who hardly remembered him because he'd hardly ever spent any time with her. He agreed to meet us at a hotel bar, then disappeared and left me with practically no money. When I divorced him, Zepaloff made a scene in court because the judge ordered him to pay $150 a month in alimony and $150 child support for Natasha. He made only one payment, then got himself transferred to a Matson cruise ship on the East Coast."

As Nina couldn't afford to take him to court, she supported herself and daughter Natasha by running a beauty shop in Healdsburg. Maria knew about this because she'd kept in touch with the Captain after he moved east. And the fact that she left Nick and Lana behind on this trip makes it clear that her plans included a visit to one of her favorite places, the edge.

In the beauty shop, Maria introduced Natalie to Nina, who introduced them both to young Natasha, then remarked (in complete innocence at the time) how alike their two girls looked.

THE RELEASE of *Never a Dull Moment* was delayed until November 1950, after new scenes had been added and the editing tightened, in a vain attempt to make the film live up to its title. Consequently, four Natalie Wood movies reached theaters that year; in the first, she's on the cusp of the awkward age, and by the last she's halfway through it.

The first began as *Beloved Over All*, became *With All My Love* during production, and was released in February 1950 as *Our Very Own*. In Natalie's most upscale movie since *Tomorrow Is Forever*, an American family that prides itself on being "as normal as blueberry pie" lives in a suburban Shangri-la: picket fences as impeccably white as everyone's teeth, mirrors as immaculate as the faces they reflect, every room in the house a designer's calling card. Samuel Goldwyn's production, shot at the Goldwyn Studios, was his answer to the suburban Shangri-la of David O. Selznick's *Since You Went Away* of 1944. The same masterly cinematographer, Lee Garmes, created its high visual gloss, and the screenplay (by F. Hugh Herbert, author of the Broadway hit *Kiss and Tell*) made the same equation of family values and patriotism.

At the center of *Our Very Own* is the eldest daughter (Ann Blyth). On the eve of her graduation from high school, she learns that she's adopted and goes into an emotional tailspin. But after hysterically rejecting her adoptive parents, she discovers where she came from and realizes that her true family is the one that cared for her. "Next to the privilege of being an American," she announces in her graduation speech on the Privileges of Citizenship, "is belonging to a family." It brings down the house.

She's arrived at the moment of truth after deciding to visit the mother who put her out for adoption and finding herself on the wrong side of the tracks. No sunlight on picket fences here, but a shabby frame house in the gray dusk, children playing in the street outside, the whistle of a train from the nearby railroad. Through the living-room window she glimpses a group of men playing poker and a tired, heavily made-up woman bringing them beer. It's too much for this material girl. She knows instantly where she belongs, and heads for home in her gleaming convertible.

Only one scene, expertly acted, makes contact with a recognizable form of contemporary life. Adoptive mother meets actual mother, and Jane Wyatt's steely graciousness confronts Ann Dvorak's sad vulgarity. But as the stereotypically smartass youngest daughter, Natalie was praised (once again) for her "natural" performance in a role that should have been unbearably irritating. Although charm and humor (once again) saw her through, she had the advantage of playing her age, unlike the actresses cast as teenagers soon to graduate from high school: Ann Blyth (twenty-two), middle sister Joan Evans (twenty-six), and best friend Phyllis Kirk (twenty-six).

Like so many emotional dramas of the 1940s and 1950s, *Our Very Own* has the fascination of a grotesquely dated artifact. Although directed by David Miller, its style is communal, with the same almost hypnotic confidence of other experts in the same genre—Curtis Bernhardt (*Possessed*), Irving Rapper (*Deception*), Edmund Goulding (*The Great Lie*). "The problems are so darling and sweet," as George Cukor remarked after seeing the Bette Davis version of *A Stolen Life* (Bernhardt) on TV. "Nothing to do with anything that's happening now. But where people make a mistake," he added, "is to think of all this as just absurd. One has to take into account what was really going on, for better or for worse."

When Natalie took this into account a few years later, she found it was on the whole for worse. Meanwhile, in May 1950, she started work at Columbia on another movie equally trapped in its period. *No Sad Songs for Me,* Margaret Sullavan's last film, cast her as a mother dying of cancer, ten years before her actual death from an overdose of sleeping pills. During her relentlessly heroic last months, she prepares husband (Wendell Corey) and daughter (Natalie) for life after her death, and even chooses her husband's second wife (Viveca Lindfors), knowing she's secretly in love with him and will make a good stepmother.

Still an off-limits word in the 1950s, cancer is never named in the movie, and Sullavan's appearance betrays no sign of any disease: another convention of the period, especially in star vehicles, and *No Sad Songs*

*Ideal screen family in* Our Very Own. *Left to right:*
*father (Donald Cook), middle daughter (Joan Evans),*
*youngest daughter (Natalie), mother (Jane Wyatt), boyfriend*
*(Farley Granger) of eldest daughter (Ann Blyth)*

was emphatically a star vehicle. Natalie, like Lindfors and Corey, has little to do except look lovingly sympathetic and grief-stricken. But Rudolph Maté, who recently had begun directing movies after twenty years as an imaginative lighting cameraman, not only made sure that the star was lit as glowingly as he'd once lit Dietrich, Rita Hayworth and Carole Lombard; he also proved skillful in monitoring tears, and Sullavan—whose voice Louise Brooks compared to "a voice singing in the snow"—hit the self-sacrificial notes without holding them too long.

Natalie remembered Sullavan as "very kind" and "maternal" but was mystified when she became edgy and impatient with other actors for no

*Ideal screen father: with Fred MacMurray in*
Father Was a Fullback

apparent reason. In fact, the deafness that would eventually end her career was already in its early stages. When Lindfors or Corey lowered their voices during an intimate scene, Sullavan accused them of not "giving" enough, because she was determined to conceal the fact that she couldn't hear what they said.

OUT OF PIGTAILS but into the awkward age, Natalie ended 1950 with yet another negligible family comedy at Fox. *The Jackpot* was released in November, two months after *No Sad Songs,* and starred James Stewart as an "average" American father, euphoric when he wins first prize in a radio quiz show, desolate when he learns he'll have almost nothing left after paying taxes. As his daughter, Natalie again has little to do, and the part marks a kind of turning point in her career. Beanpole thin, she's clearly under strain, directed to act and react as a pigtailed eight-year-old when she's really twelve. And she's not quite plain but not quite pretty, with nothing in her appearance to suggest she'll ever become a great beauty.

*Ideal screen mother: with Bette Davis in* The Star

Not surprisingly, she'll be less in demand for the next few years: something that had already happened to Peggy Ann Garner (so memorable in *A Tree Grows in Brooklyn*) and was happening at the same time to Margaret O'Brien (so fiendishly talented in *Meet Me in St. Louis*). For them, it's a dying fall; but although Natalie will never join the ranks of child stars for whom the bell tolled, she will spend more time at Van Nuys High, in a world far distant from a movie set and with a family distinctly less normal than blueberry pie, where her mother consulted the tarot for a sign that a change of fortune was on the way and Nick Gurdin still raised Cain four or five times a year—sometimes so violently that Maria drove Natalie and Lana to a nearby motel for the night.

Of the three movies that Natalie made over the next two years, with three new star mothers, the first was an RKO weeper, *The Blue Veil*. Directed by the eternally self-assured Curtis Bernhardt, and adapted by

Norman Corwin from a 1942 French film, it centers on a former governess who recalls her life over the past thirty years in a series of flashbacks. The producer, Jerry Wald, had tried unsuccessfully to interest both Garbo and Ingrid Bergman in the role before casting Jane Wyman. Thirty-six at the time, she spent the framing episodes graciously aged in latex, and the earlier ones adroitly key-lit, as a penniless young widow who becomes a governess after her husband dies in France in World War I.

Natalie appears in a flashback as one of her charges, the neglected daughter of a New York musical comedy star (Joan Blondell, splendidly costumed in a Cossack-style ermine hat, ermine wrap slung across a black tunic and diamond-studded black stockings). In the movie's weepiest scene, the governess persuades Blondell to give up her fading career for her child. Tearfully overcome with joy at finding her real mother again, Natalie is equally tearful at losing her substitute one, while Wyman bravely and tearfully prepares for another sacrificial goodbye. But the scene is far less embarrassing than it sounds, thanks to Joan Blondell's tact and skill as she reveals the simple heart beneath her tarnished brassiness, and to Natalie once again getting under the skin of a lonely child.

On September 5, 1951, *The Blue Veil* had a gala premiere at the Carthay Circle Theater. It was promoted as a family picture, and Wyman made the event a family affair by bringing Maureen, her daughter by her former husband Ronald Reagan. But she was upstaged by Joan Crawford, who brought her *two* adopted children, Christina and Christopher. Freighted with jewelry, the glaze of a loving maternal smile on her face, she took over (until the movie began) as the star attraction.

Thirty years of lonely courage in the leading role gained Wyman an Academy Award nomination, but most of the reviewers praised Blondell and Natalie above the rest of the cast (which included Charles Laughton and Agnes Moorehead). The period detail in *The Blue Veil* is vague, but Natalie's episode is presumably set in the early 1930s, as at one point Blondell sings "There'll Be Some Changes Made." Natalie plays her only sustained scene in a frilly white confirmation dress, and at this stage in her life it makes the awkward age look less awkward.

She's also starting to look prettier, and although her next movie allowed her to play her age and seem relaxed in contemporary jeans and sweater, it did nothing else for her. With a script by Robert Carson, co-author of the 1937 *A Star Is Born,* and an uncredited "polish" to the New York theater scenes by playwright John Van Druten, *Just for You* was in production at Paramount from mid-October to mid-December 1951. The director was Elliott Nugent, who had collaborated with James Thurber on his only work for the stage, *The Male Animal,* and later directed the film version. The songs were by Harry Warren (*42nd Street*) and Leo Robin (*Gentlemen Prefer Blondes*), and the cast included Bing Crosby as a producer of Broadway musicals, Jane Wyman as the star of his latest hit, Ethel Barrymore as the principal of a snobbish girl's school and Natalie as Crosby's neglected daughter. But after noting "the talent line-up" when *Just for You* was released in May 1952, the reviewer for the *Hollywood Reporter* found nothing to praise except Wyman's legs ("whistle bait") in her "Zing a Little Zong" number with Crosby. In spite of the bait, the movie failed to lure an audience.

Meanwhile, Natalie had been shipped back to Monogram Studios for the tackiest B picture she ever made, and the last and most tiresome of her brattish-kid-sister roles. In *The Rose Bowl Story* Vera Miles played her older sister, a Rose Princess at the Tournament of Roses in Pasadena, and Marshall Thompson a quarterback who falls in love with her while training for the Rose Bowl football game. Quickly shot during the last twenty days of May, it was quickly released and instantly forgotten in September—the same month that Natalie reported for work on another movie with a schedule only four days longer.

By this time she had celebrated her fourteenth birthday (on July 20) and also had her first period. But as Maria had never explained the facts of menstruation, the flow of bloody fluid terrified her.

> *Natasha Gregson Wagner: My mother was convinced she was dying and screamed for help. She never forgot that moment, as she told me thirty years later. When I was eleven, she made a point of talking to me about sex and periods.*

A few weeks after her first period, Natalie experienced another trauma. *The Star,* in which she played Bette Davis's daughter, was shot entirely on actual locations, one of them a sailboat belonging to Sterling Hayden, who played Davis's lover. The director, Stuart Heisler, evidently decided to add a moment when Natalie dives into the Pacific and swims toward a nearby raft. It doesn't occur in the script, and when Heisler proposed it, Natalie assumed he would use a double. But Heisler wanted a close shot and refused to listen when she explained her fear of the ocean. When he insisted, Natalie began to scream hysterically, and the sound brought Davis out from her dressing-room cabin. At a 1977 American Film Institute tribute to the star, Natalie recalled Davis's threat to leave the picture unless Heisler employed a double. "This was the only time I saw the famous Bette Davis temperament surface," she said, then smiled at her as she added: "And it was not in her own behalf."

Later, Maria claimed that *she* was also on board the sailboat and threatened to halt production unless Heisler used a double. If nobody bothered to call her bluff, it was surely because, in the release print of *The Star,* nobody dives off the sailboat, and there was no double on call, as the scene wasn't in the script. Like a few others, the sailboat scene looks hastily shot; and the number of abrupt dissolves throughout the movie suggests that a tight budget dictated a number of cuts during production. As well as saving money on the sailboat loaned by Hayden, producer Bert Friedlob economized by using his own home for the Beverly Hills mansion once owned by the fallen star.

The script of *The Star* was the work of two magazine writers, Dale Eunson and his wife, Katherine Albert; and they based the character of Margaret Elliot, who can only relate to life as portrayed in her movies and believes she's still young and attractive enough to play romantic leads, on Joan Crawford. (Albert had worked for a contentious time as her publicist at MGM.) One scene even makes an unmistakable physical reference to Crawford in her current *Harriet Craig/This Woman Is Dangerous* mode. Convinced that she's tested successfully for a role that will launch her comeback, Elliot adopts a stern upswept hairstyle, enlarged eyebrows and mouth. Davis herself was obviously in on the joke.

The movie itself has a few sharply written scenes that survive blunt direction; effective when she holds back, Davis verges on self-parody when she lets rip. And Natalie's insipid role is apparent from her first line of dialogue, when Davis pays her a surprise visit: "Oh, Mother, Mother! I have the most beautiful mother in the world!" But by now she can fall back on more than uncomplaining professionalism. The awkward age over, a swimsuit reveals her perfect figure, and although not yet a beauty, she's more than pretty, with the "elusive" and "insidious" grace that Nabokov's Humbert Humbert found in his Lolita.

Friedlob had raised money for *The Star* on a distribution guarantee from Fox, whose publicity department devised a slogan for its release during Christmas week of 1952: "She Was a Star from Start to Finish When She Finally Became a Woman." In the 1950s, of course, becoming a woman meant becoming a wife and mother, so Margaret Elliot surrenders her fantasy of a glamorous comeback to marriage with her patient, down-to-earth lover, and grants her daughter's wish for security and a normal family life.

LIKE HER FIRST MOVIE, Natalie's education in the actual world had begun as a test of strength. At Burbank Public Elementary, Maria had made sure that she maintained her "Little Star Big Future" image, and in a new pinafore dress, with new ribbons in her pigtails, Natalie seemed absurdly out of date. Nine-year-old girls in her class were wearing sweaters or blouses and skirts; prepubescents in higher grades styled their hair; a few teenagers wore lipstick; and most students were as impatient to grow up as Maria was determined that Natalie remain an eternal Child of the Year.

Although not unfriendly, her classmates kept a distance from the strange little girl taught by her mother to curtsy when introduced to her teachers; and her first sustained contact with life beyond a studio stage made the strange little girl realize, as Natalie said later, that she and her mother had been "living on an island," and that kids in the actual world behaved very differently from kids (and parents) in her movies.

By the time she transferred to Robert Fulton Junior High in the winter of 1950–51, Natalie had persuaded her mother to let her wear a sweater and skirt. Less than a month later, her agents transferred her to Paramount for ten days' work as a supporting brat in *Dear Brat* and added almost $2,000 to the Gurdins' bank account. And toward the end of 1951 she developed a crush on the son of a dairy farmer, a student named Jim Williams.

After Natalie died, more than one man cast himself as her first love, but only Williams claimed the role of her first lover. In the Williams version, their affair began soon after Natalie transferred as a sophomore to Van Nuys High in January 1953; and toward the end of the year, when Maria discovered that he'd taken her daughter's virginity, she made Natalie desperately unhappy by insisting the lovers must never see each other again. The reason for a lack of credibility here begins with Olga's denial that the affair had become so "intense" (as Williams claimed) that Natalie phoned her for advice: "Natalie never told me that she was in love with any boy at this time. I had one call from her to say she'd decided to break up with a boy she'd been dating called Jim Williams, wanted to give him a ring as a parting present, and could I lend her the money as she'd spent her allowance that month. I sent her about twenty dollars." Olga was equally certain that Natalie and Williams were never lovers: "After I went to live in San Francisco I stayed in close touch with my mother, who called regularly and often very dramatically with family news. If she'd found out Natalie had lost her virginity, the call would have been very dramatic indeed. Besides, Natalie made it very clear to me that it was her own decision not to see this boy anymore."

DURING HER SOPHOMORE YEAR, Natalie had two experiences (neither of them with Jim Williams) that would affect her whole life. The first was her discovery of various gaps in her education. Eager to catch up on any subjects that interested her (art, drama, history), she learned quickly, and would never lose her appetite for knowledge. And because learning, like acting, appealed to her sense of pride, she made a private resolution to graduate from Van Nuys High.

The second experience was the mutation of a child star into a former child star, who knew that the Gurdins had never been on the same planet as the happy-ever-after families she'd pretended to belong to in so many movies. Another warning signal flashed in 1953 when Famous Artists sold her to TV for *Playmates,* an episode of *Schaefer Century Theatre.* Nineteen-year-old Bonita Granville, a former child star (*These Three*) with a foundering adolescent career, got solo top billing. Fourteen-year-old Natalie, her career on the brink of foundering, was featured in smaller letters below.

Another thing she knew: all those Children of the Year and growing girls she'd played, and believed in, and won praise for making so "natural," now felt like somebody else. As for her real self, with all those false selves accumulating inside her over the past eight years, she had never been allowed the time or opportunity to discover it.

But she couldn't know, of course, that she was just two years away from the movie role that would introduce her to herself. If you accept

Jung's belief that coincidence may be more than a chance event, this movie becomes a startling example of screen life and personal life making instant and far-reaching contact. Most obviously, Natalie will play a high-school teenager who rebels against her family at the same time as Natalie the high-school teenager begins to rebel openly at home. Less obviously, by introducing Natalie to her first two lovers, the movie will release a sexual drive that colors the rest of her life; and its director and leading actor will unlock the door to her future as an actress.

Meanwhile, although Natalie also knew that ambition had deformed her mother's life, she didn't yet know how to deal with the situation. Their relationship was already tragic, with Natalie aware of how much she owed to a mother who could be wonderfully loving and formidably angry; and she was torn between a need to love her and a need to repress the reasons for not loving her. It was the kind of relationship that could only become more tragic, until her mother's urge to control (which Maria herself was unable to control) would force Natalie to put a terminal distance between them.

The situation with Nick was less complex, in spite of his sometimes terrifying physical violence. At least she had witnessed his other side: his love of reading, the emotion in his voice when he talked about the suffering that the Russian Revolution caused his family, the look of mingled respect and sadness on his face when he showed her the iconic portrait of Tsar Nicholas II.

But Maria's emotional violence was the more dangerous, to herself as well as to Natalie. It gradually overpowered her other side; and like anyone with consuming obsessions, Maria could never let go—not only of her daughter, but of her romance with the Captain and the life of intrigue it obliged and excited her to lead. And when she thought it important, the "con artist" could also put on a great show of charm, respectability and distinction as the "former ballerina of Franco-Russian descent," and even convince Maureen O'Hara that "she wasn't a stage mother at all."

Until her memory began to fail, Maria would tell anyone willing to listen that her own unswerving determination was mainly responsible for making Natalie a star. It's one of her claims with more than a grain of truth; but Maria could never admit (and never understand) that she was also mainly responsible for Natalie's deepest, most persistent fears.

# 3

# Growing Pains

*One day, at Big Sur, we sat looking at the ocean, and I told Natalie: "The ocean's always seemed to me like a huge rocking chair or a cradle. It always soothes me." And Natalie said: "Don, I've never been able to make friends with the ocean."*

—DONFELD

O N THE LAST WEEKEND of August 1981, MGM chartered a private bus to take director Douglas Trumbull, producer John Foreman and three members of the cast of *Brainstorm* from Los Angeles to the Esalen Institute near Big Sur on the Pacific coast. The cast members were Natalie, Louise Fletcher and Cliff Robertson (but not Christopher Walken, who was detained in New York), and Natalie had asked her friend Donfeld, costume designer on the movie, to accompany her.

Near the end of the journey she glanced out the window at a solitary house overlooking the ocean and suddenly remembered herself as a child of eight playing Gene Tierney's daughter in a hoop skirt. "I'm sure that's the house they used for *The Ghost and Mrs. Muir,*" she said. Now forty-three, Natalie was about to play the wife of a scientist who invented a "sensory experience" machine that enabled its user to relive, and be transformed by, a key personal experience from the past.

Trumbull, who had devised the special effects for *2001* and *Star Trek,* was interested in a seminar at the institute on the "death and rebirth" experience, and hoped to get some ideas from its slide-show illustrations of images from ancient Greek, Egyptian and Mesoamerican cultures. The seminar also included supervised group exercises in accelerated breathing and deep meditation, which Natalie didn't attend. In fact, she

*Another ideal screen mother, gravely but bravely ill:*
*Margaret Sullavan, with ideal husband Wendell Corey and*
*daughter Natalie in* No Sad Songs for Me

had been unsure what to expect, as a visit to Esalen twelve years earlier had provided Paul Mazursky with a point of departure for his comedy *Bob & Carol & Ted & Alice,* his first feature film and Natalie's last successful one.

But Stanislav Grof and his wife, Christina, who created the seminar, and the illustrated lecture that she attended with Donfeld, made a deep impression on her. A former assistant professor of psychiatry at the Johns Hopkins University School of Medicine, and researcher for the U.S. government into LSD as a therapeutic drug, Grof had also explored the spiritual disciplines of Zen, Siddha Yoga, and Native American and Mexican shamans. By the time he became scholar-in-residence at Esalen, he was no longer interested in drug therapy, and like Christina he disassociated himself from the current fads of New Age, a phrase that she pronounced to rhyme with "sewage."

The slide-show images, according to Stanislav, "reflected the night journey of the self to the underworld, and its return." For Natalie they proved an unexpectedly helpful experience, not only on account of a scene that she'd have to play in *Brainstorm,* but because of her own personal night journeys over the years, and of the death of Nick Gurdin a few months earlier. The images also stirred thoughts of "facing mortality," and she told the Grofs that when the movie began shooting in a month's time on location in Raleigh, North Carolina, she would like to invite them to visit her for a private talk.

Although the ocean had always seemed unfriendly, as Natalie told Don when they took an afternoon walk before the lecture, then sat on a cliff overlooking the Pacific, a swimming pool never aroused the same fear. But during that weekend at Esalen, he remembered, she not only had the pool lights turned on an hour before sunset while she exercised in the water to firm her waistline; she asked Don to hold out a small brick and clutched it tightly with one hand.

Fear of dark waters, of course, had haunted Natalie since the age of ten, and extended to the ocean after Maria confided that the Gypsy's warning made her so afraid of it that she refused to learn to swim. But lately both these fears had intensified, like the fear of betrayal that was first aroused by Maria's complicity in the secret of the bridge timed to collapse during the storm scene in *The Green Promise.* Also more pronounced now was the occasional flicker of anxiety and unrest in Natalie's eyes. As an actress, it had always given her a touch of mystery; as an adult, it became a secret warning signal from the buried child, whose need for love was in perpetual conflict with the fear of love betrayed.

Or lost. The child had occasionally made a friend on a movie set, but friendship ended when shooting ended. The closer you got, it seemed, the more you had to lose; and as Natalie the adolescent grew increasingly wary of getting too close to people, she was left with no long-lasting relationships outside her far-from-happy family.

Maria always acted on her feelings, but Natalie often kept them to herself, partly because she had no close childhood friend to confide in, partly because her feelings about her mother would have been too troubling to confide. Not surprisingly, after years of inward solitude, adult

Natalie found it difficult to express her deepest emotions. When they were too strong to hold back, they could emerge in an outburst of hysteria, and when she felt betrayed, the wound and the anger were correspondingly, unforgettably deep.

Another fear that haunted Natalie for many years was Maria's warning about the serial killer who prowled movie theaters and knifed young girls in the back. As a teenage actress under contract to Warner Bros., she only felt safe watching movies in one of the studio's screening rooms, or at premieres with armed security guards in evidence. But fear as a reproductive organism is often indiscriminate. After psychoanalysis helped Natalie exorcise Jack the Jabber, a relatively trivial danger connected with movie theaters replaced him. When Natalie Wood the star wanted to see a movie during its regular run, she feared the humiliation of being turned away at the box office if the house was full, and either notified the theater in advance to reserve seats or asked the friend she was with to notify the manager that he was escorting Miss Wood.

In her late teens she also developed a fear of flying, although it wasn't until 1970 that she actually refused to board a plane for a few years. And another serious fear lodged in her mind after Natalie became a wife and mother. On Halloween, many of the privileged children of Beverly Hills were only allowed to tour the neighborhood in their trick-or-treat costumes under the protective supervision of armed security guards, and sometimes a police car cruising alongside. Returning home one evening to the house on North Canon Drive where she lived with her husband Robert Wagner, Natalie witnessed one of those bizarre processions. It aroused an immediate fear that her own children might be kidnapped, and she acted on it right away by ordering the latest, most elaborate security system for the house, as well as bulletproof walls and windows for the children's bedrooms upstairs.

In seeking assurance that the world of her marriage and family was safe, whatever dangers might exist in the world outside, Natalie was responding to another signal from the buried child. It's now a commonplace that popular movies have a unique power to absorb and transform reality. But for the child actor as opposed to the audience, their power is even greater and more insidious. During her earliest, most impressionable years, Natalie spent much of her time on studio sets that were wonderfully convincing facsimiles of the world outside, populated by equally convincing facsimiles of ideal mothers, sisters, fathers and father figures. It was in their company that she felt most secure, admired and loved, until she grew up and never entirely forgot the shock of discovering a world outside that only *looked* uncannily like its studio facsimile. It might not be Sodom or Gomorrah, but it certainly wasn't heaven; "success as a human being" was not everybody's idea of the most important kind of success; and even if "the thing you do for yourself always gives you the most satisfaction," there was no guarantee that you'd be allowed to do it.

An adult movie star has at least two selves, a private one (if he or she is in touch with it) and a public image created by the roles he or she plays. In Natalie's case there was a third image, imposed on her by Maria. By supervising Natalie's publicity, especially in relation to her family background, Maria succeeded in fabricating a persona (former ballerina, exemplary mother) for herself; and Natalie felt obliged to validate it. In public, Maria's eye was always on the photo opportunity to pose lovingly beside her daughter; and when interviewed about her childhood, Natalie kept up the pretense by thanking her parents for making it so wonderfully "normal."

But by the time she lay in the pool at Esalen, lights switched on although there was still an hour of sunlight left, one hand clutching the brick held out by Donfeld, the old fears and denials, some half-remembered or half-forgotten, a new fear about the state of her career, grief over the death of a supposed father she had come to love, overdependence on alcohol and sleeping pills—all these things had sent Natalie on one of the longest night journeys of her life. In the past those journeys had been interrupted by stopovers of great happiness; and the memory of them allowed her to retain a zest for life, as well as her sense of humor, even on that late afternoon at Esalen when she was secretly fighting a state of panic almost as extreme as the never-forgotten moment when she clung for dear life to a shattered bridge above a raging torrent.

IN THE ABSENCE of any movie offers by May 1953, several months after *The Star* opened, Natalie's current agent again sold her to TV; and in a deal approved by Maria, the fourteen-year-old former child star would earn $400 an episode for twenty-six episodes of a sitcom. Back in the best of all possible domestic worlds as a cute airheaded teenager, she completed the entire series of *The Pride of the Family* during the summer, rehearsing and recording each episode in two days. The show premiered on October 2, and although no copies appear to have survived, its reviews (like those of *Playmates*) suggest that there's no reason to send out a search party. But at least Natalie found another congenial screen mother in Fay Wray, unjustly relegated to a footnote in film history as the beautiful screamer in King Kong's paw, instead of acknowledged for her touching performance in von Stroheim's *Wedding March*. Wray not only admired her screen daughter's "uncanny ability," but sympathized with Natalie's restless impatience to be allowed to grow up.

In fact, there was another reason for the teenage veteran's impatience. The idea of acting as escape had begun to give way to the idea of acting as drudgery, and her next chore did nothing to change her mind.

The TV series was not renewed for a second year, and in the spring of 1954 an offer from Warner Bros. returned Natalie to the big screen, now bigger than ever before. The success of *Quo Vadis?*, with a script officially blessed by Pope Pius XII, had inspired a revival of the religious epic on a scale of DeMille-times-ten; and although each epic was publicized with sanctimonious references to the importance of faith, its true faith lay in the anamorphic CinemaScope lens as a way to aggrandize spectacle and recover audiences lost to TV. Warner Bros.' first entry in the Christian sweepstakes was *The Silver Chalice*, adapted from Thomas B. Costain's best-selling novel. Paul Newman made an unhappy film debut in the leading role of the silversmith who designed the cup that Christ passed to his disciples at the Last Supper, and that subsequently disappeared; and Natalie (with fourteenth billing) played Helena, a teenage slave girl who grows up to become Virginia Mayo.

*The Silver Chalice* was originally planned as an American-Italian-British co-production, with "authentic" location work in Rome, Antioch and Jerusalem. But financial negotiations with overseas production companies broke down, and it became 100 percent Warners, shot entirely at the Burbank studio apart from one location scene near Palm Springs, a stand-in for the Syrian desert. Natalie's hair was dyed blond to match Mayo's, and she was fitted with blue contact lenses to match Mayo's eyes. But two days later she began to suffer from eye inflammation and refused to wear the lenses anymore.

When the movie opened during Christmas week, none of the reviewers commented on the mysterious change in young Helena's eyes from blue to very dark brown, then back to blue for Mayo's first appearance. Most likely they were too bored by a relentlessly pedestrian movie to notice the discrepancy—although they should have noticed the production's one positive feature: the sets by Rolf Gerard, a theatre designer chosen by Victor Saville, the British producer-director. Unlike the stiff, literal attempts at period reconstruction of *Quo Vadis?* and *The Robe,* Gerard's designs created a postmodern biblical world muted in color, elegantly stylized, light and uncluttered.

Saville had been one of the very few adventurous directors of British films during the 1930s, but you'd never have guessed it from his later work in Hollywood. As for Natalie, the best thing about her role was that it took only two weeks to complete; the worst, that her blonded hair and slathered makeup were almost brutally unbecoming. The role itself was something to get through rather than act, but it gave her a prophetic moment during a scene with Peter Reynolds, the actor who grows up to become Paul Newman. Shocked by the way her master treats young Helena, he asks why she allows it. "Because," she whispers, "I'm a slave."

Four months after the movie opened, but for reasons totally unconnected with it, Warners signed Natalie to an exclusive long-term contract. It was dated March 30, 1955, and the terms included a weekly salary of $250 for the first year, less than she'd earned on *Pride of the Family;* but a regular income was the deciding factor for those who always decided on Natalie's behalf. Warners had an option to renew the contract every year for seven more years, with a weekly salary increase of $250 each year, minus twelve weeks of annual unpaid layoff.

The contract also stipulated that Natalie must "comply promptly and faithfully with all requirements, directions or requests," including the studio's decision to loan her out and send her on publicity tours. Furthermore, she was required "to act, sing, speak, or otherwise perform as an actress in such roles and such photoplays and other productions or assignments as Producer may designate, [and] to perform and render such services whenever and wherever and as often as Producer may request or deem necessary."

In other words, Producer owned her. Did Natalie know what she was getting into? Years later, she couldn't remember if she ever read the contract (as a minor, of course, she couldn't sign it), only that she understood it was "standard." Anyway, she had no choice. Unless she agreed, she couldn't play Judy in *Rebel Without a Cause.*

MEANTIME, after her two weeks' work on *The Silver Chalice,* Natalie returned to Van Nuys High for the fall and winter semesters of 1954–55. But she interrupted her studies to appear in a couple of TV productions, the first (aired on November 14, 1954) for *General Electric Theater,* a CBS dramatic anthology hosted by Ronald Reagan.

*I'm a Fool* was adapted from Sherwood Anderson's story by Arnold Schulman, who would later write one of Natalie's best movies, *Love with the Proper Stranger.* "Put up a good front and the world is yours," a midwestern farmer advises his young son when he leaves home to work as a racetrack groom in a neighboring town. And when the poor country boy falls in love with Lucy, a young girl visiting wealthy friends in the town, he duly reinvents himself as the heir to a family fortune.

The leading role was played by James Dean, himself a country boy from Indiana, who had filmed *East of Eden* on a nearby Warners soundstage while Natalie was making *The Silver Chalice.* Elia Kazan's movie had not yet been released, and Natalie saw Dean for the first time when he rode up (late) on his motorbike and climbed into the rehearsal studio through an open window instead of entering by the door. He wore horn-rimmed glasses and a pair of scruffy old jeans held up by a safety pin, and Natalie's first impression was of someone "totally weird," but after they began working on their first scene together, she found him totally fascinating.

Instead of a fixed approach to each scene, Dean liked to improvise a series of different ones, until he felt that he'd explored every possibility. This was the opposite of what Natalie had been taught all her life, by directors who expected her to do exactly as she was told and by a mother who warned her never to argue with them. But the director of *I'm a Fool* worried about completing the show on schedule, and what excited Natalie made Don Medford accuse Dean of lacking discipline. As a result the two young actors bonded, and in retrospect the intimacy of their final scene seems like a rehearsal for the scene in the deserted mansion in *Rebel Without a Cause.*

*General Electric Theater* was a half-hour show, and the story is inevitably fragmented as it moves between present and past, with Eddie Albert as James Dean thirty years on, recalling an episode from his earlier life. The farewell scene at the railroad station, almost entirely in close-up and close two-shot, is not only the strongest in the show, but gives Natalie her most sustained opportunity. About to return home, Lucy suddenly realizes she's in love with this mysterious, lonely boy, and as the train pulls out, she promises to write. But he knows that he'll never get her letters, because he's never told his real name or address.

It's beautifully played, Dean already the archetypal troubled outsider of his generation and a constantly inventive actor, Natalie displaying an emotional depth that so many shallow teenage roles had denied her. The ache of loss and missed connections also seems personally resonant for both of them, youthful romantics at once eager and wary, as if they suspect that the world may never be theirs.

Like all TV shows then, *I'm a Fool* was very briefly rehearsed before it aired, but as Natalie remembered later, she had enough contact with Dean to realize that "he was proud of being an actor." This was something she felt personally very unsure about at the time; but although she found it a revelation to work with a twenty-three-year-old actor at once so passionate and so relaxed about his craft, she could find no cause for pride in her next assignment. *The Wild Bunch* was a segment of another dramatic anthology, *Four Star Playhouse,* and took her back to domestic sitcomland. She played one of two spoiled, vacuous sisters (Gigi Perreau was cast as the other) who at first resent their widowed mother's second marriage and her introduction of a stepfather (Charles Boyer) into the family. Directed by William A. Seiter, one of many veteran Hollywood workhorses put out to TV pasture in the 1950s, the show was as instantly disposable as a plastic spoon. Boyer, Perreau and Natalie acted with no visible signs of involvement in heart or mind, and in Natalie's case it was doubly understandable. By then her heart and mind were otherwise deeply engaged.

*The Wild Bunch* was aired on February 17, 1955, the same week that Nicholas Ray began testing several young actresses for an important role opposite James Dean in his next film for Warners, *Rebel Without a Cause.* Dean, of course, was one reason that Natalie wanted the part; the other was the part itself. She had obtained a copy of the script through the agent currently in Maria's good graces, Dick Clayton of Famous Artists, and for the first time in her life announced what *she* wanted—an interview with Nick Ray.

The script that Natalie read (dated January 21, 1955) was only two-thirds finished, with the rest in synopsis form. To develop a screenplay from his own story outline, Nick had first engaged Irving Shulman, author of *The Amboy Dukes,* a novel about juvenile delinquents from apparently "normal" middle-class families. But although Nick liked some of Shulman's ideas, director and writer disliked each other personally. For a second draft Nick turned to Stewart Stern, who had written a movie he admired (*Teresa,* directed by Fred Zinnemann) and was also friendly with Dean.

After their first script conference, Stern realized that "Nick had a vision of what he wanted to say" but was unable to articulate it clearly. Fortunately, Stern had his own vision after reading Shulman's material. In the story of three young people deeply alienated from their families, he saw the possibility of "a modern version of *Peter Pan,*" with the trio pooling their frustrations and inventing a world of their own. This way, Stewart suggested, they could make a film about "the nature of loneliness and love."

As well as connecting immediately with Nick, Stern's way drew an immediate emotional response from Natalie. She identified strongly with Judy's rebellion against her family and her discovery of something that Natalie herself had been denied: friendship with her own kind. But Jack Warner wanted a star (actual or, in his view, potential) for the role. By the time Nick agreed to interview Natalie, he'd been obliged to test Debbie Reynolds, Jayne Mansfield, Pat Crowley (1954's "Star of Tomorrow"), Kathryn Grant (soon to marry Bing Crosby and retire from the screen) and Margaret O'Brien, who amused him by confessing that she'd never been a rebel and always respected her parents. He rejected them all, and had almost made up his mind to cast Carroll Baker, whom he'd tested in New York on the recommendation of Elia Kazan.

At sixteen, Natalie was at least six years younger than all the other candidates except O'Brien, who was seventeen; and when she arrived at Nick's office on the Warner lot, it was not only her youth that appealed to him. How quickly did Natalie realize that he found her extremely desirable, and how soon did Nick make his move? Possibly later that day; certainly not long afterward. The interview took place in the first week of February, and by the time she made her first test ten days later, they were lovers.

Talented dreamer, obsessive gambler, with a wearily handsome face, robust physique and fractured psyche, Nick Ray had mood swings that took him to the verge of manic depression. But his sexual appetite was

*Natalie, James Dean and Marsha Hunt before the first cast
reading on the set of* Rebel Without a Cause. *After the reading,
Hunt decided she didn't like the part and was replaced by Ann Doran.*

not yet dulled by twenty years of heavy drinking. He had married and
divorced two wives, initiated and broken off affairs with many women
and a couple of men. Natalie, although a virgin, had already developed
highly responsive sexual antennae, and they picked up Nick's signals. He
seemed mysterious, laconic and powerful, like an aging Heathcliff, and
the timing was right for an act of open rebellion. Her parents, she knew,
would be horrified when they learned about it, and Maria might have a
convulsion; but the Star Mother would keep quiet for the sake of her
daughter's career.

When Natalie made her first test, James Dean was in New York.

Dennis Hopper, already cast in *Rebel Without a Cause* and signed to a
Warners contract, had taken his place in previous tests and did so again
with Natalie. Although it was a rainy night, Nick shot the test on the
studio back lot. Warners had decided that the movie would be shot in
black-and-white CinemaScope, and as Hopper recalled, Nick wanted to
see how the new lens would register darkness and rain: "By the time we
finished, Natalie and I both felt like wet unhappy animals. Next day she
phoned and asked for a date. I was astonished. We'd never met before, I
came from a very conventional middle-class family in San Diego—
although not as restrictive as Natalie's—and this was the 1950s, when
girls who'd turned sixteen only a few months earlier just didn't do things
like that."

But Natalie did a thing like that, because Nick Ray had awakened her
sexual drive, and she'd also tasted the excitement of release from convention. Freedom of choice—responding to her own needs instead of defer-
ring to the needs of others—had existed only in her imagination until
now. Hopper, recently turned twenty, was on the same road to emanci-
pation. Once over the shock, he caught Natalie's excitement and agreed
to pick her up at the Chateau Marmont the next day. She planned their
assignation like an experienced conspirator, asking him to wait outside
in his car at five o'clock, when she'd be leaving Nick's bungalow. (He
liked love in the afternoon.) Obviously they couldn't go to the Gurdin
house, and Dennis shared his apartment with a roommate, so as night
fell they drove up to the Hollywood Hills and, on the unlighted, rustic
"Lovers' Lane" stretch of Mulholland Drive, made love for the first time.

WARNER AND HIS executive assistant Steve Trilling were moderately
impressed with Natalie's test, but not convinced that she could sustain
the role of Judy. Nick was convinced that she could and insisted on making a second test, which he directed after a week's coaching.

Shortly afterward, on an unseasonably warm evening in February,
Dennis Hopper took Natalie out to dinner, with one of her classmates
from Van Nuys High whose name, years later, he is no longer sure of:
"Later that night I was driving both girls back to their homes in the Val-
ley when an oncoming car collided with my open convertible on Laurel
Canyon Boulevard. All three of us were thrown out of my car, and

although I escaped with minor bruises, like the classmate, Natalie had a slight concussion. I got scared because she was unconscious for maybe a minute. Then she recovered consciousness, and her wits, and asked me to call Nick, not her parents."

But the emergency room receptionist at the hospital called the police, who arrived within a few minutes. They released Hopper and Natalie's classmate after questioning because they had no serious injuries, then insisted on calling Natalie's parents because she appeared slightly dazed. In Myron Meisel's 1974 documentary on Nick Ray, *I'm a Stranger Here Myself,* Natalie claimed that she "kept saying 'Nick Ray, Nick Ray, the number is . . .' I just kept repeating the number of the Chateau Marmont, so that's what they did call. Nick sent his doctor down to the hospital, then he came down himself, and I said: 'Nick, they called me a goddamn juvenile delinquent, *now* do I get the part?' And I got it."

In the documentary, Nick also told the story about someone at the hospital calling Natalie a juvenile delinquent, although both he and Natalie knew it had been invented by the Warner Bros. publicity department almost twenty years earlier. Neither of them ever talked publicly about their affair, and fell back on an old story for the sake of "respectability." And for the same reason, Nick also pretended that he called the Gurdins before driving Natalie home.

Almost two years after the event, toward the end of 1956, Nick Ray told me privately why Natalie kept insisting that the police call him from the hospital; she dreaded the scene her parents would make if they learned about the accident. Coincidentally, Nick added, when he drove Natalie home after his doctor pronounced her fully recovered, he mentioned that he'd tried to call her from the studio earlier that afternoon. Warner and Trilling, he said, had seen the second test and agreed to cast her as Judy.

The classmate from Van Nuys High was in fact Jackie Eastes, one of several who promoted themselves to "close friend" after Natalie's death and came forward like a legion of Forrest Gumps with accounts of happening to be present at various important moments in Natalie's life. (Eastes even claimed that she recommended Sal Mineo for Plato in *Rebel Without a Cause,* after seeing him play a small part in his first movie, and Nick rewarded her with $200.) But the level of credibility in the case of all these "close friends" is on a par with the "inside stories" in fan magazines.

*Dennis Hopper: When I think about those early days with Natalie, the way she called me up for a date after that first test in the rain, the cool way she handled two affairs at the same time, how quickly she told me to notify Nick and not her parents after the accident, I realize Natalie was way ahead of her time. Incredibly progressive. And maybe the first passive-aggressive.*

She was certainly "way ahead of her time" in responding so directly to her need for sexual adventure with Dennis, and again when she realized that the affair with Nick was also *his* sexual adventure, not a deep involvement. In fact, as Dennis remembered, when Nick learned about the situation, "he accepted the threesome."

At least until Maria learned about it.

STEWART STERN'S SCRIPT note on the character of Judy was an uncannily predictive comment on Natalie herself. "At sixteen," he wrote before he'd met her, or Natalie had met Nick Ray, "she is in a panic of frustration regarding her father—needing his love and suffering when it is denied. This forces her to invite the attention of other men in order to punish him." And perhaps not coincidentally, Natalie's first lover was a man old enough (at forty-three) to be her father, with the same first name as Nick Gurdin.

WHEN JACK WARNER approved Natalie for the role of Judy, he made two conditions: she must sign a long-term contract with the studio, and must begin lessons with a voice coach as soon as possible.

The studio head now in control of Natalie's career for the next ten years was a shrewd administrator who liked to meddle in creative matters, even though he once remarked that he'd rather "go on a fifty-mile hike than crawl through a book." But his jovial smile and fondness for terrible jokes concealed more than a hard bargainer. He had surprising flashes of perception about the popular appeal of scripts and actors, and he also spotted Natalie's one drawback: a lack of vocal range. She'd never before had to sustain an emotionally complex scene with abrupt changes of mood; and one of her test scenes (at the police station) for *Rebel With-*

*out a Cause* was virtually a monologue veering between confusion and loneliness, defiance and appeal for help.

Nick's friend Robert Ryan recommended his former voice teacher Nina Moise, a retired theater actress who had also coached Rita Hayworth. As well as exercises to develop vocal resonance, Moise gave her students a crash course in psychology: "Actors must learn to listen not just with their ears. Listening is the impact of mind on mind." And if an actor only learns to *look* as if he's listening, she explained, his voice will *sound* self-conscious.

Although Natalie studied with Moise for only six weeks before shooting started, she was once again quick to learn. In *Rebel Without a Cause* her voice is more varied in tone than before; and although not always as expressive as her face, it avoids the occasional lapses of a Joan Crawford or a Lana Turner, whose elocution lessons caused them to fail the Moise test: "In the best speech, you are not aware that an actor's voice is trained."

Essentially, Moise taught that speech and body language depend on more than external skill and that "the impact of mind on mind" involves an actor's sense of his character's inner reality. This was something very much in the current Hollywood air. "The early 1950s," Stewart Stern remembered, "were an exciting time, with all those new young actors coming out from New York—from the Actors Studio, Stella Adler's classes, theater, live TV. Nobody had talked about 'truth' and 'preparation' on a movie set before." Brando, Montgomery Clift, James Dean, Julie Harris and Eva Marie Saint were among the new avatars. All had worked at least once for Kazan; Nick Ray had once worked as Kazan's assistant. And nine years after winning an award as "The Most Talented Juvenile Picture Star of 1946," Natalie had her first induction into the rites of that world.

A MONTH BEFORE *Rebel Without a Cause* was due to start shooting, when Nick Ray had still not cast the role of Plato, several young actors answered a casting call for two minor roles. Among them was sixteen-year-old Sal Mineo, a former child actor on Broadway. Nick had considered only one other juvenile actor, Billy Gray (who'd played "Bud" in *Father Knows Best*) for the part; and as well finding that Mineo "looked more like a Plato than Billy Gray," his looks and personality reminded

Rebel Without a Cause. *Sal Mineo, James Dean and Natalie form
a triangle in the deserted mansion.
James Dean and Natalie huddle on the deserted mansion
set as Nick Ray watches.*

Nick of his own son Tony, "a Plato of sorts." After Mineo auditioned at
the Chateau Marmont, and improvised a scene with James Dean, Nick
tested him at the studio on March 16; and this time he played a scene
with Dean and Natalie on the set of the deserted mansion.

At the suggestion of a Warner Bros. executive, Nick first tested
another actor that day, and sixteen-year-old Richard Beymer remembered him as "gruffly unhelpful because he didn't want me." Nor did
Beymer want the part, "because I was so much taller than James Dean,
and we'd have looked ludicrous together." But he vividly recalled the
Nick Ray–James Dean–Natalie–Dennis Hopper "gang" on the set: "I
was completely unfamiliar with the kind of improvisation they were into.
Dean kept changing his moves; suddenly I couldn't find him—he'd gone
halfway up the staircase. And Natalie gave me no help either. Dennis
Hopper was around, although not in the scene, and the four of them were
always whispering together, schmoozing, whatever. I was the outsider."

It was "a disastrous experience" for Beymer, who left the studio determined "to learn how to deal with that kind of acting," but a success for
Sal Mineo, who began rehearsing several scenes with Natalie and James
Dean in the living room of Nick Ray's bungalow the next day. Nick had
asked the art director (Malcolm Bert) to design the living room of Jim
Stark's parents as a replica of his own; and this enabled the three actors
to work out their moves, as well as explore the script, as if they were on
the actual set. Nick also encouraged them to improvise as well as
rehearse, and recorded the results on audio tape. Then, as Natalie
explained at the American Film Institute seminar, they listened to play-
backs: "That was the first time I'd been exposed to that kind of work,
because I had worked for many years as a child, and most directors never
asked me my opinion, my thoughts. The less they heard from me, the
better. And suddenly Nick Ray began saying, 'What do you think?' He
would encourage me, and get annoyed if I didn't bring in lots of notes or
ideas, or even changes of dialogue, or I didn't challenge certain scenes."

To rehearse the night scene in the deserted mansion, Nick moved his
three actors to the soundstage at Warners and filmed the final rehearsal
in black-and-white. A copy of it preserved by the studio reveals an
almost exact blueprint for the scene as it appears in the movie. The
actors reworked a few untidy improvised details, but duplicated all the
important moves.

Asked about Nick's method of work with actors, Natalie said he never talked in "conceptual" or abstract terms: "He always felt it was important to know a lot personally about the actor, so that at a given moment, if he needed something in a scene, he might say something not totally relevant to it, but relevant to the person."

During rehearsals, Natalie also learned something important from Dean: "He told me to relax before playing an emotional scene. It seemed like a contradiction, but it worked." She found the same contradiction in Dean as a person: "He seemed very introspective and quiet, but he was always very accessible and friendly." And perhaps because she was so fascinated by his talent, or "perhaps because I was too young," she was never aware of the "doomed self-destructive figure that many people see." But she did become aware that he was an emotional loner, "intensely determined," as Nick Ray said, "not to be loved or love."

Like everyone else connected with the movie except Nick Ray and the Warner executives, Natalie never knew that on March 25, five days before *Rebel Without a Cause* was due to start shooting, Dean suddenly vanished. He couldn't be reached at his New York apartment (a one-room fifth-floor walkup); his agent and various friends claimed not to know his whereabouts; and the Warner executives began consulting with Nick about a replacement, as well as talking among themselves about suing Dean for breach of contract.

A ritual of Stewart Stern's friendship with Dean was that they always imitated an animal sound instead of saying hello when they met. Three days after the disappearance, Stewart's phone rang, and a moo from a cow came over the line; he mooed a greeting in return. Then Dean said: "I'm not sure I should do this movie, because I'm not sure I can trust Nick."

Although *East of Eden* had not yet opened, Dean had seen it at a couple of private screenings, and compared his experience with Kazan, whom he trusted completely, with his doubts about Nick: " 'I have to trust who I'm with,' Jimmy said. 'Remembering Kazan, am I making a mistake to do this movie?' I told him, 'I can't answer that.' In fact I could understand Jimmy's doubts, because I'd had my own problems with Nick. 'But I can't take the responsibility of saying you should or you shouldn't,' I said."

Stewart never told anyone at the studio about this, and heard nothing more from Dean until a day or two later, when he finally decided to take the risk and appeared at the studio in time for his first call. The rea-

*Natalie and James Dean at play
between setups*

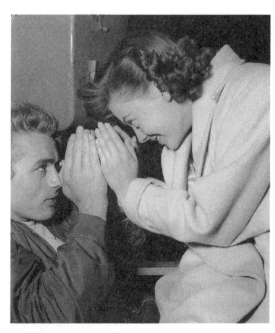

*Natalie and James Dean at rest
between setups*

son for his doubts, he told Stewart, was that Nick kept changing his mind about the direction of a scene, but never explained why, unlike the highly articulate Kazan, always in charge and always sure of what he wanted. "I understood this all too well," Stewart remembered, because he'd been disturbed by the way Nick would profess complete satisfaction with a scene in the script, then ask the actors to ignore it and improvise instead. This led to several changes that Stewart protested and a few more that he discovered too late. Unwilling to become involved in any problems between Dean and Nick, he stayed away from the set.

Perhaps no movie that communicated so directly with audiences, especially the young, emerged from so many conflicts in the making. To Dennis Hopper, it often seemed that Dean was "the real director of *Rebel,* and controlled every scene he was in." To Natalie it seemed that Nick got everything he wanted from Dean because "he absolutely understood him, and Jimmy reminded Nick of himself a great deal." I remember Nick saying the same thing to me a year or two later; but similarities can create friction as well as rapport. Dennis remembered that Nick once called "Cut!" when Dean thought it premature, and the actor turned on him. "I'm the only one who says fucking 'Cut' here!"

To arrive at the heart of a scene, actor and director both liked to explore it from different angles; and if Dean suddenly became unsure about the angle they'd agreed upon, he refused to shoot the scene until he'd thought it over. Nick understood this, and before calling "Action!" he always waited for Dean to signal that he was ready. In one way this validates Dennis Hopper's impression that Dean "controlled every scene he was in," but in another it confirms Natalie's belief that Nick controlled Dean's performance because "he absolutely understood him."

As deeply introverted loners, distrustful of all authority (but especially studio executives), hungry for love but wary of involvement, both Nick and Dean took refuge in self-dramatization. Nick liked to confuse and unnerve strangers with long, mysterious silences. Dean preferred to disconcert them by turning a cartwheel when he entered a room. But of all the misunderstandings that occurred before and during the shoot, the most ironic was that Dean felt he could trust Kazan, while Kazan had warned Nick that he'd found Dean surly and narcissistic on *East of Eden* and advised against using him on *Rebel Without a Cause.*

AS WELL AS CROSS-PURPOSES, erotic crosscurrents developed on the set. The "threesome" situation described by Dennis began with "the three of us often having dinner together," but soured when Maria "somehow found out about it. She knew about Natalie and Nick, didn't like it, but kept quiet because he was the director. But she made a fuss about Natalie and me to an executive at the studio, and I was told to lay off."

After the tabloid magazine *Confidential* first appeared on newsstands in 1952, and proceeded to expose the alleged sexual intrigues and kinks of Joan Crawford, Frank Sinatra, Lizabeth Scott, Ava Gardner and beloved Lana Turner, Maria became increasingly alarmed by the power of scandal. Throughout her life she suffered from nightmares, and perhaps one of them was about an exposure of teenage Natalie's simultaneous affairs with Nick Ray and Dennis Hopper. She certainly attempted to lessen that danger by eliminating Dennis.

"Maria never mentioned Nick to the executive, and he came out pure as snow," Dennis recalled. "I resented this, and showed it." On the night that Nick shot the famous "chicken run" (drag race) scene, the tension between them neared breaking point when Nick impatiently dismissed a question from Dennis about the way he was being directed: "I accused him of taking it out on me because of the situation with Natalie, and warned him we were heading for a fight. Nick said it was time I started using my mind as well as my fists if I wanted to become a serious actor, and ordered me off the set. That's when I stopped being aggressive."

Another crosscurrent developed when Sal Mineo echoed the character he played by becoming strongly attracted to Dean. Both Dean and Nick were aware of it; and Nick, who was also aware of Dean's bisexuality, asked him to "use" it in their scenes together. Accordingly, Dean told Mineo "to look at me the way I look at Natalie," and a subtle erotic tension develops when the screen threesome spend a night in the deserted mansion. Mineo's Plato glances longingly at Dean's Jim Stark, who gives him a quick smile with an undercurrent of flirtation, while Natalie's Judy is too involved with Jim to notice.

Natalie, like Mineo, was still a minor, legally obliged to attend studio school three hours a day; and she also continued her extracurricular education on and off the set. After working with Nick and Dean, making movies no longer seemed like drudgery. Later in life she often

*Natalie and Dennis Hopper at a studio screening of* A Streetcar
Named Desire, *starring her favorite actress, Vivien Leigh*

described *Rebel Without a Cause* as the experience that fired her to
become a serious actress, an ambition that her Academy Award nomination as Best Supporting Actress would endorse six months later.
(Although Mineo was also nominated, the Academy inexplicably failed
to honor Dean.) And off the set, Natalie even resumed the affair with

Dennis Hopper—"without anyone knowing," according to Dennis, who remembered that they continued the relationship as "great friends who occasionally went to bed together."

Evidently the studio never even suspected what was happening. Over the next twelve months, Natalie and Dennis played lovers in a Warners live TV show and were sent to New York to play lovers again on loan to *The Kaiser Aluminum Hour* and to attend the premiere of *Giant,* a Warners production. Newsreel coverage of the premiere showed them arriving at the theater, and while the commentator's voice-over introduced Dennis as a supporting player in Dean's final movie, Natalie made a private gesture of defiance by turning to kiss him, then turning back to smile brightly at the camera.

"I never had a friend like Natalie again," Dennis recalled. "She was a very important part of my life until we lost touch after I left Warners." Then he gave a thumbnail sketch of the person he remembered: "Apparently very vulnerable, yet somehow in control."

In fact, although Natalie sometimes lost control, she nearly always managed to regain it. But otherwise the sketch exactly defines the tightrope that Natalie walked for the rest of her life.


ALTHOUGH *REBEL WITHOUT A CAUSE* was an extraordinary popular success, Warners barely acknowledged Natalie's part in it. By the time the movie opened on October 6, 1955, James Dean had made an impact in *East of Eden* as great as Brando's in *A Streetcar Named Desire* and Montgomery Clift's in *A Place in the Sun;* and by dying a week before *Rebel* opened, he also became a legend-in-the-making and the focal point of the studio's publicity machine.

Nick had directed *Rebel* for only two days when Jack Warner and Steve Trilling viewed the rushes of the scene at the planetarium and ordered it reshot—but not because they were displeased. Sniffing a hit, they decided to promote the movie from black-and-white to color. (Incidentally, Nick had asked Dean to wear his eyeglasses for the planetarium scene. Now he changed his mind, and Dean took them off when it was reshot in color.) The studio also commissioned a promotional documentary on the making of the movie (in black-and-white, as Jack Warner always looked for costs to cut), and apart from the chicken run, it focused almost entirely on Dean in confrontation with his parents. Mineo was scarcely glimpsed, and Natalie's interview outside her trailer at the planetarium lasted long enough for her to say a line that surely emanated from the publicity department: "In this movie I play a bad girl."

By the first week of May, Natalie had completed her major scenes, and Warners loaned Natalie to Universal for a movie already in production. It was an abrupt switch to another of the stereotyped roles that made acting seem like drudgery, and worst of all, it put her back in the dreaded pigtails. In *One Desire,* produced by Ross Hunter, directed by Jerry Hopper, and adapted from a best-selling novel (*Tacey Cromwell*) by Conrad Richter, she was only a subplot character in a 1910 romantic drama. Tacey (Anne Baxter), the manager of an Oklahoma City gambling house, and the faro dealer (Rock Hudson) fall in love. But soon after they start "a new life" in Colorado, he runs off with a rich girl, leaving her to bring up a homeless fourteen-year-old orphan (Natalie) they've unofficially adopted. Under Tacey's wing the brat loses her pigtails, goes through a tomboy phase, becomes a cutely feminized junior miss, and witnesses the unsurprising reunion of Tacey and her lover after the rich girl dies in a fire. Released in late August 1955, six weeks before *Rebel,* the movie did well at the box office and nothing at all for Natalie's career; but this, as she discovered later, was exactly what Jack Warner intended.

In 1934 he had loaned Bette Davis (after sixteen movies of contract bondage) to RKO for *Of Human Bondage.* It was her first opportunity for a major success, and when movie reviewers rebuked Warners for wasting Davis in run-of-the-mill pictures, Jack took it personally. In the future he approved a loan-out for the sake of a profitable deal, but never if it threatened to offer an actor the opportunity to advance his career at a rival studio.

Although the ever-developing businesswoman didn't profit directly from Natalie's loan-out, she found her way to an incidental perk. When she read the script of *One Desire,* Maria took note of a bit part for an eight-year-old girl. She immediately presented Lana to the movie's casting director, who accepted the bait, and her daughters posed together for publicity shots.

ONE DESIRE, but for a total of only two weeks, as Natalie was shuttled back to Warners for an occasional day's work on *Rebel Without a Cause.*

*Rebel* completed production on May 25, when the unit worked overtime until almost midnight on the studio back lot, filming pickup shots of James Dean, Natalie and Dennis Hopper for the chicken run sequence. And by June 16 Natalie was free to keep the promise she'd made to herself to graduate from Van Nuys High.

Her last report card, noting her considerable number of absences while at work, awarded her B's in every category and E's (Excellent) for Work Habits and Cooperation in every category except one. In drama, the teacher noted that she was frequently tardy and graded her a mere S (Satisfactory). If it seems unlikely that Natalie really fell below her usual level of cooperation in drama, no doubt the answer lies in her memory of a teacher who disapproved of child actresses and looked even further down her nose when Natalie's classmates wanted to know all about James Dean.

For Natalie, graduation was an achievement that had nothing to do with Blue Ribbon citations or acting with Dean. It was a matter of personal pride, and she naturally wanted her family to be present. What she didn't want was any publicity connected with movies; but thanks to Maria, who alerted the publicity department at Warners, she came out of the school building in her white cap and gown after the ceremony and was confronted by a battery of reporters and photographers.

It wasn't the only bitter moment. Earlier, Maria had warned Natalie not to expect her father to be there. Nick Gurdin (whom Warners agreed to employ in the property department when the developing businesswoman signed Natalie's contract) had disappeared on a bender that day; and with Maria not only cornering a reporter and talking about a mother's pride, but posing to kiss Natalie for the camera, the double betrayal became even more painful.


WHEN GEORGE ZEPALOFF returned from his five-year assignment on the East Coast, he'd saved enough money to build a place for himself and Maria. It faced Clear Lake, forty miles north of San Francisco, and followed his own architectural plan: main house with a large living room that featured an open fireplace in the center, guest cabin nearby. And a few days after Natalie's graduation, Olga received one of her mother's "highly emotional" phone calls. Marriage to Nick had become unbearable, Maria said, and she wanted to live with the Captain, whom she'd always truly loved.

"My mother came up to Camp Rose for the weekend, leaving Lana in my care, and went off to see Zepaloff. By then she'd almost made up her mind to leave Nick, but a few days later I had a call from his brother Dmitri to say that Nick had suffered a heart attack. Luckily Natalie was in the house at the time, and sent for an ambulance. My mother, who got back later that day, had a convulsion when she heard the news. Then she went to the hospital and stayed there every night with Nick."

In another "highly emotional" phone call after Nick was released from hospital, Maria told Olga that she'd definitely planned to leave him until she learned about his heart attack. The only explanation she gave for changing her mind was to quote a Russian saying that translates, according to Olga, as "You get used to a dog." At first Olga wondered if her mother "cared for Nick more than she was willing to admit." Then she suspected that Maria had also weighed love in the country with Zepaloff against life as Star Mother, and tilted the scales in favor of Natalie and Hollywood.

But Olga had no idea that Maria believed Zepaloff to be Natalie's biological father, and no way of knowing that her fear of scandal must also have tilted the scales. If she left Nick for the Captain, even though he never wanted to acknowledge Natalie, there was always a danger that *Confidential* with its network of "researchers" would discover the truth. Putting her daughter's career at risk was out of the question; and so, finally, was the prospect of giving up the status in life that she'd worked so hard to acquire.

When Maria returned to Star Motherhood and a husband who aroused feelings that veered between angry disappointment and guilty fondness, the Captain evidently understood. He went back to his old ship, and their "great romantic love" continued as before.

AT THE END of June, Natalie left for Monument Valley to start work on her next assigment for Warners. Her role as Debbie, the niece of Ethan Edwards (John Wayne) in John Ford's western *The Searchers*, was even smaller and only fractionally more rewarding than her role in *One Desire*. The story begins with a Comanche raid on the homestead of

Ethan's brother. They slaughter the entire family, except his eight-year-old daughter, and Natalie doesn't appear during the movie's first hour (eight years in actual time), until Debbie has become the Comanche chief's squaw.

Maria had not only persuaded the casting department at Warners to let Lana play Debbie as a child, but cast herself as official location chaperone to both underage daughters. By joining Lana on the studio payroll for a month, she earned some useful pocket money, but Natalie was still rankled by the graduation episode, and the last thing she wanted at this time was an isolated life in close quarters with her mother. She began *The Searchers* in a dark mood, and the location experience did nothing to lighten it.

Like the rest of the cast (mainly Ford's stock company) and crew, the family stayed at Goulding's Lodge, then a fairly primitive compound of tents and cabins with dirt floors. Water was scarce, hot water available for showers three days a week, and Natalie waited two weeks for her first call "with nothing to do. For recreation you could walk to the dining room and back." In fact she found something else to do, and occasionally flirted with John Wayne's son Pat over a game of Scrabble. But as an outsider in the company, she told the AFI seminar, she was terrified of Ford himself: "Every day they'd go out on location and they'd come back with these horror stories of somebody changing one word of dialogue, and 'Pappy had them put in the barrel' is what they used to say. So I was terrified because I had a tendency to change lines, and thought I was going to get in the barrel."

Ford had originally devised the barrel as a literal punishment: a barrel of cold water into which he ordered an offending actor to be dumped. In his relatively mellow later years, he made the actor assume various kinds of uncomfortable positions instead. And a day before she was finally on call, Natalie unintentionally risked the barrel. She felt her own skin was improbably pale for a girl who had lived with the Comanches since childhood, decided to get a suntan, and got badly sunburned instead. She fainted, was carried back to her cabin and put to bed, where the location doctor treated her burns. While he bandaged them, Pat Wayne came into the room. "Uncle John [Ford] says you've got to go to the dining room and rehearse," he told her. Not only in pain, but "very irritable after two weeks of playing Scrabble in Monu-

*First ethnic role: kidnapped by Comanches and*
*brought up as a squaw. Left to right: Natalie,*
*John Wayne and Jeffrey Hunter in* The Searchers

ment Valley and hearing about everybody being put in the barrel,"
Natalie told Pat to inform Uncle John that if he wanted to rehearse, he
must come to her cabin.

A few minutes later Pat came back, looking very embarrassed, and
told Natalie that he couldn't repeat what Uncle John had said. "And I
said, 'Well, what did he say?' And Pat said, 'Well, he just gave a terrible
message. He said to tell her to go shit in her hat.' And I said, 'Well, I
don't want to be talked to that way, and screw him, and just put me on a
plane and send me home. I hate it here. I hate my part. I don't want to
be put in the barrel. Send me home.' And [the doctor] was saying, 'Now
calm down, calm down,' and at this point John Ford appeared in the
doorway. And when he saw that I was badly burned, and the doctor was

wrapping me in bandages, he couldn't have been more kind. 'Don't worry,' he said. 'We wouldn't dream of making you work. We can easily shoot around you.' "

But this was Natalie recalling her experience with Ford almost twenty-five years later, at the AFI seminar, and after saying that he was never mean to her, discretion intervened. In fact she continued to hate her part and developed a strong dislike for Ford himself. Rightly convinced from the start that she was miscast in *The Searchers,* she'd hoped that working with the legendary director would bring some reward, but as she said in private, Ford did nothing to help her with an unclear and underdeveloped role. Like the romantic subplot featuring Jeffrey Hunter and Vera Miles, she's a weak point in a movie that remains extraordinarily gripping as long as it concentrates on the story of Ethan Edwards. But in spite of his lack of interest in Debbie, Ford could at least have objected to the makeup department's insistence on coating the face of a desert squaw with heavy eyeliner and orange-red lipstick.

When she made the *The Searchers,* Natalie hadn't met the actor she would fall in love with and marry two years later, and was unaware how cruelly Ford had treated him. After he told her about it, she disliked the man even more in retrospect, but preferred not to air a personal grudge at the seminar, and remained characteristically discreet.

In 1951, Robert Wagner was under contract to Fox, and cast in its production of Ford's *What Price Glory?* On each movie he made, Ford arbitrarily selected a whipping boy, and unluckily Wagner landed this role as well. Among other humiliations, the director invariably called him Boob instead of Bob; but when Ford offered to interview him for the part of Martin Pawley in *The Searchers,* Wagner accepted. Eager as any young Hollywood actor for a role in an important movie, he couldn't know that Ford had privately decided to cast Jeffrey Hunter, and was in the mood for a sadistic game. "You'd like to play this part, wouldn't you?" he asked, deceptively benign at first. "Yes, Mr. Ford, I would," Wagner replied, and Ford changed his tone. "Well, you're not going to." Wagner abruptly turned away and started to leave, but turned back when Ford called after him: "You really want to play this part?" "Very much, Mr. Ford." Ford stared at him for a moment, then went for the jugular. "Well, Boob, you're not going to."

By July 13, Ford had finished location work on *The Searchers,* and Natalie returned to Sherman Oaks with her mother and sister. During the next four weeks, she worked on her few studio scenes at RKO-Pathé in Culver City, and her one remaining exterior near the end of the movie. When John Wayne picks Natalie up and says, "Let's go home, Debbie," they're in a canyon area of Griffith Park, just a few miles away from the planetarium of *Rebel Without a Cause.*

In mid-July, coincidentally, Nick Ray had begun filming *Hot Blood,* a disastrous musical about American Gypsies with Jane Russell and Cornel Wilde; and by the time shooting ended on August 30, his affair with Natalie had ended as well. Partly because Nick was in a phase of particularly heavy drinking, it had started to wind down almost as soon as it started up again, and the end-all was an episode of black comedy when Natalie missed a period and feared she might be pregnant. On the night before her pregnancy test, she placed a urine sample in the fridge at Nick's bungalow, but he woke up thirsty as well as fuddled in the small hours, mistook the sample for a glass of fruit juice and drank it down without realizing what he'd swallowed.

Fortunately the pregnancy test was negative, and Natalie had her delayed period the next day. By this time Nick had left for London, to confer with the Warner Bros. publicity department about the forthcoming British release of *Rebel.* And in the third week of September the studio sent Natalie, Sal Mineo and small-part player Nick Adams to New York for the usual round of publicity interviews before the movie opened there. (James Dean, who had just finished *Giant,* decided to enter his new Porsche Spyder in an auto race at Salinas instead.) Thrifty as ever, Jack Warner covered the studio's expenses (and then some) for the publicity trip, with the fee he demanded for loaning Natalie to NBC for a bland supporting role in a live "all-star" musical version of *Heidi* (songs by Schumann, with new English lyrics). Alongside Jo Van Fleet, Elsa Lanchester, Wally Cox and Jeannie Carson as the orphan of the Swiss Alps, she was called for rehearsal the day after she arrived.

On the evening of September 30, Natalie, Mineo and Adams went to see Arthur Miller's *A View from the Bridge,* with Richard Davalos (Dean's brother in *East of Eden*) in a leading role. They had dinner afterward with Davalos at a Chinese restaurant near the Warwick Hotel, where Natalie, Mineo and several members of the *Heidi* cast were staying. A few hours earlier (during the performance of the play, in fact) James

Dean had died on the way to hospital after another car broadsided his Porsche at an intersection north of Bakersfield. But none of them knew it yet.

As *Heidi* was due to air next day and Natalie had an early call, Mineo and Adams walked her back to the hotel immediately after dinner. She went straight to bed, and the studio chaperone, who was waiting in the lobby, took Mineo and Adams aside to break the news about Dean, then ask them not to disturb Natalie. Next morning she joined Jeannie Carson and Jo Van Fleet outside the hotel entrance as the company limo drew up to take them to Brooklyn Studios. The driver got out to wish them good morning and open the rear door, then asked if they'd heard about James Dean's death.

> *Jeannie Carson: It was news to us all. You can imagine what it was like for Natalie, and for Jo Van Fleet, who'd played his mother in* East of Eden, *to hear about it that way. They were absolutely stunned, and could hardly speak during the drive to Brooklyn.*

As well as rehearsing for most of the day, Natalie faced reporters clamoring for a statement ("I remember him very fondly," "He was wonderful to work with," etc.) and asking about the rumors that they'd "been more than friends" ("Completely untrue," she told them, truthfully and more wearily each time). In the early evening, the cast assembled for the live performance, and Natalie had her final the-show-must-go-on moment. As Jeannie Carson remembered: "Natalie was playing my best friend, and in one scene I had to sing a song to her at night, after we saw a shooting star outside the window. In a typical live-TV hitch, the star was late. So I started to ad-lib, and like a true professional Natalie calmly helped me out until it arrived."

When the telecast was over, Natalie went back to the Warwick, sat alone in her room. Delayed reaction to the sudden death of someone still very young, and a major influence on her own young life, made the shock even more devastating. She remembered one of Dean's favorite sayings: "Dream as if you're going to live forever, live as if you're going to die tomorrow." Then Sal Mineo called, and in an ironic variation on the scene of Judy and Jim consoling each other over the death of Plato in *Rebel,* Natalie and Sal mourned the death of Dean together.

FIVE DAYS LATER, on October 6, *Rebel Without a Cause* opened to mixed notices, ranging from "strange and forceful" to "boring" and "appalling." The most hostile reviewer of all, in the *New York Herald-Tribune,* condemned it as "turgid melodrama, written and acted so ineptly, directed so sluggishly," that he declined to name anyone connected with it apart from Dean, whose talent he acknowledged. But young audiences identified passionately with the movie, and of course with Dean himself, who seems now to have anticipated the 1960s, with his anger at a world gone wrong tempered by a wistful longing for some way to set it right. Young audiences also responded, above and beyond her performance, to Natalie herself. As Jim Stark's kindred spirit and first love, she became the girl that would-be Jim Starks dreamed of dating and would-be Judys dreamed of becoming.

"Actress, 17, Takes Pet to Sign New Contract," the *Los Angeles Examiner* announced on October 27, after Famous Artists renegotiated Natalie's contract with Warners in the wake of her success in *Rebel.* Still a minor, she had to appear in court to obtain approval of a salary increase from $250 to $400 weekly, but a courtroom entrance with her French poodle on a leash showed Natalie beginning to take stardom seriously, or half-seriously. (Soon she'll be waving a cigarette holder.) Adept at handling reporters by now, she told them that as well as Fifi she owned another dog, a cockatoo and a pair of finches; that her career and her pets were the most important things in her life; and that she "wouldn't even consider marriage" until she was twenty-four. Although Fifi proclaimed Natalie Wood a movie star, her love for animals was genuine. By surrounding herself with them, she created an illusion of family life, and when she created the real thing as wife and mother, animals were included.

But in spite of paying a higher price for Natalie, Warners gave no sign of appreciating her value. Determined to get their money's worth during the first year of her contract, they loaned her out for two more TV shows, assigned her to an episode of a Warners TV series, and cast her opposite another contract actor in a terrible B movie.

In *A Cry in the Night,* directed by Frank Tuttle, a psychotic voyeur, played by Raymond Burr, is so obsessed with Natalie and her boyfriend that he kidnaps her. Its widely publicized sneak preview, advertising a personal appearance by the star of *Rebel Without a Cause,* was a display of misguided confidence that Natalie later recalled as "sort of traumatic. The whole audience was laughing and jeering and talking back to the screen."

The first TV show was *Feathertop* for *General Electric Theater*, based on Nathanael Hawthorne's fable about a scarecrow (Carleton Carpenter) whom a good fairy grants a term of human life. He falls in love with a girl (Natalie), but when she meets her true love (John Carlyle), he has to become a scarecrow again.

Natalie, as Carpenter recalled her, was "terribly sweet but terribly sad, still distraught over the death of James Dean." At the same time, she was "marvelous to act with, very quick and very responsive." But when he also wondered at the way "she took live TV in her stride, and never seemed nervous," she was surprised by his surprise, and explained that she'd been doing it since she was thirteen.

Carpenter, who lived in upper New York State, returned there after the show aired on December 2, but Natalie and John Carlyle had developed a rapport and met socially over the next few months. He described Natalie at seventeen as "a girl about to become a woman and desperate to do so. I've never seen anyone blossom so quickly"—so quickly, in fact, that just as they were about to play a scene in *Feathertop*, she suddenly asked: "John, do men like women to go down on their toes?"

Carlyle also remembered Natalie as "sometimes melancholy and sometimes horny. But always"—that word again—"adorable." He thought she wore too much makeup, and once told her she'd look much prettier without it, then realized "it was part of her impatience to grow up." Additionally, of course, it was the style of the Warners makeup department at the time.

By late 1955 Famous Artists had merged with Ted Ashley's agency to become Ashley-Famous, and the agents assigned to Natalie were Dick Clayton and Henry Willson. Willson, formerly a talent scout for David Selznick, had a reputation for "discovering" young actors and seducing them, but "discovery" was never conditional on seduction. According to Carlyle, also one of his clients, "until his decline Willson was basically a very decent man. When a client he believed in didn't seem to be catching on, he wouldn't give up." He was also very concerned about "respectability," and pressured his gay actors to go out on dates with actresses; and since that concern extended to himself, he chose Carlyle "to go out on double dates with Natalie and Henry and Natalie's mother."

As Maria liked him ("He made her laugh," according to Carlyle), enjoyed being invited to "go out on the town" and was naturally impressed that Lana Turner had been a Willson client, she became a willing beard. "But Natalie's mother didn't laugh too often," Carlyle recalled, "and Natalie was always trying to lighten the proceedings. They both had very 'Russian' lapses into melancholy, but I noticed that the film of sadness that occasionally covered Natalie's face only happened in her mother's presence. Mrs. Gurdin, by the way, had striking looks, like a Louise Brooks gone askew, but she was the formidable controlling presence when the four of us went out to nightspots like Cyrano and the Mocambo, and always the first to announce, 'Time to go home.' "

At parties without her mother, Carlyle often saw Natalie "necking on a bed with a guy—hardly ever the same one—although I'm pretty sure, in spite of what some of them claimed later, that was as far as it went." His most lasting impression was of someone "working a room in search of love."

It was always a different room. Unconditional love, from her family or a lover, was something Natalie believed she had never been given.

FOR HER NEXT TV show of 1955 Natalie was loaned to *Studio One* and flown to New York immediately after Thanksgiving. In *Miracle at Potters Farm,* directed by Franklin Schaffner and aired on December 19, she played the teenage daughter of a widowed farmer. His death leaves her an almost penniless orphan, with three younger brothers to care for. The farm is insolvent, the family in danger of being split up, but although a long way geographically from Thirty-fourth Street, they're saved by the same kind of "miracle." And the movie delivers a more homespun but similar message: "You put your faith in something, everything turns out pretty well in the end." "Everything" in this case means everything needed to make the farm operative again: truckloads of chickens, cows, animal foodstuff, seeds for growing crops, fertilizers, power tools and a new tractor.

With a star's mandatory eye shadow, lipstick and impeccably styled hair, Natalie seems far too groomed for an impoverished farm girl, and has little to do except act nice and normal, worried and finally joyful. No pigtails, but otherwise she's back where she started, in never-never land. A minor point of interest (there are no major ones) is that the eldest of her brothers is played by Burt Brinckerhoff, later to direct Natalie in one of her finest performances, in *The Cracker Factory.*

Two days after Christmas she was on the small screen again in an episode of *Kings Row,* one of three TV series recently launched by the studio under the collective title of *Warner Bros. Presents.* Like *Casablanca* and *Cheyenne* (the only one that ran for several seasons), it was a low-budget spinoff from a big-screen hit, padded with additional characters that bore no relation to the original movie; and in "The Wedding Gift," Natalie played Dennis Hopper's mail-order bride.

The end of her first year under the new Warners contract, in fact, marked the beginning of a professional life that often felt like another night journey. After the revelation of her talent in *Rebel* (to herself as well as to audiences), the studio would exile her from substantial acting roles for five more years. Now that she'd reached her full height of five foot two, with a tiny, finely proportioned ninety-five-pound figure that emphasized her large, exotically dark eyes, Warners decided that Natalie looked "ethnic" and cast her as a half-Mexican spitfire in her first movie of 1956. *The Burning Hills* was a western shot from mid-February to mid-April, and her opening lines, delivered from a horse and cart to a group of cowboys who flirt with her, are a preparation for the kind of dialogue she'll have to struggle with: "You dirty gringos! You're no good! None of you! You make a rathole of this town!"

Her co-star was Tab Hunter, playing a man on the run from a group of cattle thieves he's threatened to expose, and he remembered that "Natalie had a lot of trouble with her accent. It was pretty terrible, and at one time the studio thought of getting a Hispanic actress to dub her." As a child, she'd imitated a German accent unquestioningly and successfully in *Tomorrow Is Forever,* but as an adult in *The Burning Hills* she had "to begin all over again," and acquire the technique of appearing to believe in a role that she found absurd.

With the help of a dialect coach, Natalie's accent improved enough to become acceptably inauthentic, but as a half-breed on the range she faced yet another reality problem: as well as the standard orange vermilion lipstick, she wore thick mascara, a heavy black wig, and Latino body makeup as deep as an Acapulco tan—accessories dictated by the studio, of course. As Connie Nichols, Natalie's hairdresser on several of her early Warner movies, recalled: "1950s makeup was always too heavy and garish, and Natalie was far more beautiful offscreen at this time. Unbelievably beautiful, in fact."

Although almost as obsessed as MGM with the way its stars had to look, Warners was less successful at making them look their best, or even look the part. The only "creative" suggestion on record of Richard Whorf, producer of *The Burning Hills,* is his memo to the hairdressing department: "Natalie's hair should be shorter, fluffier and not so coarse, [and] Tab Hunter is to grow no whiskers." Whorf either didn't know or didn't care that in the pioneer West a half-Mexican girl with short fluffy hair was as improbable as a man on the run who managed to shave every day. But Natalie knew that she had to devise one authentic detail for herself. Always determined to conceal her distended wristbone, she circled it with a rawhide band.

*The Burning Hills* was one of several Warners movies made by a director who gave actors no help at all. "One thing Natalie and I agreed on," Tab Hunter recalled, "was that being under contract to Warners, you learned who's a hack and who's the real thing." And they agreed that Stuart Heisler, who directed *The Burning Hills,* was emphatically not the real thing. Hunter found him "completely unable to communicate with actors. In a film I made later, Heisler came over to Jack Palance, who was also in it, as he was starting to prepare a scene. The only thing he said was, 'Remember, you hate cops!'" And Natalie had not forgotten Heisler's behavior on *The Star.* This time she disliked him and her role so much that Heisler complained to Jack Warner about the way she deliberately overate during lunch breaks so she could "suddenly get sick," and he threatened to "really bawl the hell out of her."

Miscast and undirected in *The Burning Hills,* Natalie seems distinctly amateurish. It took Warners to dent her professionalism, and the studio did nothing to repair it by continuing to assign her to mediocre pictures and directors.

ALTHOUGH NATALIE and Tab Hunter were doomed to co-star in another terrible movie a few months later, at least they liked each other and even managed to enjoy working together. "We both wanted better material," he recalled, "and agreed to try and make the best of what we were given." They also enjoyed each other's company offscreen, and

*Another ethnic role: as a half-Mexican spitfire (with Tab Hunter,
as a man on the run) in* The Burning Hills

were happiest in their roles when the studio cast them as "dates" at movie premieres and events. "Although you could go on suspension for refusing a part," Tab Hunter explained, "you could refuse an arranged date, and Warners didn't insist or penalize you for it. But there was no question of that with Natalie, who was always stimulating to be with."

At the 1956 Academy Awards ceremony, they saw the award for Best Supporting Actress, which Natalie had hoped to win for *Rebel,* go to Jo Van Fleet for *East of Eden;* and near the end of the show, Ingrid Bergman received the Best Actress award for *Anastasia,* a part Natalie would choose for her theater debut only a few months before she died.

"The awards were naturally on Natalie's mind," Tab Hunter remembered. "But she was also worried about the way her hair looked. We were shooting [*The Burning Hills*] very late that day, and it left her no time for a session with the hairdresser. 'Why don't you just cut it short?' I said. 'I was recently in Europe and saw a lot of girls who looked great with short hair.' So she did, and it worked. Typical of the way Natalie picked up on things right away."

And over the next few years, columnists will note Natalie's frequently changing hairstyles, from European short cut to debutante, long mane to upswept; they will also comment on her series of wardrobe changes, from all-American teenager (capri pants and striped sweater) to glamour girl (low-cut black satin evening gown). Denied the challenge of variety in movie roles, the frustrated actress also develops a variety of life roles: simple teenage girl and animal lover with her dogs, birds and toy leopards; dedicated artiste who places career above romance; movie star hiding behind enormous dark glasses in her red Thunderbird; girl-about-town "romantically linked" by Hedda and Louella with almost every young actor on the Warner lot and (this is when the long cigarette holder first appears) "hoping to own a real leopard one day."

All these life roles, of course, were only surface experiments, monitored by Maria and the publicity department at Warners, and the studio treadmill limited Natalie's time for exploring life outside the gates of Burbank. In any case, she wasn't ready for it. As a minor with no control over her money until her twenty-first birthday, she couldn't leave home even if she wanted to; and with relatively little knowledge of the great world, she was still very insecure about her ability to function as an independent adult. With so many of her everyday needs taken care of by Maria or the studio, there were curious gaps in Natalie's everyday practical knowledge. It would take her another ten years to learn what to pack when traveling alone; and another gap would become the subject of a joke: "Sure I'm domestic—I know how to order room service."

But the strongest roadblock in Natalie's present life was that she hadn't yet freed herself from the childhood reflex of doing as she was told; and she now faced, in the person of Jack Warner, an authority figure even more powerful than her mother.

Shortly after *The Burning Hills* finished shooting, Maria took Natalie to Hawaii for a week. "She was very excited about it," Tab Hunter remembered, "and told me it was the first real vacation she'd ever had." But it wasn't a vacation from authority, as the studio paid for it, and in return Natalie had to pose for publicity shots with Hugh O'Brian, the popular star of its TV series *Wyatt Earp*. They were photographed dancing together on the beach at Honolulu, Natalie in a swimsuit, O'Brian in swimming trunks pressed tightly against her. "He's too fast for me," she told Olga later, adding that she refused his invitation to a dinner date.

Back at the studio, where Jack Warner had begun to increase production of movies for TV under the *Warner Bros. Presents* umbrella, Natalie was immediately assigned to *The Wife of Bath's Tale*. Publicized as "a modern version of Chaucer," it aired May 22, but apparently no copies have survived. And on June 12 Natalie began her second picture with Tab Hunter, written by Marion Hargrove, who specialized in comedies of army life. *The Girl He Left Behind* was the last and least of them; Natalie later referred to it as "The Girl with the Left Behind." Tab Hunter remembered that she grew increasingly impatient with the material and its workhorse director, David Butler: "She hated every moment because she wanted something better. But she was always very prepared, very professional, even for dreck. At times I thought she even worked too hard at 'exploring a character' when there was no character to explore."

A few days before shooting ended, Hunter introduced Natalie to Scott Marlowe, an actor friend from New York who had studied at the Actors Studio and just completed a small role in his first film, *Men in War*. They "clicked," according to Hunter, "both personally and because Scott was serious and knowledgeable about acting." After a spy for Louella Parsons reported seeing them at several little theaters (Hollywood's equivalent of off-Broadway), she announced that Marlowe was "the great love of Natalie's life." He wasn't, but Natalie had begun a relationship as unconventional (in 1956) as her affair with Nick Ray.

Her first studio-arranged date with a gay or bisexual actor had been with Nick Adams, whom the publicity department considered a more likely "beau" than Sal Mineo for the New York premiere of *Rebel*. His amiable manner and eagerness to please gained her confidence for a while, and he also played up to Natalie's girl-about-town role by blatantly seizing every photo opportunity to put his arms around her and making sure the gossip columnists took note. (Later she had reason to agree with Nick Ray's verdict: "The most ambitious actor I've ever known.") Her next arranged date, after *A Cry in the Night*, was with Raymond Burr, who played the sophisticated Older Man of the World and escorted her to Romanoff's and La Rue. "We had escargots for dinner last night," Natalie told Hedda Hopper, playing up to Burr as expertly as she would play down Adams, when he became too persistent, by describing him as "always more like a brother."

*Robert Wagner: From the first, Natalie had no problem accepting something still taboo at the time, and formed many*

*lifelong friendships with gay men. And she was always totally
loyal, never talked about their private lives.*

But Scott Marlowe was Natalie's first gay friend to become an object
of attraction; and as with Dennis Hopper, her first heterosexual friend,
they "occasionally went to bed together." Career-minded to an almost
obsessive degree, but an adept sexual politician, as Dick Clayton, his
agent at Famous Artists recalled, Marlowe was a regular at Hollywood's
leading gay bar of the period, the Red Raven. Jack Larson (playing
Jimmy Olsen in the *Superman* TV series with George Reeves at the time)
remembers Marlowe as darkly handsome, fashionably sullen, beer bottle
in hand, always dressed in black, "with something desperate in his
aggressive pose as a sex object, and a glazed look in his eyes, as if he really
hated being gay."

Before James Dean definitely committed to play Jim Stark in *Rebel*,
Marlowe had been one of several members of the Actors Studio interviewed by Nick Ray as a possible second choice. He tasted movie honey
and moved to Hollywood, but adopted the defiant anti-Hollywood
stance of some of his New York colleagues—not a good idea unless
you've already proved your talent (like Dean in *East of Eden*), and
although Marlowe impressed several directors, producers and acting
teachers as talented, his behavior alienated them.

Trent Dolan, another of Dick Clayton's clients, went to the same acting class as Marlowe, and "saw him do a scene as a fucked-up teenager.
He was brilliant, but he played every part the same way, it was all he
could do. When [acting teacher] Charles Conrad finally said, 'Scott,
now try and do something we haven't seen you do,' he got furious,
walked out, and never came back."

Marlowe created a good deal of publicity for himself as Natalie's
"great love," but his career was virtually over five years later, after only
one leading role in a superior low-budget movie, *A Cold Wind in August*.
The remaining forty-five years of his life brought one more good role in
a TV movie, *No Place Like Home*, a handful of routine supporting parts,
and a final decade of violent mental disturbance.

"I was always telling Scott to lighten up," Tab Hunter recalled, but
Natalie responded to a fellow rebel with the allure of an Actors Studio
background, and admired his open contempt for the Hollywood
machine. As for his sexuality, Hunter (as discreet as Natalie herself)

*Natalie and Tab Hunter as themselves during a break*
*on location for* The Girl He Left Behind

never talked about his own or his friends' private lives; but whether or
not Marlowe confided in Natalie, her sexual radar seldom failed to pick
up signals. And Marlowe's signals would certainly have aroused her sense
of adventure and her curiosity.

By 1956 "Child Star Grows Up" and "Love Smites Natalie Wood"
had headlined gossip columns often enough to alarm her mother, who
viewed a romance (as she'd already proved in the case of Dennis Hopper)
as even more threatening than a close friendship. Maria knew that some
of Natalie's dates were orchestrated by the studio, but she couldn't be
sure about all of them; and although no longer able to exercise total control over her daughter's life, she found ways to monitor it. Like the time-
keeper who clocked studio employees in and out of Warners, she waited
for Natalie's return from a date, examined her daughter's skirt for wrin-
kles, then inspected her underwear for possible stains.


JACK WARNER LOANED Natalie and Dennis Hopper to the *Kaiser
Aluminum Hour* that summer for *Carnival,* a live TV show directed by
George Roy Hill, with Natalie playing a hoochy-koochy dancer and

Dennis a barker. It aired from New York on August 24, and no record of it survives, but according to Dennis the loss is not for mourning.

In mid-September Warners released *The Burning Hills,* to instant commercial success and a notable increase in fan-mail for its stars. The studio quickly prepared a more ambitious publicity campaign for the November release of *The Girl He Left Behind,* and sent Natalie and Hunter to New York for press interviews and a joint TV appearance on the October 15 *Perry Como Show.* The protocol for these shows was that the host promoted the movie and his guests "entertained," and for Como's audience Natalie and Tab ice-skated to music.

Nick Adams, who happened to be in New York that week, had recently managed to ingratiate himself with Elvis Presley. He told Natalie that the singer wanted to know if he might ask his favorite actress for a date. "Natalie was all shook up after Presley called and asked her to go out with him when she got back to Los Angeles," Tab Hunter remembered; and the dinner date led to an invitation to visit Presley at home in Memphis.

Natalie at eighteen was no longer obliged, as she remarked later, "to have a welfare worker following me around everywhere, including the bathroom." On November 1, wearing movie-star dark glasses, scarf around her head, sweater and jeans, she flew to Memphis under an assumed name. But she was unofficially chaperoned by Nick Adams, who had maneuvered an invitation for himself as well, and alerted the press. Hundreds of fans assembled outside Presley's mansion for Natalie's arrival, and when the couple went out to dinner at the Hotel Chisca, hundreds more waited outside the entrance, then screamed their names when they arrived. Next day Presley took Natalie for a ride on his new motorcycle, with Adams following on one of the singer's older models.

On their first date Natalie had discovered that twenty-one-year-old Presley (who had just completed his first Hollywood movie, *Love Me Tender*) was personally very shy. In Memphis he seemed even more unlike his performing self, and many years later she told her friend (and stepdaughter) Sarah Gregson that "going out with Elvis was like going out on a high-school date. He took me to ice-cream parlors and we drank sodas."

Elvis's mother, no less possessive than Maria, believed that Natalie was a schemer who hoped to "snare" him for publicity purposes; and

Gladys Presley assigned her a bedroom as far away from Elvis's as possible, in the opposite wing of the mansion, while her own room, halfway between the two wings, became a strategic lookout point.

"I'm sure my girl is not seriously involved," Maria (who was seriously worried) told a reporter. In fact, neither Star Mother had cause for alarm, and although a week with Elvis in Memphis was exciting in prospect, it failed to measure up in reality. Indoors, Gladys played guard dog to her son day and night, and outdoors he seemed content to take Natalie for rides on his motorcycle and wave to fans. On the third day, Natalie invented an urgent reason for returning to Los Angeles, where she assured Maria that "nothing happened," then braced herself for Louella Parsons, who demanded and got an interview on the Elvis situation.

Parsons began by reminding Natalie that she'd "taken her to task" more than once for "cheapening herself with all this romance activity with Nick Adams, Tab Hunter, Raymond Burr and heaven knows who else." Apparently forgetting that only a few weeks earlier she'd described Scott Marlowe as "the great love of Natalie's life," the columnist wanted to know if the romance with Elvis was "serious."

"Not right now," was Natalie's cool answer. "But who knows what will happen?"

By this time Natalie had learned an important lesson in handling the press. Titillating curiosity without satisfying it was always more effective than the standard denial of "We're just good friends." As for the charge of cheapening herself, it was Parsons who'd cheapened Natalie by constantly trumpeting the news of her "romance activity" at the request of studio publicists. But the young old hand knew better than to point this out.

"Miss Parsons," she said instead, "naturally I meet other young actors around the studios. If we go out to dinner or a premiere, the photographers take our picture, and the first thing I know I'm having a romance with my escort." By pretending to take Parsons seriously, she let both of them off the hook, and enabled the columnist to deny all the silly rumors about "my dear young friend" without admitting that she'd been the first to spread them. "Natalie dropped by my house," Parsons concluded the interview, "and spoke up spunkily in her own defense."

But a week later she was reviving the old rumor as well as spreading a new one. Hundreds of Natalie's fans, Parsons reported, were writing her and calling her names because they feared she might marry Elvis Presley, while the eighteen-year-old star was secretly dating forty-two-year-old actor John Ireland.

IN VIEW OF NATALIE'S ambition to become a serious actress, it was ironic that while promoting a movie she despised, she made an important career move without realizing it. Norman Brokaw, then a junior agent at William Morris, had seen her ice-skating performance with Tab Hunter on *The Perry Como Show* and was struck by the vivid personality of "this beautiful girl," whom he remembered as a pretty but rather ordinary adolescent in *Pride of the Family.* (Apparently he hadn't seen *Rebel Without a Cause.*) Brokaw contacted Maria, and after the stories he'd heard about her imperious attitude toward Natalie's agents in the past, found her not at all the kind of person he expected. "I never had any problems with her," he recalled. "She liked and respected me."

Naturally, Maria knew when she was on to a good thing, and the situation called for the "con artist's" best show of charm. Eager, successful and important, Brokaw was of great potential value to her daughter's career; and on the personal level, the Russian connection was an additional point in his favor.

In 1898, the Haidabura troupe had been the first Russian dancers to arrive in the United States. A family affair, consisting of Nicholas and his wife, three sons and three daughters, the troupe toured the vaudeville circuit for many years. By the time Nicholas retired and the troupe dissolved, he'd changed the Russian-Jewish family name to Hyde. One of his sons married Brokaw's mother. Another, known as Johnny, became an agent who briefly represented the very young Marilyn Monroe and in 1943 had steered his fifteen-year-old nephew to his first job as a mailroom clerk at William Morris. Five years later Brokaw, who took his mother's maiden name, had risen to the rank of junior agent; and by 1956 he was able to impress Maria by dropping the names of the agency's most illustrious female clients: Barbara Stanwyck, Susan Hayward, Kim Novak, Loretta Young—none of them perhaps quite as dazzling as Lana Turner, but bright enough to light a few stars in Maria's eyes.

With Natalie about to start another contract movie at Warners, Brokaw could do nothing for her at first. But a daughter represented by the William Morris Agency had obviously risen in value, and could do something for Maria. The ever-developing businesswoman's hand is apparent in a memo from Jack Warner to Steve Trilling, dated November 20: "Talk to me today about lending Natalie Wood the money for the house. I believe it will be good business if we do so. We will do it direct with Natalie and her Mother, and we will make the best arrangements we can on the repayment."

It was good business for the studio, of course, because Warners increased its power over Natalie by putting her in its debt; and Trilling saw the point so quickly that he arranged for Natalie and her mother to discuss it with a studio lawyer that afternoon. The non-negotiable price for 3331 Laurel Canyon Boulevard was $12,500, and the owner accepted Trilling's offer of "$3,000 advance with our guaranteeing the $9,500 payment later." This made Natalie little more than the new owner in name only, burdened with a $12,500 debt for a house that was large enough to provide her and her mother, father and sister with separate bedrooms. Constructed only a few years earlier of stucco trimmed with volcanic rock, its ranch-style layout at least allowed Natalie to occupy her own private bedroom suite, with an entrance leading to the pool area, where a tiled mermaid perpetually smiled from the depths.

IN THE SECOND WEEK of December, Natalie started work on *Bombers B-52,* a studio potboiler directed by another studio workhorse, Gordon Douglas. Although the credits announced "Starring Natalie Wood," her part was relatively small, and although the movie was supposed to be her third with Tab Hunter, he turned the part down, went on suspension, and was replaced by the less congenial Efrem Zimbalist Jr.

Fortunately, Natalie developed a personal rapport with Karl Malden, who in fact had the most important role, as a sergeant engineer in the U.S. Air Force, "proud of a job that keeps U.S. bombers up in the air." When his daughter falls in love with his superior officer, Malden objects, and Natalie accuses him of being jealous because Zimbalist is a younger and more important man. All ends well, of course, and there's a gung-ho Cold War subtext to the formula junk; but as its America-needs-to-be-prepared spokesman, Malden gives a disturbingly authentic performance.

The scenes with Malden allow Natalie's performance to catch fire, partly because they're the most dramatic in the movie and parental dis-

*Hollywood, 1957. Natalie, age nineteen, with Nick Gurdin*

cord was once again a stimulant, partly because she's playing opposite an actor she likes and admires. Their rapport, as Malden recalled, was mutual: "The boys hung around Natalie all the time. I used to kid her about it. But she always came prepared, unlike most of the young contract stars at Warners, and she worked very hard as well as having fun. We both liked the confrontational scene when she came home late from a date, and really worked at it."

Also under long-term contract to Warners, Malden was "grateful" when they eventually let him go, but grateful for the experience as well. "It was a test, and only real professionals passed it. I feel it must have been the same for Natalie, in spite of all the frustrations."

Before they met, Natalie knew that Malden had worked with Kazan in both theater and movies, and was particularly impressed that he'd played Mitch in the original production of *A Streetcar Named Desire* and won an Oscar for his performance in the film version. She first saw the movie in a screening room at Warners with Dennis Hopper, after hearing Nick Ray, James Dean and Dennis talk about Kazan; and during her years under contract to the studio she screened it several more times, to remind herself that there was life beyond *A Cry in the Night* and *The*

*Burning Hills,* to admire the direction and acting, and simply to watch Vivien Leigh, who fascinated her above all other movie actresses.

On a personal level, Natalie was only moderately curious about other actresses, but after we became friends she asked many questions about Vivien. She was fascinated to learn that they shared a "wrist problem," as Vivien thought her wrists too thick and usually wore bracelets or long sleeves to conceal them. Natalie seemed to find every detail important, from Vivien's favorite couturier to her favorite role.

The extent of Natalie's curiosity suggested some kind of personal identification, to an extent that became apparent only after both lives had ended too sadly too soon. Although Vivien's life was the higher-wire act, they had the same delicate balance in common: unhealed wounds and undying humor, surface poise and subterranean disorder. Vivien's favorite theater role was Marguerite in *The Lady of the Camellias,* and Natalie's first theater role would have been as *Anastasia:* feverish romantics, ultimately, both of them, living in a climate too cool for their kind.


NATALIE'S FIRST encounter with Robert Wagner, deeply romantic on her side, took place in the spring of 1949 and was over almost before it began. Neither spoke to the other, and the nineteen-year-old actor, who had just signed a contract at Fox, was unaware of the impression he made on the child star in pigtails. Natalie, who was filming *Father Was a Fullback* at the same studio, recalled later that they were walking along the same hallway in the administrative building. "He was going in one direction, I was going the opposite way. As we passed, I looked up at him, he smiled at me and naturally I smiled back." Then she stopped and stared after him. Wagner didn't turn back, but there was no emotional turning back for Natalie: "At age ten, crushes can be very vivid."

Maria the fabulist, who was with her daughter at the time, claimed later that Natalie turned to *her* and said, "That's the man I'm going to marry." In fact, Natalie told Mary Sale, who was on the set of *Father Was a Fullback* that day, that she'd fallen in love with an incredibly handsome and charming man, but had no idea who he was.

After working as an extra for a year, Wagner had recently made his first movie, playing a baseball catcher in *The Happy Years,* directed by William Wellman, a friend of his father's. But as Wagner wore a mask over his face, and the role was almost as brief as his first encounter with Natalie, it led nowhere. A few weeks later, though, Famous Artists agent Henry Willson was at dinner in the Beverly Hills Gourmet when RJ (as everyone called Robert John Wagner) began singing a popular hit, "About That Girl," a capella with a group of friends. He noted RJ's good looks and high spirits and asked him to call his office at Famous Artists for an appointment. RJ did so, signed with the agency, and soon afterward made a successful screen test at Fox.

Although RJ was aware of Willson's reputation as a sexual predator, it never bothered him, especially as two other Famous Artists agents, Charles Feldman and Ray Stark, managed his career from the start. But Willson had "discovered" him, and the usual rumors began to circulate: "Over the years, I've been linked sexually with Jeffrey Hunter, Burt Lancaster, Dan Dailey, Clifton Webb and, my God, even Clark Gable." He could shrug the rumors off because he felt secure about his own sexuality, and like Natalie had many gay friends throughout his life.

Their second encounter took place in June 1956, almost seven years after she'd cut out his photo from a fan magazine and tacked it to her bedroom wall; and by then his fan mail at the studio was second only to Marilyn Monroe's. They were formally introduced at a star-studded fashion show at the Beverly Wilshire Hotel, and a photographer asked them to pose together for a few pictures. Natalie had just started filming *The Girl He Left Behind,* and she thought RJ must have noticed that she'd grown up since their first encounter. But if he did, he gave no sign; and that, she supposed, was that.

A month later, when Natalie had almost decided to remove RJ's picture from her bedroom wall, he called to invite her to a screening of his latest movie, *The Mountain.* The date of the screening was July 20, which he didn't know was her birthday. At dinner together afterward, Natalie found him not only more physically seductive than ever, but thoughtful, witty and a brilliant movie-star mimic, whose Cary Grant imitation was the high point of his repertory.

Although many people commented that RJ had the same kind of relaxed, sophisticated, man-about-town humor and charm as Grant, no one was yet aware that they also had a dark side in common. The older star had already revealed it in life as well as in several movies, notably *Suspicion* and *Notorious.* The younger would soon give an unexpectedly chilling performance in *A Kiss Before Dying*. But while his personal dark side was not yet apparent to Natalie, or even to RJ himself, there was a deep mutual attraction that at first unnerved both of them.

In RJ's case, he was a popular bachelor, much in demand socially and otherwise, whose only serious affair, with Barbara Stanwyck (they met in 1953, on the set of *Titanic*), had ended painfully. It left him unprepared to risk another, and was partly responsible for a bet he made with his father, that he wouldn't consider marriage until he was thirty. The day after his first evening with Natalie, he sent her flowers, then called to say how much he'd enjoyed seeing her, and ended the conversation with a casual "I'll see you again sometime." Over the next five months, Natalie recalled, "every time the phone rang I would say, 'Well, this time it's RJ,' but it never was." Finally they met by accident at a CBS awards cere- mony, and "casually, as if we'd talked the night before," RJ invited her to join him for lunch the next day at the studio.

They agreed to meet at noon. She arrived at three and found him still waiting for her. She apologized. He astonished her by not being angry. Or was he only pretending not to be angry? And although Natalie later insisted that she hadn't *intended* to keep RJ waiting, maybe she had. In any case, he asked her to dinner the following night, December 6, a date that became significant in both their lives. It produced the first entry in an occasional journal that Natalie began the next day: "Our first serious date."

Over the next three months they continued to meet and make love, but there were still barriers. Unlike Natalie, RJ came from a well-heeled family. Robert Wagner Sr., a steel executive in Detroit, became the com- pany's West Coast representative when RJ was nine. The family moved to La Jolla, near San Diego, and although Wagner Sr. wanted his son to enter the steel business, RJ was determined to become a movie actor. At first Wagner Sr. objected strongly. He didn't disapprove of acting as a profession—in fact he was friendly with several actors and directors in the movie industry—but an only son was expected to follow in his father's footsteps. Finally Wagner Sr. relented and introduced him to William Wellman.

Not surprisingly, RJ soon felt "alien" to what he called "Natalie's group—Nick Ray, Dennis Hopper, Scott Marlowe. My friends were Bogart, Bacall and Spencer Tracy, and later, because of Tracy, Katharine Hepburn. I was eight years older than Natalie, and more successful, but

*Natasha Zepaloff at age seventeen:*
*graduation picture*

*Natalie, age seventeen,*
*with Nicky Hilton*

to her group *Prince Valiant* was a joke. I found this frustrating." *Prince Valiant* was the absurd and absurdly popular movie that had made RJ a star; but although the Actors Studio way was not the way of RJ or his friends, he was serious about an acting career. Tracy had recognized his potential when they first appeared together in *Broken Lance* (1954); and two years later he persuaded Darryl Zanuck to cast RJ as his young brother in *The Mountain.*

From his family situation and Wagner Sr.'s connections, RJ had acquired a sense of security that Tracy's friendship and encouragement naturally reinforced. From her family situation Natalie had acquired a chronic sense of insecurity, and the closer she felt to somebody, the stronger her fear of betrayal. And although RJ could forgive her for arriving three hours late for a lunch date, she later did something that at the time he couldn't pretend to forgive.

One evening after they'd had dinner, she asked him to drive her to the Chateau Marmont. "Scott's staying there now," she explained. "I want to see Scott." RJ knew they'd had an affair, but didn't know how serious or how casual, or that Marlowe was gay. "I was so furious, I dumped her, and didn't see her again for a while."

During that while, Natalie stopped seeing Marlowe and began an affair with Nicky Hilton, son of hotel magnate Conrad Hilton and stepson of his former wife, Zsa Zsa Gabor. Fatally rich and handsome, Nicky Hilton had been briefly married to Elizabeth Taylor, and was a lord if not a prince of darkness, endowed with equal parts of charm, sexual expertise and cruelty. The practicing Catholic kept a rosary, a handgun and pornographic books on his bedside table, and according to Taylor, became physically abusive when drunk.

Although Natalie had heard at least some of the stories about Hilton, she was not deterred; and Maria, eyes and ears on constant alert, certainly heard some of them as well. But when the affair began in December 1956, she made no attempt to discourage it. Like movie stardom, wealth was sacrosanct.


IN JANUARY 1957, fifteen-year old Natasha Zepaloff and her grandmother (the tsarist general's widow) spent a few days in Los Angeles; and one afternoon, when Natalie was at the house on Laurel Canyon Boulevard, Maria invited them over. By coincidence, Natasha was wearing her hair in a short cut similar to Natalie's in *The Girl He Left Behind*. Natalie noted this at once and laughed, then said she had to get ready for a date with Nicky Hilton and asked Natasha to help her choose what to wear. She opened her extensive bedroom closet, and Maria watched approvingly as they agreed on a white dress, silver shoes and ermine wrap.

Later, Natasha recalled this as the first time "I felt a strong connection with Natalie without knowing why." When she felt it again, the occasion was always stage-managed by Maria, with an imprudent relish for intrigue. Once she drew Natasha's attention to a framed photograph of Natalie and Nick Gurdin. "There's Natalie with her father," she said, and accompanied the word "father" with a broad wink.

BUT WHAT SUDDENLY propelled Natalie to change lovers in midstream when she was so powerfully attracted to RJ? Several years later, after their divorce, she began the second most serious affair of her life, with Richard Gregson; and it seems more than coincidental that before she married him, Natalie came close to repeating the pattern. The episode again involved Hilton, and Gregson remembered that "she couldn't figure it out, and was overcome with deep pain." Even though she was in analysis by then, there were two things that Natalie apparently hadn't yet figured out. Like her mother, she was sometimes compelled to court danger; and she wasn't simply undeterred by Nicky Hilton's reputation, but excited by it. Another compulsion was also a legacy from Maria, who had repeatedly warned Natalie as a child to mistrust anyone who tried to get close to her. Consequently, Natalie as an adult drew back from emotional fulfillment at the same time as she pursued it.

> *Robert Wagner: Natalie had moods that would sometimes drive me up the wall.*

But it was only after marrying her that he began to analyze them. Earlier, in his man-about-town role, he told a reporter: "There were so many boys around Natalie that you had to beat a path to her door." But by the time he'd beaten the path and the competition, and Hilton had decided to beat a path to Joan Collins's door, RJ was about to leave for Japan and *Stopover Tokyo*.

On March 12, 1957, their last date before he left, he gave Natalie a gold charm bracelet with "Wow Charlie" engraved on one of the charms. (They'd picked up the expression from *On the Waterfront,* and "Charlie" had become their private nickname for each other.) The prospect of separation had evidently made RJ accept the reality of a serious affair; the fact of separation intensified it; and over the next four months he called Natalie almost every day from his Tokyo hotel.

"I think we both realized how deeply in love we were during the time RJ was in Japan," Natalie said later. "I dated occasionally, but my heart was not in it."

Apart from RJ, her heart was mainly occupied with her career, and she enlisted the help of the William Morris Agency in persuading Jack Warner to cast her in the title role of *Marjorie Morningstar.* She had read Herman Wouk's best-selling novel soon after Warner acquired the rights and was discouraged when the agency reported that he planned to sign either Elizabeth Taylor or Audrey Hepburn.

Natalie was encouraged again when Tab Hunter, who had recently enjoyed a jukebox success with a song he recorded for Dot Records, suggested that she follow his lead and take singing lessons. The idea of a new career as recording stars was a pipe dream for both of them, of course, but at the time it promised a way of escape from Warners.

Meanwhile, in the last week of March, the studio loaned Natalie out to Bob Hope Enterprises for an appearance on one of his occasional TV specials. (This time she wasn't even promoting one of her own movies. The deal guaranteed the studio $7,500 and "a 30-second plug for *The Spirit of St. Louis.*") Natalie and Hope performed a 1920s Charleston and a 1950s rock-and-roll number, and a record of the show makes it clear how much she owed to her early training as Natasha Gurdina at Ermolova's "dancing studio" and her later classes with Michael Panaieff and Tamara Lepko. They not only developed her instinct for graceful movement, but supplied her with the basic elements of technique (as Jerome Robbins discovered when they worked together on *West Side Story*). While Hope clowns along, she really dances: fluid, rhythmical, with perfect coordination. Also, she's obviously enjoying this performance far more than her recent roles at Warners.

Two weeks later, there was encouraging news from the *Morningstar* front: as neither Elizabeth Taylor nor Audrey Hepburn would be available for the movie, the Morris Agency had arranged for Herman Wouk to interview Natalie in New York. But discouragement followed. Wouk found her beautiful, alluring, precocious and very determined—the polar opposite of his naive, insecure Jewish girl with a hopeless dream of becoming a famous Broadway actress. The author had casting approval, and his rejection seemed final; but in late April, when the "right" actress still had not been found, the Morris Agency convinced Milton Sperling, producer of the movie (and Jack Warner's son-in-law), to test Natalie.

The test, like the movie itself, was directed by Irving Rapper, whom Wouk had approved after turning down Michael Curtiz (who was eager to make it) as "too old-fashioned," and preferring Daniel Mann, on the crest of the wave after the success of *I'll Cry Tomorrow,* with Susan Hayward in one of her flamboyant lady-on-the-skids roles as Lillian Roth. But Mann proved unavailable, and everyone agreed on Rapper, "who used to hold the script for me," as Bette Davis once remarked to Robert Wagner about the director of *Now, Voyager.*

Since the role of the young writer who falls in love with Marjorie had not yet been cast, a hopeful unknown was hired for the test; and Rapper, who seemed out of humor, made Natalie feel unnervingly tense. But in spite or perhaps because of the tension, she played a love scene with the hopeful unknown so effectively that both Sperling and Warner decided to bring Wouk out to Burbank to see the test. A typical example of Jack Warner's thrift, it was shot in black-and-white against a couple of flats, with lighting that Wouk described as "harsh and slovenly," and clumsy, hurried camerawork that allowed Natalie to move out of frame several times. All the same, three minutes into the scene, Wouk realized how naive he'd been to reject Natalie because he couldn't imagine her in the role when they met for lunch in New York: "My Marjorie would have been stammering and feeble talking to a novelist 20 years older than herself. She would have spilled coffee or dropped a fork. Natalie Wood wore a seductively cut red dress [and] carried off the interview with unshaken aplomb. She took charge. But [in the test] she was absolutely electrifying! *This* was my Marjorie, yearning for a career she clearly would never have, irresistibly appealing in her awkward immaturity."

No copy of the test has survived, although a couple of stills from it certainly suggest the "electrifying" Marjorie that Wouk saw. But it was not the Marjorie of the completed movie, for reasons that include a series of often contradictory revisions to Everett Freeman's script throughout the shoot (from August 19 to November 17); the lack of

connection between Natalie and Irving Rapper, by then a tired workhorse; and a drastic change, ordered by the producer, in the character of
the young writer who falls in love with Marjorie. Natalie had hoped for
Montgomery Clift in the role as originally conceived, but the writer
mutated to an actor-dancer played by forty-six-year-old Gene Kelly.

Wouk's novel is a long, bulky, sentimental package, which the movie
packaged even more sentimentally. For Wouk to make Marjorie (née
Morgenstern) Jewish seems more a gimmick than an essential part of her
star-is-not-born story, and in the movie the Jewish element is so diluted
that it has no effect on her WASP lover, who's only momentarily restive
at the Morgensterns' Passover dinner. And when the aspiring actress
changes her name to Morningstar, so she won't be thought Jewish, it
passes without comment or explanation. Worst of all, as Natalie remembered, "I was in tears during the whole movie. They couldn't decide on a
point of view. One day Marjorie was desperately serious about becoming an actress, a few days later it wasn't important to her. So you'd play
her one way for several scenes, then they'd change."

A palpable lack of chemistry with Kelly, who knew he was miscast
and felt uncomfortable in his role, was an additional problem; and it no
doubt accounts for Natalie's unexpectedly flat reaction when he says he
can't marry her. Partly because family confrontation scenes always
sparked a strong personal response, her performance is at its best in the
scenes with Claire Trevor, who played her mother and somehow managed to be believable even when miscast and misfitted with a dark brown
wig. And in the movie Natalie even *looks* different than she did in the
test, too groomed and styled and lipsticked—another example of
Warner Bros. putting her through its glamour blender.

When *Marjorie Morningstar* was finally released in April 1958 (after
four months in the editing room), it received cool reviews and barely
escaped box-office failure. Natalie saw it as the latest and greatest in a
series of career disappointments since *Rebel Without a Cause*. Unlike the
others, it had seemed to offer serious possibilities, all dissipated in production.

"NATALIE AND I first became good friends in the late 1950s," Donfeld
recalled, "after meeting socially a few times." In those days he was
designing album covers for Capitol Records, among them Frank Sina-

tra's. "I knew she had this idea of becoming a recording star, and asked Capitol's top producer, Voyle Gilmore, to meet with her and discuss the possibility of making a test cut for the label. He was very enthusiastic about the idea, and suggested we meet her during a break in the filming of *Marjorie Morningstar*.

On the day that Donfeld arranged to pick Natalie up on the set and walk her over to the studio commissary, where Gilmore would join them, Rapper was rehearsing a scene between Claire Trevor and Howard Bert, who played Marjorie's young brother, and "humiliating him cruelly for his inexperience." An angry Claire Trevor told the director to leave him alone. "For God's sake, he's doing his best!" she said, and put her arms around the boy. Suddenly Natalie appeared at her side, put her hand on the boy's shoulder and joined Trevor in fixing the director with an accusing stare. Embarrassed, Rapper turned abruptly away. "I loved Natalie for that," Donfeld remembered; and although the two actresses didn't become friends until several years later, Trevor recalled the scene "as the moment I knew that one day we would."

But the test cut of "Little Girl Blue" that Natalie agreed to make for Gilmore was the end of a pipe dream. Throughout her life, whenever she wanted to succeed at something, from acting to graduating from high school to motherhood, she really worked at it. But in spite of singing lessons, vocal exercises and sheer determination, "she just didn't have much of a singing voice," according to Donfeld, "and the test was no good. More than a few off-pitch notes. Even though it was typical of Natalie to continue working on her voice, and improving it, she could never sing well enough to record her own songs for *West Side Story* or *Inside Daisy Clover*."

DURING THE LONG shoot of a boring movie in Tokyo, RJ satisfied an occasional urge for release "with a couple of Japanese girls." And soon after Natalie began work on *Marjorie Morningstar*, Nicky Hilton seized the chance to resume his affair with her (while his other object of affection, Joan Collins, was co-starring in *Stopover Tokyo*). Did Natalie and RJ feel they needed a last diversion before accepting total commitment to each other? In any case, it should be apparent by now that a sexual history of Hollywood in the 1950s would reveal patterns of behavior that looked ahead to the "liberation" of the 1960s, and were far more unorthodox than the professional gossips discovered, or reported, or were bribed not to report.

RJ returned from Japan while *Marjorie Morningstar* was still in production at Burbank, and Nicky Hilton, according to Olga, was hoping to marry Natalie. But when RJ and Natalie saw each other again, they knew at once that separation had only heightened their desire to commit to each other. The end of Hilton as Natalie's lover, and potential husband, was the beginning of a dialogue between Natalie and RJ, tentative at first, on getting married. And when the *Morningstar* unit moved to Schroon Lake in the Adirondacks for three weeks of location work, RJ joined Natalie there. Maria, who invited herself and Lana to join them, occupied one bedroom of Natalie's suite at Schroon Manor, a luxury hotel with its own private beach, while RJ shared the other with Natalie. Their open cohabitation made Maria uneasy, but she managed to twinkle when she served the lovers breakfast in bed. In fact she had nothing to fear, and the "scandal" was never leaked to the press—a situation unimaginable today.

Two days after *Morningstar* finished shooting, Natalie reported to Paramount for her next assignment, which came about through Norman Brokaw. Bert Allenberg, the William Morris senior agent who handled Frank Sinatra, had told Brokaw that his client would agree to appear in *Kings Go Forth* only if Warners agreed to loan Natalie to Frank Ross–Eton Productions for the picture. Although Jack Warner hesitated at first, once again fearful of a contract star doing too well at a rival studio, he was finally unable to resist a tasty offer: $55,000 for Natalie's services for a maximum of twelve weeks. As Producer would be paying his star no more than her regular weekly salary of $750, he was guaranteed a 500 percent profit on the deal.

Brokaw had assured Natalie that *Kings Go Forth,* in which Tony Curtis had also been cast, would mark an important step in her career. But she had two reasons to feel ambivalent about it. The first was the prospect of another "exotic" role: Monique, an American girl with a black father, who's been brought up in France and speaks with a French accent. The second was Sinatra himself, by 1957 a powerful combination of exceptionally gifted popular singer, movie star, charismatic bad boy and liberal hero.

Until the release of FBI files under the Freedom of Information Act,

Sinatra's political record was overshadowed by the record of his connections with La Cosa Nostra and his reputation for sexual voracity. But it's an important part of the case history of this enormously successful and troubled man, and helps to explain the fascination he held for so many people, Natalie among them. In 1945 Sinatra had produced and appeared in *The House I Live In,* a short film pleading the cause of racial and religious tolerance; and he also supported several other admirable causes that the FBI considered "subversive" (among them the American Crusade to End Lynching, the Joint Anti-Fascist Refugee Committee and the American Society for Cultural Relations with Italy). In 1947 the House Un-American Activities Committee decided it had enough evidence to accuse him of being a Communist, and although the charge was never proved, it earned Sinatra a pair of influential right-wing enemies in the media. Columnist Walter Winchell and radio commentator Gerald LK Smith repeatedly attacked him as a draft-dodging, fellow-traveling, overpaid crooner, and his career went into a seven-year decline.

But it rebounded swiftly after he won an Academy Award in 1954 for his performance in *From Here to Eternity.* Over the next two years Sinatra recorded a series of best-selling albums in collaboration with arranger Nelson Riddle, received an Academy Award nomination for his performance in *The Man with the Golden Arm,* bought an elaborate home in Palm Springs, acquired an interest in the Sands casino in Las Vegas in partnership with a former associate of Al Capone and became friendly with Senator John F. Kennedy.

When Lord Byron acquired the reputation of "mad, bad and dangerous to know," it only increased the number of people, especially women, eager to know him. The same thing happened to Sinatra, and like Byron he took advantage of it. Perhaps not coincidentally, their recent biographers have concluded that both men, with their apparently uncontrollable mood swings from warmhearted to cruel, generous to vindictive, lived on the cusp of manic depression.

As well as a private call sheet of prostitutes and Vegas showgirls, Sinatra had a list of star conquests that included Lana Turner, Ava Gardner, whom he briefly married, Lauren Bacall and Marlene Dietrich. On *Kings Go Forth,* it soon became clear that the forty-five-year-old bad boy expected to add Natalie to the list, as she herself had expected and feared. And if she hadn't been in love with RJ, she might even have responded to the call of sexual adventure, or at least enjoyed a serious flirtation.

Throughout her life, Natalie was a compulsive, charming flirt, and "flirting is a quest for approval, like acting," as one of her later friends, actor James B. Sikking, pointed out. "It fills a pocket of insecurity. The more response you get, the more you flirt, and Natalie loved to swish her tail." But by holding out against Sinatra, she risked his anger, which she knew could be brutal. In the event, he was intrigued by a vulnerable sweetness that he perceived behind Natalie's tail swishing. And while kindly Sinatra eased the pressure and grew genuinely fond of her, ruthless Sinatra determined to try again later. At the same time, Natalie was fascinated by a "bad boy glamour" with more substance than Nicky Hilton's; and for a few years during the 1960s, their relationship became another case of "friends who occasionally went to bed together."

By the time Natalie reported to Paramount, *Kings Go Forth* had been in production for two months. Its story took place in the south of France during the last months of World War II, when a company of American soldiers (headed by Sinatra and Curtis) was dispatched to eliminate a pocket of German resistance in the mountains above Cannes. The action sequences had to be shot there before winter set in, and with Natalie busy on *Morningstar,* the script was adjusted so that only her double would be needed on location—a change that no doubt partly accounts for the excessive voice-over narration (by Sinatra) in Merle Miller's final script, and incidentally doubled Producer's profit by reducing Natalie's total work schedule to six weeks.

Everett Sloane, the brilliant Mercury Theater actor brought to Hollywood by Orson Welles for *Citizen Kane,* had sounded authentically Hebrew in the small part of a rabbi in *Morningstar;* on the strength of this, and his reputation as an expert in foreign accents, he was engaged to coach Natalie to sound authentically French. The result was sometimes successful, sometimes not. And it's never clear why she has to sound French in the first place: her late father came from Georgia, and her mother (Leora Dana), who's spent most of her life in France, speaks unaccented American.

Although liberal Sinatra announced that *Kings Go Forth* "states the case for tolerance in terms of drama and humanity," it's basically a standard romantic triangle with a racial twist and a World War II back-

*Yet another ethnic role: as the mulatto girl in*
Kings Go Forth *with Frank Sinatra*

ground. For most of the movie, Natalie does what she can with an insipid character, and for most of the movie it's not very much. But the director, Delmer Daves, was a former actor with the "extra understanding of an actor's problems" that she always responded to, and he helped her in the only scenes that made contact with emotional reality: when she admits to Curtis that she's half-black and is stunned by his harsh, bigoted reaction, and when she recovers from the suicide attempt that follows. She's moving in both scenes, but especially the second, when an indelible moment reveals the true screen actress. Her eyes flutter open, and as she realizes she's still alive, the look on her face changes from confusion to intense desperation.

ON THE AFTERNOON of December 6, when she was not on call for *Kings Go Forth,* Natalie went to a jewelry store to collect a present she'd ordered for RJ. It was an engraved identification bracelet to commemorate their first "serious date" the previous year. RJ had called earlier to say he'd made reservations for dinner at Romanoff's, and suggested they meet beforehand at his apartment on Durant Drive in Beverly Hills; but on the way there, she had a typical moment of insecurity. He'd never mentioned their "anniversary," and she wondered if he'd forgotten it.

"I should have known better," she realized later. As soon as she arrived, RJ opened a bottle of champagne, poured two glasses and handed her one. A diamond-and-pearl ring glittered among the bubbles. "Read what's engraved inside, Charlie," he said, and Natalie fished out the ring. Its inscription read: "Marry me."

At Romanoff's that evening, RJ ordered more champagne, and when Natalie found a pair of pearl earrings at the bottom of her glass, she laughed. The waiter brought two more glasses, and in hers she found another charm for the "Wow Charlie" bracelet, also with an inscription on the back: "Today we're one year old."

This time she cried. Next day she noted in her journal: " 'Two lonely stars with no place in the sun found their orbit—each other—and they were one.' I sent this to R on the anniversary of our first love. It also turned out to be the day that we were engaged to be married, and the start of our real life."

# 4

# Love and Marriage

*The feeling about being in love, I learned from my mother.*

——NATALIE GREGSON WAGNER

*A single white rose because we were separated 10 hours. I met R at the airport when he came in from SF. I had come in in the morning—we missed each other. So much. I love him so much.*

——NATALIE WOOD (JOURNAL, 1958)

*If I'd been more secure, I could have handled the problems in our marriage better. I opposed Natalie's idea of going to an analyst because I felt she could work through her fears and anxieties on her own, and with my help. Ironically, after the split, I started going to an analyst.*

——ROBERT WAGNER

A FEW DAYS before the diamond-and-pearl ring and the earrings, and the charm steeped in champagne, Natalie and RJ had a serious discussion of the pros and cons of marriage. The only major con, they agreed, was the prospect of conflicting careers; the solution, they believed, was to agree never to be separated (by one having to go on location or a publicity tour without the other) for more than two weeks at a time; and after RJ proposed, they scheduled wedding, honeymoon and future career obligations and plans as precisely as a movie.

The marriage ceremony was projected for Saturday, December 28, 1957, four days after work on *Kings Go Forth* was suspended for the hol-

*"Two lonely stars found their orbit":*
*Natalie and RJ*

idays; and Natalie would not be required to complete her remaining scenes until the last week of January 1958, when RJ was due to begin *The Hunters* at Fox. So the schedule permitted three weeks for a honeymoon, and just enough time for their mutual friends Mary and Richard Sale to give the couple a shower at their house in Beverly Hills on the afternoon of December 26.

The press was invited, and the guest list made it clear that the shower was designed as an "event" for the Hollywood establishment to celebrate the forthcoming marriage of two young movie stars. Except for the families of bride and groom, it was a mainly show-biz affair, with a cast that included Frank Sinatra, Lauren Bacall, Rock Hudson, Tony Curtis, Jane Russell, Delmer Daves, Louella Parsons, various 20th Century–Fox colleagues of RJ's and/or the Sales', director Walter Lang, Clifton Webb, Cesar Romero and Virginia Zanuck, wife of the studio's former head of production.

For Natalie, the only show-biz guest who qualified as more than an acquaintance or professional associate was Sinatra. At this point in her life she had many acquaintances among her contemporaries, and five actual or prospective friends, all first met at Warners. The first of the actual friends (but not for much longer) was Nick Adams, and the next a young actress from New York who played a bit part in *Marjorie Morningstar.* Barbara Gould attached herself to Natalie, who always responded to a beginner's loneliness and insecurity; but although they became close for a while, it was another friendship that wouldn't last much longer. The first of the prospective friends was Norma Crane, who came out from New York (and the Actors Studio) to test for the role in *Morningstar* eventually played by Carolyn Jones. "They began schmoozing over coffee," according to Mart Crowley, and Natalie was instantly attracted to Norma's wit and earthy directness. The other two were Edd Byrnes, who played a small role in *Morningstar* and later starred in the TV series *77 Sunset Strip,* and his actress wife, Asa Maynor. The couple divorced several years later, but by then Asa had become part of what Natalie called her "nucleus."

All except Barbara Gould were either filming or out of town, and Jack Warner also sent his regrets, accompanied by an impressive gift. Steve Trilling had informed him by memo that the lovers "would very much like a rawhide Hartman trunk to match their luggage. There is only one on the coast and it retails for $650, which we can get for 20% off. This makes it $520 plus $73 for taxes for a total of $593." A bargain always made Warner's day, and he approved the deal with an "OK" and an enthusiastic circle around the sum total.

AFTER THE SHOWER, the lovers took the night train to Phoenix. They were accompanied by the Sales and Nick Adams, and Mary Sale was "very insistent that Natalie and RJ mustn't sleep together," as she believed it would bring bad luck. They had decided to get married at the First Methodist Church in the nearby resort town of Scottsdale, where RJ's parents owned a house. Robert Wagner Sr. was best man; Natalie had chosen Barbara Gould for her maid of honor and Lana as a bridesmaid. RJ's business manager, Andrew Maree, and his wife were the other guests, and Mary Sale remembered that Nick Gurdin unwrapped an icon he'd brought from Russia: " 'This has to be with them when they get married,' he said. Both Natalie and RJ were very touched."

Next day the couple left by train for Florida, where RJ had chartered a boat for what they hoped would be a honeymoon cruise. But bad weather caused them to reschedule, and they took a train to New York, where they saw two plays: *The Dark at the Top of the Stairs* by William Inge and *West Side Story*, "conceived, directed, and choreographed" by Jerome Robbins. Then they drove cross-country to Palm Springs, where Natalie's lawyer, Greg Bautzer, lent them his house for a few days. They continued to Long Beach harbor, planning to end their honeymoon on *My Other Lady*, the boat RJ had recently bought and anchored there.

Soon after they got under way with RJ at the helm, dense fog smothered the coast and canceled their last chance for a honeymoon cruise. But four blurred and becalmed days off Catalina seemed even more romantic for being unscheduled, and Natalie remembered them as "the best part" of the trip.

FOR THE NEXT few months, Natalie and RJ lived at his bachelor apartment on Durant Drive, too busy to do more than talk about finding a house. As well as completing *Kings Go Forth*, Natalie was loaned out for a guest appearance on Sinatra's TV series, *The Frank Sinatra Show* ($10,000 for Producer plus a thirty-second plug for *Morningstar*), and tested for a leading role she didn't want to play. The script for *The Miracle*, "based" on the Karl Vollmoeller/Max Reinhardt play that became one of Reinhardt's most famous productions, had reduced it to the story of a girl in eighteenth-century Spain torn between desire to become a nun and desire for a soldier. Irving Rapper, assigned to direct the tests and the picture, also tested Carroll Baker. To Natalie's relief, he preferred Baker, and her only fear was that Producer might not agree. Fortunately he did. (Although the movie was a dud, the studio had better luck with nuns later that year with *The Nun's Story*.)

"See if you can find something modern for Natalie Wood," Warner instructed Steve Trilling in a memo dated March 20. In the meantime, he instructed the publicity department on March 28 that he was sending

*Scottsdale, December 28, 1957: Just married.*
*Left to right: bridesmaid Lana Wood, maid of honor Barbara Gould,*
*Nick Gurdin, Natalie, RJ, Robert Wagner Sr.*

her on a six-city promotional tour for *Morningstar:* "She is going by train and may have a chaperone and hairdresser accompany her. Also, her husband, Robert Wagner, may join her before the tour is over."

Although Natalie wanted to travel by train on her honeymoon because it was more romantic, she'd already begun to develop a subconscious fear of flying. Another example of fear as a reproductive organism, it came to the surface when RJ realized he would be able to join Natalie only for the last few days of the four-week tour, when he completed filming *In Love and War.* He encouraged her to stand by their prenuptial vow, and although she hated the idea of a month's separation, she was deeply afraid of angering Warner and Maria by going on suspension when she owed the studio $12,500. "I was finally able to reassure her," RJ remembered, "because at that time I was the big earner, $3,000 a week compared to Natalie's $750, so between us there was no money problem. And she decided to go through with it."

In fact the Morris Agency broke the news to Warner and spared Natalie a personal confrontation. But as Producer was about to go on vacation in Europe, he told Steve Trilling to "straighten out Natalie" in his absence. Trilling decided against suspension, sparing Natalie (for the moment) a confrontation with Maria, and began looking for "something modern" for her instead.

He was still looking when Jack Warner sustained serious injuries in an automobile accident in France two months later. A long hospitalization and convalescence in Los Angeles kept Producer away from the studio until November; and as his deputy, Trilling hoped to "straighten out Natalie" when the Hecht-Hill-Lancaster Company requested her services on loan for *The Devil's Disciple.* Although not modern, it was "prestige": Alexander Mackendrick had been signed to direct the adaptation of Bernard Shaw's play, and Natalie would be compensated for a relatively slight role by appearing in the company of Laurence Olivier, Burt Lancaster, Kirk Douglas and Eva Le Gallienne. But Hecht-Hill-Lancaster had decided to shoot the film entirely in England, which would separate the Wagners for several months, and Natalie asked for time to "talk it over" with her husband.

By then the William Morris Agency's senior triumvirate, Bert Allenberg, Abe Lastfogel and Joe Schoenfeld, had taken charge of Natalie's career; and on June 3, Allenberg informed Trilling that the couple had again decided to stand by their prenuptial agreement. This time Trilling reacted with a threat to invoke a "demand on services" clause in Natalie's contract, which entitled the studio to sue her if she refused to accept her next assignment. And he ordered her to report to director Vincent Sherman on July 15 to discuss her role in *The Philadelphian.*

On the day before her scheduled appointment, an article in the *Los Angeles Examiner* claimed that "not since the heyday of Shirley Temple has a youngster dominated a studio as Natalie Wood does." And it quoted an unnamed Warners executive who described Natalie as "our top box-office draw and, I personally believe, our greatest acting talent." Obviously concocted as advance publicity for Natalie in *The Philadelphian,* the article misfired. She failed to keep her appointment with Sherman, and the studio dominated its top box-office draw by placing her on suspension and informing her that "we hereby refuse to pay you any compensation as of the date thereof [July 15]."

When Natalie turned down *The Devil's Disciple* for personal reasons, she couldn't foresee that it was a wise professional move. After a series of disagreements with Burt Lancaster during the first two weeks of shooting, Mackendrick was fired. His unsuitable replacement was a specialist in action movies, and star power couldn't save the project from critical or commercial failure. *The Philadelphian* (later *The Young Philadelphians,* with Barbara Rush replacing Natalie opposite Paul Newman) was a "superior" commercial picture with two effective leading roles; but in fact the Morris triumvirate had encouraged Natalie to turn it down so they could renegotiate her contract with Warners. More money was their object, not her right to be consulted about the roles she played, and the negotiations dragged on for seven months.

Meanwhile, Natalie couldn't escape a confrontation with Maria. Although a less formidable authority figure than Producer or his deputy, she could still apply strong emotional pressure. Maria's control over her daughter had suffered a serious blow when Natalie married RJ, but she managed to convey the impression that she was still in charge by telling Louella Parsons, "I thoroughly approve of Bob Wagner." When the remark duly appeared in Louella's column (as Maria intended), it carried the implication (as Maria intended) that the marriage would never have taken place without her approval.

But in private the gloves came off when Natalie went on suspension: bitter accusations of throwing her career and good money away and of ingratitude to the mother who made her a star: for Maria, the inevitable last resort of a convulsion, and for Natalie, the inevitable aftermath of guilt.

> *Robert Wagner: "You will simply not believe what you're going to see," Natalie said the first time she took me to meet her parents. I could tell they'd just had a row, could smell something going on, all that tension in the air. And if her mother was angry with Natalie about something, Nick backed her up. Later Natalie told me they'd "woven a web" around her since she was a child. One day someone was a friend, the next a no-good enemy, and she grew up never knowing who to believe or who to trust.*

On July 18 the Wagners attended the Hollywood premiere of *Kings Go Forth*. This time star power laced with doomed interracial romance ensured a moderate box-office success, although most reviewers dismissed the story as high-minded soap opera and found Natalie more expressive visually than vocally—fair comment when she was obliged to deliver so many drab lines with a French accent. Coincidentally, on the Fox lot, World War II proved even less beneficial to RJ (and the studio) that year. *The Hunters* failed to advance his career or make a profit, and he suspected that *In Love and War* was unlikely to reverse the trend.

BUT RJ'S CONTRACT with Fox proved useful that summer when Nick Gurdin was arrested for drunken driving on his way home to 3331 Laurel Canyon Boulevard after a night at the bars. He ignored a red light and hit a pedestrian who was crossing the street at the intersection. When the man died in hospital, Nick was additionally charged with manslaughter, and RJ enlisted the help of the studio's troubleshooter, who specialized in getting stars and/or their families out of trouble. He managed to get the manslaughter charge voided, although Nick's driving license was canceled for six months.

Shortly afterward, when Maria finally had to acknowledge that Natalie considered her husband's feelings more important than her mother's, RJ witnessed an alarming scene. "We hadn't yet found a house that we wanted to buy, and were starting to feel really cramped in my apartment, so Natalie suggested we move to 3331 Laurel Canyon. Her family was still living there, but we could give them the $12,500 Warners had loaned Natalie to move out and buy another house. They were both furious when we told them what we'd decided, and Mud began shouting at Natalie, until Natalie finally shouted her down—'You have to get the hell out!' Then they had to accept, but Mud felt her control slipping even further away and this time went totally berserk." Maria had now become "Mud," a nickname she owed to RJ, who couldn't remember why he invented it. (Maybe it came from "Musia," Nick Gurdin's nickname for his wife.) "But the name stuck, like mud. And when someone else started referring to Nick as Fahd, the couple became known as Mud and Fahd."

THE ROMANTIC ENTRY in Natalie's occasional journal, after RJ sent her a white rose because they'd been separated for ten hours, is undated. But it was obviously made some time in the fall of 1958, as it precedes the next entry on November 6, and follows a previous note on July 20, "My twentieth birthday." And on that day, as her lawyer Greg Bautzer pointed out, marriage made Natalie legally twenty-one. She was now entitled to pick up $27,050 in government bonds from the trust fund established after *Tomorrow Is Forever,* a gratifying windfall at the start of her unpaid suspension, although a disappointment followed.

The studio refused to loan Natalie out while she remained on suspension, and she was unable to accept the role eventually offered to Audrey Hepburn in John Huston's *The Unforgiven:* not one of Huston's best, as it turned out, but hugely superior to the "something modern" that would be waiting when the contract dispute was at last settled.

For the rest of 1958, then, no movies for Natalie Wood, who became Mrs. Robert Wagner in public as well as in private when she accompanied her husband on a promotional tour for *In Love and War.* And her next (November 6) journal entry, a letter she wrote but didn't send to RJ, reveals the depth of their feelings for each other:

Dear R, we have just returned from a three-week very hectic tour. We have been to 12 cities, had 4 hangovers, met approximately 8000 people, had three fights, one upset stomach and a wonderful time. We have emerged with battle scars, but they only add to our characters (?).

Sometimes you walk into a room after being gone only five minutes, and my heart leaps as though it were the first time we had ever met. I wonder how I could be so lucky—that you are *my husband*—that your worth as a human being is so great that it almost breaks my heart. And your indulgence with me when I am silly, or childish, or headstrong. You are my husband, my child, my strength, my weakness, my lover, my life.

On February 25, 1959, Mrs. Robert Wagner reverted in public to Natalie Wood when Warners announced "the conclusion of amicable arrangements for Miss Wood to resume her contract with the studio." The statement also mentioned "important plans" for her and expressed "confidence that with her talent, future roles would bring her to even greater heights." Under the new agreement, Natalie's weekly salary began at $750, and an annual increase of $250 would raise it to $1,250 in 1962, at the end of which her original contract was due to expire. She also gained a measure of independence by being allowed to make one picture away from the studio each year.

In fact the "amicable" negotiations were as bitter as they were long, although Natalie and Producer always made a show of cordiality and affection in public:

> The arguments were all carried on through lawyers, and when we met at parties he was always very polite, and he'd say, "Hello, Natalie darling, how *are* you?" And I'd say, "Hello, Mr. Warner, how are *you?*" On my birthday he'd send me lovely flowers, and on his birthday I'd send him a bottle of Jack Daniel's, and there were little notes back and forth, "Thank you *so* much for the lovely flowers," and "Thank you *so* much for remembering my birthday," and meanwhile the lawyers were saying that he was saying through them, "This child will only work again over my dead body, blah, blah, blah."

The first of the studio's "important plans" was the "something modern" that Warner had instructed Steve Trilling to find for Natalie, but soon after she began reading the 168-page first-draft script of *Cash McCall*, she hated it so much that she decided "to read only the scenes I was in." On March 19, her first day back on the Burbank lot, Jack Warner sent more lovely flowers and assigned her the two-room dressing-room suite with kitchen occupied by Joan Crawford for her triumphant comeback in *Mildred Pierce;* but Natalie disliked its yellow walls and champagne-pink curtains and insisted on a new color scheme of white and gold. (Her own taste in decoration would improve a few years later.) Although protocol demanded a grateful letter in return, she thanked Warner for the flowers but made no reference to the dressing room or the script, and ended: "I can't tell you how happy I am to be working again."

He had given her nothing else to be happy about, and the truth of the letter lay in what it omitted. Tab Hunter, her best friend at the studio, had grown tired of asking "How can I learn my craft without good pictures to work on?" and bought out his contract for $100,000 ("Quite a lot of money in those days"). He'd already improved his situation by playing opposite Geraldine Page in *Portrait of a Murderer* on TV, while Producer had saddled Natalie with another workhorse director, Joseph Pevney, for a movie she agreed to make only because each month that she remained on suspension added another month to the duration of her contract, and she'd already served seven.

A mixture of behind-the-scenes big-business drama and romantic comedy, *Cash McCall* was adapted (by Lenore Coffee and Marion Hargrove) from a best-selling novel by Cameron Hawley, whose *Executive Suite* had made a much better movie five years earlier. Natalie plays a fashion designer romanced by a tycoon (James Garner), but although the character has a profession, she has no character. When the tycoon breaks off their affair, he explains that he's starting to feel "serious" about her and has "more important things to do than fall in love." But instead of protesting or feeling insulted, she "understands," and passively awaits the (inevitable) change of heart.

In his first leading film role, Garner has an amiable screen presence, although he's too lightweight to be convincing as a tycoon, or as the irresistible lover who persuades Natalie to take second place to the "more important things." No need, of course, to ask what they are, after all the scenes of Cash operating his way to more and more $$$.

But in spite of generally caustic reviews after it opened on December 10, 1959, *Cash McCall* was a commercial success. It did more for Garner than for Natalie, mainly because Cash (admiring nickname) was a hero for the times. He got the girl he wanted the same way as he made a deal, on his own terms; and as the reviewer for *Time* magazine aptly noted, "they lived wealthily ever after."

BY THEN the Wagners had bought a neo-Colonial house at 714 North Beverly Drive for $150,000. When *Cash McCall* opened, they were still busy with an ambitious scheme of remodeling and redecoration that had begun in June. It would cost them more than half as much again, even though most of the rooms would never be finished. A currently fashionable decorator, Dewey Spriegel, had provided as much rose-and-white marble flooring and as many crystal chandeliers as the traffic would bear—except in the den, which Mart Crowley remembered as "the only cozy room in the house, with a wet bar and poker table."

Upstairs, Natalie's enormous marble tub in her "over-the-top movie star bathroom" eventually proved more than the traffic could bear. When the floor soon started to give way beneath its weight, an ominous crack in the ceiling of the room below shrouded it in dust. And although the floor was repaired and reinforced, hot water took so long to reach the tub that it was tepid on arrival.

At the same time, Natalie and RJ were making a movie together that would prove equally tepid on arrival. Pandro S. Berman, a resident producer at MGM, had first offered *Ever for Each Other* to Elizabeth Taylor and Elvis Presley, who turned it down. In the screenplay by Robert Thom, based on Rosamond Marshall's novel *The Bixby Girls,* the leading characters are two young lovers in the backwoods of Texas. The girl becomes pregnant, leaves for New York, has an affair with a wealthy young man from a socially prominent family and marries him after convincing him that he fathered her child. Then her former lover also arrives in New York, is "befriended" by a fortyish black singer, becomes a famous jazz trumpeter on the nightclub circuit and marries Hamilton's sister.

The only surprise was that Natalie and RJ were not ever for each other after all, but for staying married to George Hamilton and Susan Kohner. More interesting is the relationship between black singer and young white trumpeter. Three years after National Guardsmen had prevented black students from entering an all-white high school in Little Rock, and a year before the start of "Freedom Rides" to protest segregation on interstate buses and trains, no major studio production would have celebrated an overt interracial affair, but the scenes between wonderful Pearl Bailey and RJ manage to imply it.

According to MGM's publicity release for the movie, eventually retitled *All the Fine Young Cannibals,* the character played by Robert Wagner was "suggested by" the early life of Chet Baker. But their only points of resemblance are youth, good looks and playing jazz trumpet. The movie's overheated dialogue was underdirected by the British Michael Anderson (presumably chosen on account of his Academy Award nomination for *Around the World in 80 Days*), who seemed no more at home in backwoods Texas than in New York nightclubs, and the luridly emotional melodrama could only have been rescued from bathos by a dialogue rewrite and the sardonic touch of Douglas Sirk as director.

Or Vincente Minnelli, who in fact directed two additional scenes that Berman ordered after viewing the rough cut. Wagner, who couldn't identify them as he didn't appear in either, recalled that "Natalie was excited about working with Minnelli." One likely contender is the elegant stylization of her drunken soliloquy at night. Wearing a red dress, she sits at a long table littered with bottles, no other furniture visible in the room. The camera remains stationary while city lights glitter beyond a picture window, and she pours a shot from each bottle into her highball glass.

Dramatically well photographed in this scene, and looking more beautiful throughout than in any of her movies at Warners, Natalie salvaged two object lessons of less-as-more from the wreckage: the understated skill of MGM's makeup department and of Sydney Guilaroff, who designed her simple, shoulder-length hairstyles.

Although she had misgivings about the project from the start, she went along with it, partly to recoup the expenses of North Beverly Drive and partly because RJ found his role more promising than any he'd recently been offered at Fox. Ironically, his reviews were almost without exception as negative as Natalie's, in contrast to the positive ones for his most recent (commercially unsuccessful) contract movie, *Say One for Me.* The studio had first offered the part of a nightclub owner on the make for a young dancer (Debbie Reynolds) to Sinatra, who declined to recycle his role in *Pal Joey.* But as well as displaying a pleasant Sinatra-ish baritone, RJ proved such a lively hoofer that he won the 1959 Golden Taps Award for "Outstanding New Dancer of the Year" (previously won by Gene Kelly). The prize for this bizarre honor, voted by three thousand female instructors at the Arthur Murray dance schools, was a pair of gilded dancing shoes.

Far from enough, of course, to revive Wagner's stalled career at a studio whose president, Spyros Skouras, was infatuated with Cinema-Scopic spectacle. His determination to splurge on epics led to the ultimate folly of *Cleopatra* and the downfall of Skouras himself, but first to unsettling rumors for several leading contract players, Wagner among them, that their contracts would not be renewed.

For someone accustomed to security, RJ's first experience of insecurity was exceptionally disturbing; and at the same time, Natalie was struggling with her own anxiety attacks and sleepless nights in their unfinished showplace of a home. Although *All the Fine Young Cannibals* had not yet been released, it was no secret that MGM executives had written it off as a disaster; and in her personal life she had begun to suspect, as she said later, that "when the bathtub fell through the floor, so did our marriage." From the start, fan magazines depicted the Wagners as the happiest and most glamorous young couple in movieland, and were soon exaggerating the movieland glamour of 714 North Beverly Drive. One saltwater pool became two, with antique statuary presiding over His and Hers; two live poodles kept company with Natalie's "collection of stuffed tigers"; and "genuine old master paintings imported from Italy" decorated the walls, instead of side-by-side paintings of Natalie and RJ commissioned from Margaret Keane, specialist in portraits that looked like airbrushed color photographs, their subjects usually in pensive mood. But now the house had no need of *Silver Screen* and *Datebook* fantasies to become a set for a couple trying to escape from themselves by assuming movie-star lives.

A few months earlier, the couple had still believed in their roles. "My first image of Natalie was pure movie star," Asa Maynor remembers. "She was sitting by that famous saltwater pool in a wide-brimmed straw hat and huge dark glasses." In July 1959, the Wagners were the star guests at a lavish party thrown by Frank Sinatra at the Claridge Hotel in Atlantic City, to celebrate his appearance at the 500 Club. (They never suspected that the event was under FBI surveillance, and its files would list "actress NATALIE WOOD" and "actor ROBERT WAGNER" as well as several notorious underworld figures "in attendance at this affair.") On October 10, shortly before *All the Fine Young Cannibals* began production, Sinatra threw an equally lavish party at Romanoff's, a dual anniversary celebration of Natalie's twenty-first birthday and the fifteenth year of a movie career that had started with *Happy Land.* A band serenaded her, RJ and Sinatra toasted her, Spencer Tracy embraced her; but the marriage and the career that seemed so secure that night had become equally precarious by the end of the year.

And by then two incidents had deepened Natalie's fear of betrayal. Barbara Gould, shy and deeply insecure herself, abruptly ended her friendship with the Wagners. Being in their company, she said, made her feel that she had "nothing to contribute," and as she felt the same way about Hollywood, Gould returned to New York in the (never realized) hope of a career in the theater. Even more wounding was the behavior of Nick Adams, at the start of a descent into drugs and alcoholism. He asked Natalie for a loan and threatened to blackmail her when she

The twenty-first birthday party:
Natalie and RJ, both happy.
Later during the party: Natalie's
"Russian" lapse into melancholy,
RJ's concern

refused. "I know a lot of stuff about you that I could sell and get the money I need," he said. RJ sent Adams packing, but the psychological shock magnified all her fears and anxieties, her sense of a lost self, of being unable to make decisions. And RJ, the one person she turned to for help, was unable to provide it.

For Natalie, the only solution was psychoanalysis, which RJ opposed because it implied that he'd failed as a husband; and she suspected that his parents, of whom she'd become very fond, would oppose it too. During a recent lunch at the Brown Derby, RJ's sister had announced that divorce was the only solution to her unhappy marriage. "Mary," said Mrs. Wagner, "I wouldn't be interested in that," and added that there had *never* been a divorce in the family.

RJ also objected to the idea of marriage counseling. The couple's increasingly violent arguments, always ending in deadlock, caused him to start drinking too much. Alcohol only increased his anger, as much with himself for being unable to handle the situation as with Natalie for creating it, and this anger drove her to the verge of hysteria. RJ always apologized the next day with flowers or a gift, but always emphatically refused to change his mind; and Natalie feared that if she went to an analyst against his will, she would lose him.

Although they both knew the movie-star game was over, neither could make the next move. They were paralyzed by simultaneous but separate insecurities, a couple who still loved but no longer understood each other, or themselves.

WHILE THE supposedly happiest young actress in Hollywood lay awake at night wondering why she was so unhappy, Mud was making one room of the Gurdins' new house on Ventura Canyon Avenue in Sherman Oaks into a Natalie Wood temple. An enlarged studio portrait hung in a wall niche like an icon, lit by a row of candles on the mantel below; and a walk-in closet was lined with shelves of scrapbooks and photograph albums, all proudly assembled by the Keeper of the Fan Mail.

At the same time, because Natalie had begun to distance herself from her mother, Mud attempted to create another star in the family, and fourteen-year-old Lana auditioned without success for the Elizabeth Taylor role in MGM's TV series based on *National Velvet*. Later, although it became clear that Lana would climb no higher than a supporting role in the TV series based on *Peyton Place* and another as a James Bond bimbo, Mud frequently blamed Natalie for not doing more to help her sister's career. In a "memoir" of Natalie, hastily written after her death, Lana claimed that she never wanted to be an actress, then proceeded to devote considerable space to her modest career from the mid-1960s to the late 1970s. But she probably gave her most effective performance offscreen, as Natalie's shy, neglected, unambitious little sister. It convinced Robert Banas and Gigi Perreau, among others, that "Lana was pushed into the background," but never convinced Olga Viripaeff. In her opinion, "Lana simply didn't have what it takes," and in private Natalie agreed. Finally, when Mud accused her once too often of not doing enough to help Lana, she hit the ceiling. "Why does everyone have to be a movie star?" she wanted to know. "Why can't she sell silk stockings? Or something?"

But in public Natalie remained brightly discreet about the jealous intrigues and tensions of her family life. "It's amazing," RJ would comment in retrospect, "how much she had to sit on and deal with. From the time she was a child."

THE FAILURE of *All the Fine Young Cannibals* made Warners unsure how to sell Natalie, and Producer made no definite plans for her next movie. Instead, he loaned her out for an appearance on *The Bob Hope Show:* scripted "spontaneous" comedy chat between Natalie and Hope, $10,000 and a plug for the studio's forthcoming production *The Sundowners.*

Meanwhile, Elia Kazan had been working for almost a year with William Inge on an original screenplay, *Splendor in the Grass.* After reading the first draft, Jack Warner agreed to distribute the picture, and Natalie first heard about the project when she was returning by train to Los Angeles with RJ after Sinatra's party in Atlantic City. Inge, also on the train on his way to meet with Kazan, told Natalie that she'd be "ideal" for the leading female role. But *Splendor in the Grass* wasn't scheduled for production until early 1960, as Kazan had contracted to start filming *Wild River* for Fox in September.

In August, however, he discussed casting possibilities for the two leading roles in an exchange of letters with Jack Warner. For Bud Stam-

*Lana ("Natalie's got the brains but I got the*
*tits") Wood, with her sister*

per, the male lead, Kazan strongly inclined to twenty-five-year-old Jody
McCrea (son of Joel McCrea and Frances Dee), whom he'd interviewed
in New York; but Warner asked him to consider the studio's "new boy"
Troy Donahue ("I feel he is great") and offered to screen the hugely popular *A Summer Place.* For Deanie, Kazan's first choice had been the talented Diane Varsi, who'd impressed him in the movie of *Compulsion,*
but she suddenly decided to give up acting and left Hollywood. His next
idea was Jane Fonda, whom he wanted to test, then changed his mind
on Inge's recommendation that he test Natalie Wood instead. Producer
gave permission, but thought Diane McBain, another new contract star,
a more promising candidate, "very vivacious, with a lot of 'it,' 'that' and
'oomph!' "

    "As well as always trying to screw Natalie, and to screw her out of
more money at the same time," Wagner recalled, "Jack Warner also tried
to stop her getting the part in *Splendor,* because she'd defied him by

going on suspension all those months. It was Kazan's insistence that got her the part."

It was also because Natalie decided to play a game. Aware that Warner enjoyed ordering her into a movie she disliked, she pretended that she didn't want to play Deanie. She even kept up the pretense with Kazan, who preferred to interview rather than test her. Although she knew that Deanie was a girl from a middle-class midwestern family, she wore a tight satin dress, false eyelashes, high heels, and plenty of bracelets. Fortunately Kazan was more intuitive than Herman Wouk, and perceived "a terrible desire for excellence" behind the glamour front. "You say she's only been good in *two* pictures?" he remarked to a journalist from the *Los Angeles Times.* "Then I say she's got it. Two pictures is a hell of a lot of pictures."

Warner proved more amenable than he expected, and Inge was equally influential in steering Kazan to his personal candidate for Bud. During 1958, twenty-one-year-old Warren Beatty acted in two East Coast repertory companies, played small parts in TV productions, studied (briefly) with Stella Adler and earned extra money as a cocktail pianist at Clavin's bar in Manhattan. For the company run by Robert Ludlum (who later became a best-selling novelist) at the North Jersey Playhouse in Fort Lee, Beatty played the Loeb counterpart in *Compulsion,* and his performance impressed both Inge and Joshua Logan. In the spring of 1959 Inge cast him in *A Loss of Roses,* the playwright's first Broadway failure and the actor's last appearance on any stage. But Beatty's favorable reviews resulted in the offer of a contract from MGM, which he turned down. Eventually, Warner approved Kazan's choices for both Bud and Deanie in *Splendor in the Grass.*

The movie's starting date, in the second week of March 1960, was postponed for another six weeks when the Screen Actors Guild went on strike from March 7 to April 15; but Producer found a way to turn the situation to his studio's advantage. He saved thousands of dollars by suspending all its contract players (including Natalie) for the duration of the strike.

Kazan shot *Splendor* entirely on the East Coast, interiors at Filmways Studios in New York, exteriors on Staten Island and upstate New York, which doubled effectively for Kansas in 1928. Landscape, Kazan realized, was not a vital part of a story whose important scenes, with one excep-

Splendor in the Grass.
*Deanie breaks down in the schoolroom.*

tion, were all interior. A few carefully chosen locations—Deanie's parents' gingerbread house with its cupola, "art glass" and front porch; the
sanitarium that looks like a larger and more pretentious gingerbread
mansion; the country club; and the desolate ranchland (with an oil der-
rick added) for the final scene between Bud and Deanie—created all the
necessary exterior atmosphere.

Inge's story of two high-school seniors who fall passionately in love,
but never consummate it because of the oppressive puritanism of time
and place, is a coded version of personal experience, his own "forbidden"
love for a handsome high-school senior. At first even Inge's best plays, *Bus
Stop* and *The Dark at the Top of the Stairs,* seem skillfully conventional.
Then, unlike the skill, the convention begins to subvert itself. It leads to
scenes, in Kazan's words, of "exceptional poignancy and quiet terror,"
and as Tennessee Williams wrote, the plays "uncover a world within a
world [by] not ripping but quietly dropping the veil." In this way they
echo the Sherwood Anderson of *Winesburg, Ohio,* which was set in
another part of the Bible Belt ten years earlier than the 1928 of *Splendor in
the Grass,* and reveals a similar "world within a world" whose placid surface rumbles and quakes when a subterranean tension disturbs it.

*Splendor* jump-started something that Natalie had waited for since *Rebel Without a Cause:* her career as an adult actress. It also coincided with an emotionally fractured period in her life. There was no separation due to career conflict for the Wagners, as Fox had no immediate plans for RJ, and the couple lived together at an apartment on Sutton Place found for them by Inge, who lived in the same building. But a month after *Splendor* began production, Fox decided not to renew RJ's contract. He found himself out of work just as Natalie's career was about to renew itself, and the roles of husband and wife at the start of their marriage were now reversed.

With time on his hands, RJ spent some of it in discouraging phone consultations about his career prospects, and more of it on the set of *Splendor,* particularly during the love scenes between Deanie and Bud, which made husband and wife equally stressed.

Beatty, of course, was a "new" kind of actor, in the wake of Brando, Clift and Dean, and although the gap between them was only one-third of a generation, RJ seemed to belong to an earlier era. When his affair with Natalie first began, he'd felt "alien" because she was close at the time to Nick Ray and Dennis Hopper; and on the set of *Splendor,* he felt "alien" again, but less equipped to deal with it because of the dent in his professional confidence. And as Mart Crowley observed, when any movie truly involved her, Natalie developed a "fixation" on the director or leading actor. It was basically creative, as in Kazan's case, although sometimes (as with Nick Ray) sexual as well. But RJ had never worked this way, and during Natalie's intimate huddles with Kazan, he felt even more of an outsider.

Natalie's only New York friend, Norma Crane, was in Hollywood filming *All in a Night's Work,* but she soon found a confidential shoulder in Mart Crowley, one of Kazan's assistants. His main job was to pick Natalie up every morning she was on call and drive her to the set. Five years earlier, as a drama student at the Catholic University of America in Washington, he had introduced himself to Kazan, who was filming *Baby Doll* on location near Mart's hometown of Vicksburg, Mississippi. Kazan gave him a pass to observe the filming, told him to "look me up when you finish school"; and after Mart graduated in 1957, Kazan got him a job as a production assistant on *The Fugitive Kind.*

Although he hardly knew Natalie's work as an actress, they very quickly became close friends. Mart had the humor, directness and insight that always appealed to her, and they were soon exchanging tales of unhappy families (in Crowley's case, an alcoholic father and psychologically fragile mother, who became the models for the leading characters in *A Breeze from the Gulf* ) and exploring each other's anxieties and guilts (in Crowley's case homosexual, and the subject of his first play, *The Boys in the Band*). Mart was also quick to perceive tensions in the Wagner marriage: "RJ's career was on the downslide while Natalie's was suddenly on the up, a seesaw effect of career swings that often failed to coincide throughout their lives. Natalie sometimes cried in her dressing room because she wanted to go into analysis and RJ was opposed to it. 'What drives me mad is that he just won't *listen* to me,' she said once. 'But I need *help,* or this marriage will fall apart.' "

To Mart it seemed that "both RJ and Natalie were falling apart." He remembered an evening when he joined them for dinner with Elizabeth Taylor and Eddie Fisher, "another marriage on the rocks, but all four from the outside playing the happiest married couples in the world." He also detected signs of tension between Warren Beatty and his fiancée, Joan Collins, who frequently visited the set and kept a sharp eye on his love scenes with Natalie until she reluctantly departed for Italy and a caftan-and-sandals biblical epic, *Esther and the King.* Kazan's personal life was yet another source of anxiety: he was still married to his first wife, Molly, but had become involved with Barbara Loden, who played Warren's sister. "Kazan also used Natalie's relationship with Mud for the scenes with her movie mother, played by Audrey Christie. It was very draining for her, and another reason why she sometimes got very depressed. In fact, just about *everybody* on that picture seemed on the emotional edge."

But although Warren's relationship with Joan Collins, like the Wagner marriage, was under strain, Crowley insisted that the affair with Natalie didn't start until a year later: "I was very close to Natalie, I never saw him come on to her, and if he had, I'm sure she would have told me. What she did tell me was that she didn't like Warren at first, and particularly disliked playing love scenes with him because she suspected he didn't bathe enough." Beatty later confirmed that he never "came on" to Natalie, and pointed out that in fact he became engaged to Joan Collins during the shoot of *Splendor.* But his proposal style was in telling contrast to RJ's. One Sunday afternoon, Warren asked Joan to make him a chopped liver sandwich. When she opened a plastic carton from the

Splendor in the Grass. *Mother
(Audrey Christie) comforts daughter.*

fridge, she found a diamond-and-pearl ring gleaming, like only half-buried treasure, among the chopped liver.

ALTHOUGH NATALIE "went along with the production's Actors Studio non-Hollywood work methods," Crowley remembered that she drew the line at a non-Hollywood hairdresser. She called Elizabeth Taylor, who was making *Butterfield 8* for MGM in New York, and asked to borrow Sydney Guilaroff to design her main hairstyles: a fall for the early scenes, tight elaborate curls for her imitation of Barbara Loden's flapper, and a more "mature" look for the final scene with Beatty.

To Kazan, this was an example of movie star taking over from actress.

*"Everybody seemed on the emotional edge."*
*Left to right: Joan Collins, Warren Beatty, Kazan,*
*Natalie and RJ during a set break*

But a few weeks later the non-Hollywood hairdresser "almost wrecked Barbara Loden's hair when he dyed it blond for the New Year's Eve party scene, and Kazan rather sheepishly asked Natalie to ask Guilaroff to come in again and perform damage control. Which he did, and really saved Barbara Loden's hair."

But movie star *did* occasionally attempt to take over from actress, Mart noted, "by sneaking in a touch of eyeliner or more lipstick." But Kazan always made her remove it, as he wanted Deanie to look completely natural until her attempt at imitating Loden's flapper. And Natalie's strange anxiety that she couldn't look her best without elaborate makeup was relieved when she went to dailies and liked the way Kazan wanted her to look.

At first, Natalie trusted Kazan unconditionally. The first time he tricked her "to bring out the performance," she told the AFI seminar, it was acceptable: "The bathtub scene, in which I was to be hysterical, always frightened me. And I told Kazan I was very worried about it. His response absolutely threw me for a loop, because he said, 'What you do, I'll let you see the film, and we'll go back and do it again. Or we can play it on Audrey's reactions.' And I was so enraged and offended that I became hysterical. That was his way of dealing with me, and it was obviously the correct way, because we only shot it once." But after Kazan tricked her again in filming Deanie's attempted suicide, Natalie no longer admired or trusted him unconditionally. The scene required her to walk along a low rocky ledge above a lake with a nearby waterfall, then step into the water and attempt to drown herself. Several days earlier, Natalie had told Kazan that she was terrified of water, especially dark water, and begged him to use a studio tank. Kazan, who said later that he thought her fear "perfect for the scene," promised to arrange for a plank to be nailed to the floor of the lake, which was not deep enough for Natalie to get out of her depth. He also promised that Charlie Maguire, his assistant director since *On the Waterfront* and now one of his associate producers as well, would stand in the water just out of camera range, ready to catch her if she fell.

Kazan's version claims that Natalie finally agreed to do the scene, "did it well," then laughed hysterically with relief after he called "Cut!" But it denies an important part of Natalie's version. She told Mart Crowley (who was not present because "Kazan sent me on an errand to New York that day") that Kazan promised to cut to a long shot of a double after she reached the end of the plank. But at that point Maguire left her side, and Natalie found herself completely alone in the water with no double. Although a poor swimmer, she managed to get through the scene and was "half proud of herself, and half furious at Kazan's duplicity."

Yet another version emerged in an alleged interview with a New York tabloid. According to Natalie, it reported, the double was there as Kazan promised, but couldn't swim, and she had to finish the scene alone. Shortly afterward, a bit player in the movie claimed that Kazan had engaged her as Natalie's double. She described herself as a very good swimmer and threatened to sue Warner Bros. for "defamation." But as she couldn't explain why she held the studio responsible for something Natalie was alleged to have said, and Kazan continued to deny that he'd ever promised or employed a double, she dropped the suit.

*1961: Kazan, Natalie and Warren Beatty at a Warner Bros.*
*celebration in the studio screening room*

Like the litigious bit player, the "interview" with Natalie is more than
suspect, and not only on account of its source (the *New York Sunday
Mirror,* June 12, 1960). Natalie knew how much she owed to Kazan, and
while the film was still in production, she certainly knew better than to
accuse him publicly of lying.

In private, Natalie's story never varied. She told RJ (also not present
that day) that there was no double, and told Karl Malden the same thing
in 1978, when they were discussing Kazan on the set of *Meteor.* She also
told RJ that in spite of her admiration for Kazan she considered him "a
trickster," and would always remember that scene by the lake in the fading afternoon light as another encounter with betrayal.

IN THE FIRST WEEK of August, as *Splendor in the Grass* neared the end
of shooting, Jerry Robbins and Robert Wise, co-directors on the movie

of *West Side Story,* had almost completed filming the dance numbers on location in New York (some of which had previously been rehearsed and test-filmed in downtown Los Angeles). But the two leading roles of Maria and Tony had not yet been cast. After Carol Lawrence (who played Maria on Broadway) had been tested and rejected as looking too old for film, the wide net of casting director Lynn Stalmaster hauled in Pier Angeli, Elizabeth Ashley, Diane Baker, Susan Kohner, Gigi Perreau, Suzanne Pleshette and Ina Balin. They were all interviewed or tested and rejected, except for Balin, who'd played a few small parts since Fox signed her to a contract, and who became a "possibility."

But Walter Mirisch and Max Youngstein, co-producers of the movie for United Artists, had always wanted a star name for at least one of the leads, and they asked Robbins and Wise to look at some of Natalie's footage in *Splendor in the Grass.* Robbins was particularly enthusiastic about the material he saw, and said later that when he met Natalie, "we clicked at once. There was immediate understanding."

Although eager to play the role, Natalie insisted on a clause in the contract that would allow her to record Maria's songs to a playback, then give Robbins and Wise the right to decide whether to use her voice or employ a professional singer to dub it.

On Friday, August 16, she completed her final scene in *Splendor.* On Saturday she took a tranquilizer before flying back to Los Angeles with RJ. (By now Natalie kept her fear of flying under control with Valium and by never traveling alone.) On Sunday she met with Robbins, and on Monday, August 19, she reported to Goldwyn Studios, where she met the vocal coach, Miriam Colón, appointed to give her lessons in a Puerto Rican accent.

"AS SHE KNEW I'd written a couple of TV scripts that hadn't sold," Mart Crowley recalled, "Natalie offered me a job as her secretary when she went back to L.A., said I could stay in the garage apartment of the house on North Beverly, and promised to introduce me to the guys at William Morris." By this time Mart and RJ had also become good friends, with RJ as eager as Natalie for a sympathetic presence, confidant and buffer zone.

On *Splendor,* the tensions had been mainly personal and occurred off the set. On *West Side,* the set was professionally troubled as well. Robert

Splendor in the Grass.
*Kazan discusses the party
scene with Warren Beatty
and Natalie "trying to
imitate Barbara Loden's
flapper."*

Splendor in the Grass.
*The farewell scene*

Wise had at first been uneasy about working with Jerry Robbins as co-director; but Robbins had the right of first refusal to be involved with the movie, and accepted only on condition that he co-direct. Because Mirisch considered him indispensable, Wise met with Robbins and "agreed that he would direct all the musical numbers, and I would do all the book stuff."

According to Richard Beymer, who played Tony, Robbins did more than that. "He also worked out the transitions, getting into the numbers, then back into the nonmusical scenes." Beymer was signed for the role two weeks later than Natalie, after George Peppard, Richard Chamberlain and Scott Marlowe had been rejected as respectively too old, too lightweight and too neurotic.

In a gallantly misguided attempt to revive her husband's career, Natalie had proposed RJ, although he was unmistakably wrong for the part. So, in his own estimation, was twenty-one-year-old Beymer: "I was a country boy from Ohio cast as street-smart New York. And I needed more character motivation from a director with more psychological insight than Robert Wise. All he ever told me was, 'Walk faster, talk faster, pick up your cue faster, be more sincere, be more loving.' And I knew Natalie didn't want me for the part, but had to tell her 'I love you' in almost every scene." With no help from Wise, only occasional contact with Robbins because he had little dancing to do, and Natalie keeping a politely firm distance, Beymer "took refuge in arrogance and didn't try to break through." Offscreen, the extent of Maria and Tony's personal contact was a perfunctory "good morning" to each other.

> *Richard Beymer: I think there was a residue of animosity toward Natalie because of that test for* Rebel, *and it contributed to our situation. But a few years later we caught sight of each other at a nightclub on Sunset Strip. Natalie waved, came over to my table, and we talked for a few moments. She was incredibly sweet, left me thinking what a lovely person she was, and I felt genuinely attracted to her.*

By the time Natalie and Beymer began work on *West Side Story,* it was almost three weeks behind schedule, mainly due to Robbins, who often made twenty takes of the same shot. "Although he devised some incredible shots," according to associate producer Saul Chaplin, not all of them proved usable, and "the pace of shooting was incredibly slow."

From the first, Robbins had little rapport with Wise, and totally ignored him while directing the dance numbers. "So Wise just sat there as Robbins got further behind schedule," according to Mart Crowley, "and waited for Mirisch to do something about it." When the unit moved to Goldwyn, Mirisch sent Robbins a memo congratulating him on the New York material, "even though it went over budget," but cautioning: "Now you're back in the safety of the studio, *you must pick up the pace of shooting*."

Robbins never acknowledged it, and never replied to another memo a week later, when the movie had gone two more days over schedule: "Do keep strongly in mind the necessity of holding the picture within a budget we can manage." And Crowley recalled that when he rehearsed and choreographed Natalie's rooftop dance, and her number in the bridal shop, he continued to ignore Wise.

The rooftop dance, when Maria anticipates meeting Tony later in the evening, was not in the Broadway production. Robbins created it for Natalie. "She was musical, she'd had some training as a dancer," he said, and his understanding of her limits resulted in a charming but incongruous solo, much closer in style to a *pas seul* by Balanchine for the New York City Ballet than to a dance on a Puerto Rican family's rooftop.

Natalie's pale blue dress for the rooftop dance was the occasion of a sharp disagreement with Irene Sharaff, who had also designed the costumes for the Broadway production. Natalie repeatedly claimed that Sharaff's fondness for puffed sleeves was unflattering to her tiny figure, and although Sharaff modified them this time, she usually held her ground. But their frequent clashes, according to Donfeld, added to the professional tensions on the set. "Sharaff tried vainly to convince Natalie that no girl in a Puerto Rican ghetto would even faintly resemble a young Hollywood star, but the more she pushed, the more obstinate Natalie became. Finally, her personal dresser helped Natalie sneak some of Sharaff's most integral work off the lot to the dressmaking shop of Howard Shoup, who'd designed costumes for several of her movies at Warners. When Natalie arrived on the set for the dance at the gymnasium, where Maria first meets Tony, her dress was so poorly altered that Sharaff and her two key assistants walked off the set."

By the time Robbins started to rehearse the dance at the gym, he'd completed all the other numbers. But the movie was more than four weeks behind schedule, and on October 21 Mirisch fired him. When Natalie heard the news, "she marched right in and told Walter Mirisch what she thought," Robbins later recalled. "Typical of her. When there were difficulties, she was right there with you."

As telling Mirisch "what she thought" included a threat to leave the picture unless Robbins was reinstated, he called in Abe Lastfogel at William Morris to mediate the situation. Lastfogel warned Natalie against making a disastrous career move, and after Robbins gave her the same advice, she reluctantly backed down.

The problem for Mirisch, and for Robbins himself, was that in the man who "conceived, directed, and choreographed" the Broadway production of *West Side Story,* talent, charm, homosexual guilt and a compensating arrogance were evenly matched. From the start, he had antagonized both Mirisch and Wise, and Robert Banas (who danced one of the Jets) remembers that when Robbins came on the gymnasium set after being fired, he even slighted the dancers he'd worked to the verge of collapse. "I'm indispensable, but you're not!" he shouted at them, then walked out again.

Howard Jeffrey, his personal assistant, left with Robbins, and Natalie lost (but only temporarily) another new friend. A former dancer who had assisted Robbins on the stage production, Jeffrey supervised the first cut of all the movie sequences that Robbins directed, and coached Natalie in the more complex steps. At Robbins's suggestion, she turned for help to Tony Mordente, another of his assistants and one of the Jets dancers. As Robbins had only worked out the choreography for the male dancers in the gym scene, Mordente created the steps for the girls as well as rehearsing Natalie on weekends. According to Crowley, he was also very helpful when Robert Wise took over: "It seemed to me that Wise had no idea how to shoot a dance number, where to put the camera. His only instruction to Rita Moreno and the girls was, 'Okay, girls—hot peppers!' "

Fortunately, Robbins retained some creative control over the editing, including the right to make suggestions after he viewed the semifinal cut. The notes he made focus mainly on the dance at the gym, which he described in a memo to Wise as "looking like general dance confusion." The idea of "the rival gangs competing to take over the dance floor had been lost," he pointed out, and "Tony and Maria must meet at the *fiercest* moment of the gangs' crescendoing competitive dancing. This is terribly important to remedy."

He also criticized the way Wise had re-edited "Maria," making the dialogue on the balcony "so short and brief that when Tony and Maria begin to sing you're back in an old MGM musical and you have Jane Powell and Howard Keel singing *at* each other rather than having the great emotional surge of a longer scene." According to Natalie: "When [Robbins] was taken off the picture and later brought back for advice, he didn't give technical advice. He would say, 'Cut to the emotion, cut to the people, cut to the movement.' I also found he was a fantastic actors' director, [and] was so clever about film that he'd sometimes say to the cutter, 'It's ten frames off' or something, and [the cutter] would say, 'It's impossible to know that,' and he would say, 'I'd like you to check it,' and it *would* be ten frames off. And the way he moved the camera with the dancers was truly innovative."

Although Wise took Robbins's advice, "Maria" remains the most conventional number in the movie. Its romantic scenes, in fact, have not worn well. When Robbins cast Natalie, he realized he was taking a chance, because "you didn't think of her as this naïve young Hispanic girl," and at times her performance suggests that Natalie found it difficult to think of herself this way. But the role itself is blandly written until the final scene, when Maria denounces the rival gangs over Tony's dead body—and Natalie brings a strong emotional charge to a love affair that neither she nor Beymer could bring to it while Tony was alive.

As Natalie still hoped to perform her own songs, she took singing lessons when she wasn't on call, but an outtake of her recording "Tonight" to a playback is excruciatingly shrill and frequently off-pitch. (Maria Gurdin, as Olga Viripaeff remembered, also "couldn't carry a tune.") According to Rita Stone, a nightclub singer and Saul Chaplin's lover, "Natalie's insistence on recording all her numbers was the only thing about her that drove Saul crazy. But Rita Moreno *really* drove Saul crazy. It took a lot of pressure to stop her putting on weight, because Rita was convinced that a fuller figure and especially a bigger butt would make her more sexy."

This obsession was most likely a by-product of Moreno's more serious cause for alarm about her appearance. A thyroid malfunction sometimes caused her eyes to bulge slightly, as well as creating dark shadows under them. At the time there was no effective medication for the problem, and although the makeup man was able to conceal the shadows, it seems probable that anxiety was partly responsible for the "friction" (Banas's word) that Moreno generated with Natalie. Several members of the original Broadway cast felt that Hollywood stardom was Natalie's only qualification for the role of Maria, and Moreno emphatically agreed; but as an actress eager for stardom, she also seemed jealous of an actress who'd achieved it, was seven years younger than herself and seductively slim.

When Chaplin and Wise heard Natalie's test recordings, they pretended to approve them rather than disillusion her with the truth. Then, after the movie completed production, they brought in Marni Nixon to dub her singing, and Natalie had no recourse except to make clear, once again, what she thought. Unfortunately, Nixon's semioperatic style, well suited to Deborah Kerr's governess in *The King and I,* seemed no more Hispanic than the rooftop dance.

But as a whole the Robbins dances remain among the most imaginative sequences in any film musical; and when *West Side Story* opened at the Rivoli Theater in New York on October 18, 1961, the greater part of its success was due to him and his collaborators, dancers George Chakiris, Russ Tamblyn and Rita Moreno, and to Leonard Bernstein for his score. (Although Robbins directed all but one of the dance sequences, Wise objected to his credit of "musical numbers staged by," and it was changed to "choreography by.") In the *Saturday Review,* Arthur Knight thought the movie's only failure was "when it attempts high tragedy," and several other reviewers found the Shakespearean parallel of Tony/Romeo and Maria/Juliet unconvincing. It seems more artificial on the screen, in fact, than in the theater, because *West Side Story* is the only important movie musical whose stars are not professional singers or dancers.

Although the Morris triumvirate was right to advise Natalie not to walk off the movie after Mirisch fired Robbins, they were less shrewd in negotiating her contract. As Wagner recalled, United Artists had offered Natalie $200,000 plus a choice between an extra $50,000 or 5 percent of the profits. "I advised her to take the percentage, but Abe Lastfogel con-

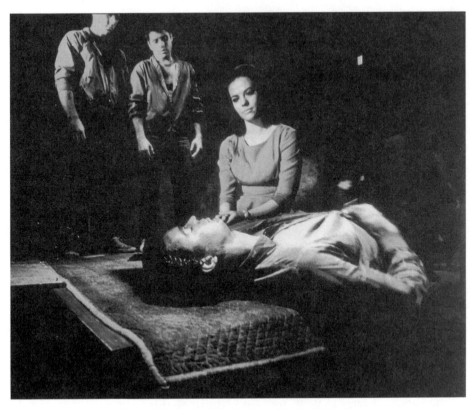

West Side Story. *Final scene: Maria (Natalie,
in her last ethnic role) after Tony (Richard
Beymer) has been killed*

vinced her that musicals never made much money, and the $50,000 was
a much safer bet. She took it, and of course regretted it bitterly after the
movie proved an enormous commercial hit."

WHEN *SPLENDOR IN THE GRASS* opened in New York a few days
before *West Side Story*, it received three important negative reviews.
Bosley Crowther in the *New York Times*, John McCarten in *The New
Yorker* and Stanley Kauffmann in *The New Republic* unanimously dismissed the story as "incredible" and objected to its "hysterical" tone.
None of them, of course, had grown up in Kansas in the 1920s, or had
any experience of the sexual problems of teenagers in the heartland. But

it seems they were equally unfamiliar with *Winesburg, Ohio,* and failed to detect Inge's nod to Sherwood Anderson, whose characters talk of passion "with a strained, eager quality," whose George Willard is left, like Bud at the end of *Splendor,* "hearing voices outside himself whisper a message concerning the limitations of life," and whose Alice Hindman fears she "will do something dreadful" after her lover leaves town, but finally accepts "the fact that many people must live and die alone, even in Winesburg."

For the leading players the reviews were more generous, and Natalie's performance would earn her a second Academy Award nomination. Like *Rebel Without a Cause,* this powerful and touching movie by Kazan and Inge found a strong response among youthful audiences, and a lesser but still considerable one among parents curious to know what their teenage sons and daughters were responding to.

MEANWHILE, in February 1961, Mart Crowley had moved into the garage apartment of the Wagners' house; and day by day "their marriage seemed to be hanging by a thread." A month later, both Natalie and RJ were relieved when he was offered a starring role in *Sail a Crooked Ship* at Columbia. Although RJ found the script of this crime-caper movie only moderately promising, he was encouraged by the offer of an option for two more pictures; but when Natalie visited the set, she was privately discouraged by its B-movie atmosphere. After completing two major movies herself, she saw RJ having to take what he could get, and a visit designed to boost her husband's morale ended by lowering her own.

Producer's idea for Natalie's next major picture was *Lovers Must Learn* (later retitled *Rome Adventure*), with Troy Donahue as her leading man. "I'm sure it's terrible," she told Crowley when the script arrived, and asked him to read it for her. In a recycling of David Lean's *Summertime,* Natalie would have played a younger Katharine Hepburn, on vacation in Rome instead of Venice, where two potential lovers instead of one awaited her. (Rossano Brazzi, repeating his role from *Summertime,* was cast as the other.) When Mart confirmed that the script was terrible, Natalie found a way to reject it without going on suspension again. "Now is the time for that tonsillectomy," she said. During the last week of filming *West Side Story* she'd developed a mild sore throat, and although her doctor had warned that surgery would be necessary after she finished the picture, she hadn't yet consulted him again: "So now she asked her doctor to write a letter advising her that postponement had made surgery essential, and she'd need several weeks to recover. Then she went to see Jack Warner, played a very effective scene pretending to feel devastated at losing the chance of a great role in a great picture, and showed him the letter."

It worked, and Suzanne Pleshette took over the great role. But the surgery caused unexpectedly heavy bleeding, and Natalie remained at St. John's Hospital in Santa Monica from April 6 to 15, and the unresolved crisis in her marriage, combined with two long, arduous, back-to-back shoots followed by a hemorrhage, lowered her morale even further. When she returned to North Beverly, she usually needed a sleeping pill at night and a tranquilizer to calm daytime attacks of panic.

On May 22 Natalie was due to report for *The Inspector* (later retitled *Lisa*), the first of two pictures for Fox that Warner had assigned her to make on a loan-out deal. It was yet another foreign-accent role, a Dutch-Jewish girl on the run from ex-Nazis at the end of World War II, and this time she got out of it by telling the truth. On May 20 she asked Abe Lastfogel to inform Warner that she was in no condition to work.

For once Producer was sympathetic, no doubt partly because the favorable advance buzz on *Splendor* and *West Side Story* had made his contract star a valuable property. He instructed the studio lawyers to send Lastfogel an official letter granting Natalie indefinite leave of absence without pay "for personal reasons," and as discretion was in his own interest, he managed to cancel the deal with Fox on a technicality. Dolores Hart replaced Natalie for the first picture, and Joanne Woodward for the second, Jerry Wald's production of *The Stripper,* adapted from Inge's *A Loss of Roses.*

To keep the press off the scent, Warner gave Louella Parsons a scoop that the Wagners were about to vacation in Italy. She duly printed the imaginary news in her June 9 column, shortly before Natalie told RJ that she'd reached breaking point, and if he wanted to save their marriage, he must agree to let her consult a psychoanalyst.

By now RJ suspected that *Sail a Crooked Ship* was no more likely to advance his career than his last three movies at Fox, and it made him as insecure as Natalie. If he'd felt able to allow someone else to help her, it might have changed both their lives. But desperation left Natalie with nothing to fall back on except a wish for professional help, and RJ had only his pride. On both sides it was too late for a breakthrough, and the day after what RJ described in retrospect as "our final and most explosive fight," he moved out of the house.

LIVING BY HERSELF in a showplace with half its rooms unfurnished and unfinished made Natalie even more depressed, and she asked Mart Crowley to find her a house for rent. Until she moved out, she frequently asked Asa Maynor if "it would be all right with Edd if I spent the night at her house. She hated the idea of waking up alone, so I slept on one side of her king-size bed."

In the second week of June Natalie made her first appointment with a psychoanalyst, Dr. Stephen Hacker, and asked another member of her support group to drive her to his office. Guy McElwaine, like Mart Crowley, was a friend of RJ's as well as Natalie's. When the Wagners made *All the Fine Young Cannibals*, he was a publicist at MGM, and shortly afterward he went to work for Rogers and Cowan, Hollywood's leading public relations specialists; then, at Natalie's suggestion, he formed his own public relations company, with the Wagners as his first clients.

> *Guy McElwaine: Before that first session, Natalie was determined but terrified, like someone about to go in for major surgery. When we got to the office, she asked me to have a preliminary talk with the analyst, and although I was reluctant, she was so insistent that I agreed. "Tell that son of a bitch not to fuck with my talent," she said. So I did, more or less, and incidentally did not have a favorable impression of the man.*

"Devastated" was the word that several of RJ's friends used to describe his condition after the breakup. Mart Crowley: "He was so devastated, he'd come knocking at my door at night, then collapse in tears on the couch." McElwaine: "He was so devastated that he sometimes slept on the couch in my office." Asa Maynor: "Every time I saw RJ after the breakup, he was devastated. The first thing he asked was, 'Have you seen Natalie? How is she? What's she doing?' " Linda Foreman, the actress wife of talent agent John Foreman, who later became a producer:

*RJ in 1962, after the breakup*

"He used to sit in a chair in our living room, not talking, almost cata-tonic. I'd seen husbands or wives suffer after a breakup, but never any-one as devastated as that."

On June 21, the Wagners announced their separation. They had "no immediate plans for divorce," according to the official statement. "Both are hopeful the problems that exist between them can be worked out sat-isfactorily." Two months later, they signed a community-property settle-ment (a fifty-fifty division of the spoils, including half of each other's salaries, and the eventual sale price of the house and its contents), and repeated that they still had no plans for divorce. When Natalie eventu-ally filed suit and went to Los Angeles Superior Court on April 16, 1962, she charged "mental cruelty," and Maria insisted on taking the witness stand to testify (against her daughter's wishes) that "Mr. Wagner was even rude to *me.*"

By then RJ was in Europe, and the house had been sold for $185,000, a loss of more than $50,000 after the cost of remodeling, redecorating, furnishing and installing the saltwater pool.

In July 1961, Natalie moved to a secluded house on Chalon Road in Bel-Air. It belonged to British producer Jimmy Woolf, and Mart Crowley had discovered that it was available for rent. Although he took an apartment of his own, Natalie soon felt "very unhappy and scared living alone" and asked him to move in with her. Over the next few months, a basic support group of Crowley, Howard Jeffrey and Asa Maynor kept Natalie company there; and later, when Norma Crane moved to Los Angeles, Natalie named the four of them "the nucleus."

For admission to the nucleus, there were five essential qualifications: humor, intelligence, emotional directness, independence of spirit and what Norma called "the kindness test." (Natalie often quoted her comment on a theater director Norma admired: "He's very talented, but he fails the kindness test.") Troubled childhood was a bonus, and all except Asa qualified on that level as well.

Many years later, RJ described Mart Crowley and Howard Jeffrey, themselves best friends, as "just about the two best friends Natalie ever had." Both had problems about coming to terms with their homosexuality, although Jeffrey lived for several years with Robert Lewis, who founded the Actors Studio in partnership with Cheryl Crawford and Kazan; and Crowley would use Jeffrey's bitter, self-deprecating wit (although not his charm or basic kindness) for the character of Harold in *The Boys in the Band.* Jeffrey's mother, a formidable obsessive, was determined that he should become a famous actor and/or dancer. He joined the corps de ballet of Ballet Theatre at the age of fifteen, then danced with the Roland Petit company for the movie *Hans Christian Andersen,* and in 1957 became Jerry Robbins's assistant on the Broadway production of *West Side Story.*

Norma Crane, born Norma Anna Bella Zuckerman, was three months old when her mother died and left her with a terror of being abandoned. She never entirely got over it, and like Natalie with her

nucleus, was in search of a "family." They also shared a belief in work as
an essential aid to survival, and an extremity of feeling (more volcanic in
Norma's case) that Stella Adler categorized as inherently Russian.
"Affairs of the heart," Norma used to say, giving Natalie another favorite
quote, "are more mysterious than how they make movies."

In the case of Natalie and RJ, Norma's remark was right on target.
Separation, followed by divorce, left two people respectively unstrung
and devastated, each disenchanted with the other, each seeking help in
psychoanalysis. But the longer they stayed apart, the more they began to
suspect that each was still the only deep, complete love of the other's life.

# 5

# Love and Marriage (Encore)

*I always envied Natalie her love of fun. She didn't have a Puritan ethic.*

—LESLIE CARON

*If she'd lived, she'd have made a great Cleopatra.*

—BURT BRINCKERHOFF

*For a long time I didn't see the full extent of Natalie's darkness, her fears.*

—RICHARD GREGSON

SOON AFTER NATALIE'S affair with Warren Beatty ended, he became involved with Leslie Caron; and one morning at five a.m. he woke Caron up and said: "You're sleeping! You're not thinking about me!"

"Flattering in a way at first, but tiring in the long run," she said later, and her comment reveals an aspect of Beatty's character that suggests why (in the not-so-long run) both affairs ended.

This demand for total attention, which he was not always ready to reciprocate, was a compound of egotism and insecurity. "Warren was obsessive about going after whatever—person or project—he wanted," according to Caron. "And once he got the person or project, he was obsessive about being in complete control." At the same time, Guy McElwaine recalled, "Warren was very irresolute, and often couldn't make up his mind about anything, from the movie he'd just been offered to what to choose from a dinner menu." The irresolution, he might have added, extended to whatever affair was on the menu. In Freudian terms,

Warren's libido had "a large amount of aggressiveness at its disposal." In Hollywood terms, he was always ready to cut to the chase.

Intelligent, talented and cunning as well as physically seductive, Warren seemed determined from the start to stand above the crowd and to work with the best. He followed *Splendor in the Grass* with *The Roman Spring of Mrs. Stone*, adapted from Tennessee Williams's novella, starring Vivien Leigh and directed by José Quintero, and his third movie was again written by Inge, an adaptation of James Leo Herlihy's *All Fall Down*. A series of bold career moves established Warren Beatty the actor as a hero/antihero/outsider figure in the wake of Brando, Clift and James Dean; and at the same time he established himself as a public figure who insisted on evading public scrutiny, something that only Garbo had brought off so well in the past. Mystery soon became part of the fascination. Was irresolution the reverse side of Beatty's deviousness, or a mask to conceal it?

FOR NATALIE, Warren's appeal was the opposite of RJ's. It reflected a lifelong conflict in her affairs of the heart, between a need for security and family and for adventure and danger. She met Warren for the first time since *Splendor* when he came to dinner at 714 North Beverly, accompanied by his fiancée, Joan Collins. This was shortly before he left (with fiancée) for Europe and *Roman Spring*, and Natalie was still at work on *West Side Story*, and (like RJ) keeping up the appearance of a happy marriage.

By the time Natalie and Warren met again in June 1961, he'd had a brief affair in Rome with Susan Strasberg while Collins was visiting her mother in a hospital in London, then returned to Los Angeles with Collins, only to break up with her a few weeks later. Natalie was living on Chalon Road, seeing very few people apart from Crowley, Howard Jeffrey, Asa Maynor, McElwaine, her analyst and Maria, who arrived for an occasional visit (during which she opened Crowley's letters before bringing in the mail). And Natalie occasionally went out to a dinner party, once at the house of agent Minna Wallis (sister of producer Hal B.), where Garbo put in a late, charming, disappointingly brief appearance. Beatty was not present, but they met soon afterward at another party. Like so many men who had made passes at Natalie since she was fifteen, he found her extremely desirable, and after the failure of her marriage, she was once again "in search of love" or at least the illusion of it.

When their affair began, RJ had left for Europe, where he would remain for two years, making movies (one of which would help revive his career) and keeping in touch by phone with Dr. Gerald Aaronson, his Los Angeles analyst. Mart Crowley, who drove him to the airport, recalled him confiding that "he was still in love with Natalie, but we agreed it was time to get out."

In August, Natalie invited Crowley to fly with her to Florida, where Beatty was on location for *All Fall Down*. Shortly after arriving, she realized that she forgot to pack her diaphragm. They stopped at a drugstore, and to avoid the risk of a leak to the tabloids if she bought a replacement herself, she put on a pair of huge movie-star dark glasses and asked Crowley to buy it for her. The situation struck both of them as wonderfully absurd, and Natalie found it hard to stop laughing while she waited in the car.

In October, Natalie and Warren made their first public appearances together in quick succession, at the New York premieres of *Splendor* and *West Side Story*. Although the Wagners had not yet divorced, it was six years since Hollywood "forgave" Ingrid Bergman for her adulterous affair with Roberto Rossellini, and movie stars had become even more glamorous as extracurricular lovers than as man and wife.

When they were photographed together with Natalie smiling a little anxiously, it was not due to any fear of a "moral" backlash in the gossip columns. But why did Beatty usually look away from her, and appear enigmatic? Was he secretly preoccupied, or bored, or distancing himself from the kind of attention that he claimed to find unwelcome?

In November a major Bel-Air fire almost reached the house on Chalon Road and scorched the surrounding area. Natalie moved to director Peter Glenville's house on St. Ives Drive above Sunset Strip; and Warren, who preferred living in hotels or "house guesting" to renting houses or apartments, moved in with her. (He had previously moved into Susan Strasberg's apartment in Rome and Joan Collins's house on Sunset Plaza Drive.) When Natalie received her second Academy Award nomination for *Splendor*, RJ wrote from Europe (in a note dated March 6, 1962) to congratulate her: "I hope with all my heart that when they open up the envelope, it's you."

But it was Sophia Loren for *Two Women*, as Natalie and Warren

*Ethel Merman, Broadway's original Mama Rose,*
*meets Natalie and RJ; Sinatra is on the left.*

learned when they sat together at the Academy Awards ceremony on
April 9, 1962. By that time Natalie had started work on another movie
for Warners, based on the Broadway musical based on the autobiography of Gypsy Rose Lee.

PRODUCER HAD FIRST approached Delmer Daves to direct *Gypsy,*
but he turned it down. "I simply *cannot* pull for the selfish mother in
this story to continually exploit her two daughters," his memo to
Warner and Trilling explained. But Leonard Spigelgass, assigned to the
script, believed he could solve the problem. "Keep Rose the bitch she is,"
he suggested in a memo to Mervyn LeRoy, who took over as producer
and director, "a funny bitch, occasionally a warm and touching bitch—
but a bitch."

After Spigelgass completed his first draft, he met with Gypsy's sister,
June Havoc, to discuss it. "Her feelings about her mother are very deep
and very bitter," he reported. "She hates the play because she says it
wasn't true." Although Havoc wanted Spigelgass to make it clear that

*Natalie and Warren Beatty at the*
*Cannes Film Festival in 1962*

Gypsy's younger sister was only thirteen when she escaped from her mother, he objected that it would make Mama Rose "appear to be a monster. 'Why not?' Havoc replied. 'That's what she was.'" But LeRoy and Warner agreed with Spigelgass, and Baby June becomes sixteen when she leaves the nest.

Jule Styne, who composed the songs for *Gypsy,* thought Natalie "too mature" to play Louise (Gypsy's real first name) and begged Warner to substitute either Shirley MacLaine or Debbie Reynolds, because they were "singer-dancers." In fact, Natalie was younger than both, by respectively four and six years; Louise was a stripper, not a professional singer or dancer; and the miscastings that Styne should have objected to were LeRoy as director and Rosalind Russell as Mama Rose.

A jack-of-all-trades, LeRoy began his career as a vaudeville actor, but lacked the flair that Minnelli or Cukor would have brought to the vaudeville scenes. Russell was married to Frederick Brisson, who owned the movie rights and sold them to Warners with his wife as "part of the package."

According to Karl Malden (who played Mama Rose's devoted suitor), "LeRoy seemed to spend more time on the phone than directing the picture. Once he said to Natalie and me, 'All right, now give me a nice warm scene.' By then we both had the measure of him, and after we did a run-through, I said, "Okay, Mervyn, we're ready to give you a nice warm scene." Natalie recalled LeRoy as an Actors Studio–phobe, who "hated any talk of the Method or anything about it . . . So I would quietly try to do a preparation without letting him know that I was doing it, and walk around to get in the mood. One time I was starting a scene in which I had to be emotionally upset. And just before the take started, he had already said, 'Roll 'em,' and the camera was rolling, and Mervyn came running over to me all of a sudden and said, 'Cut!' Then he asked me, 'What's the matter? You look so upset!' "

She didn't specify the scene, but most likely it was Gypsy's confrontation with Mama Rose near the end of the movie. "I'm getting no help at all from Mervyn," she told Crowley on the day it was shot, and he advised her to think of her most explosive confrontation with Mud. But this had already occurred to Natalie. Her problem with LeRoy, she said, was that "he doesn't seem to understand that I have to get into the scene gradually, then build to the climax." Evidently LeRoy's idea of "confrontation" was to encourage both actors to shout at each other from the start; and it resulted in an over-the-top contest between Natalie and Russell that ended in a draw—a flagrant contrast with Natalie's subtle underplaying in the rest of the movie, which to Malden was proof that "anyone who works with Kazan advances enormously. Natalie got better and better as an actress."

Although a more intuitive director would have held Natalie back for the confrontation scene, by this stage in Russell's career over-the-top had become her unstoppable approach to every role. "Natalie and I discussed Roz's performance," Malden recalled. "I said what was missing was that she just *pushed*—but you never understood why. Natalie agreed." In fact, only an actor as skillful as Malden could make it believable that he continued to love this strident virago, who incidentally never aged by a gray hair or a day, and was never the warm or touching bitch, and seldom the funny one, that Spigelgass imagined.

Russell also insisted, according to Malden, "on doing all the songs herself. They brought in an orchestra on the set. But her voice wavered a lot when she had to hold a note, so they brought in a professional singer [Lisa Kirk] to dub her." In Natalie's case, the original Gypsy was not a professional singer, so her voice sounds exactly right in "If Mamma Was Married," the duet with Ann Jillian's precocious and more accomplished Baby June, and the solo "Let Me Entertain You." For the movements and gestures that reflect Louise's progression from uncertain first-timer to seasoned stripper in that sequence, she *did* get help—from Gypsy Rose Lee herself, who demonstrated various trade secrets, among them how to peel off an elbow-length glove for maximum allure.

BY THE TIME of *Gypsy*, Mud had managed never to hear anything she didn't want to hear. Like the deaf person who switches off his hearing aid, she perfected a mechanism of denial. The parallels between Mama Rose and herself, and Natalie's awareness of them, aroused no spark of recognition, not even when she visited the set and calmly watched Mama Rose take charge of her daughter's career. As usual, she was there to establish Mama Maria as an important presence in the movie world.

In 1918, as she often recalled, she was six-year-old Maria Stepanovna who saw her half-brother hanging from a tree; and at nineteen she was Maria Tatuloff living on the edge of penury with her estranged husband and baby daughter in a meager San Francisco apartment. But five years later, in 1936, she wore a white evening gown for her coronation as Queen of the Veterans Ball, and she still loved to display the photos of that first transforming moment. By 1962, of course, the transformation was complete. The public Maria Gurdin had achieved status and security as a Star Mother as well as the secret satisfaction of a "great romantic love."

She was also the undisputed head of her own household. Nick had lost his license after a third drunken-driving offense, and lost his job in the studio property department because he could no longer drive to work. To get out of the house he depended on a friendly neighbor or (less frequently) the busy Keeper of the Fan Mail; and it reduced him to more of a silent "background figure" than ever, alone with his balalaika, his Russian novels, his drunken outbursts, an indelible memory of his

Gypsy. *Natalie as the young Louise*

father's death during the revolution and an increasingly desperate belief that his life was in ruins because of the Bolsheviki.

A FEW DAYS before *Gypsy* began shooting, Natalie's analyst, Dr. Hacker, suffered a fatal heart attack. For the next eight years she was a patient of Dr. John Lindon, and her daybooks record almost daily appointments or phone calls as well as long-distance consultations when she was in New York or Europe.

*Natalie as Gypsy Rose Lee*

Although Lindon continues to maintain an ethical silence about his patients, it's clear that he dispelled any of Natalie's remaining doubts that analysis would "fuck with my talent." In 1979 she told the AFI seminar, "I know a lot of actors who just prefer to remain screwed up rather than run the risk of any tampering with their talent. I don't agree with that, because I feel that if you get too sick, then you can't function." As well as making her "think in a different way about characters, about your own work," she added, analysis helped her to become "more aware of others instead of being self-involved."

The sessions with Lindon began at what Guy McElwaine remembered as "a time when Natalie was very troubled by her lack of rapport with Mervyn LeRoy, and the ride with Warren had started to get bumpy." After Peter Glenville returned to Los Angeles, she had moved to a house on Coldwater Canyon and become seriously dependent on sleeping pills. "She sometimes went to bed early, took her Dalmane, and I would sit on her bed and hold her hand until she went to sleep," McElwaine recalled. "She looked incredibly beautiful without makeup, but when I said so, she told me she was wearing a special undetectable makeup that she'd devised for bed. I realized then that Natalie was even insecure about her beauty."

One of the first things Lindon told her, Natalie confided to Asa Maynor, was that "she must make commitments." He soon perceived that her habit of being late for appointments, or sometimes canceling them at the last moment or even not showing up for them, was part of a general fear of making her own decisions. And this fear, he believed, was at the heart of her instability. Ironically, when he explained this to Natalie, she was involved with someone whose habit of *not* making (or keeping) commitments, from relationships to dinner dates, was at the heart of his stability. For Warren, keeping his partner of the moment on edge was an effective way of keeping control, until Natalie finally rebelled against plans often changed at the last moment, and unexplained disappearances for a night or two. Then she realized, as Leslie Caron did later, that Warren's strongest needs were for power, and for fulfilling his ambition to be taken seriously as an actor, not just a movie star.

One early result of Lindon's advice to Natalie was the emphatic commitment that she made one evening at a nightclub with Warren. President John Kennedy and a group of friends, including his brother-in-law Peter Lawford, were sitting at another table. After Kennedy spotted her, Lawford came over. "Number One would like to invite you to join his party," he said. Natalie replied that she and Warren would be honored. Then Lawford explained that Warren was not included, and she declined the invitation. "But it's Number One!" Lawford said with a mixture of astonishment and reproach that Natalie found so comic, she was barely able to hold her laughter until he turned away.

IN THE SECOND week of May, Natalie accompanied Warren to the Cannes Film Festival, where *All Fall Down* was shown on the thirteenth. It was the first trip to Europe for both of them. On the seventeenth Natalie's daybook recorded: "London. *Stop the World, I Want to Get Off*"—the musical starring Anthony Newley, with whom Joan Collins had just become involved. On the twenty-third: "Paris. Drinks Jules Dassin Raphael bar." They stayed longer in Paris than anywhere else, and on the twenty-eighth (a busy day): "Go to Louvre. Habitation Victor Hugo (musée). Versailles-Trianon. Balmain, 5.30." Pierre Balmain was not the only haute couture salon Natalie visited that week, but the French style never became a major influence. According to her friend Linda Foreman, "The perfect understated Chanel suit was never her style. But even when I didn't like her style, I had to admit she looked wonderful." Micky Ziffren, soon to become another important friend, agreed: "She had an instinct for chic. It wasn't infallible, but it was always very personal. She had a very definite idea of herself as a star, and how a star should look—*and* how well she should be paid."

From June 1 to 6 Warren and Natalie stayed in Rome, where Natalie recorded visits to two famous villas, d'Este and Hadrian's, and one famous director, Fellini. But she didn't record an unplanned meeting when she and Warren went out for dinner at the Hostaria dell'Orso in Vecchia Roma. In the restaurant's secluded back room, where visiting celebrities always sat, they encountered RJ and Marion Donen, formerly Marion Marshall, whom he'd first met when they played bit parts in *The Halls of Montezuma* at Fox.

> *Robert Wagner: The conversation was stilted-conventional. "How are you? How's your mother? Where are you staying?" That kind of thing. But there were strong vibes in the air. On both sides. And over the next eight years there'd be several more of those brief encounters, and each time the vibes would be stronger.*

At the time of that first encounter since the separation, RJ had been living in Europe for three months, and regular consultations by phone with his Los Angeles analyst "had already helped me a lot, through a period I would describe as not my finest hour." He'd left California mainly because it was "time to get out," but also with a career move in mind. The new wave in Britain (*A Taste of Honey, Saturday Night and Sunday Morning*) had followed the new wave in France (*Breathless, Jules and Jim*) and he hoped to find better roles in so-called Swinging London.

But his first picture there was a fairly routine assignment under the option clause in his contract with Columbia. A few notches above *Sail a Crooked Ship*, it did nothing to harm his career and little to advance it. *The War Lover* cast Steve McQueen and RJ as RAF pilots during World War II, both of them (surprise) in love with the same girl, and its fifteen minutes of aerial photography were far more dramatic than its ninety on the ground. Halfway through shooting, when he wasn't on call for two weeks, RJ marked time in another World War II picture, Darryl Zanuck's epic of the all-star Anglo-American invasion of Normandy on D-Day. In *The Longest Day*, he joined John Wayne, Robert Mitchum, Sean Connery, Richard Burton, Henry Fonda, Rod Steiger and Roddy McDowall—and Zanuck himself as a five-star general.

Also playing a small part was twenty-seven-year-old George Segal, who remembered RJ as "desperate that Natalie was with Warren." But soon after RJ returned to London to complete *The War Lover*, he began what he described as "a serious affair" with Marion Donen, formerly married to director Stanley Donen. The divorce settlement awarded her custody of their sons, Josh and Peter, and visitation rights for Donen, a British resident at the time; and Marion, who lived in Rome, had brought the young boys over for a visit.

While Josh and Peter stayed with their father in London, RJ and Marion took a trip to Paris, where she introduced him to Blake Edwards. *The Pink Panther*, which Edwards planned to start shooting in Rome that summer, was a comedy about a heroically inept police inspector (Peter Sellers) on the trail of an elusive international jewel thief (David Niven). After meeting RJ, Edwards cast him as Niven's suave and devious young nephew. Niven had become a good friend of the Wagners soon after they first married. As an actor, his strongest card was not depth of character but casually elegant "presence," and during the shoot, RJ noted the skill with which Niven played the same card in many different ways.

Marion found RJ an apartment close to her own in Rome, but soon after *The Pink Panther* began shooting, he had a painful accident on the set. For a bathtub scene, a studio worker laced the bubbles with a strong detergent, and RJ's eyes were burned so badly that he became almost blind and had to wear eye patches until the corneas healed.

Fortunately, Mart Crowley had arrived to stay with him before the accident occurred, and "led RJ around Rome" for three weeks. But they were unaware, like Marion, that Stanley Donen had employed a private detective to shadow his former wife. To gain sole custody of their sons, he hoped to prove her an unfit mother, and the detective obliged by reporting that she was exposing them to moral corruption in the form of Marion's homosexual houseguest, decorator Peter Shore ("a longtime friend of myself and my family," according to Marion). The detective also cast a slur on RJ by reporting that *his* houseguest was another homosexual, Mart Crowley, who occasionally baby-sat Josh and Peter when Marion and RJ went out for the evening.

According to Linda Foreman, the Donen divorce had been "very ugly." Its aftermath threatened to become even uglier. The prospect of a public confrontation with her ex-husband had brought Marion to the verge of public breakdown when she arrived at a London court to answer his charges. But Donen failed to appear, the case was dismissed and the barrister hired to represent him later told RJ "it was probably the most ridiculous case he'd ever worked on."

While *The Pink Panther* was still shooting, RJ's agent in Rome arranged a meeting with Vittorio de Sica, who offered him a role in *The Condemned of Altona.* Derived from French source material (the play by Sartre), with American, Italian and Austrian leading players (Fredric March, Sophia Loren, Maximilian Schell, Wagner), the movie was a product of "Hollywood on the Tiber," the period of commercial and (sometimes) cultural exchange that began in the early 1950s. *Quo Vadis* had proved that spectacular sets could be built at a fraction of U.S. labor costs; *Three Coins in the Fountain,* that authentically gorgeous contemporary locations were another bargain. When RJ arrived in Rome, Hollywood on the Tiber was in high season, and "*la dolce vita*" an everyday expression in at least half a dozen languages.

*The Condemned of Altona* began shooting at Cinecittà shortly after *Rome Adventure* (which Natalie had escaped) completed location work in and around the city. In spite of a mainly positive critical reception in Italy, the film was a commercial failure; but the U.S. release of *The Pink*

*Panther* made RJ's Rome adventure a professional and personal success. Although Peter Sellers dominated the reviews, RJ's favorable notices encouraged him to return to Los Angeles.

Wagner once said that David Niven helped him develop "a sense of style," but in fact that sense was partly innate. He'd begun to find it by watching Cary Grant on the screen, begun to lose it after the divorce from Natalie, and begun to find it again not only with Niven's encouragement and his role in *The Pink Panther,* but with his mutually supportive relationship with Marion Donen. She guided his "discovery" of Rome and Mediterranean Europe, and when they returned to California in 1965, the young man-about-town of *Say One for Me* had become a man of the world.

BACK IN THE HOUSE on Coldwater Canyon a week after the chance encounter with RJ in Rome, Natalie made a note to remind herself in her daybook for June 18: "Call Joe [Schoenfeld] re *Sunday* [*in New York*]." He had offered to propose a deal with MGM for Natalie and Warren to star in the movie of Norman Krasna's Broadway hit, and although Warren appeared to favor the idea at first, he changed his mind when MGM expressed interest. Throughout the summer, the daybook contains various reminders to check with Schoenfeld on various possibilities for the "outside" picture allowed by her contract with Warners: *The Unsinkable Molly Brown;* Tony Richardson's *Laughter in the Dark;* an unspecified role in George Stevens's *The Greatest Story Ever Told;* Otto Preminger's *Bunny Lake Is Missing;* and Hitchcock's *Marnie.* She decided against all of them, even though Mart Crowley had read and recommended *Marnie.* But Natalie had heard that Hitchcock's treatment of Tippi Hedren on *The Birds* was a spectacular example of an artist failing the "kindness test."

In November, *Gypsy* opened to (undeservedly) favorable reviews and simultaneous release to more than a thousand theaters across the country. But after her experience with LeRoy, Natalie told Guy McElwaine, "I want to do things for myself," and suggested they form a company. By then McElwaine had become an agent at ICM, and he made an appointment with Lew Wasserman, head of Universal. They agreed on a three-picture deal, and Wasserman immediately contacted Schoenfeld to discuss terms. Next day, Schoenfeld summoned McElwaine to his office.

"I've been debating whether you should ever work in this town again," he said, coldly matter-of-fact. "But I've killed the Universal deal instead." McElwaine was outraged. When he demanded an explanation, Schoenfeld told him in the same tone of voice: "You didn't come to me first."

APART FROM NOTING almost daily appointments with Dr. John Lindon, Natalie's daybook for the winter of 1962–63 records a second wave of "Possible Pics," including Robert Rossen's *Lilith* (in which Beatty had agreed to appear); a remake of *Alice Adams,* the 1935 George Stevens movie with Katharine Hepburn (abandoned after Natalie decided against it); and a "René Clément Pic" (which eventually became *Joy House* with Jane Fonda and Alain Delon). The mention of Clément reflects her growing interest in foreign movies. Over the same period, Natalie noted that she saw Claude Chabrol's *Les Cousins,* Resnais's *Last Year at Marienbad,* Jean-Luc Godard's *Breathless* and François Truffaut's *Jules and Jim.*

Perhaps not coincidentally, the project she finally chose became the most "European" film of her career. Except for a final week at Paramount studios, it was filmed in black-and-white on New York locations as deliberately ordinary as the Paris of *Breathless.* And there was also a distinctly "un-American" element in the screenplay by his client Arnold Schulman that Abe Lastfogel sent Natalie. "It was her willingness to commit to the project," Schulman recalled, that decided the producer-director team of Alan J. Pakula and Robert Mulligan to become involved, and Paramount to provide financing.

Robert Mulligan was immediately attracted to the basic situation of *Love with the Proper Stranger,* which he described as "falling in love in reverse—of having an affair, and then, through the stress and results of the 'affair,' falling in love." In fact the "affair" began as a one-night stand with a jazz musician that resulted in Angie becoming pregnant; and the "stress" occurred, as Schulman commented later, when "a funny thing happened on the way to the abortionist." At the seamy backstreet premises, the musician sees the fear in Angie's eyes and realizes he can't let her go through with it. "Morality" never intrudes on a scene that becomes a turning point in their relationship and that, when the movie opened, would provoke several American reviewers to take the moral high ground.

Mulligan first met Natalie at Romanoff's for lunch. He'd told Lastfogel that he preferred meeting actors "one to one, as a way of getting to
know each other," but while waiting for Natalie to arrive, he felt sure
that she'd be accompanied by an "Assistant Somebody" or one of her
agents: "Suddenly, there she was. Alone. Mike Romanoff greeted her,
and escorted her royally through the place to our table. Heads turned. A
real star entrance. Natalie seemed to love it. She looked very young, and
literally glowed in a bright summer dress. As Mike seated her with a bow
and a kiss of her hand, he murmured to me, "The Princess has arrived."
The moment he left, Natalie rolled her eyes at me, made a face, and
laughed." Mulligan liked her instantly for her humor, and the cool way
she dealt with "the Hollywood game" of red carpets and hand kissing
that always followed a star of three hit movies in a row. But work, he
soon realized, "was serious. She had a quiet determination to grow as an
actress. No declarations. It was just there."

At Lastfogel's suggestion, Warren Beatty was approached to play
opposite Natalie, but as he'd already committed to *Lilith* and didn't care
for the part anyway, Mulligan and Pakula got the actor they originally
wanted. Both felt that Steve McQueen, whom Mulligan had directed
years earlier in live television, would make an interesting partner for
Natalie. She agreed, and so did McQueen, who "read the script
overnight and committed the next morning."

Before rehearsals began, Natalie met several times with Arnold
Schulman: "But not about the script. She knew I'd been in analysis, and
wanted to know how it helped me. She talked about her own experience, and her progress in figuring out who she really was, what she really
wanted out of life, with an almost sexual excitement. She also told me
about her family situation, her fear of dark water, and how she hated
playing 'the Hollywood game,' which I soon discovered she played quite
brilliantly—but had been trained to feel that 'I had to win and make
people love me.'"

Rehearsals for *Love with the Proper Stranger* began in New York in
March 1963, and Mulligan soon discovered that "Natalie was always
open to exploring her character or a scene. She was unafraid and would
try anything. She never once said, 'I can't do that.'" And McQueen, he
recalled, hadn't yet acquired the mannerisms and temperamental "star
personality" that he developed later. "He had a wonderful comedic talent, wanted to show it and let it come out."

Love with the Proper Stranger. *Natalie and Steve McQueen*

Schulman, who was present at rehearsals, noted that Natalie was very open in discussing the personal resonance of Angie's conflict between the desire to rebel against her family and a fear of living on her own, as well as her need to find commitment in love. But although she never talked about Warren, "Their affair appeared to be almost over." In fact Warren had recently left for Paris with Robert Rossen to interview Jean Seberg for *Lilith,* the actress he suggested after Natalie turned the part down, and from Paris he flew back to Los Angeles.

By the end of *Love with the Proper Stranger,* Angie has succeeded in finding the commitment she needs, and Natalie has failed. *Lilith* began shooting on location in New York three weeks after the start of *Love with the Proper Stranger,* and the lovers saw each other several times before the Rossen unit moved to Maryland. Each time, Natalie reiterated her need for someone she could trust not to disappear without warning, and Warren his need to live a freelance life; and each time, the storm clouds darkened.

When I asked Beatty about the final breakup, he was brilliantly evasive, and engaged me in a semantic discussion of the word "breakup." But I soon realized that his evasiveness was strategic, a way of discovering what I knew, or thought I knew, which he could then confirm or deny. So progress was made when he denied the tabloid gossip du jour that Natalie burned his clothes after he abandoned her during dinner at Chasen's and went off for the weekend with a hatcheck girl. He'd heard that fabrication many times before and was weary of it.

But to get Beatty to say anything about the emotional temperature at the end of their affair, I had to give my own reading first. By the time he left for Maryland, I suggested, they both surely knew the affair had run its course and knew why, so the storm clouds had almost dissolved and the parting was relatively friendly. Yes, Warren said, it was friendly; and there's no reason to doubt him. Natalie's subsequent breakups were usually friendly, and her serious affairs always ended for one of two reasons: they were exciting, as in Warren's case, but offered no security; or they offered security but were not exciting enough.

Although Natalie never talked to Schulman about Warren, he suspected that she "used" him during *Love with the Proper Stranger* in the scenes with Steve McQueen, the jazz musician with a similar reluctance to commit himself emotionally. And during the shoot, Schulman recalled, "Natalie began to flirt openly and charmingly with Steve. But neither Steve nor his wife took it seriously." With Natalie, as James Sikking remarked, flirting was a need for approval, but it could also be a game that allowed her to put deeper feelings (this time, about Warren) on hold, and also (this time) to relieve the tension of an ironic coincidence.

Soon after Warren left New York, Natalie received an offer of commitment in the form of a marriage proposal from Jerry Robbins. Guilt about his sexuality had previously led to his unsuccessful proposal to dancer Nora Kaye, over the same "romantic candlelit dinners" that Natalie later described to Mart Crowley. "It made her very nervous, but she remained in control," he recalled, and because of her tact and their genuine affection for each other, the friendship survived.

ALTHOUGH *LOVE WITH THE PROPER STRANGER* earned Natalie a third Academy Award nomination, Producer was slow to decide on her next contract movie; and as she wasn't allowed to make an "outside" picture of her own choice for another year, her career marked time.

After a divorce and a failed love affair, her personal life was also on hold, and she lost an important member of her nucleus when Mart Crowley decided to remain in Europe for a while. Another secretary succeeded him, then another, but "they didn't work out," Mart explained, "because Natalie needed someone she really liked to work for her, someone to have a drink with at the end of the day, and so on." Then, as Howard Jeffrey had been out of work for several months, she offered him the job. As Robert Mulligan noted, the affection between Natalie and her "staff" (which by now included Bob Jiras, her makeup man since *Splendor in the Grass*) was mutual: "You could feel the people who worked for Natalie genuinely liked her. It was never a star entourage, the kind that bowed to her every wish and secretly disliked her. These were real friends."

Whenever Natalie felt low, humor became an essential tonic, and in the case of Arthur Loew Jr., an essential bond in the affair that began shortly before they attended the June 15 premiere of *Cleopatra*. A droll and charming dilettante, Arthur was born to the Hollywood purple. His maternal grandfather, Adolph Zukor, founded Paramount. His paternal grandfather, Marcus Loew, founded Loews Theaters and MGM, and his father established MGM as the leading international movie studio by creating a network of overseas offices during the 1920s.

Arthur Jr. had worked as a sports reporter before producing two movies: *The Rack,* with Paul Newman as an American soldier taken prisoner and brainwashed during the Korean War, and *The Affairs of Dobie Gillis,* whose star, Debbie Reynolds, he consoled after the breakup of her marriage with Eddie Fisher. Although Arthur loved pretty women, and especially unhappy pretty women, he was not sexually demanding. His greatest pleasure was to become the Great Consoler, listening very attentively to their problems, being very generous with gifts and keeping them amused.

But Arthur's drollery was also a very effective way of disguising his feelings, and Natalie never realized how deeply he'd fallen in love with her. Neither did most of her friends (including this biographer), because he only let down his guard to his cousin and close friend Stewart Stern. "He was insane about Natalie," Stewart recalled. "I'd never seen him like that before, very serious, very concerned." He soon gave Natalie a diamond "engagement" ring, and although she agreed to wear it, she warned him that she wasn't ready to marry again. But this was enough for Arthur to send a photograph of himself and Natalie to various friends and describe it as their "engagement picture," in spite of the fact that the engagement was never officially announced.


BY THE END OF JUNE, Producer had still not chosen Natalie's next contract picture. He'd bought the rights to *The Sparrow*, J. P. Miller's screenplay about Edith Piaf, and planned to assign her to the project after Leslie Caron proved unavailable; fortunately, Trilling (or somebody) dissuaded him. And by that time Natalie had been sent—not by Warners or her agents—a script that she liked.

Before Mart Crowley left for Rome, she'd asked him to read a novel by Dorothy Baker sent to her by Martin Manulis, a contract producer at Fox. *Cassandra at the Wedding* was the story of twin sisters, with a subtle but unmistakable slant on the repressed lesbianism of one twin, and Mart thought it contained two strong roles for Natalie. He took the novel with him to Rome, and when RJ invited him "to stay on and write," he decided to adapt it on speculation, and sent a copy of the script to Manulis. "I wrote this for Natalie Wood," he explained in an accompanying note, and as Manulis had never heard of Mart Crowley, he called Natalie to ask if she knew him. Natalie laughed, said she knew Mart very well and asked to see the script. When she told Manulis how much she liked it, wheels began to turn very quickly because, as Crowley discovered, "*Everybody* wanted Natalie for something then."

Darryl Zanuck, back in charge of production at Fox, approved the project after asking Manulis "to cut the dykisms to a minimum." Joe Schoenfeld found Warner amenable to negotiating a loan-out deal, and Fox sent Crowley to Paris to meet Zanuck's director of choice, Serge Bourguignon, whose *Sundays and Cybèle* had won the Oscar for Best Foreign-Language Film that year.

"Not my choice," Crowley decided after the meeting. "Too dapper, and self-assured to the point of almost incredible egotism." But he kept this to himself when he returned to Los Angeles for further meetings on the script and a more crucial meeting on the costumes. *Love with the Proper Stranger* was the first picture for which Edith Head had designed Natalie's costumes, and she liked them so much that she insisted on Head as her designer on *Cassandra*. After Head completed her first sketches, Manulis arranged a lunch for her to display them to Natalie, Bourguignon and Crowley. Bourguignon rejected them all, and proceeded to sketch his own ideas in pencil on the tablecloth, while Man-ulis, Crowley and Natalie (who'd quickly decided that she disliked him) watched in silence. "To show their different characters, I make sketches in very different styles for each twin," Bourguignon announced, and turned to his star for approval. After a moment, she smiled very sweetly. "And then," she asked, "will you wear them?"

Apparently humor was not a language that Bourguignon spoke or understood, and he wasn't shrewd enough to perceive a danger signal. He changed the subject by telling Natalie, "You were good in *West Side Story*, but you'll be great in my picture." No smile this time, and no answer. She left the table abruptly and called Schoenfeld to say she would not make *Cassandra* with Serge Bourguignon. Zanuck reacted by canceling the project, and Arthur Loew, who had never liked the idea of Natalie playing a closet lesbian, advised her not to pursue it any further.

SHORTLY BEFORE the end of the year, Natalie learned that RJ and Marion planned to get married when they returned to Los Angeles; and in early February 1964, the couple arrived with Josh and Peter Donen, now free to travel with their mother. By this time RJ had heard about Natalie's involvement with Arthur, whom he'd known for several years, and he decided to drop by Arthur's house on the chance of finding her there. Both of them were home, and RJ recalled that while Arthur did most of the talking in an effort to keep the occasion light and easy, he exchanged only "a few conventional remarks" with Natalie. But the vibes of Rome resonated strongly for both of them.

ON THE LAST DAY of February the lease expired on Natalie's rented house, only a few blocks away from Arthur's on Coldwater Canyon. She rented a hillside house only a couple of miles away, on San Ysidro Drive, and Arthur moved in with her. But he wasn't there the day Mud phoned to tell Natalie that Natasha Zepaloff had come to stay for a long weekend.

Natalie responded with an invitation to bring Natasha to the house that same afternoon. And almost as soon as they arrived, Maria contin-ued to play the games she'd started on the first day of Natasha's visit.

Another broad wink when she drew Natasha's attention to the photograph of Natalie and "her father." On the Warner lot, where Maria proudly displayed her studio pass, a visit to the set of *Mary, Mary* and an introduction to Debbie Reynolds: "This is my niece, Natasha." Later, in response to Natasha's question "Why did you say I'm your niece?," Maria informed her: "But you *are*. On your father's side." And then, as Natasha remembered, "She just wouldn't say any more."

When Natalie began questioning Natasha about her family, Maria moved closer to the edge. She reminded her that Natasha was "the Captain's daughter" and gave her niece what she intended as a surreptitious wink. But Natalie (who knew all about her mother and Zepaloff) noticed it, and as Natasha recalled: "She looked at me sort of quizzically. After that the conversation became general. I took some photographs of her, and when it was time to leave, she gave me a warm goodbye hug that made me feel very special inside." A few years earlier, Natasha had the same "special" feeling when Natalie sent her a silver bracelet with a medallion engraved "Natalie" on the back. Natasha assumed it had belonged to her, but wondered about the reason for the gift, because "it wasn't my birthday or any other kind of occasion like Christmas."

This biographer also wonders. Obviously the gift was a sudden impulse on Natalie's part, but also a surprisingly personal gesture to someone she'd met only three times in the past. And obviously something has been going on here.

For several years, as we know, Natasha had felt a "connection" with Natalie that she couldn't account for; and it's impossible not to suspect that Natalie also felt it. If physical resemblance was the starting point on both sides, what followed was the "extreme sensibility of reacting, caring, feeling" that Stella Adler defined as an essential part of the Russian character. Although Natalie never asked Natasha "any specific questions" about her father (unaware of Maria's belief that they had the same father), she knew that Nina's marriage to the Captain had been almost as disastrous as Maria's to Nick. Her own childhood had made Natalie acutely sensitive to signs of loneliness or abandonment in anyone her own age, or younger; and here again the "connection" ran deeper than she knew. Nick Gurdin had been too weak and troubled to give Natalie the attention she so often longed for, and Natasha had seen the Captain so seldom that she used to call the Matson Line to find out when his ship was due in port, then wait at the dock to watch him bring it in, and be granted a few minutes of recognition: "The only long time we ever had together was when I was eleven and a half. He took me to Hawaii for two weeks. But he was in Hawaii when I graduated from High School 9 in Berkeley. Later, when he was in Los Angeles, he saw Maria frequently and she told me he always asked about me. But because I was growing up, he wouldn't see me. Vanity! He didn't want people to know he had a grown-up daughter."

Did Mud occasionally drop a sly, teasing hint about Zepaloff to Natalie as well as to Natasha? The risk was probably too dangerous even for Mud; but if she proved unable to resist it, Natalie's gradually increasing affection for Nick Gurdin makes it clear that the hint miscarried.

SOON AFTER NATALIE'S affair with Arthur began, he advised her to place her legal and financial affairs in the hands of Paul Ziffren, lawyer and business manager to many leading Hollywood figures. Ziffren replaced both her attorney, Greg Bautzer, and Andrew Maree, RJ's business manager, who had worked for Natalie as well after they married and whom she'd retained since the divorce.

"Natalie told Paul that she'd supported the entire Gurdin family from *Tomorrow Is Forever* on," his widow, Micky Ziffren, recalled, "and after twenty years of work had almost no money at all. Paul was shocked when he realized how she'd been used, and began by advising her to buy a house, and arranged for a bank loan."

In the first week of March, Natalie bought a house at 191 North Bentley Avenue in Brentwood. Unlike 714 North Beverly, it was neither large nor pretentious: the exterior was standard French provincial, the interior accent was on comfort. The house stood on a secluded, fairly steep hillside; a lawn sloped down to the pool, and a short driveway led to the street. For a while, after Natalie moved in, the Gurdin family car was sometimes parked further down the dimly lighted street at night. Since Dr. Lindon had advised Natalie to keep a distance from her family, partial exile had turned Mud into a spy. From the driver's seat, with Nick at her side, she would keep watch on the house for several hours and note the arrival and departure of visitors.

In the third week of March, Natalie began work on Producer's choice for her next "obligation" picture. *Sex and the Single Girl* was based on

Helen Gurley Brown's best-seller, and Norman Brokaw originated the project. He had known Gurley Brown since they both landed their first jobs at the William Morris Agency, as mail clerk and secretary, and handled the movie rights to her book. He sold them to Warners for $200,000, entirely on account of its title and its sales, as it was not a novel and had no story line.

The first credited writer to work on the script created its unappetizing central situation: handsome young journalist sets out to seduce pretty young sex expert to prove she's a virgin and expose her false credentials. Joseph Heller was brought in for an injection of comedy, a tall order even for the author of *Catch-22*. His most notable contribution was a comic car chase, extraneous to the story and all the more welcome for it.

*Sex and the Single Girl* was not an agreeable experience for Natalie, partly because she despised the script, and partly because Tony Curtis played the journalist. She'd found him aggressively self-important on *Kings Go Forth,* and the second time around did nothing to change her mind. The result was a total absence of romantic feeling in scenes intended as romantic comedy; and in the post–*Sex and the City* era, most of the movie seems pathetically coy.

Stewart Stern recalled an incident from that time that shows how far Natalie had begun to distance herself from the Gurdins. When Maria insisted that she join the family for a Russian Easter lunch, Natalie dreaded the prospect, but knew how guilty she'd feel if she refused, and asked both him and Arthur to keep her company. They picked her up at 191 North Bentley and headed for the San Fernando Valley. Arthur was driving, and when they reached Ventura Boulevard, he asked for directions to the Gurdin house. But Natalie had forgotten to bring the address with her, and because it had been so long since she last visited her parents, she'd forgotten the name of the street where they lived. Finally she recognized a tree at the Ventura Canyon turnoff, and they arrived just in time for lunch.

ON APRIL 13, Natalie and Arthur and Warren Beatty and Leslie Caron were among the couples attending the Academy Awards ceremony. Natalie was nominated for *Love with the Proper Stranger,* Leslie for *The L-Shaped Room* ("Warren always had this weakness for Oscar nominees," Caron recalled), and they both lost to Patricia Neal for *Hud.*

On May 8, shortly after *Sex and the Single Girl* finished shooting, the ever-unreliable Louella Parsons reported that Natalie had broken off her engagement to Arthur Loew. In fact, she had decided to end the relationship, and although Stewart Stern remembered that for a while his cousin "was just wrecked," Arthur managed to conceal his pain from Natalie, and kept up his usual jokester façade on the social circuit. Like Warren, he was a lover testing for the role of husband; and although genuinely in love with Natalie, he lacked the ardor that might have won him the part. But they remained friends, and Natalie never forgot to be grateful for the way "he made me laugh at even the saddest things."

> *Micky Ziffren: It was humor that helped Natalie survive the terrible years. She was always able to see the joke.*

Not quite always. Over the next nine years her life was full of very "Russian" highs and lows, and to recover from some of the lowest, she needed strength as well as humor. The end of a love affair, being alone at night with her unresolved fears after the party ended or the endurance test of a particularly disagreeable "obligation" picture always created a low. And a week after the low of parting from Arthur, another followed. She'd made a dinner date with Mart Crowley, and as they walked into La Scala, they saw RJ with a group of friends. A few days earlier Marion had given birth to a daughter, Katharine, and RJ was celebrating fatherhood. "Natalie went over to his table and pretended to be very happy for him," Crowley remembered, "but she felt deeply sad." For some time she'd longed to have a child, and RJ's happiness only intensified the longing, as well as the stab of regret that she always felt after a chance encounter with "my strength, my weakness, my lover, my life."

AT THE MOST civilized Hollywood parties of the 1960s, the hosts had no agenda beyond liking to entertain the people they liked; and the party givers in question were Dominick Dunne and his wife, Lenny, at their house on Walden Drive in Beverly Hills, Roddy McDowall at his rented beach house in Malibu, and Natalie herself at 191 North Bentley.

At Natalie's and Roddy's parties, many of the guests overlapped: George Cukor, Mart Crowley, Mia Farrow, Ruth Gordon and Garson Kanin, Rock Hudson, Howard Jeffrey, Hope Lange and Alan Pakula, Tom Mankiewicz, Juliet Mills, Stewart Stern, Tuesday Weld. At Walden Drive the guests included some but not all of these, and some only encountered there: Irene Dunne, Vincente and Denise Minnelli, Merle Oberon, Rosalind Russell and Freddie Brisson, Billy and Audrey Wilder.

"Natalie loved getting dressed up to go out," Dunne recalled. "She wasn't the kind of star who would sit down and expect *hommage* to come to her." She also loved games and party turns, and her parody of Louise's first appearance as a stripper in *Gypsy* became famous. "You're going out there a lady, but you're coming back a star," Mama Rose tells her in the movie, but Natalie inverts the line. "You're going out there a star, but you're coming back a lady," she announces, and the lady opens her strip routine with a series of outrageously unladylike bumps and grinds.

Natalie also devised a spectacular game for deflating the inescapable bore across the table at a sit-down dinner. During his relentless monologue, she takes a cigarette from her case, fits it into a long holder, and every male within reach snaps out a lighter. Cigarette lighted, holder extended like the handle of a lorgnette, she appears to give the bore her full attention, but from time to time uses her free hand to flick imaginary ash from her decolletage. Then, with her center and index finger, Natalie gently squeezes one nipple, tossing back her head and rolling her eye as if on the verge of orgasm. It reduces the bore to astonished silence, transfixes the other guests, and she wonders innocently why everyone is staring at her.

Another game was to rate the performance of sexual partners on a scale of one to ten, and Asa Maynor witnessed a telling round during a girls' luncheon at the Bistro, the fashionable Beverly Hills restaurant co-owned by Billy Wilder. Apart from talent agent Sue Mengers, all the girls were actresses, among them Joan Collins, Samantha Eggar, Hope Lange and Asa Maynor. Natalie and Joan Collins had two previous partners in common and awarded them diametrically opposite scores: for Collins, Warren Beatty rated a ten to RJ's five; for Natalie, RJ rates a ten to Warren's five.

But one night at North Bentley, another party for the girls became a psychological test for Natalie. Someone suggested a skinny dip in the pool; they all stripped enthusiastically and ran down the lawn. Then

Natalie switched on the pool lights, explained that she never swam in dark water, and the game was over. Cries of protest as bodies are exposed to the harsh glare, a quick retreat to the house, the girls put on their clothes, and the party was over as well.

Although psychoanalysis had helped Natalie in many important ways, it would never erase that fear of dark water; or the habit, when the party's over and she's alone, of taking a sleeping pill, and sometimes, when she still couldn't sleep, a final glass or two of white wine. And sometimes, when she arrived alone at a party, she lacked the heart for games, and remained profoundly alone.

> *Richard Gregson: I have one vision of Natalie before I met her. A party at [producer] Ray Stark's house, lots of people. Late in the evening I saw this beautiful young woman in a sherry-colored dress, standing all by herself and looking so lonely and*

*Natalie with costume designer Edith Head*
*at one of Dominick Dunne's parties*

*Natalie with David Hockney (left) and writer George Axelrod
at a party given by Marguerite Littman in London*

*unhappy. I asked who it was. When I was told, I was
astounded that someone so beautiful and so famous could look
so miserable and so alone in the middle of so many people. I
was naïve in those days, I guess.*

But psychoanalysis and humor were not Natalie's only antidotes by
now. With Dr. Lindon's help she had also started to conquer her fear of
betrayal and developed several passionate friendships. They included,
beyond the nucleus, Donfeld, Hope Lange, Guy McElwaine, Arnold
Schulman and Tom Mankiewicz, who described her as "the best friend
you could possibly have": "Natalie helped me decorate my house as soon
as I bought it. I had very little money at the time, but she had a decorator's license and terrorized dealers into selling me stuff at cut prices.
Then she threw a housewarming party and invited some famous stars I
hardly knew or didn't know at all, 'because they'll have to bring housewarming presents.' "

When Norma Crane set herself up in the decorating business to earn
money in the intervals of unemployment as an actress, Natalie obviously
didn't have to worry about unemployment, but her eagerness to learn
was aroused. She decided to follow Norma's example and, according to

her mentor, "developed a good eye for furniture. And I think I helped Natalie out of her white-and-gold period."

Mart Crowley, out of a job when *Cassandra at the Wedding* was canceled, was eventually hired to rewrite a few television scripts, but then began drinking heavily, and "my career went on hold." Once he got very drunk at a party given by Natalie, and a guest aroused her anger by criticizing him. "Don't you dare criticize Mart! He's not your friend, he's *my* friend, and that gives me the right to criticize him *if* I want!" But what she really wanted was to help. " 'You've got to get your life in order,' she told me, and offered to pay for my first six months with an analyst. Coincidentally, our mutual friend Diana Lynn and her husband, Mortimer Hall, were going to Europe, and she offered me their house while they were away. And that's when—thanks to Natalie, my analyst, and sobering up—I started writing *The Boys in the Band,* a play I'd been thinking about for some time."

As for self-help, one way that Natalie found to relieve a low was to reclaim her lost childhood for an hour or two. Lastfogel had a contact at the Disney studio, who loaned her 16mm prints of *Snow White and the Seven Dwarfs, Pinocchio* and *Dumbo.* And if she knew Tom Mankiewicz was also feeling low, she used to invite him over. "Together," he recalled, "we lost ourselves in that wonderfully simple, unreal world of tears and laughter, where laughter and a happy ending always came out on top, and brought out the child in Natalie."

She developed a good eye for painting as well as furniture with the help of Micky Ziffren, who guided her first steps as an art collector: "I liked the house she bought, but not the paintings on the walls. Most of them were chocolate-box sentimental, like those Keane portraits she commissioned. 'So how do you find out about art?' Natalie asked, and I advised her to start going to the best galleries and look at a lot of paintings. Very quickly she built up an original and personal art collection, a Matisse lithograph, a Giacometti sketch, a Bonnard, a Courbet." And in a memory flashback to her studio schoolhouse days with Frances Klampt, Natalie also built up a collection of pre-Columbian ceramics, all from an archaeological site recently excavated in Guanajuato, Mexico. Later she placed them on indefinite loan to the Ethnic Art Galleries at UCLA, and at a reception after the preview, she recalled how she learned to work with ceramic materials. Then she added that she had always "liked to sketch"—an interesting aside in view of Zepaloff's avo-

*Cutup time for former child stars and current friends:*
*Natalie and Roddy McDowall*

cation for painting, and Olga Viripaeff's memory of him as "something of an artist. He painted a landscape with snow on the mountains so real that it made you cold to look at it."

ALL THESE NATALIES, the light and the dark, contended with each other during the twenty-seven-week shoot of *The Great Race;* and by the end of it, 1964 had become one of her darkest "terrible years." From the start, she made no secret of her dislike for the prospect of working on a movie "that my contract forced me to do. I was in analysis, and the picture was going to be made mainly on location, and I didn't want to be away from my doctor." Additionally, the "outside" movie that she wanted to make, *Inside Daisy Clover,* had been set up at Columbia, and Producer threatened not to release her for it if she refused *The Great Race.*

Like Natalie, the production was troubled from the start. The Mirisch Brothers originally planned to produce it for United Artists, with Paul Newman as the Great Leslie and Burt Lancaster as the malignant Professor Fate, rivals in an auto race across half the world during the early 1900s. After Newman dropped out, he was replaced by Charlton Heston, who later dropped out, and Tony Curtis finally stepped in. After Lancaster dropped out, he was replaced by Jack Lemmon, and the project transferred to Burbank as a Blake Edwards production for Warner Bros., on a fifty-fifty basis of cost and profits.

Edwards's first choice for the role of Maggie DuBois, the feminist reporter who covers the race, was Jane Fonda. After she preferred to make *Cat Ballou* instead, his second choice was Lee Remick, currently starring on Broadway in Stephen Sondheim's *Anyone Can Whistle.* She wanted the part but was committed to a run of the play and couldn't guarantee that she'd be available. It didn't improve Natalie's mood to learn that she was third choice; or that, because the movie was a co-production with Warners, Producer had economized by charging the Blake Edwards company only $15,000 for loaning her out and that under the fifty-fifty agreement, she would receive only $7,500.

Her relationship with Blake Edwards soon deteriorated, although not before he learned how Warner had shortchanged her, and gave her 1 percent of the company's share of the profits. Jack Lemmon, who had his own profit-sharing deal, did the same; the antipathetic Tony Curtis refused. But Natalie's open complaints about the deal, and the script, evidently inspired an act of revenge from the studio. Donfeld, who was engaged to design the female costumes, remembers that Martin Jurow, the co-producer, showed him a memo from Steve Trilling: "Do not overestimate the importance of Natalie Wood on Prod. #476, THE GREAT RACE." Unfortunately, Donfeld's relationship with Natalie deteriorated when she arrived for her first day of fittings (May 6) in the company of

Edith Head: "Not coincidentally, Edith was a William Morris client, and she'd lobbied unsuccessfully to have Orry-Kelly removed as Natalie's costume designer on *Gypsy*. As I knew that Natalie had liked her Edith Head wardrobe on *Love with the Proper Stranger*, I wasn't altogether surprised when Martin Jurow informed me that I was to design all the female costumes except Natalie's. 'Edith feels *terrible* about this,' he added. 'She's such a *great* fan of your work, but Natalie asked for her.' "

Surprised and offended that Natalie had never spoken to him directly about the situation, Donfeld made a point of ignoring her when she emerged from her trailer after a conference with Edith. In return, "she looked at me as if looking through glass." For someone so sensitive to betrayal, it was a curious lapse on Natalie's part to act as if a friend had betrayed *her*; and as well as creating a long estrangement, it marked the beginning of a downward spiral in her life.

*The Great Race*, she said at the AFI seminar, had "the kind of sense of humor that didn't appeal to me." Her resentment increased as the movie went and remained considerably over schedule, and "[William] Wyler had asked me to do *The Collector*, which I had to turn down to be allowed to do *Inside Daisy Clover*." What Natalie didn't mention was that Blake Edwards reacted to her open dislike of the project by concentrating his attention on Lemmon and Curtis, and she retaliated by attempting to play an offscreen role in addition to Maggie DuBois.

Her first attempt at imitating Joan Crawford ended in humiliating failure. Because Donfeld had to supervise the costuming of several hundred dress extras, as well as create costumes for the saloon entertainer played by Dorothy Provine, he was frequently on the set. His presence made Natalie uncomfortable, and she marched into Trilling's office to complain about it. But he was unresponsive. "You created the problem," he said, "and now you've got to live with it."

A few days later she learned that Edwards had commissioned Johnny Mercer and Henry Mancini to write a special number for Dorothy Provine, and Hermes Pan to choreograph it. A further turn of the screw was that Provine, an accomplished singer, would record the number herself, and Natalie reacted by making an ostentatious entrance on the set midway through Provine's rehearsal for the camera. Donfeld recalled: "Right before the take, she carried her folding canvas chair closer to the action, alongside the camera's dolly tracks, and directly in Provine's sightline. Provine began strutting her stuff on the stage of the saloon,

COSTUME DEPT. PROD. *4 79*
NAME *NATALIE WOOD*
PART *MAGGIE*
CHG. *MONTAGE 6*

The Great Race. *Wardrobe test for*
*an Edith Head costume*

then headed along the proscenium runway straight toward the camera. And there, instead of the offscreen audience, was Natalie clapping her hands in rhythm to the song."

When Donfeld saw this, he blocked Natalie and Provine from each other's view by quietly placing himself in front of her chair. After Edwards called "Cut!," Natalie got up, glared at Donfeld, then headed for her portable trailer. Later, as Provine began rehearsing the next shot, the overture from *Funny Girl* resounded at full volume on Natalie's record player, followed by Streisand singing "I'm the Greatest Star."

This was "the child in Natalie" coming out with a touch of the bad seed, and although it gave her satisfaction at the time, the tables were turned later. When Edwards commissioned Mercer and Mancini to compose a love song for Maggie, Natalie had to lip-sync to a prerecording of "The Sweetheart Tree" by Jackie Ward.

BEFORE THE *GREAT RACE* unit moved to Europe for location work, Natalie's mood on the set had been lightened by the start of a friendship, and the downward spiral of her life temporarily arrested by a romantic adventure. "We became good friends, but never close," Jack Lemmon recalled. "But it was typical of Natalie that she knew Felicia [his wife] and I loved antiques, and when we came back from location in Europe she presented us with a fine antique inkwell she'd bought over there."

The romantic adventure began in the third week of May, a few days after Natalie shot her first scene. Her makeup man, Bob Jiras, invited David Lange to visit the set and introduced him to Natalie. "On both sides, a tremendous infatuation sprang up almost at once," David Lange remembered. "But I couldn't sustain it. I was going with the most popular girl in the biggest high school in the world, and I didn't have the ego or the means."

The brother of Hope Lange, David was working as personal assistant to her husband, Alan Pakula, and "one thing I did have going for me was that I was a Harvard graduate." He noted that Natalie was "very chameleonlike with her lovers," and his Harvard background, combined with Pakula's plan to produce a film of *The Wapshot Chronicle,* meant that "she began reading a great deal, especially John Cheever—and even wore reading glasses." One Saturday night, when the infatuation was at its peak, they had dinner with Jim Henson, creator of the Muppets, and his wife, Sally. " 'You two are obviously crazy about each other,' Jim said. 'Why don't I arrange for a plane to take you to Las Vegas to get married?' Natalie and I looked at each other as if to say, 'Who's going to stop this first?' Luckily, fate stopped it. Jim couldn't get us a private plane."

The competition that finally proved too strong for David came in the form of Natalie's occasional lover Frank Sinatra. "One night during the third week of our affair, she said she had a date with Sinatra that she couldn't break, and I should come to the house later. I got there around eleven o'clock, and Sinatra's limo was still outside. I waited in the bushes until midnight—until two a.m.—until four, and then the voice of self-protection told me to give up and go home." By the time Natalie left for Paris at the end of June, the affair had "wound down," but they remained close friends for several years, and today David remembers her as "funny and kind and beautiful."

The night after the unit arrived in Paris, the French production manager took the stars, Blake Edwards, Martin Jurow and Donfeld on a nightclub tour that ended at the transvestite cabaret Elle et Lui. The house lights had started to dim as they arrived, and a line of not-very-young chorines appeared onstage, wearing flamboyantly tacky costumes and wigs. Natalie applauded each number loudly, but when they began dancing and stripping to a playback of her own voice singing "Let Me Entertain You," her hands freeze-framed in midair. Once over the surprise, she bounced up and down to the music, and when the performers came over to pay their respects, she congratulated them warmly and even pretended to admire their cut-rate costume jewelry.

The rest was downhill all the way. *The Great Race* shot for almost four months in France and Austria, and Natalie wasn't always able to phone Dr. Lindon when she felt a need to consult him. Throughout the shoot she struggled with a mainly passive role, and throughout the race disagreeable things happened to Maggie. The first occurred on location in California when her automobile broke down in the Mojave Desert. Later she was kidnapped by Professor Fate in his "Hannibal 8" and hoisted on a hydraulic lift above his contraption that contained a hidden machine gun and a fire-breathing cone to melt Arctic icebergs. She was stranded on one of those icebergs with a polar bear, chased through a Bavarian forest, and (for two days of filming) chained to a medieval dungeon door. Finally, by the time of the barroom brawl that culminated in a custard-pie fight, Natalie's relations with Edwards had become so sour that he personally aimed the pies at her face and made sure they smacked the target. She retaliated by playing diva again. In Salzburg, she demanded to stay at the Hotel Imperial, in the suite favored by Hitler when he visited the city. But it was already occupied, and on August 3 a memo to the Austrian production manager records Natalie's terms for staying at the Goldener Hirsch instead: she requested a two-bedroom suite on the top floor, for herself and secretary Mona Clark (who had replaced Howard Jeffrey when he found work as a dancer again); a single room for her makeup man, Bob Jiras; a double room with twin beds for her wardrobe woman, who had brought her daughter along; a single room for her hairdresser; and a room for "Miss Wood's wardrobe."

On September 3, a production report by Martin Jurow mentioned "an extremely irritating morning in view of the fact that Natalie Wood,

The Great Race. *Blake Edwards (by camera) right on target
(Natalie) with a custard pie*

concerned about what she was going to wear, resulted in a hold-up of
work." But the delay of a few hours was trivial. *The Great Race* had run
twenty-four days over schedule by the time the unit returned to Burbank on November 10, for five weeks of further work in the studio.

"On Monday, November 23rd," a memo from Jack Warner informed
the production manager, "Natalie Wood advised the Assistant Director
that she would not be able to work in the scheduled Ext. Lake sequence
as the action required her to go in the water and her menstrual period
had begun." Menstruation was sometimes acutely stressful for Natalie,
partly no doubt on account of the trauma of that first periodic flow at
the age of thirteen, and the stress increased when her mood was low. But
she returned to work for the lake sequence on November 25, and seemed
in good spirits on Friday, November 27, when she asked Mart Crowley
to join her for dinner at La Scala.

This time, when they entered, it wasn't RJ but Warren whom they
saw at a table with a group of friends. He came over, "light, polite, and

charming," as Crowley recalled, and they exchanged a few words. Although Crowley was unaware that signals had also been exchanged, Natalie's radar had picked them up; and as he drove her back to North Bentley, she mentioned that Warren would be coming by the house for a drink. Then she added that her live-in housekeeper, Frances McKeating (known as "Mac"), was away for the weekend, and asked Mart to sleep over in the downstairs den, as she didn't want to be alone in the house that night. Soon after they arrived, the doorbell rang. Crowley answered it, let Warren in, and after a few minutes of social conversation, he said a tactful goodnight. Around two a.m. he was woken by a series of weak but insistent knocks on the door. When he opened it, he found Natalie on the threshold in her nightgown. She looked very pale, took a few uncertain steps into the room, then fell to the floor. "What's happened?" Crowley asked, still only half-awake, but there was no answer, and he realized she was unconscious.

He slapped her face and she didn't react. He sniffed her breath and there was no whiff of alcohol. "Pills!" he thought, and started to panic. He dragged her to the shower, turned on the cold water, and there was still no response. "Same thing when I dragged her to the toilet bowl and put my finger in her mouth to make her throw up. I dragged her back to the room, both of us (me in my jockey shorts) drenched by now, and called Howard Jeffrey. I told him to call Rex Kennamer, Natalie's doctor, ran to open the front door and switch on lights, then ran back to cover Natalie with a blanket."

Before Dr. Kennamer arrived, Mart had time to put on his clothes, check Natalie's eyes and pulse, realize she must have taken an overdose, and call the emergency department at Cedars of Lebanon to summon an ambulance. Then Kennamer gave Natalie a shot and asked Mart to think of a false name for her at the hospital: "First I thought, Natasha Gurdin, then no, that won't do, and after a moment, for some reason that eludes me to this day, I thought, Nancy Gordon."

The ambulance and Howard Jeffrey arrived almost simultaneously, and Kennamer accompanied Natalie in the ambulance to Cedars of Lebanon. Mart drove with Howard and waited outside the room where an intern pumped out Natalie's stomach under Kennamer's supervision. "Seconal," Kennamer said when he came out. "I don't know if she'll make it. It's close."

When Mart explained that Natalie was due back on the set of *The*

*Great Race* on Monday morning, Kennamer suggested he call Abe Last-fogel. "I'll be right over," Lastfogel said. "Don't let anyone else know." He arrived with Joe Schoenfeld and Norman Brokaw and immediately asked Kennamer: "If she pulls through, what are the chances she can make it to Warners by six-thirty a.m. Monday?" Kennamer declined to commit himself and suggested that Lastfogel call Dr. Lindon. "But *not*," he added, "Natalie's mother or sister."

After Lindon arrived, Howard Jeffrey drove Mart back to Natalie's house, where they found an empty Seconal bottle in her bedroom. They agreed not to call Beatty, then drove to Jeffrey's apartment. Mart went to sleep for a few hours, and they returned to the hospital around ten a.m. Lastfogel was still there, and told them that Natalie had just started to come around, but Lindon would be staying with her for several more hours. Back at North Bentley around noon, Mart noticed that the light on the answering machine was flashing. He played back but didn't answer several messages from Beatty, asking where Natalie was and if she was all right.

Over the next twenty-four hours, Mart and Howard waited for news from the hospital, and intermittently dropped off to sleep. Around three p.m. on Sunday, Natalie herself called. In a surprisingly matter-of-fact voice, she told Mart that she was due for release, but had only the night-gown she arrived in, and needed clothes. He brought her some and drove her home. She said nothing about what had happened, and he knew better than to ask. He told her about the messages from Warren, and she said that she wouldn't call him back for a while. Then, again very matter-of-fact, she announced her intention to report to the studio the next morning.

Mart was stunned. "But you look terrible," he said. "I'll get by," Natalie said. "There aren't any close-ups scheduled. And I have to go to work because I don't want any word of this getting around." For Mart, it was a moment that revealed Natalie's "extraordinary strength": "She was humiliated, depressed, but determined to finish a movie she'd been working on for over six months, and hated. 'It's a six-thirty call for eight,' she said. 'I'll have time to get some sleep.' And she did. Was on time at the studio and picked up the scene they'd left off on Friday evening."

Meanwhile, the phone rang several more times at North Bentley, and on Monday night Natalie finally took a call from Warren. Later she reported the conversation to Mart. Warren: "What happened? Where have you been? I've been trying to find you for two days." Natalie: "Nothing happened. After you left, Mart and I suddenly decided to drive down to Palm Springs for the weekend." "He didn't believe me," she told Mart, "and asked if I'd been in the hospital. 'That's crazy,' I said, and stuck to my story."

Natalie never discussed her suicide attempt with the nucleus, or with RJ after their remarriage, and never, of course, with her family; and as I knew that Dr. Lindon would never discuss it, I hoped that Beatty might provide a clue to Natalie's state of mind that night. At first he was defensive, because he'd heard Mart Crowley alleged that "Natalie and I had a violent row before I left." I assured him that Mart never said anything of the sort to me, and the "violent row" was a story that first appeared in Lana Wood's "memoir," Natalie, and that Mart always dismissed it as an absurd fabrication.

When I explained what Mart had told me (omitting the messages left on Natalie's answering machine, and his phone call later, in case he became defensive again), he challenged two points. "I drove Natalie back to her house, and I never went inside, but said goodnight at the door." After a moment he added, "That's all. Everything was very friendly." After another moment he corrected himself: "I did go inside, but only for a few minutes. We chatted about unimportant things, and I said goodnight. Everything," Warren repeated, "was very friendly." Then he changed the subject and evaded any return to it with his usual brilliance.

Warren's claim that he and not Mart drove Natalie home, like his initial irresolution to admit that he went inside the house, is unimportant. What's important is that Natalie remained on friendly terms with him—an unthinkable situation if she'd tried to kill herself on account of anything he said or did that night. But equally important is that Warren would not have left those anxious messages on the phone the next day if he hadn't realized that Natalie was at a very low point when they said goodnight.

A week or two later, Mart met Warren by chance. "I know what happened," Warren told him, and Mart denied that "anything happened." By then Warren was no doubt aware that rumors had started, although only one appeared in print. (Today, of course, reporters, photographers, and TV trucks would have kept an all-night vigil outside Cedars of

Lebanon.) On November 30, a cryptic item appeared in Mike Connolly's column in the *Hollywood Reporter*, evidently leaked by a hospital employee who recognized "Nancy Gordon." "Natalie Wood," Connolly wrote, "is fine after a slight siege—under her square nom de Natasha Gurdin—of mal-de-motorcycle or something at Cedars." "Square" was Connolly's code name for a visiting or business card, although he was misinformed about the "nom." "Mal-de-motorcycle" was his code name for a drug overdose, though he was also misinformed about the "slight siege."

The only person apart from Dr. Lindon whom Natalie talked to about that night was David Lange, and thirty-seven years later he could only remember part of what she said. "I think," he explained, "I tried to block out the whole painful episode." Most likely Warren felt the same way, especially after all the rumors that circulated because he was the last person to see Natalie before she overdosed herself. And most likely, as David suggested, Natalie herself tried to block out the episode because she couldn't really explain it.

David principally remembered that Natalie talked about the very fine line between truly wanting to kill yourself and "falling into it in a state of confusion." He believed she was feeling low that night for "a combination of reasons," and attributed the confusion to her habit of "taking a sleeping pill, then getting up to drink a couple more glasses of wine, and when the wine acted against the pill, taking another pill." If Natalie truly wanted to die, he wondered, why would she have asked for help by knocking on Mart's door, and would she have summoned the will to insist on returning to life and work two days later?

The powerful "combination of reasons" included three failed love affairs over two years; the loss (forever, it seemed at the time) of Donfeld's friendship; the missed opportunity of working with Wyler because *The Great Race* was running weeks over schedule; and two residual emotions: the surge of longing and regret after her encounters with RJ, and the guilt and resentment created over the years by her family.

Why did Natalie ask Warren to drop by her house that night? The only convincing explanation is a sudden, desperate hope of renewing their affair—desperate, of course, because she knew that Warren was involved with Leslie Caron and due to leave for London very shortly to join her in a movie, *Promise Her Anything*.

There's no cause to doubt Warren's account of a "very friendly" goodnight when he decided to leave after a few minutes—something Natalie clearly had been afraid of when she asked Mart to sleep over. Not long afterward, I was third party to a similar episode between Natalie and Warren, and there was no ill feeling on either side. It was more of a game that time, and although Warren seemed to enjoy it, he played a very gentlemanly game. And I suspect that gentlemanliness (the reverse side of his evasiveness) partly accounts for his refusal to discuss the night of November 27 in detail.

AFTER COMPLETING her role in *The Great Race,* Natalie decided to go to Europe for the holiday season. During the location shoot she had met David Niven's son, a William Morris agent based in Rome. One of his jobs was to "take care of" the agency's major American clients when they came to Europe, and while Blake Edwards filmed the palace ballroom scene in Vienna, David Niven Jr. took care of Natalie well enough for her to call him a week before Christmas.

He offered to take care of her again during the holidays in Gstaad, where his father had a chalet; and when he returned to the Morris office in Rome on January 3, 1965, Natalie decided to go with him for a few days. The few days became two weeks, and the couple said goodbye ("with many kisses," according to local journalists) at Fiumicino Airport on the eighteenth. The affair was Just One of Those Things; but at a New Year's Eve party in Gstaad, Natalie had met a guest whom she would later identify, for a few unhappily misguided months, as The Man I Love.

Ladislow Blatnik, a Hungarian based in Caracas and known as "the Shoe King of Venezuela," raised his glass of champagne and drank a toast to her. Then, after gulping it down, he performed his party trick, crunching the glass between his teeth and swallowing the pieces, stem as well as bowl.

NATALIE HAD read my novel *Inside Daisy Clover* as soon as she heard that Pakula and Mulligan were going to film it, and called me to announce, "I'll kill for that part." Don't bother, I said, you're the first choice of everyone concerned.

I didn't know Natalie well at that time, and we were friendly without becoming real friends. I first met her in the fall of 1956, when I was working as Nick Ray's personal assistant and living with him in his Chateau Marmont bungalow. She dropped by one day to say hello to Nick, and he introduced us. She looked extraordinarily young, seemed totally unaffected, wore very little makeup, and was casually dressed in a sweater and jeans. We talked briefly about nothing in particular, but I was aware of an occasional gleam of curiosity in those dark eyes. After she left, Nick described in his laconic way how they were quickly attracted to each other when he interviewed her for the part in *Rebel Without a Cause;* and he seemed offhandedly proud of having taken her virginity.

Two years later I became friendly with Barbara Gould, and before going out to dinner one evening, we stopped by 714 North Beverly Drive. The place seemed less like a house than an elaborate movie set still under construction. This time Natalie was heavily made up, and jittery. RJ, whom I'd met and liked while working on Nick Ray's *The True Story of Jesse James,* was more relaxed. They were both friendly, but seemed not quite real, like the house. Later, I wondered if they seemed that way to themselves.

Over the next few years Natalie and I met socially from time to time, but our real friendship began early in February 1965, when she called to suggest having dinner to discuss *Inside Daisy Clover.* This time she was as open and unaffected as I remembered from our first meeting, but with the patina of movie-star glamour, and she made a very acute, very personal comment on the script: "At every important moment of Daisy's life, she's alone. No one to turn to, no one she can really trust."

The secretly bisexual movie star Daisy fell in love with, and who abandoned her the day after their marriage, obviously didn't strike a direct chord; but there was an echo in the situation of Natalie's failed marriage and the transient affairs that followed. The most recent and transient, I knew, had been with British actor Tom Courtenay, in Hollywood to film *King Rat.* They had met at a party given by the film's producer, Jimmy Woolf, and I first met Courtenay, who was clearly ill at ease with "Hollywood," at a party given by Natalie about two weeks before our dinner.

Thirty-five years later, when I asked this deeply reticent man about the affair, he first of all said: "You've really caught me offguard!" Then, after a reflective pause: "I knew Natalie very briefly, and I think that's all

I really want to say." It's probably all there is to say. By the time Natalie and I had dinner that night, Courtenay had left for Madrid and *Doctor Zhivago,* and she never mentioned him. But like several others, he seemed to be on her mind when our discussion of the script led her to ask: "How long has 'true love' in *your* life lasted?"

To date, I said, I've had three "true loves," and each lasted two years, give or take a few months. Then I recalled our first meeting at the Chateau Marmont, and the gleam of curiosity in her eyes. "I was wondering exactly what was going on with you and Nick Ray," Natalie said. "What was going on," I said, "was exactly what you wondered."

By this time we'd both drunk a good deal of white wine, and Natalie again switched the subject (but not really, as its subtext had been the same all evening): "Let's go see Warren!" When she said this, there was another kind of gleam in her eyes, excited rather than curious.

Warren was then living in a penthouse apartment at the Beverly Wilshire Hotel. I drove Natalie there, we walked to the lobby, and I waited while she talked to him briefly on the phone. Then she announced with another gleam of excitement: "He wants us both to come up!"

My presence, I realized, was a kind of security. If Warren gave her a signal to stay, it would be a signal for me to leave; no signal, and we would leave together. Which is what happened. Warren was very cordial, very charming, we talked agreeably and unimportantly for a while, and the situation seemed to amuse him—Natalie too, who became lightly flirtatious. After perhaps twenty minutes, she got up to leave, and they said a friendly goodnight. When I drove Natalie home, she made no reference to Warren, *her* signal that she preferred not to talk about it.

She never did, but seemed not at all apprehensive about going home alone, as if to flash another signal—that she would never again entertain the hope, or illusion, of stirring the embers of that affair.

ON FEBRUARY 16, *Inside Daisy Clover* began two weeks of rehearsal with Natalie, Christopher Plummer, Robert Redford, Ruth Gordon, Katharine Bard and Roddy McDowall. After disagreements with Columbia, Pakula and Mulligan had made a distribution deal with Warners; but although filmed at the Burbank studio, it remained an outside picture for Natalie, as her contract was with Park Place, the

Inside Daisy Clover. *Robert Mulligan confers with Natalie as the early Daisy on the Santa Monica Pier location.*

Pakula/Mulligan production company. It specified "seven hundred and fifty thousand dollars against ten percent of the gross," approval of director, co-star, cameraman, costume designer, makeup man, hairdresser, stills photographer, publicist, "portable and permanent dressing rooms." The same terms would apply to Natalie's next two movies; and 1965 was the year that she came as close as she would ever get to realizing the ambition she once confided to Guy McElwaine: "I want to do things on my own."

At the end of the second week, Natalie gave a party and introduced her guests to a man none of us had met before. Ladislow Blatnik, who was visiting Los Angeles, had called to remind her of their meeting in Gstaad, and invited her to dinner. Their affair had apparently begun that same night, and was viewed as a puzzling aberration by Natalie's friends, especially the nucleus and myself. We found him amiable, clownish and (as I remember Howard Jeffrey saying) "an unbelievable comedown" after Warren and Arthur Loew. Although there seemed "nothing seriously wrong" with Ladi that night (it was the best we could say of him), later we were not so sure. Rumors began to circulate that the reputed millionaire and Shoe King of Venezuela had financial problems and hoped to solve them by marrying a wealthy movie star, like his friend Gunther Sachs von Opel, who briefly snagged Brigitte Bardot.

Meanwhile, he became a frequent visitor on the set of *Daisy Clover.* Although Mulligan and Pakula had contracted me to be on hand every day in case of script problems, I hardly saw Ladi, as he always disappeared into Natalie's trailer between takes. But I saw a good deal of Mud, still a fixture in all Natalie's contracts as Keeper of the Fan Mail, and a guest at the larger North Bentley parties, where Natalie loyally kept up the pretense that she was a wonderful mother.

In both places Mud reminded me of exiled royalty, fallen from power but still expecting homage (however brief) to be paid. As if in mourning for her lost throne, she usually wore black; but her occasional choice of an embroidered peasant dress, or the royal purple, offered a glimpse of the flamboyance she'd once been famous for. Although the same height as Natalie, she had heavier shoulders and hips, more noticeable as she started to put on weight in middle age. On the rare occasions when Nick accompanied her, he rarely spoke a word. He was still handsome, but worn, and more solidly built than the "slim-waisted" and "perfectly proportioned" Zepaloff.

Mud was fascinating to talk to, although what she said was dull. At a party her eyes were always working the room, in search not of love but of information, registering the number of stars among the guests, and sometimes missing a presence that she expected. Then she would ask, "Is Elizabeth Taylor coming tonight?" or "I wonder, where is Mia?"

On the set of *Daisy Clover* I had an almost daily opportunity to watch Natalie at work. But as George Cukor once said, "Real talent is a mystery, and people who've got it know it. The very best actors never talk very much about acting itself—and above all they never talk about it until they've done it." This was certainly true of Natalie and Robert Redford, whose rapport was obvious from the start. His cagey charm proved an ideal match for the role of Wade Lewis, and Mulligan was the kind of director, like Nick Ray and Kazan, who only talked to his actors in private. So all I saw were the actual takes, not the preparation.

Once, I remember, Natalie said that the movie "seemed to be going dangerously well." A prophetic remark, as we discovered when a few important changes were made without consulting us. The first was during a climactic scene when the producer's wife (Katharine Bard) drunkenly reveals Wade's bisexuality. Anticipating censorship, Pakula-Mulligan had cut several lines, and some but not enough were restored only after I pointed out that the scene no longer made sense. The second change was equally damaging. In the script, I used Daisy's offscreen voice, not as narrator, but to make an occasional ironic comment on her situation. Example: Impeccably groomed and gowned, transformed into a sweet little ingenue for her coming out as a star, Daisy catches sight of her reflection in a mirror and her eyes flicker with surprise. "I don't think we've met," her voice comments offscreen before she turns abruptly away.

Natalie learned about the elimination of her voice-overs, except for the opening and closing shots, when she discovered that a rough cut of the movie was being previewed in Glendale. She sneaked into the theater (back-row seat) after the lights went down, and told me afterward, but more angrily, what she told the AFI seminar: "It was like cutting out half my performance—the other side of Daisy."

At that preview, which I didn't see, the movie ran two hours and thirty-four minutes. Twenty-six minutes were cut, including an important scene where Wade Lewis casually warns Daisy not to fall in love with him, and the musical number Natalie and I liked best, "Back Lot Kid." But the final version previewed well enough in Riverside for Producer to congratulate Pakula, Mulligan and myself, and for Warner executive Walter McEwen, misguidedly optimistic, to inform Abe Lastfogel that the picture would "open locally for a special engagement at Christmas in order to qualify for Academy Awards."

WHILE *INSIDE DAISY CLOVER* was in production at Warners, RJ was filming *Harper*, adapted from Ross Macdonald's *The Moving Target*, on a neighboring set. One afternoon, during a long break, he walked over to Natalie's set, accompanied by the screenwriter of *Harper*, William Goldman. Natalie was performing a musical number, "You're Gonna Hear from Me" (later revoiced, like her other numbers, by Jackie Ward). As they watched, RJ climbed several steps up a nearby ladder for a better view. After Mulligan approved a final take, Natalie walked to her dressing room and passed (by accident or design? Goldman wondered) close to the ladder. Goldman wrote an account of the dialogue that followed, and RJ has confirmed its accuracy.

> WAGNER [*from above*]: Hi.
> WOOD [*stopping, looking up*]: Hi.
> WAGNER: That looked good.
> WOOD: You think?
> WAGNER: I do. Yeah.
> WOOD: Hope so. [*Little smile, starting off*] Bye.
> WAGNER [*watching after her*]: Bye.

"Not very telling dialogue," Goldman commented. "But the subtext sure let you know a lot." "It sure did," RJ said later, and described it as "the most loaded yet."

ON A WARM summery night at the end of May, shortly after *Daisy Clover* finished shooting (which was also shortly after the encounter with RJ), Natalie threw an elaborate party to announce her engagement to Ladislow Blatnik: buffet in a tent erected on the lawn, long tables set up outside to accommodate around forty guests, and a task force of waiters serving food and drinks. Toasts were proposed and drunk, and while the guest of honor performed his party trick, the nucleus and I hoped that something would occur to change Natalie's mind.

Fortunately it did. After the engagement party, Natalie and Ladi left for a two-week vacation in Caracas, where the Venezuelan minister of tourism offered to throw a wedding party for the couple, then take them on a tour of Venezuelan beauty spots. Blatnik was eager to accept, but the press reported angry protests from opposition members of the Venezuelan Parliament when they learned that the proposed celebrations would be at government expense.

When Natalie sidestepped the invitation by announcing that they hadn't fixed a definite date for the wedding, it was the first sign of second thoughts. Asa Maynor witnessed another soon afterward. One evening at Natalie's house, they heard the sound of a car turning into the drive-way. "Oh my God, that must be Ladi!" Natalie said. "Quick, turn out all the lights so he'll think no one's home."

IN JULY, *The Great Race* opened to mainly negative reviews. Although Bosley Crowther of the *New York Times* found it "roaring fun," *News-week* summed up the majority verdict: "An incredibly overblown imita-tion of old-time comedy." Meanwhile, Donfeld's comment circulated widely in private: "About as funny as a baby's grave." Natalie was praised by some reviewers for her sense of comedy and damned by others for her lack of it, but all agreed that she looked exceptionally beautiful. It was a task that Natalie the professional had set herself. Playing a role she found totally unrewarding, and in a state of personal turmoil, it was the only satisfaction she could hope for. According to Donfeld, "Edith Head seldom bothered with historical accuracy when designing period films, preferring to create a 'look' of her own invention, for better or worse." On *The Great Race* it was definitely for better. For a journalist constantly on the move, Natalie's wardrobe was improbably high-style and varied, but a welcome distraction.

Mindful of her percentage points, Natalie agreed to make a publicity appearance with Blake Edwards at the Indianapolis 500 race, where she posed beside period automobiles from the movie. But her reward was relatively modest. *The Great Race* had an enormous budget for the time and exceeded its original $5,250,000 by more than $2 million, and its box-office receipts were less than spectacular.

ON OCTOBER 5, Natalie left for New Orleans to start location filming on her next movie. *This Property Is Condemned* was a Ray Stark produc-tion that John Huston had originally agreed to direct, with Elizabeth Taylor in the leading role. When Huston bowed out, so did Taylor. Natalie replaced her, and for Huston's replacement, Stark eventually set-tled on thirty-four-year-old Sydney Pollack, whose first movie, *The Slender Thread*, had just had a very successful preview. But as Pollack recalled, Natalie's contract included the right to approve her director: "I was very inexperienced in many ways then, and scared to death when I arrived at her house. I had a strong reputation in TV, but at the time few movie people paid much attention to TV, and I felt I had nothing to show. Then Natalie came into the living room, very glamorous, very movie star, and it turned out she'd seen a TV movie I made and liked it. We sat and talked for two or three hours about the script, and next day she okayed me."

As Stark was busy with other projects, he engaged John Houseman to produce the movie after signing Natalie and Redford for the leads, James Wong Howe as cinematographer, and Francis Ford Coppola, Fred Coe and Edith Sommer to write, in succession, one or more drafts of a script. Houseman was dissatisfied with all of them and contracted James Bridges to write another; Pollack, equally dissatisfied, signed David Rayfiel to write still another. Each writer, Houseman recalled, tried to "strengthen the film's dubious and contrived love story." (Tennessee Williams's fifteen-minute play serves only as prologue to the romance, ten years later during the Depression, of Alva Starr and Owen Legate.) It was finally left to Pollack "to make some sense out of more than a dozen different drafts. And as this was before the days of computers, I laid out each draft on the floor and cut out the scenes in each I thought best."

For Houseman, whose main contribution was to cast the talented Canadian actress Kate Reid as Alva's mother, all this confirmed what he'd suspected from the start: "Certain films are made with little hope of artistic quality or of popular success merely because a studio entrepreneur, for some special reason, finds it advantageous to produce them." But whatever Stark's motives, both Natalie and Pollack had serious hopes of "artistic quality."

The main problem, Pollack agreed when we discussed the movie, was that none of the writers succeeded with the character played by Redford. Owen Legate seems undefined and opaque, the love story never catches fire, and only one of Redford's scenes with Alva (written by Rayfiel) comes to life. They meet in a disused railroad coach, and the tragedy of an incurable dreamer in love with a cool, wary nondreamer is suggested when Alva describes her life dreams, and he responds by telling her flatly, "I have no dreams." But once sketched in, the situation fails to develop.

Another effectively faux-Williams scene, again by Rayfiel, was lost on the cutting-room floor. After Alva runs away from her mother's boardinghouse, the scene changes to a deserted railroad station at night. Sydney Pollack:

Alva stands at the entrance. She looks seedy, wearing a straw hat that partly shadows her face, and throws patterns of fragmented light from a street lamp nearby. She's now a prostitute, and a young traveling salesman picks her up. She talks about her life and her mother, romanticizing it, lying about it. "You're a very beautiful young person," he tells her. "Did you say beautiful?" she asks. He repeats it, and she smiles. "My name is Alva Starr," she says. "Starr with two R's."

The scene explains why Natalie described her role as "the nearest I'll ever get to playing Blanche DuBois." Although it was discarded as too "downbeat," the movie ends on an equally downbeat but much less dramatic note and leaves the audience with a sense of anticlimax. After an abrupt cut to a shot of Alva's tombstone, her sister's offscreen voice starts to explain how she died, and we return to the prologue. Like many decisions imposed for commercial reasons, it harmed the movie commercially.

Maybe the director's cut will eventually appear on video, and we'll see just how close Natalie got to playing Blanche. But even without the scene, *This Property Is Condemned* contains one of her finest performances. (A New York friend, actor Ralph Roberts, wrote Natalie that Zoe Caldwell and her husband, Robert Whitehead, had always admired her, and their reaction after seeing the movie was that "you are the greatest.")

No doubt Natalie's personal tensions contributed to her creation of Alva, restless, sexually driven, brave and fragile. Blatnik had visited her several times during the New Orleans shoot, and they were still officially engaged, but only because she'd become a little frightened of him and didn't want to end the relationship while she was deeply involved in the movie. Instead, having developed a "fixation" on Pollack as director, she took it a stage further: "One day after shooting," Pollack remembered, "Redford and I went to Natalie's dressing room to discuss the next day's scene. After a while, Redford left. I started to make a point about the scene we'd been discussing when a pillow thrown by Natalie hit me in the face. 'I don't want to talk about the scene,' she said. 'I'm hung up on you.'" Pollack was extremely startled, and at first uncertain what to do. "Although the attraction was mutual, on my side it was unspoken. I was married, with a young son; and when I explained this, Natalie understood, and nothing developed."

This Property Is Condemned. *The dreamer and the man
who never dreams (Robert Redford)*

Early in November the unit moved to Paramount Studios, and
shortly after the Thanksgiving holiday Natalie told Blatnik that the
wedding was off. He seemed to take the news calmly, but she knew he
was very angry. A few nights later, Mart Crowley came by for a visit, and
they heard a sound outside her living-room window. They crouched
below the window and saw the figure of a man not far away, prowling
the lawn. When he came close, they recognized Blatnik and began to
laugh. When he came closer, they stopped laughing: he was carrying a
gun. But then he turned away and disappeared down the driveway, having presumably parked his car on the street.

Natalie was prepared for this kind of emergency. Paul and Micky Ziffren lived in Malibu, but Ziffren kept an apartment in Westwood for occasional use. He had given Natalie the keys in case of need, and later that night she fled there with Mart, and didn't return to North Bentley until she heard that Blatnik had left the country.

IN THE FIRST week of December, while *This Property* was still in production, Natalie went to a dinner party given by publicist Rupert Allan, and found herself seated next to the man who had first glimpsed her looking beautiful and lonely at Ray Stark's party. Richard Gregson was a successful British talent agent with offices in London and New York, and like RJ he was eight years older than Natalie.

"I think I was seated next to her because I was considered 'eligible,' " Gregson recalled. Personally he was engaging and assured, and professionally he was fashionable. British movies were still on the crest of a New Wave with *Tom Jones* and *Darling;* and Gregson and his partner, Gareth Wigan, had a list of clients that included Joseph Mankiewicz, Alan Bates, John Schlesinger and screenwriter Frederic Raphael.

"Natalie was smoking cigarettes through a black plastic holder that evening," Gregson also recalled, "and I told her jade would be more elegant." Later they were among several guests who went on to the popular showbiz club and disco, the Daisy. When they danced together, he felt "strongly attracted," and the current seemed to flow both ways. But when he phoned the next day, Natalie refused to take the call, and refused when he tried again.

Then, much to his surprise, she invited Gregson to a large party at her house on the following weekend, and "during the evening became very flirtatious." When he phoned the next day, Natalie not only took the call, but agreed to go out to dinner with him. "We dated on and off for a couple of weeks, the first time she was very guarded, but the night before I was due to go back to London, we went to bed together."

When Natalie met Blatnik, she was in search of an alternative life, and by this she meant not only a life "outside" Hollywood, but a commitment to marriage and having children. She was at a low point (only a few weeks after her attempted suicide) when Blatnik impressed her as a possibility. Then she began to mistrust him, and finally to see all the way through him. Gregson, whose tough-minded sense of direction was obviously a far cry from the near-burlesque version of an "international playboy-adventurer," became a far more serious possibility. But although Natalie clearly found him attractive, she hesitated about seeing him again after they first met. Then she changed her mind and agreed to date "on and off." On their first date, the current seemed to flow both ways again, but a part of her seemed to resist it, and she only went to bed with him on the night before she knew he was leaving town.

Why did she hold back? A likely minor reason: although Rupert Allan considered Gregson "eligible," he was in the middle of an expensive and protracted divorce. A definite major reason: Natalie suspected she was falling in love. And after her experience of marriage to RJ, followed by her affair with Warren, she still connected falling in love with fear of betrayal.

ON DECEMBER 22, 1965, a few days before Gregson's departure, *Inside Daisy Clover* opened for a week's run at Radio City Music Hall to qualify for Academy Awards. The critical reception, led by Bosley Crowther's dismissal of the movie as "fatuous and vulgar," was extraordinarily harsh. Most of the other dailies and weeklies were almost as negative, with only two notable exceptions, *Newsweek* and, more surprisingly, the *Hollywood Reporter,* whose reviewer described it as "one of the best movies about Hollywood ever made."

It was a painful jolt for all of us, and particularly for Natalie, whose exceptional performance went unrecognized. But ten years later, Ron Haver, who was in charge of the film department of the Los Angeles County Museum of Art, programmed a series of films "about Hollywood" and asked me to invite Natalie to the screening of *Daisy Clover.* "I don't know, what do you think?" she said. I thought we should accept, because Haver liked the movie and thought it was time for a reassessment.

So we went, and as Natalie evidently considered the Bing Theater a screening room, she didn't ask to sit in the back row. The audience reaction was enthusiastic, she received a standing ovation, and when we talked with various people afterward, it was clear that in spite of the damaging cuts, the movie had appealed to them in the way all of us had intended, as an ironic fable. Later it reached cult status on TV and video, but too late for Natalie to know about it.

*Tom Mankiewicz: Studio life from an early age had cut
Natalie off from so much, and she was eager to make up for it,
but I often had the impression that she never knew exactly
how to live her life.*

With Blatnik out of the picture, and Gregson on suspension in London,
Natalie made another try at an alternative life. She had first met Henry
Jaglom, a twenty-five-year-old actor from the Actors Studio, at a party in
July 1965, when he came out from New York on a visit. On March 10,
1966, when he'd come back in the hope of making a career in Holly-
wood, they met again at the Daisy.

Warren Beatty was also at the Daisy that evening, and although he
and Natalie nodded to each other, they didn't speak. But when she asked
Henry to drive her home, he saw them leave together; and a few minutes
after Natalie invited Henry to come in for a drink, the phone rang.
"Warren!" Natalie said immediately. She arranged for Henry to listen in,
and "I heard Warren warn her against me. 'I'm concerned for you,' he
said."

Why? "I don't remember exactly, but I remember a lot of people,
including Frank Sinatra and Roz Russell, considered me somehow 'dangerous.' Russell actually warned Natalie that I was a 'dope-smoking
rebel.' That was the kind of reputation you could get for being unemployed, politically outspoken and smoking a moderate amount of pot."
But although Henry was unemployed, he came from a well-to-do
Russian-Jewish family, bankers and landowners wealthy enough not to
have suffered from anti-Semitism, and well enough known for Natalie
to recognize the name. "The Russian connection was important to
Natalie," he remembered, and the prelude to "a very emotional night."

At the time, as he told her that night, Henry was already involved
with a girl in New York. Although "Natalie accepted the situation," he
described her in his diary next day as "a very neurotic girl," and believed
he understood why: "She told me that ever since she was a seven-year-
old actor in *Tomorrow Is Forever,* she'd been begging for love. She was
constantly asked to cry, praised and admired when she did, realized that
if she could cry authentically, everyone adored her, and she soon established a connection between love and pain." Almost certainly Dr. Lindon had first pointed this out; but after four years of analysis, Natalie
was still unable to break the connection. And Henry, privileged rebel,

antiestablishment and anti–Vietnam War, moderate pot smoker, equally intelligent and accomplished as lover and self-lover, was not really able to help.

Jaglom found Natalie "false" when she became "Natalie Wood movie star" in public or at parties, playing what she called "the Hollywood game." But he apparently failed to understand that she'd been trained to play it, like most Hollywood stars, and *knew* she was being false. When she was depressed, a social occasion could intensify her depression, and she became the Natalie Wood that Richard Gregson saw for the first time. When she was happy, it amused her to "put on the badge," as she called it, and play glamorous movie star. She also found "the badge" useful to avoid waiting in line for a movie, but Henry recalled that she always insisted on sitting in the back row, because she "didn't want to be recognized." He never knew that the movie star was still haunted by Jack the Jabber, and that the Natalie remembered by Dennis Hopper was still walking a tightrope between vulnerability and "being in control."

Henry himself never felt the need to play "the Hollywood game" because he never sought mainstream acceptance. When he became an independent writer-director in the mid-1970s, he was able to function very successfully long before "independence" became a movement (apart from his friend Orson Welles's one-man movement) because of his access to private finance and his business skills in marketing his movies.

For a while Henry was amused by the parties that he attended as Natalie's escort, although an evening at the Daisy reinforced his doubts about "becoming part of her world." Judy Garland and Mia Farrow joined their table, "Mia in a desperate period, either about to marry Sinatra or having just married him, Garland more desperate than ever." Together they unnerved Natalie, who signaled that she wanted to leave. Driving back to North Bentley, Henry predicted that Garland would kill herself very soon, and Natalie confessed that she'd once attempted suicide, but refused to say why.

On April 2, Henry left for New York and a reunion with his girl-friend. Although Natalie was "in tears" when he left, Richard Gregson arrived in Los Angeles a few days later, and when he called her, she proposed spending Easter weekend together in Palm Springs: "She couldn't find a house available for rent, and rang Sinatra, who found us a house near his compound there, and sent his private plane. We visited the compound, where several Mafia honchos were staying, including Sam Giancana. He palmed Natalie a pair of ruby and emerald earrings, which she later gave back to Sinatra."

By then it seemed to Gregson that he and Natalie were equally "serious" about each other; and as he had to go back to London in a few days, he asked her to join him there. She declined because she was due to start work on a movie in a month's time, but it wasn't her only reason. Natalie was certainly "serious" about Gregson, but still uncertain about the kind of life she wanted to lead, and not ready to make a final commitment. Instead, she played for time by resuming the affair with Henry Jaglom; and Gregson, who was under the impression it had ended, became what he called "a long distance affair" for a while.

WHEN HARVARD UNIVERSITY'S *Harvard Lampoon* notified Natalie that they had voted her the "Worst Actress of Last Year, This Year and Next," they invited her to receive the award in person on April 23. She became the first actor to accept, because it appealed to her sense of humor; and TV coverage of the occasion records her charmingly tongue-in-cheek acceptance speech to a large undergraduate crowd.

The presenter begins by asking Natalie if she realizes that the *Lampoon*'s is really "a lifetime award." "Oh yes," she replies with a deceptively innocent smile. Then why did she come? "Well," she explains, clearly enjoying herself, "I thought you should accept any award that's ever given you. They invited me and I thought it was only polite to accept." She looks very demure and bats her eyelids. "It's funny, last year I was nominated by the Academy for Best Actress, and this year I'm the worst." Then she bursts out laughing. The crowd laughs and applauds, a group of undergraduates hoist her on their shoulders and parade her around the campus. The look of triumph on Natalie's face reflects not only her sense of fun, but the confidence in herself as an actress that she's acquired by now.

Her success provoked a spokesman for the *Lampoon*, who evidently lacked a sense of fun. "It definitely wasn't meant as an honor," he insisted. "They wanted her to know that she wasn't the best actress around." But when Natalie appeared on *What's My Line?* in New York next day, one of the regular panelists, Bennett Cerf, congratulated her on walking off with the game.

To avoid complications with Henry's girlfriend, Natalie didn't contact him in New York and flew back to Los Angeles after the TV show. He returned to Los Angeles two weeks later, resumed their affair and noted in his diary: "I can't feel totally real with her—ultimately this will keep us apart." But Natalie, of course, couldn't feel "totally real" with Henry, and he soon found that "the very instability of our relationship attracts me." It also attracted Natalie, still weighing the possibility of committing herself to Richard Gregson.

On May 16 she left for New York, where her next movie was about to start shooting on location, and to avoid complications with his girlfriend, Henry didn't go with her. When he first read the script of *Penelope,* a feeble comedy about the neglected wife of a successful banker (played by Ian Bannen), who disguises herself as an old lady to rob her husband's bank, Henry advised her to turn it down. Then he realized "she wanted to do it for Arthur Loew," who had unwisely decided to produce the movie for MGM, and signed the unexceptional Arthur Hiller to direct. Although Henry respected Natalie's loyalty to a former lover, he thought it a mistake to make a mediocre picture "just when her career as an actress was at its peak."

"Natalie visited my parents in New York," Henry recalled, "and my father was very elegant and courteous, with an aristocratic manner. She fell hard for it." She also admired his collection of paintings—German expressionists, a Cézanne, and particularly a Bonnard. "She seems to have found a home," his mother commented later to Henry; and when Natalie returned to Los Angeles, she told him: "My life would have been very different if I'd had parents like yours."

He found her "analyst needing" after ten days away from Dr. Lindon, and alternating between "extreme connection and noncommunication. Unpredictable, yet maintaining appearance of normalcy." They discussed a mutual desire to have children (but not by each other), and "she became very emotional about this, terrified she'd be like her mother."

In the second week of June, while *Penelope* was filming at MGM, Warren Beatty came to North Bentley to offer Natalie the role of Bonnie in *Bonnie and Clyde,* which he was also producing. But she didn't want to be separated from Dr. Lindon again, this time for a much longer location shoot; and although she liked the script, she felt (rightly, and perhaps with a backward glance at the early scenes of *All the Fine Young*

*Cannibals*) that she would not be convincing as a girl from the Texas backwoods.

By this time she was totally relaxed with Warren, even on a more charged occasion when Henry escorted her to a performance by the Bolshoi Ballet. Warren was there with prima ballerina Maya Plisetskaya, successor to Leslie Caron, and suggested that the four of them drive to the Daisy afterward: "Warren sat in front with Plisetskaya, and they were very lovey. But she spoke no English, and Warren asked Natalie to translate his remarks to her in Russian. Everything he wanted her to translate was a declaration of love. 'Tell her how you say, "I love you more than life itself,"' and so on. Natalie calmly agreed, and Warren clearly found the whole situation exciting."

On June 23, Natalie called Henry from the set of *Penelope* and asked him to meet her in two hours at the Beverly Hills Hotel, then escort her to the premiere of *Who's Afraid of Virginia Woolf?*—tuxedo required, she added. When Henry arrived at the hotel in a borrowed tuxedo and bow tie, he found that Sol Hurok was hosting a party for the Bolshoi Ballet. Natalie was already there, still wearing screen makeup, and as the only Russian-speaking guest, "surrounded by the Bolshoi dancers, who had a great rapport with her and didn't want her to leave."

On their way by cab to the Pantages Theater, Natalie removed her screen makeup and replaced it with her public movie-star face. When they arrived, hundreds of fans were waiting outside the theater. "Natalie Wood! Natalie Wood!" they screamed, and she gave them her beguiling public smile. The episode confirmed Henry's dislike of "the movie-star world," and he told Natalie afterward that he "couldn't take it when you put on the movie-star badge." But it's impossible not to suspect that he'd grown restless at being upstaged, especially as he suggested, only a few days later, that they continue their affair but refrain from going out in public together.

If he'd been aware of the situation with Richard Gregson, Henry would surely have realized that his attitude was tilting the scales in favor of London. And although Natalie agreed to keep their affair private, he invited her out to the Actors Studio West a week later to hear Lee Strasberg make a speech. When Strasberg remarked, "Talent is the most killable thing in the world," Henry saw that Natalie was very moved. "She repeated it with tears in her eyes, but then Strasberg continued to speak for a very long—too long—time, and she got bored." Later, at yet another party for the Bolshoi Ballet, he became irritated that nothing else in Strasberg's speech had made any impression on Natalie; and as they drove back to North Bentley in silence, he sensed that he'd alienated her. She didn't invite him to come in, "and although it was goodnight but not goodbye, I knew it was the beginning of the end."

A FEW DAYS LATER, Richard Gregson arrived in Los Angeles for a brief visit to Natalie. Unintentionally well timed, it marked the end of the beginning of their affair, and she agreed to join him in London in September.

Before he left, Richard attended the June 30 Los Angeles premiere of *This Property Is Condemned* with Natalie. It opened simultaneously in New York, and in both cities the reviews were mostly tepid. But although the movie had flaws, it was not negligible, and as underrated as her performance. Three weeks later, a screening of the first cut of *Penelope* proved so disappointing that she turned on Henry Jaglom. "You could have stopped me," she said, forgetting that he'd advised her not to make the picture. "You *should* have stopped me!"

And in almost the last entry about Natalie in his diary, Henry noted: "She seeks help, but runs away from it."

WHEN NATALIE ARRIVED in London toward the end of September, she had booked a suite at the Carlton Towers hotel. "She didn't want to stay at my house in Pimlico because my divorce wasn't yet finalized," Richard Gregson recalled, "and she was worried about the press." (Especially the British tabloids, which Natalie had heard were even more ruthless than the home product.) But then she changed her mind and stayed with Richard, met his son Hugo and daughters Sarah and Charlotte, and made a new friend in Delphine Mann, who was married to one of Gregson's clients, screenwriter Stanley Mann.

"Natalie arrived with masses of luggage," according to Richard, "as if she'd packed every piece she owned." And when they decided to go to Paris for a few days, she asked Delphine for advice on what to pack. Delphine was astonished at first, then "realized that there'd always been someone to pack for her. But she followed my directions and, typically, she soon became a very good packer."

Anxious to get back to Dr. Lindon, whom she'd called frequently during her stay, Natalie left for Los Angeles in early November. On December 9, *Penelope* opened nationwide in the United States, a sure sign that MGM executives, like Natalie, feared the worst. They were right, but her third commercial failure in two years harmed her career much less than she'd feared. In Hollywood-speak, the star of *Gypsy* and *West Side Story* was still "huge," and as Natalie had seen the first cut of *Penelope,* the shock of unanimously dismissive reviews was cushioned.

WHEN NATALIE CALLED Olga to confide her feelings about Richard, she said that she wanted to become a wife and mother, and that she loved him (in that order). It made Olga suspect that "she wasn't in love with him as deeply as she'd been with RJ," and that she still needed time to think the situation over. Independently, Richard had suspected that Natalie would never agree to settle down with him in London, and as their affair threatened to become long distance again, he arrived in Los Angeles in mid-December and "one crucial evening" they went to a party: "Nicky Hilton was among the guests. We'd all had quite a few drinks, he made a huge pass at Natalie in front of me and his girlfriend, and on Natalie's side it became a case of fatal attraction springing up all over again. In the early morning I reluctantly agreed when she wanted us to go back to Nicky's house. I took a pee there, then came back to the living room and found Natalie and Nicky necking and dancing. I was outraged and insisted on taking her home. We had a huge row, Natalie became very wound up, full of guilt, and appalled at the way she'd behaved. Then she said she wanted to kill herself and grabbed a bottle of pills."

She had swallowed a couple before Richard was able to stop her. He immediately called Dr. Lindon, and around three-fifteen a.m. they drove to his office, where her analyst talked to both of them for an hour, then to Natalie alone. As they left, she told Richard that "she couldn't figure it out, but was overcome with deep pain." And he realized "the extent of Natalie's dark side, how deeply she'd been wounded by life. She was charming, generous, beautiful—and haunted."

Within a few days Natalie seemed "back to normal," and when Richard returned to London toward the end of February 1967, she joined him a week later at his house in Pimlico. This time she stayed longer. In the spring they took a trip to the Scottish border country to visit Richard's father, "a retired army officer who drank too much when he got overexcited." Natalie's impending arrival had overexcited him, he alerted the tabloid *Daily Express,* and a group of reporters and photographers were soon knocking on the door of his house. After they left, he apologized to Natalie, "lying in bed, his false teeth in a glass on the bedside table. Although understandably nervous, she handled the situation with great tact."

By this time Natalie also felt secure enough about her career to reject several movie offers, among them *Diary of a Mad Housewife,* and to wait for a project that she genuinely liked; and until late August she continued to live with Richard without finding one. Five months was the longest time Natalie had ever spent away from her analyst, although she continued to call him frequently; and when she decided to return to Los Angeles, it seemed clear to Richard that she would never agree to settle in London. But as it was also clear that their feelings for each other had deepened, he decided to stay behind, sell his agency, then remake his career in Hollywood.

Toward the end of 1967, the Grade Organization bought the agency. Six weeks later EMI, a larger conglomerate, acquired Grade and agreed to back Richard and his partner, Gareth Wigan, in a new agency with headquarters in Los Angeles. London International opened in January 1968, when Richard was living with Natalie on North Bentley. "She was totally supportive," he recalled, and "at first everything was fine."

NINETEEN SIXTY-EIGHT was election year in the United States, and Natalie had never been interested in politics until Micky Ziffren, an active Democrat, took her to hear a speech by presidential candidate Eugene McCarthy. "He got to her," Ziffren recalled, "and that was it. Later I changed my mind and supported Robert Kennedy, but when I tried to persuade Natalie to change her mind and do likewise, she stuck with McCarthy—typical of the way, once her mind was made up, she never faltered."

While celebrating his victory in the presidential primary on June 5, Robert Kennedy was assassinated. Two months later, the Democratic Party nominated Hubert Humphrey as its presidential candidate. Admirable but not very dynamic, he lost to the far less admirable but more dynamic Richard Nixon. It was a close contest that reflected a deep split in the national mood; and the split was reflected in Hollywood, where two friends of Natalie reacted by moving respectively right and left.

Although liberal Sinatra had been furious when Robert Kennedy, as attorney general, investigated the mob, he supported Humphrey against Nixon; but when Nixon won, ruthless Sinatra decided to court power. He became friendly with Vice President Spiro Agnew and, a year later, campaigned for Ronald Reagan's re-election as governor of California. But Warren Beatty campaigned for George McGovern in the 1972 Democratic primary, went to San Francisco (accompanied by Julie Christie) and addressed two large crowds on the need for gun control. Both times, unfortunately, the crowds had assembled for sporting events and grew impatient. Undaunted, Warren supported McGovern when he ran for president, then lost to Nixon.

Unlike Warren and Sinatra, Natalie never publicly supported a presidential candidate again, but remained (and voted) Democratic.


TWO WEEKS after Robert Kennedy was shot, EMI acquired Associated British–Pathe, a major production/distribution complex; and as American anti-trust laws had made it illegal for production companies to acquire agency holdings, the Hollywood labor unions gave London International sixty days to go out of business.

When Richard went to London to finalize the dismantling of the agency, Natalie accompanied him. Her contract with William Morris had expired at the end of May, and as she'd never forgotten or forgiven Joe Schoenfeld's behavior to Guy McElwaine over their attempt to form a company, she moved to the Freddie Fields Agency. Fields was in London when Natalie arrived, and a few days later received a call from one of his clients in Los Angeles. Paul Mazursky had written a script, in collaboration with Larry Tucker, that Fields had sold to Columbia; and he called with the news that Mike Frankovich, the studio's head of production, had agreed to let Mazursky direct. But there was one condition: Natalie Wood in the leading female role.

In spite of his doubts ("She's gorgeous, she's sexy, but will she do it, and if she does it, can she handle satire?") Mazursky asked Fields to give Natalie a copy of *Bob & Carol & Ted & Alice*. One of his doubts was quickly resolved. "She'll do it, she'll play Carol," Fields reported. "It's the first script to excite her in two years." Then he told Mazursky (this is the kind of situation that powerful agents love) to catch the next plane to London.

The three of them met for lunch at Claridge's. "I liked the fact that she was punctual, and of course that she loved the script," Mazursky recalled. "And when the two of us took a walk together in Hyde Park after lunch, I fell in love with her, the way we all did."

He told Natalie that *Bob & Carol & Ted & Alice* would be his first feature movie as director, but he'd worked in the theater, taught acting; and that Charles Lang, whom Natalie knew and admired from *Inside Daisy Clover,* had been engaged as cinematographer. She seemed "enthusiastic about everything," talked of her love for Richard Gregson and their plan to marry as soon as his divorce became final, then mentioned that she'd met Robert Wagner a few times since their divorce and still considered him "a wonderful friend." This was Natalie's way, Mazursky realized, "of establishing a genuine relationship with her director when she agreed to do a movie."

The modest budget for *Bob & Carol* made it impossible to offer Natalie her current salary of $750,000, but she accepted the deal proposed by Fields, "$50,000 up front and 15 points in the picture," according to Mazursky. "And as a result she made an enormous amount of money"—reportedly, around $3 million.

As *Bob & Carol* was due to start two weeks of rehearsal on October 15, and Richard was still involved with the dismantling of London International, Natalie returned to Los Angeles alone. In London with Richard, she had frequently called Dr. Lindon, and in Los Angeles without him, she called Richard as frequently as she saw her analyst. Her experience with analysis was one reason why she appreciated the humor of the script, whose original idea had occurred to Mazursky after reading an article in *Time* magazine, "The New Therapy," illustrated with a photograph of art dealer Fritz Perls in a hot tub at Esalen with six nude girls: "I went up to Esalen for a marathon weekend with my wife, Betsy, and our experience became the first scene in the movie. A group of us, all couples, began explaining what we felt about our relationships, and after four hours Betsy became upset. She complained that I 'didn't let her breathe,' and some of the others attacked me."

For the first week of the shoot, Mazursky remembered, "Natalie seemed nervous. She was working with a first-time director, and with three actors playing leading roles in a movie for the first time—Elliott Gould, TV star Robert Culp and Dyan Cannon." He also suspected that after the failure of *Penelope,* Natalie had doubts about her talent for comedy. "Then she relaxed, and was great, and we all knew it was going to work."

The only major problem erupted late in the shoot. The New Permissiveness was a by-product of the New Therapy, and the movie's climactic scene occurs in a Las Vegas hotel suite, where the two couples (Natalie and Culp, Cannon and Gould) decide to swap mates. Mazursky had planned to open the scene with a four-shot: in foreground, Natalie and Gould seated at the bar counter and "clearly doubtful about the 'orgy,' " and in the background, Cannon suddenly starting to strip and Culp to unzip his pants. Natalie objected that she didn't want to play her scene with Gould while the other two prepared for action in the same shot. "I explained that the humor of the scene depended on the visual contrast between one couple saying no in the foreground while the other couple are saying yes in the background. But Natalie was adamant. 'I won't do it this way,' she said, 'and I won't finish the picture unless I can do it my way.' Then she retired to her trailer."

When Mazursky informed Frankovich and Larry Tucker of the problem, they came over to the set and pleaded with Natalie, but she refused to budge. By then it was time for the lunch break, and she agreed to take a walk with Mazursky. On the spur of the moment, he found himself telling her "the story of my life," his Brooklyn background and determination to break into the theater. "I guess I was really trying to explain how I always followed my instincts, and if you ignore them you're lost." As usual, Natalie's radar was quick to pick up signals. She looked thoughtful for a moment, then said, "Okay!" They embraced, and when he shot the "orgy" scene, with the four of them in a king-size bed, "she had no problem at all."

THE DISSOLUTION of London International had left Richard Gregson with no American income when he returned to North Bentley while Natalie was filming *Bob & Carol.* And as British currency restrictions were still in force, he could transfer only a few hundred dollars to the United States. He had planned to become a producer in Hollywood, but his reputation as a tough, aggressive agent meant that he was greeted

*The marriage between Bob (Robert Culp) and*
*Carol (Natalie) starts to unravel during group therapy*
*in* Bob & Carol & Ted & Alice.

with a series of cold shoulders. Then Robert Redford, who had formed
his own company to make *Downhill Racer,* about a fanatically competitive professional skier, offered Richard the job of producer.

On January 20, 1969, the movie began shooting in Kitzbühel, Austria, and Mart Crowley described Natalie's situation there as " 'the producer's wife,' although they weren't married yet." Crowley had moved to
New York shortly before *The Boys in the Band* began its successful off-
Broadway run a year earlier, and he arrived in London for its opening
night there on February 11. Natalie flew in to join him, they had dinner
afterward with Billy and Audrey Wilder, and she gave Mart the impression that "although she enjoyed her 'role' on location at first, she was
growing restless."

At the end of March, after *Downhill Racer* completed shooting,
Richard was at last legally divorced: "And over drinks in the bar of the
hotel, she suddenly said, 'I've got to talk to you. I think it's time we got

married.' I asked her, 'What made you suddenly make up your mind?' And she told me, 'Because I think it'll work.' I said, 'Okay. When do you want the wedding to be?' And she said, 'As soon as possible. Can I go and arrange it?' And I said, 'Sure.' "

Natalie's first call was to Norma Crane, whom she wanted for her matron of honor, and her second to Paul Ziffren, who offered his Malibu beach house for the wedding. But she had decided on a traditional Russian ceremony, and asked Olga for details of her own Russian wedding in San Francisco.

Fifteen years before Ermolova, the Gurdins and the Lepkos arrived in Hollywood, several thousand White Russian refugees (including Rasputin's daughter Matryona) had settled in the Silverlake area of Los Angeles. Like the San Francisco immigrants, these tsarist army officers, nominal aristocrats, artists, engineers and other professionals formed their own clubs and created a demand for Russian restaurants: Boublichki, the Moscow Inn, the Two-Headed Eagle. But by 1969 all traces of the original colony had vanished, apart from the Holy Virgin Mary Russian Orthodox Church, built in 1928, an ornate and nostalgically detailed replica of a cathedral in the motherland.

Looking as beautiful and happy as I'd ever seen her, the bride walked down the aisle of the church in a wedding gown she'd designed with the help of Edith Head. It was also a replica, based on an illustration of a dress at the court of Catherine the Great that Natalie had found in a book on Russian costumes. In the same book she found an illustration of a Russian wedding, where the bride decorated her long hair with blades of wheat, the Russian symbol of fertility. Natalie copied this as well, and also gathered a strong Russian contingent for the ceremony: Maria and Nick Gurdin, Olga and Lana as bridesmaids, the Viripaeff family and Nick's brothers, Vladimir and Dmitri.

The two sides of Natalie's life, Russia and the movies, were united on May 30, 1969, along with the bride and groom. Robert Redford and Gareth Wigan shared the honors of best man; the guests included two more movie stars, Warren Beatty and Julie Christie; and I was among the group of Natalie's Los Angeles friends that included Mart Crowley, Edith Head, Howard Jeffrey, Hope Lange, Tom Mankiewicz, Roddy McDowall and Guy McElwaine.

*Just married: Natalie and Richard Gregson,*
*May 30, 1969*

"NINETEEN SIXTY-NINE, from our time in Kitzbühel to New Year's Eve in Paris," Gregson recalled later, "was our happiest together." Natalie wanted to rent a boat in the Caribbean for their honeymoon, was recommended a company that provided a boat with a German captain, and they sailed to a privately owned island. "Disaster!" Gregson recalled. "No provisions, nothing. A couple supposed to be working for us who behaved more like guests. After three days, when we wanted out, the couple demanded full payment and things got hostile. It made Natalie very nervous. 'How do we know they won't come for us in the middle of the night?' she said, and burst into semihysterical laughter. Then she called Claudette [Colbert] at her house in Barbados. We had a great week there, then went back to L.A."

Almost immediately they went on publicity jaunts for *Bob & Carol*
and *Downhill Racer* in Los Angeles, New York and Paris. Natalie had
recently read *I Never Promised You a Rose Garden,* Joanne Greenberg's
autobiographical novel about a young girl under treatment for schizo-
phrenia in a mental hospital, and it became the first project to excite
her since *Bob & Carol.* In Paris she met with Simone Signoret, who
agreed to play the girl's psychiatrist, and Natalie planned to ask Guy
McElwaine for help in setting up the movie when she returned to Los
Angeles.

Meanwhile, on New Year's Eve, the Gregsons attended a party given
by the oil sheik Adnan Khashoggi, with a guest list of fifty that included
"at least a dozen oil-sheik colleagues and Joan Collins." In the early
hours of 1970 they went back to L'Hôtel, where "Natasha was conceived."

Seven weeks later, Natalie was "thrilled" to discover she was pregnant: "rich and pregnant," as Richard described her after *Bob & Carol*
became a popular success. But impending motherhood put all thoughts
of a movie career, even of *I Never Promised You a Rose Garden,* on hold.

At the same time *Downhill Racer* barely made a profit and failed to
advance Richard's prospects as a producer in Hollywood. "Guy McElwaine tried to help me out by organizing an executive position at
MGM, then another at Fox," he recalled, "but they weren't real jobs,
Natalie was against them, so I turned them down." And with a career as
blocked as his British bank account, "my situation became very difficult,
I began to feel very low and frustrated, and inevitably it affected my relationship with Natalie."

# 6

# First and Last Things

*There's nothing quite like finding out for the very first time that you're pregnant. There's nothing ever quite as miraculous as that.*

—NATALIE WOOD

*Although Natalie took time off to be a mother and devote herself to her family, I would watch her when we sometimes went to the movies together. It was like watching a racehorse seeing another racehorse get to the gate first.*

—TOM MANKIEWICZ

*Dearest, Here's to smooth sailing for us from now on! I love you with all my heart and it belongs to only you.*

—NATALIE WOOD,
EASTER GREETING TO ROBERT WAGNER, 1975

*I didn't go to the mortuary when they were preparing Natalie's body, or when they finished. I knew if I saw her dead, I couldn't take it.*

—ROBERT WAGNER

D URING THE LAST WEEK of June 1970, John and Linda Fore-man, friends of Natalie and RJ's during their first marriage and of each of them separately after the divorce, gave a Saturday-night party for about fifteen guests. When Linda called to invite the Gregsons, she told Natalie that RJ and Marion Wagner would also be coming. "I had no ulterior motive," Linda insisted. "We were friends of both couples, and they didn't object."

The day before the party, Marion called Linda from the house that

RJ had bought in Palm Springs to say that she wasn't feeling well and RJ would be coming alone. And on the night of the party Natalie arrived alone. She explained that Richard had left for New York with his partner, Gareth Wigan, to discuss an offer to form a production company with Wall Street capital.

Natalie, who was six months pregnant, went to sit in an armchair. A few minutes later, RJ arrived. "The moment he saw her, he went over and sat at a stool at her feet," Linda remembered. "As it was the kind of party where everybody could sit where they wanted, and talk to whomever they wanted, those two were never apart the whole evening." RJ couldn't recall in detail what they talked about, except that it was "like a replay of all our previous chance meetings, lasted much longer, and was far more intense." He'd heard rumors of "problems" in Natalie's marriage, his own marriage ties had started to loosen, "and we found ourselves sharing memories of all our good times together."

It was a rainy night, Natalie had arrived by cab, and John Foreman offered to drive her home when the party broke up. Then RJ said, "Why don't I drive you?," and she accepted. Once again he couldn't recall specifically what they talked about, no doubt because once again the subtext was more important than anything they said. But by the time he pulled up outside the house on North Bentley, they were both at "emotional high tide."

"I guess I shouldn't come in," he said, and after a moment Natalie said, "I guess you shouldn't." Then they said goodnight, and after driving half a block down the street, RJ stopped the car and began to sob.

In her living room, Natalie told Linda soon afterward, she "burst into wild sobs and wondered how she could ever have been so stupid." She was still crying when Sophie Irvin (wife of TV and movie director John Irvin, a friend of Gregson's), who was staying with Natalie at the time, came into the room. "What's wrong?" Sophie asked. "I've fallen in love," Natalie said.

Next day a bouquet of roses from RJ was delivered to the house. Natalie sent him a brief note of thanks, and there was no further contact between them for over a year. On September 29, Natalie gave birth to her first daughter, Natasha; and the memory of her latest encounter with RJ, as well as her anxieties about Richard's future, receded for a while. "The first experience of motherhood," Leslie Caron recalled, "made it seem the most important thing in Natalie's life," and David Lange joked that "she adopted a Madonna-and-Child hairstyle, parted in the middle and drawn back chastely behind her ears, that made Natasha seem the result of an Immaculate Conception."

By the end of 1970 the deal for Richard's production company in partnership with Gareth Wigan had fallen through, leaving him with "nothing to show for three years of work and only two hundred dollars in the bank." Natalie, he remembered, was "supportive but helpless— not working and completely into motherhood."

In February 1971, Richard read *The Headshrinker's Test,* a novel that he thought had strong possibilities as a movie with a good role for Natalie. She helped him secure an option, and with her name attached, "both Warners and the Richard Zanuck–David Brown company at Fox expressed interest." At Natalie's suggestion, he sent a copy of the novel to Robert Moore, who had directed *The Boys in the Band* and was currently working in television in New York. Moore also expressed interest, and agreed to come out to Los Angeles in July to meet with Richard and Natalie.

Meanwhile Richard's son and two daughters came over from England, and as there wasn't enough room for all of them at North Bentley, they spent the month of June in a house at Lake Tahoe that Natalie had bought a few years earlier. Sarah, who was eleven years old at the time, became especially close to Natalie and remembered her as "very into being a wife and mother. The rest of us went snowmobiling, but not with Natalie. After Natasha was born, she didn't come out to play."

A new housekeeper had succeeded Mac, whom Richard remembered as "a holy terror. Natalie fired her after a God-almighty row, mainly to do with drink—Mac liked a drink, as they say—and a little misuse of housekeeping money." Natalie also had a new secretary, twenty-two-year-old Ann Watson, "with long dark hair, and a round face with a John Lennon look," according to Sarah. "My father used to call her Mo, and one day I saw him put his arms around her. I told him it wasn't right, and he had to stop it."

Natalie seemed unaware of what was happening, but Guy McElwaine believes "she'd begun to suspect the situation" after Richard's children went back to England at the end of June and the Gregsons returned to North Bentley. "I was at the pool one day with a few other guests," he recalled. "We were all in swimsuits. Ann came out of the house in a mumu and Natalie said, 'You're one of the family, why don't you change into a swimsuit?' The girl said she didn't have one, Natalie told her to wear one of hers, Ann went back to the house, then returned still wearing a mumu—none of Natalie's suits fitted her, she said. Natalie insisted she take the mumu off, and although Ann was fairly ordinary-looking, in her underwear you could see she had a great body." Although Natalie was "friendly and charming on the surface," McElwaine sensed an undercurrent of tension in the way she insisted that her secretary undress.

Three weeks later, another poolside scene proved him right. By that time Bob Moore had arrived from New York with his lover and assistant, George Rondo. "The four of us became very good friends," Rondo recalled. "We made a couple of trips to scout locations in San Francisco, where *The Headshrinker's Test* was set." On the last Sunday in July, Moore and Rondo arrived for a barbecue around the pool, "and after greeting us, Richard said he had work to do until lunchtime and went back to the house." While Moore lay in the sun, Natalie went into the pool, holding ten-month-old Natasha in her arms, and Rondo joined her. Then the poolside extension phone rang. Natalie handed Natasha to Rondo, picked up the receiver and listened for a moment. Then she said very matter-of-factly, "I'll take this inside," buzzed Richard on the house phone and hurried to the house without a word to Rondo or Moore.

"I want you to know your husband is screwing my girlfriend." This, Natalie told Sophie Irvin later, was the first thing the caller had said. And this, according to Gregson, is what happened in the house: "Ann's ex-boyfriend, who was very jealous, had started to blow the whole situation on the poolside phone, and everything came out on the phone in the house when Natalie arrived. She reacted with a kind of anger I'd never seen before, and immediately called the police. They arrived within half an hour and gave me an hour to pack up my stuff and get out of the house."

"I'm sorry, the barbecue's off, please go home," Natalie told Moore and Rondo. Then, after calling Ann Watson and firing her, she ordered twenty-four-hour security guards for the house, gave them instructions not to admit Richard if he attempted to return, and sent for a locksmith to come over at once and change all the exterior locks.

Actress Elizabeth Ashley, a friendly acquaintance of Natalie's, admired her "for having the courage and strength to make the kind of decision right away that it took me far too long to make." (At the time Ashley was having her own marital problems with George Peppard, who coincidentally had been writing drunken love letters to Natalie.) Leslie Caron found Natalie's reaction to infidelity "rather extreme at first. Then she explained that because of Richard's financial problems, it had become her responsibility to support the family, and she'd begun to suspect that Richard wanted her to work to pay for everything." But here Natalie's antennae picked up a false signal. Always alert to the possibility of betrayal, she was remembering the way her family had exploited her financially and imagined Richard was doing the same thing.

But when David Lange and his (then) wife, Gillian, invited Richard to stay at their house for a few days after the breakup, Natalie's reaction was truly extreme. It led, David remembered, "to a major falling-out, and we hardly ever saw each other again." Perhaps she never forgave David because they'd been lovers. Although she accused Tom Mankiewicz of "betrayal" because he went out to lunch with Richard, she soon backed down. "I understand how you feel," Mankiewicz said, "but I can't live my life according to whom I'm supposed or not supposed to see." Natalie thought it over, saw the point and apologized. And when she told Guy McElwaine, "I know you've been working for Richard, but now you either work for him or for me," he remembered, "I told her to stop it, and she did."

Although Richard complained to Mart Crowley and Delphine Mann, among others, that he felt neglected on account of Natalie's "obsession" with Natasha, Mankiewicz believed there was another reason for the affair with Natalie's secretary. "She was quite attractive, but it wasn't like Richard was betraying Natalie with Elizabeth Taylor. So maybe it was also a form of revenge because he felt overshadowed by her stardom." In retrospect, Gregson felt this might be true, although he was unconscious of it at the time. It was only later that he realized "the dichotomy in Natalie. Sometimes, when we were married, she wanted to be another person—the producer's wife—but couldn't. In the end she was always a star."

Although the dichotomy certainly existed, many women with successful careers have felt it. There's a nub of truth in that enduring cliché "Her career came between us," and if Richard's "fling," as he called it, was partly a form of revenge, it was also an equally unconscious form of self-destruction. When Natalie agreed to star in *The Headshrinker's Test,* it was his last chance for a career as a Hollywood producer.

A very different side of Natalie, tender and generous, appears in a letter dated August 9, 1971, that she wrote jointly to Sarah and Charlotte Gregson:

> The only important thing I want you both to know is that I love you both and Hugo very much, and the failure of Daddy and myself together doesn't in any way change my loving feelings towards you. Knowing you and being your "stepmother" and friend has been very important to me. And maybe when you are grown-ups you will be able to be more loving and compassionate toward the people you love than Daddy and I are able to be at this time. You are very young to be asked to forgive us for bringing unhappiness to you out of our own unhappiness and so I will not ask you to forgive us. Just know that I do love you. If you feel like it please let me know how you feel. And if you're mad at me or at us tell me that too.

Sarah's "very sweet letter" in reply touched Natalie deeply. "In my heart I will always feel and be your loving stepmother," Natalie wrote back, "and I feel quite sure that you and I will see each other again." They did, more than once, and although a residue of tension subsisted whenever Natalie met Richard again, they had a "friendly" discussion not long after the breakup: "I said that I felt a professional failure, no money, no future in Los Angeles. She suggested I go back to England, and when I finally decided to start a production company there, Natalie offered to put money in it."

At the same time, according to Richard, the new maternal side of Natalie "made life very difficult for me, because she wouldn't allow me to see Natasha." Toward the end of August, in fact, she took their daughter to Europe, sailing from New York on the Italian liner *Michelangelo* with Olga and Mart Crowley as her guests.

By then life had also become very difficult for Natalie. Soon after changing the locks on her house, she returned from a visit to Norma Crane, realized she'd forgotten to take her new keys, and cut her wrist when she had to break a window to get in. On the boat, Olga remembered, she seemed "devastated" by the collapse of her marriage, but also

*Mother and child, Natasha Gregson Wagner,*
*age 5 months*

"very touched that RJ had called before she left to say how much he felt for her, and she was thinking about him a lot."

Natalie had planned to stay at the Hôtel du Cap in Antibes, and as David Niven owned a house on the Riviera, she asked him to book rooms there. When he cabled during the crossing that the hotel was full, she decided to stay at Cala di Volpe, the Aga Khan's recently opened hotel in Sardinia. They disembarked at Naples, took a train to Rome, then a plane to the island. To Natasha, one year old at the time, Cala di Volpe "felt like being in a dark house," and her mother, who had lost weight, seemed "very fragile." After a week, Natalie told Mart Crowley that she found the hotel too remote and isolated, and decided to return to Los Angeles by way of Rome.

AT THE END of September, Natalie and Richard's lawyers finalized their property settlement, whereby "each of said parties hereby waives any and all rights to the estate of the other." Natalie was awarded custody of Natasha and granted Richard "reasonable visitation rights." He also agreed to pay $200 monthly for child support until Natasha was twenty-one and to create a trust of $15,000 in her name. Of their community assets, Natalie retained her art collection and assigned two items to Natasha, "1 Maillol sculpture (of a crouching woman) and 1 Bonnard oil painting."

On October 14, RJ divorced Marion on grounds (which she didn't contest) of "irreconcilable differences." "We both knew we'd reached the end of the road," RJ recalled. "At first we felt very passionately about each other, but when the passion subsided, friendship wasn't enough to keep us together, especially as I spent so much time working in L.A., away from my house in Palm Springs."

By the time of the divorce, RJ had begun an affair with Tina Sinatra, "but we were never engaged, as the gossip columnists reported." And three weeks later Natalie gave her first party at North Bentley since her marriage ended. Among the guests was Jerry Brown, the secretary of state for California. "We've been out on a few dates," she told me. Not long afterward, when we had dinner together, she said: "It took a long time to happen, but a couple of nights ago it finally happened."

"How was it?" I asked.

"If you mean 'it'—like a wand."

Natalie had heard about RJ's affair with Tina Sinatra, of course, and reacted by searching for diversion rather than love. Ironically, with the secretary of state soon out of the picture, Tina's father picked up his cue as Natalie's occasional lover, but he proved less of a diversion than she'd hoped. After one of their rendezvous, she told Asa Maynor: "Frank spent the whole time telling me what *I* could do for *him*."

"La Ronde" continued as Natalie began an affair with Steve McQueen, who recently had separated from his wife. By mutual agreement it was a sometime thing, and she hinted as much to RJ when he called from London. He had gone there to produce as well as co-star with Bette Davis (playing the Oriental head of an espionage ring) in *Madame Sin,* a pilot for a TV series that failed to sell. "I'd heard about the divorce, and after the usual condolences I asked Natalie, 'Are you involved with anyone now?' And she said (meaning Steve), 'A little bit.' Then she asked, 'Are *you?*' And I said (meaning Tina), 'A little bit.' And then I said, 'But maybe we could sort things out and get together in the future?' And after a moment Natalie said, 'Maybe we could.' "

By November she had started thinking about her career again, but although Guy McElwaine tried to interest several studios in *I Never Promised You a Rose Garden,* it was considered "too risky," even with the names of Natalie and Simone Signoret attached. Another project with Natalie's name attached was *Wait Till the Sun Shines, Nellie,* from a novel about a fragile, self-destructive nightclub singer with a sad and intimate voice in the style of Helen Morgan. Ray Stark had optioned the rights and commissioned me to adapt it for Natalie, but when he read the script, he decided to offer the role to Barbra Streisand, whose persona was far from fragile or self-destructive. Fortunately, she proved unavailable. Less fortunately, Stark shelved the project, and both Natalie and I knew why. She hadn't made a film in over two years, and he doubted that she was still a major box-office draw.

It was the first sign of changing times, but a more important change was in the wings. Just before Christmas, RJ returned to Los Angeles and brought presents for mother and daughter at North Bentley. "There were other people around, so everything was subtext again. But a couple of weeks later I broke up with Tina, Natalie broke up with Steve, and I called to invite her to my house in Palm Springs for the weekend—and she stayed until the end of March."

Before she joined RJ at the end of January 1972, Natalie worked for one day on *The Candidate,* playing herself in a political satire about an idealist running for election to the Senate, as a gesture of friendship to Robert Redford, the movie's producer and star. It would be almost three years before she appeared on the big screen again.

WHEN NATALIE and RJ decided to remarry, "the seesaw effect" of their careers, noted by Mart Crowley at the time of *Splendor in the Grass,* had left RJ on top. On the strength of his performance in *Harper* six years earlier, Lew Wasserman, head of Universal, had offered him the lead in one of the studio's TV series. At first he was reluctant to abandon the big screen, but two things changed his mind. David Niven, who had

*Olga Viripaeff's house in San Francisco, January 1972.*
*A visit from Natalie, with Natasha, after the divorce from Gregson.*
*Left to right: Olga, Natalie, Maria and Alexei Tatuloff*
*(only a day before his fatal heart attack)*

produced a successful TV series in partnership with Charles Boyer, advised him that the small screen was a safer career investment for the over-thirties. Then RJ tested for the role of the husband in *Rosemary's Baby*, and was deeply disappointed not to get it. (He would have been far more effective—as *A Kiss Before Dying* proved—than John Cassavetes, too saturnine to surprise anyone when he was unmasked as a Satanist.)

*It Takes a Thief*, with Fred Astaire as RJ's father and equally elegant partner-in-crime, aired from 1965 through 1969. Although it made RJ a major TV star, he became involved in a lawsuit with Universal over residuals after its final season; and the studio secured an injunction to prevent him from working in TV until the suit was settled. He appeared in a theatrical movie, *Winning*, that did nothing to improve his prospects on the big screen, and was soon paying alimony and child support to Marion after the court granted her custody of their daughter, Kate.

When Steve McQueen called Natalie and RJ in Palm Springs to say,

"You're back together again, that's great," she was a wealthy movie star with an uncertain future and only one recent offer (which she rejected) of a mediocre role in a mediocre film-noir parody, *The Black Bird;* and RJ was a financially strapped but successful TV star, whose career would not be stalled for much longer by Universal's injunction. But after many ups and downs, they had both got off the emotional seesaw, and as Natalie said when she called me from Palm Springs: "We're back where we started, and where we should have stayed."

TWO YEARS after they remarried, and were on vacation in Provence, Natalie wrote a letter to John Foreman: "I woke up in the middle of the night and started thinking about how great '73 had been for me and RJ, and how really happy I am." And then, the letter continued, she started thinking about "a certain night at your house" and realized that she owed her present happiness to the party John and Linda gave: "This is all by way of saying thank you for making that evening happen which made everything start happening for us. As things in life sometimes have a way of turning out, you've turned out to be my best friend and I just wanted you to know that I know it. And I hope you get everything you ever wanted—like I did!"

On February 10, 1972, Natalie and RJ left Palm Springs to stay at North Bentley Drive for a few days. "She wanted to throw my forty-second birthday party there," he remembered, "and invite our friends to make it official that we were back together again." On April 10, when they arrived at the Academy Awards ceremony (where they jointly presented the Oscar for Best Actor to Marlon Brando for *The Godfather*), the almost hysterical media reaction astonished them. It was like a replay of the time when they were Hollywood's golden young couple, and Mary Sale remembered that even the "valet parkers at Chasen's, who had been very upset when they broke up, said to me and my husband, 'Guess who just came in? They're together again!' "

On July 16 they were remarried on a chartered boat, *Ramblin' Rose,* offshore from Catalina. No professional photographers were present, as they purposely chose a small boat that could only accommodate their respective families and a few close friends. "We honeymooned around the Isthmus, Avalon and Emerald Bay," RJ recalled. "No fog this time. It was incredibly beautiful."

But they returned to an incredibly disagreeable surprise. Lana had begged Natalie and RJ to allow her current husband, Richard Smedley, to photograph the wedding ceremony, and they agreed on condition the photos were kept private. But no less than twenty-seven had been sold to a fan magazine. "I cannot begin to tell you how very hurt and disappointed RJ and I are to have found out that you have sold our personal photographs to *Silver Screen* magazine," Natalie wrote Smedley. "Apart from our personal hurt feelings toward you as a relative, we are just astounded that you would do such a thing." The letter also accused Smedley and Lana of "betraying our trust" and noted that she hadn't even received copies of several of the photos they sold.

It was not the first time that Natalie had accused Lana of betrayal. "In those pre-credit-card days," according to Peggy Griffin, who was RJ's secretary at the time, "Lana used to charge many things she bought at department stores to Natalie's account." Even before her modest acting career virtually ended in the early 1970s, Lana's persistent requests for loans had deepened their estrangement; and the tone of Smedley's letter, which Natalie felt sure had been written with Lana's approval, made it all but final.

Smedley denied that Natalie "explained anything about privacy" and asked her not to consider him a relative. "From my observations of being a relative," he wrote, "one must either be afraid of you, as your parents are, or bear the scars of past hurts as both your sisters do." This was more wounding than Lana's jealousy (at its crudest in her remark to Donfeld, "Nat's got the brains, but I got the tits") or the clothes charged to her account or the loans that were never repaid. It was bitter confirmation that Lana's affection was as conditional as her mother's.

When Lana persisted with her demands for a loan, RJ advised Natalie to respond only in case of serious need; and over the years she often paid the school fees and medical bills of Lana's daughter. But she seldom saw Lana again. Elizabeth Applegate, who became Natalie's secretary in 1975, soon after Peggy Griffin left to work for director Gil Cates, could recall "only three times, until Natalie's death, when Lana was invited to the house." The estrangement caused Natalie the same feeling of guilt as her decision to keep Mud at a distance, although RJ (and no doubt Dr. Lindon) assured her there was no reason for it. In public, as usual, she remained loyal to both, and in private never told anyone, not even RJ, what Olga had confided about Lana's father.

*Just remarried: Natalie and RJ on board*
Ramblin' Rose, *July 16, 1972*

"The second time around was mostly the best years for both of us," according to RJ, "and the most deeply emotional time of my life." As the Palm Springs house was only half-furnished, Natalie used her money and her decorator's license to complete it; and when RJ's lawyer advised him that Universal's injunction could not prevent him from working in England, he was free to film a new TV series there. In December they sailed to England on the *Queen Elizabeth II,* and during January and February 1973 he starred in the first thirteen episodes of *Colditz.*

Before they left, the Wagners had agreed (after some hesitation) that Mud could move into the Palm Springs house and look after Natasha during their absence. Natalie knew that her mother was genuinely fond of children, and believed she could be trusted with them, as long as they weren't her own. "She also felt guilt about divorcing my father," according to Natasha, and by allowing Mud to stay in the house, hoped to maintain a semblance of family life.

Instead, she created an opportunity for disruption. Mud convinced three-year-old Natasha that she was in mortal danger if they didn't stay close to each other at all times, because neither Natalie nor RJ could be trusted. "And in other subtle ways," Natasha remembered, "she tried to turn me against my mother." When the Wagners returned, they found the locks had been changed on most of the doors in the house, Mud had locked Natasha in her room, and RJ had to break down the door.

This explosion of resentment at being sidelined in Natalie's life was the last occasion when Mud became, in RJ's words, "as close to certifiable as you can get." It was also her last attempt at asserting control, and left her more sidelined than ever. Natalie continued to invite her to Thanksgiving and Christmas dinners, but not to the New Year's Eve parties that became the Wagners' most important celebration. Mud also got to play Star Mother when she was included on the guest list at a reception honoring her daughter's charitable activities. Always quick to seize a photo op, she was recorded not only cheek-to-cheek with Natalie, but bestowing a kiss on Cesar Romero.


THAT SUMMER, after RJ heard that *Colditz* would not be renewed for another season, the Wagners accepted an offer from producers Aaron Spelling and Leonard Goldberg to appear together in a TV movie for ABC. In *The Affair* Natalie plays Courtney, a songwriter crippled by polio, who's never trusted herself to fall in love until she meets an unhappily married corporation lawyer (RJ). He reciprocates, but their love doesn't last, because they come from different worlds, etc., and after the pain of breaking up, Courtney consoles herself with: "He touched me. I touched someone. We knew each other—for a while."

A soap opera tastefully underwritten to the vanishing point by Barbara Turner, *The Affair* was soberly directed by Gil Cates, and the Wagners received better notices than the movie when it aired on November 20. Thirteen years earlier, in *All the Fine Young Cannibals,* the Wagners had seemed to make little connection with each other or the material. In *The Affair,* they find a between-the-lines connection with each other. It's

*RJ and "nucleus" wedding guests Norma Crane,
Howard Jeffrey, Mart Crowley*

as if they're making their own private movie, and the movie on the
screen is only a pretext.

It's also a pretext for Natalie to use her own voice to record Courtney's undemanding song "I Can't See You Anymore." By this time her
persistence with singing lessons has resulted in a voice that's at least
acceptable, a long way from the playback for *West Side Story.*

TWO WEEKS before *The Affair* began shooting, Natalie discovered she
was pregnant. It was one reason that she turned down a leading role in
an all-star big-screen disaster movie, *The Towering Inferno.* The other
reason was that she found the script mediocre. So did RJ, who accepted
a supporting role for the money. He might have turned it down if he'd
known that *The Affair* would deliver an unexpected bonanza for himself
and Natalie, as Tom Mankiewicz explained: "Part of their deal was that

they'd get 50 percent of the next TV series produced by Goldberg and Spelling. It turned out to be *Charlie's Angels.* RJ thought the script was terrible and the series wouldn't make a penny. So did everyone at ABC, and they finally aired the pilot in a non-prime-time slot. It was a huge success, and made a lot of money for everyone involved."

THAT FALL, while filming *Fiddler on the Roof* on location in Dubrovnik, Norma Crane discovered a lump in her breast. Rather than jeopardize her first major role in a movie, she waited until the unit moved to a studio in England to consult a doctor; and he diagnosed cancer. As surgery was out of the question before Norma finished the movie, she began radiation treatment. A close friend, Sue Barton (formerly a publicist in Rupert Allan's office), drove her from Pinewood Studios to the hospital every day after she finished shooting. But the treatment had started too late, and shortly after returning to Los Angeles, Norma died at the age of forty-two.

When she was buried at Westwood Village Memorial Park, Howard Jeffrey took charge of the funeral arrangements, and Natalie was one of several friends who spoke at the ceremony. She recalled how Norma "always made me feel what it's like to be alive, how you have to take the bad with the bad, and in spite of everything, never lose your capacity for enjoyment."

ON MARCH 9, 1974, Natalie gave birth to her second daughter. Her doctor in Palm Springs had warned her to expect a cesarean delivery, and RJ drove her to Los Angeles, where she checked into Cedars of Lebanon. Due to the baby's misplaced umbilical cord, the operation lasted several hours. They named her Courtney, after the character Natalie played in *The Affair,* and once again motherhood became the focus of Natalie's life. "Look at this beautiful thing!" Mart Crowley recalled her saying when Courtney was only a few weeks old. "Who needs movies?"

Natalie Wood, for one. In July she began filming *Peeper,* a clone of the *Black Bird* film-noir parody that she'd turned down a year earlier. She accepted the role of a glamorous femme fatale partly for the chance to act with Michael Caine, whom she liked and admired, and partly to test the practicality of combining marriage and motherhood with a career. Before the movie started production, the Wagners had decided to move to Beverly Hills, and *Peeper* would be shot in the studio at Fox and on location at the nearby Harold Lloyd estate.

When she brought both daughters to the set or the location, Natalie was still breast-feeding Courtney and completely unselfconscious about it. But it made five-year-old Natasha very curious: " 'You can taste if you like,' she said to me. So I did, and hated it."

But although *Peeper* succeeded as a personal test, it failed as a movie. Low-grade direction (Peter Hyams) met low-grade script (by W. D. Richter), and Natalie was uncomfortably miscast. Fox held up its release until December 1975, but no amount of tinkering in the cutting room could save it from what Caine bluntly described as "a disaster."

Never seriously involved with her role or the project itself, Natalie was not seriously disappointed. She took refuge in motherhood, domesticity and bonding with other mothers, notably actress Juliet Mills. "We'd first met when I was rather lonely and between marriages," Juliet remembered. "Natalie was incredibly kind, and when I married again and gave birth to a daughter, she suggested to RJ that they send over a special dinner to the hospital. It was catered by Chasen's and served by two Chasen's waiters."

By this time RJ's lawsuit had been settled, and he'd started filming a new TV series. *Switch,* which would run for three years, cast him as a reformed criminal who operates a detective agency in partnership with a retired cop. He always enjoyed being the provider and welcomed Natalie's return to "Who needs movies?" The Wagners' two-story, nine-room neo-Colonial house at 603 North Canon Drive also marked the return of Natalie as decorator; and the change from the showplace grandeur of their first home was as great as the change from the emotional climate of their first marriage: floral-patterned upholstery and needlepoint pillows instead of satin drapes and chandeliers; no marble bathtub adjoining the master bedroom with its quilted floral bedspread and wicker armchairs, but a dressing room on one side and an alcove that served as Natalie's office on the other.

Upstairs, connected by a playroom, were bedrooms for three children. The third was Kate Wagner, who planned only to stay temporarily at first. She needed to establish residence in Beverly Hills to attend Beverly Hills High, but Josh Donen had moved into the garage apartment, and "there was a real family feeling, Natalie's warmth and directness brought us all together, and I wanted to stay."

When the Wagners decided to buy the house, Mart Crowley remembered, the deciding factor for Natalie was its huge walk-in bedroom closet. For the dressing room, she decided that she must have "one of those expandable 1930s makeup mirrors, that you could see yourself reflected in at various angles, and remembered that her makeup man on *All the Fine Young Cannibals* at MGM had used a mirror of this kind." She asked Mart to go with her on a foray to MGM, where "the guard at the studio gate recognized her at once and waved us through. Then we stole one of those mirrors from the makeup department during the lunch break, when no one was about."

This was not Natalie's first commando-style studio raid. When Fox announced it was selling off its back lot for developers to raze and turn into Century City, she asked Mart to accompany her on a last nostalgic tour of the suburban street with its false-fronted houses where she'd made so many movies as a child. As they drove down the western street, she spotted an old-fashioned shoeshine stand outside the Last Chance Saloon. "That would look great in RJ's study," Natalie said, so they loaded it into her station wagon and drove out past a smiling, waving guard.

She ordered the stand covered in leather to match the leather furniture in RJ's study, "and like all the dogs and cats," Mart recalled, "it became one more example of the total family feeling in that house." According to Asa Maynor, Natalie's need for "family atmosphere" increased after her estrangement from Mud and Lana, "and it was especially noticeable at Christmas, when she invited the nucleus (except for Norma, of course) and a few other close friends to trim the tree. Babies and small children were always welcome too."

But when Richard Gregson came to visit, there was still residual tension. Sarah remembered Natalie's "frozen smile" and her too-polite "How are you?" So did Sue Barton, who accompanied Richard on one visit during their brief marriage. "Natalie was truly friendly and charming, but you couldn't miss the undercurrent."

It was an undercurrent with an intensity as variable as El Niño's, and sometimes Natasha decided to risk swimming against it. One day she ran away from home with her friend Tracy, whose house was "very casual and free in contrast to Natalie's," and where they used to sing Billy Joel's song "My Life": "this is my life . . . leave me alone." After leaving notes for their respective parents, they went to the house of a mutual friend. Tracy's mother guessed where they'd gone, and informed Natalie. "She drove up in her Mercedes, wearing tight boots and jeans, and was furious, thought I'd betrayed her and made her feel a failure as a mother."

"But what made Natalie feel like a failure made Natasha feel how much she was loved," according to Elizabeth Applegate. "I remember her triumphant smile when she told me, after Natalie brought her back home, 'I've been grounded for a week!' " And as Natasha came to realize, "My mother was really fine in expressing feelings, whether she was angry or loving or afraid. 'If you're scared, explain,' she would say. She always wanted Courtney and me to have opinions. She used to tell me, 'You're so smart,' and because I looked like her, 'We're the same.' She'd write me letters and say, 'I'm thinking of you.' "

Natalie also wrote RJ when she was thinking of him with a special love, on his birthday, on the anniversary of both their marriages, at Christmas and Easter. February 10 (his birthday), 1974: "This is always my happiest day, too—because of *you*. I love you." December 28 (date of their first marriage), 1974: "This was the happiest day of my life in 1957—but I didn't know you'd make me doubly happy in July of 1971." February 10, 1975 (when she had a fig tree planted in the garden): "This fig may look bare now, but soon it will bear fruit—as we have. I love you with all my heart and I hope this tree grows as beautifully as my love for you does every single day." Easter 1976: "I love you more than love."

In the summer of 1974, the Wagners acquired a new housekeeper, Willie Mae Worthen, who became a trusted friend (like Elizabeth Applegate) and still works for RJ today; and after a three-year search, RJ bought a new boat that he and Natalie decided to call *Splendour*, in honor of the Kazan movie. Large enough to sleep eight, it had a spacious deck, saloon and galley, and a motorized dinghy (called *Valiant* in ironic homage to RJ's star-making movie) attached to the side. But to Guy McElwaine, the boat had two curious features. "The master stateroom was aft, and close by it, two steps led down to the dinghy, the only way off and on the boat when it was offshore. And the lower step, that they called the swim step, became very slippery when it was below the waterline."

Natalie helped decorate the boat, installing French doors to the aft

*One eye on the camera at a charity event in the late 1970s,
Maria creates a photo opportunity with Cesar Romero.*

deck and Early American furniture in the master stateroom; and when
guests stayed over the weekend, Delphine Mann recalled, "the galley
became the only time Natalie ever spent in any kitchen. She enjoyed
cooking huevos rancheros for breakfast." In spite of her fear of dark
water, "Natalie loved being on the ocean but not in it," according to RJ.
They also spent many weekends "with the Newport Beach boat
crowd"—Claire Trevor and her husband, Milton Bren; Rock Hudson;
Mary and Richard Sale.

In those years, Karl Malden recalled, "Natalie looked more beautiful
than ever," and the Wagners were "a golden couple" in public: "Charming, glamorous, in love—and it was real. The first time around, you

sometimes got the impression they were playing it. But this time they just enjoyed letting people see how happy they were."

From a private angle, they made the same impression on George Segal. He came to know Natalie when he resumed the friendship with RJ that had begun on *The Longest Day*, and remembered spending a day on the boat, along with David Niven and Arthur Loew. "RJ couldn't join us because he was filming, but he talked with Natalie on the phone about every forty minutes." It also made no difference to the Wagners that they were "establishment" and Segal was "new": "When my wife and I gave a party and invited them, RJ would joke, 'We'll provide the glitter.' And they did. Nobody else had Natalie's pizzazz, and the Wagner parties were really an extension of the George Cukor times, with the same mix of younger and older people, the same intelligence and glitter."

IN 1977 RJ first noticed a "change" in Natalie. "Natasha was seven years old and less dependent, Courtney was three and had become very attached to Willie Mae, and I could see the career demon starting to take over." He believed that Natalie's career was "her only security, and apart from her daughters, she considered it her only real accomplishment."

But the "change" was preceded by three events that almost certainly acted as subconscious preparation. The first, a televised American Film Institute tribute to Orson Welles, occurred on February 9, 1975. Welles's longtime friend Frank Sinatra acted as master of ceremonies, and Natalie joined Ingrid Bergman, Peter Bogdanovich, Joseph Cotten, John Huston and others in honoring the man who played her guardian in *Tomorrow Is Forever*.

A clip is screened of six-year-old, blonded and pigtailed Natalie crying hysterically on Welles's lap; then Sinatra welcomes thirty-seven-year-old Natalie to the stage, and movies become a time machine. Dark-haired, at the height of her beauty, she smiles at the director who made *The Trial* when she was starring in *Love with the Proper Stranger*. Thirty years have passed since they acted together; he's grown considerably heavier and wears a genuine beard instead of glued-on whiskers.

Natalie's speech is brief and graceful. "That was a scene with me on Orson's lap," she tells the audience. "Of course I'm a little bigger now, and so is Orson's lap." Welles laughs; then she addresses him directly: "It was as delightful to sit on your lap then as it's been to sit at your feet now. I'd like to thank you from both angles."

Welles had hoped that the occasion would result in an offer of completion money for his current project, *The Other Side of the Wind*. (He got a standing ovation but no offers.) In Natalie's case, a reunion obviously aroused memories of the past; but her last substantial role had been in *Bob & Carol* six years earlier, and listening to Bergman, who'd won two Oscars, and Cotten, who spoke of the excitement that Welles communicated to actors, was bound to arouse thoughts of the future as well.

The next event occurred in October 1976, when Natalie herself was the subject of a tribute at the San Francisco Film Festival. Although excited by the recognition of her work, she wondered apprehensively how a program of clips from her film career would hold up, especially as Jack Nicholson was also being honored and she feared he would seem more "contemporary."

For moral support at the tribute, she had RJ, Mart Crowley, Howard Jeffrey, Peggy Griffin, me and her new agent, Arnold Stiefel, who replaced Freddie Fields after he dissolved his agency to become a producer. A compilation of clips from Natalie's performances (as child star, adolescent, and adult actress) made a strong impression; her entrance onstage for the question-and-answer period cued a standing ovation, and when it was over, another for the way she handled herself—charming, poised and funny. Leaving the theater, she was literally besieged by fans with one more question to ask, one more congratulation to offer, one more autograph book to sign. It was an example of how, in RJ's words, "people gravitated to Natalie. She always seemed to be at the center of whatever was going on, not because she sought it, but it just seemed to be her natural place. And of course she enjoyed it."

The night before the tribute, Mart Crowley had checked into the same hotel as the Wagners and witnessed a different kind of "change" in Natalie. He told her that a rent boy would be coming to his room after dinner, and toward midnight she made an unannounced drunken entrance, wearing a nightgown, went straight over to the boy and castigated him. "You're not good enough for my friend!" Mart was stunned and asked her "not to be rude." "I'll give you rude!" Natalie shouted, ran to a table set with sandwiches and chocolate cake that Mart had ordered for the boy, and whipped off the cloth. Food flew across the room; then she ran out and slammed the door.

In the past, Mart commented later, Natalie had sometimes drunk too much, but he'd never seen her lose control before. Hindsight suggests a connection between the return of her "career demon" and the wildness that too much alcohol would continue to arouse from time to time in the future.

The third event was Natalie's appearance as Maggie the Cat, with RJ as Brick, in a TV production of *Cat on a Hot Tin Roof.* Taped in England six months before the San Francisco tribute to Natalie, it would not be aired in the USA until six weeks later, on December 9.

*Cat* was a co-production of NBC and Granada in Britain, and part of a TV series of outstanding twentieth-century plays with Laurence Olivier as host, actor and "artistic director." The series had opened with Alan Bates, Malcolm McDowell, Helen Mirren and Olivier in Harold Pinter's *The Collection;* and Natalie was "astonished and delighted," as she said later, not only by Olivier's invitation to star herself and RJ in the second play, but his admiration for her talent as a film actress.

For RJ, the role of Brick was his first serious acting challenge in a long while, and so important to him that he persuaded Universal to suspend production of *Switch* for two months. Like all the plays in the series, *Cat* was rehearsed and taped as an actual stage production, act by act, and RJ had never worked this way before, unlike Natalie, with her experience of live TV that began in the 1950s.

After two weeks of publicity interviews and costume tests in London, followed by a month of rehearsal, the cast moved to Granada's studio in Manchester for nine days of taping by four cameras. The day of the dress rehearsal, Natalie felt that "we could have gone onstage and played it," but the American director, Robert Moore, was disagreeably surprised by the rigid British union rules. "When Bob asked for overtime, it was refused," according to Derek Granger, who produced the series. "Even when he explained that he hadn't finished the scene, the union representative wouldn't budge. As each scene was taped in a long take, it wasn't always easy to sustain the emotional continuity."

And Natalie was surprised by her makeup artist, who proved far less cooperative than Bob Jiras and others she'd worked with in Los Angeles. One day, Granger recalled, "she was very tight-lipped, and at first didn't want to tell me when I asked what was the matter. But finally it turned out that Natalie had asked for a particular brand of foundation and the makeup woman assured her it wasn't available in England. So she went to Boots [drugstore], found it, came into the makeup room and shook it in the woman's face."

Unlike the movie version with Elizabeth Taylor and Paul Newman, which Williams disliked because it omitted every reference to Brick's guilt over a latent homosexual attachment in the past, the TV production respected the original text. Although Natalie found it ironic that "things you couldn't do in movies in 1958, you can do now on television," no reviewer commented on this when *Cat* aired on NBC. Most reviewers, in fact, were extraordinarily hostile, scoffed at the idea of a couple of movie stars in a Tennessee Williams play, and dismissed both leading performances; and as Williams had fallen out of fashion by the 1970s, some dismissed the play as well.

> *Interviewer: How do you feel about negative reviews? Does it*
> *bother you a lot?*
> *Natalie Wood: No. After the first few suicide attempts, you get*
> *right over it.*

In fact *Cat on a Hot Tin Roof* is a strong production with strong flaws, notably sets that fail to convey the Delta plantation style of a mansion that Williams defined as "Victorian with a touch of the Far East," and the miscasting of Olivier as Big Daddy. He lacks the vulgarity of the self-made patriarch, and also the swaggering power, partly because illness has begun to deplete his own power as an actor. He's at his best in moments of reacting rather than acting, notably in the last act, when Maggie claims that she's pregnant with Brick's child. "He played it differently every time," Natalie said later. "Once he just looked at me. And looked and looked." It was the take that Moore chose, although Natalie conceals *her* reaction when the look "went on so long that I began to feel faint."

Sudden, unnervingly enigmatic looks had become one of Olivier's most effective devices for the camera (*Wuthering Heights* and *Carrie* are full of them), and as Maureen Stapleton, who played Big Mama, told Natalie: "Honey, when you've been looked at by Olivier, you *know* you've been looked at." Stapleton's own performance is occasionally uncertain, as if she can't decide whether she's playing Big Mama or little Birdie in *The Little Foxes,* but she's splendidly pugnacious in the climactic family brawl. And RJ is very persuasive in conveying the two sides of Brick, his air of weary detachment and the moments of emotional disorder that contradict it.

"Natalie was even better in the dress rehearsal, when her nervousness added to the tension," according to Derek Granger; but in the taped performance she seems electrically charged, powered by the kind of role she's longed for over the past ten years. And in the final scene with Brick, as Maggie realizes "I'm stronger than you," there's an echo of Natalie's favorite actress, Vivien Leigh. "Oh, you weak people, you weak beautiful people!—who give up with such grace," Maggie says as she switches off the lamp at Brick's bedside. "What you want is someone to take hold of you—Gently, gently . . ." Gently, yes, in the delicate seductiveness that both actresses shared; but less gently in the fierce determination they so exquisitely conveyed.

A year later, when Olivier came out to Los Angeles to make *The Betsy,* the Wagners often entertained him at 603 North Canon, and Delphine Mann had a strong impression that "he saw the young Vivien in Natalie."

THE ONLY MOVIE offer that Natalie had received by the spring of 1977 was for *Meteor,* a late and (as it turned out) mediocre offering in the big-budget disaster cycle. Two actors she liked, Sean Connery and Karl Malden, had accepted the other leading parts; and she was also tempted by the chance to play her first Russian role, as interpreter for a group of Soviet scientists who cooperate with NASA in an attempt to liquidate "Orpheus," a meteor heading toward earth. But the special effects were the movie's real stars, and literally overwhelmed most of the cast when a hefty chip off Orpheus devastated part of Manhattan and buried them up to their necks in mud.

Natalie had learned from experience that it wasn't quality of performance, Academy Awards or nominations that kept you in demand, but your record of appearing in movies that consistently made money; and when she ventured into blockbuster country for the first time, she hoped for a commercial success that would restore her value at the box office. She approached the chore with her usual professionalism, took a

*With cigarette holder and bracelet, c.1970*

crash course to polish her Russian (which she spoke "very fluently," according to Natasha Zepaloff, "with a slight but definite American accent") and even called Vladimir Zacharenko at the Westinghouse Corporation in Sunnyvale to make sure the Russian technical terms in the script were correct.

MGM's enormous Stage 30, which had once housed the world's largest swimming pool to accommodate the aquatic spectaculars of Esther Williams, was converted to an equally spectacular set of a New York subway terminal, complete with train, that would later collapse under a million tons of mud. At Paramount, NASA Control Center was reproduced on a set only marginally less huge, to be deluged in its turn with another million tons of mud. The script called for the three leading players to be stuck in it, and they endured seven days of filming in the studio tank, trying to keep their heads above mud until a rescue team arrived.

*Meteor* began shooting on October 31, and it soon became clear that both schedule and budget ($17 million) were inadequate. The movie exceeded both by several weeks and several millions, and although Natalie completed her role at the end of January 1978, the remaining scenes took another two months, special effects another six months, and *Meteor* wasn't released until October 1979. By that time Natalie was more creatively employed, and distance had erased a disagreeable memory.

*Meteor* became an equally disagreeable memory for its director, Ronald Neame. "I left after principal photography, and was appalled when I saw the third-rate special effects, the only thing that could have saved the picture." Natalie's role, according to Neame, "was forced into the script by the producers." Dissatisfied with the way it was written in the first draft by Edmund North and the second by Steven Bach, "I came up with the idea of making her a Russian interpreter, and worked closely with Stanley Mann on the final draft."

But the role still lacked color, and Natalie's two "romantic" scenes with Connery's NASA scientist (married, of course) were beyond tentative. After the movie completed production, Neame was surprised when "RJ deliberately cut me at a party." He claimed to have no idea why, and could recall "only one moment that might have given Natalie offense. She seemed overly concerned about the way she looked, and one day took so long worrying about her face that I got a bit impatient and said, 'It's more important to worry about the character you're playing.'"

In Natalie's view, she had no character to play or worry about, and Neame's attitude struck her as devious and patronizing. "She didn't like it when people blew smoke at her," according to RJ, "and she felt that Neame blew a lot." He also had a personal reason for the cut: "I'd recently been on a panel with Neame, who remarked at one point, 'You have to treat actors like children.' I found this an offensive thing to say in front of an actor, and it also made me understand why Natalie was unhappy working with him."

*METEOR* WAS not the only frustrating experience for Natalie. She'd recently been passed over for two roles she longed to play. The first was a TV drama, *Sybil,* about a girl whose childhood traumas had created a case of multiple personality. Stewart Stern had written the script, and she hoped for his support in her bid for the part. But although Stewart inclined to an unknown actress—"like an ordinary-looking woman you

*As Maggie, with RJ as Brick, in* Cat on a Hot Tin Roof

*With Laurence Olivier as Big Daddy*

might see getting off a bus"—he was careful "not to take sides" when Natalie was under consideration. "Then Sally Field came in, wearing glasses, did an extraordinary audition playing two Sybils, and everyone agreed on her."

Convinced that Stewart had talked against her, Natalie accused him of betrayal. Although he denied it, she refused to speak to him anymore. "But we soon reconciled, and with the generosity that was so typical of her, she offered to help me decorate the house I'd just bought."

A few weeks later *I Never Promised You a Rose Garden,* which Natalie had once hoped to make with Simone Signoret, became the first film of TV and stage director Anthony Page. He disliked the existing script and asked me to rewrite it. When Natalie proposed herself for the role she'd offered Signoret, and asked me to discuss the idea with Anthony Page, I was placed in the same situation as Stewart. Although I'd often hoped to work with Natalie again, I couldn't see her as an ordinary-looking European psychiatrist on the brink of middle age. Neither could Anthony, and when I told Natalie that he wanted an older, less beautiful actress (which was true), she accepted the news gracefully.

By this time, I realized, her "career drive" was in high gear, but it was a drive for parts that excited her. Acting had become a creative experience as essential to her life as psychoanalysis.

> *Sydney Pollack: Natalie was very fulfilled as wife and mother, but increasingly restless because she was finding it difficult to get worthwhile parts just when she was really blossoming as an actress. And after being put on a pedestal when she was young, she became a victim of changing times, when the new stars were "people like ourselves" rather than iconic.*

It was one reason that she began to drink more heavily. The other was her anxiety about approaching the age of forty, when iconic stars were considered over the hill. But until her final movie, she never drank during a shoot, exercised beforehand to make sure she looked her best—and, as Tom Mankiewicz commented, "heavy" drinking in Natalie's case was relatively light. "Being so tiny, she filled up so quickly, and could get seriously drunk after a fourth glass of white wine."

In November 1977, Natalie heard that Julia Phillips, co-producer of *The Sting* and *Taxi Driver,* had acquired the film rights to Erica Jong's

novel *Fear of Flying.* She asked Arnold Stiefel to arrange a meeting with
Phillips over lunch at La Scala, and although Phillips expressed interest
in discussing the project with Natalie, she arrived forty minutes late.
"That showed how things had changed," Stiefel commented. "A few
years earlier, the producer would have been waiting for Natalie."

During lunch, Phillips sprinkled cocaine on her side plate, broke off
the filter from a cigarette, dipped it in the cocaine, then inhaled. After
she left, Natalie (who had never been part of the drug scene and knew
almost nothing about it) asked Stiefel: "What was she doing?" When he
explained, "Natalie was appalled that a producer would be smoking
coke in public during a meeting."

Phillips, whose addiction had brought her career to the cusp of
decline, was unable to set up *Fear of Flying;* and in late March 1978,
Natalie took Natasha and Courtney to Hawaii, where RJ was filming
*Pearl,* a miniseries about Pearl Harbor. Two weeks after she arrived at the
house he'd rented on Diamond Head, she was offered the role of Karen
in an ABC miniseries based on *From Here to Eternity.* (Mysteriously,
Pearl Harbor was in and on the air that year.) At first "there seemed
something wrong about playing Deborah Kerr's part in a TV remake of
a famous movie," but when Natalie weighed *Cat on a Hot Tin Roof*
against a movie industry obsessed with sharks, volcanoes, earthquakes
and (especially) meteors, it seemed that TV had more to offer.

During the first week of June, when *From Here to Eternity* began
filming, Tom Mankiewicz flew in from Los Angeles to offer Natalie and
RJ the leads in another Spelling-Goldberg production. It was based on
an unproduced script by Sidney Sheldon that Spelling had signed Tom
to rewrite and direct as a two-hour pilot for a TV series. Although RJ
liked the pilot script of *Hart to Hart,* he told Tom that Natalie didn't
want to get involved in a regular series, and that he didn't want her to.
"But I'm happy to do a series," he added, "and make enough money for
Natalie to feel she has to work only when she really wants to."

Natalie read and reread James Jones's novel as well as the TV adaptation, then went to look at some of the places it described—downtown
Honolulu streets, Schofield Barracks, the Moana Hotel. She made a lot
of notes, not only on Karen's character, but "things that I felt could be
incorporated in the scenes that I had." They reflect her habit of typically
detailed preparation, cover more than twenty handwritten pages of an
exercise book, and concentrate on the development of Karen's relation-

*On a cold day in L.A. Left to right: Kate Wagner,*
*RJ, Natasha, Natalie and Courtney*

ship with Milt (William Devane in the Burt Lancaster role). In their first scene together, "She's attracted to him but not wanting him to see through to her pain, trying to maintain icy calm and control." During a phone conversation soon afterward, "She's trying to be the aggressor—new color—more open, tantalizing, less sure of herself, trying to keep her defenses but letting them down." And their love scene in the ocean demands "false brightness, revealing deep insecurity, total spilling of all emotions."

For the following two-hour segments of the six-hour series, the notes chart Karen's gradual disillusionment with Milt. "Frustration at affair leading nowhere" leads to their "bittersweet" parting, which Natalie compares to the "last scene in *Splendor*." There are also notes on her costumes, and on two scenes that she considers "*absolutely unacceptable*" (underlined) because they "emasculate" Karen's character.

When she discussed *From Here to Eternity* at the AFI seminar, Natalie mentioned that the director, Buzz Kulik, was "very open" to all her suggestions, and William Devane "had his bible [the novel] and I had mine, and if we ever had a problem with a scene, we would always refer to the book." She was also relieved to find Don McGuire's adaptation very different from Daniel Taradash's screenplay: "I hadn't seen the film recently, but my husband had, and I said, 'I'm afraid to see it,' and he said, 'You shouldn't feel that way, because you'll see that it's very different.' He'd read the script also, so it really wasn't a problem, and Kulik and the producers were very aware of the fact they didn't want to be imitative of the film."

Partly because the TV adaptation is more faithful to the book, and includes several important scenes omitted in the movie, and partly because censorship was far less powerful in 1978, the relationship between Karen and Milt becomes more complex. The TV version emphasizes the social gulf between them, and Karen's painful insecurity, most powerfully in a scene when she explains how she contracted gonorrhea and had a hysterectomy that left her "feeling unwanted as a woman." At the same time, Milt becomes more nakedly crude in his sexual rapacity, as well as more bitter in his hatred of the officer class.

Natalie and Devane bring excitement and urgency to these scenes, but they caused a violent disturbance in the Wagner marriage. When Natalie first arrived in Hawaii, Natasha remembered, "She was very solid and safe as a mother." But then her frustrated career drive began to take its toll, and she drank heavily. "It was sometimes scary. When she was really drunk, she didn't know who we were." After RJ completed *Pearl*, and the children went back to Los Angeles with Willie Mae, the Wagners moved to the Colony Surf Hotel. There RJ began to drink heavily out of frustration at Natalie's frustration, and in another seesaw effect, Natalie went on the wagon to begin costume fittings for *From Here to Eternity*.

By this time Mart Crowley had arrived as their guest and buffer zone, and he soon realized that Natalie was developing a "fixation" on William Devane. So did RJ, who became increasingly jealous and made a point of visiting the set for their scenes together. Although several of them had a high sexual charge, and there was a sexual element in Natalie's fixation, it went no further than "swishing her tail." But this was enough to arouse RJ's suspicion, "particularly when she didn't want me around watching her nude love scene in the ocean with Devane."

James B. Sikking, an actor friend of RJ's, was also making a TV movie in Honolulu and staying at the Colony Surf. One evening at the Outrigger bar attached to the hotel, he remembered, RJ's jealousy drove him "to get as drunk as you can get before you lose consciousness." Natalie, completely sober and increasingly on edge, retired to the Wagners' suite on the eighth floor. "How could she *do* this to me?" RJ asked Sikking, then wandered out to the beach, "flailing, weepy-eyed, so totally irrational he could have walked out into the ocean. Anything!"

Sikking persuaded him to come back to the hotel and, with Mart's help, walked him to an elevator, then up to the suite. Natalie, who had an early call, was getting ready for bed. But RJ's jealousy flared up again, as Mart recalled: " 'Don't lie to me about Devane!' he said. Natalie got furious, went into the bedroom, and slammed the door. In a drunken dramatic gesture, RJ ran to the window as if to throw himself out. While Jim and I pulled him back, Natalie came out from the bedroom. 'Are you out of your mind?' she said to RJ, then we locked the windows and put him to bed."

> James B. Sikking: At that time, drinking was the bane of RJ and Natalie's existence. But next day RJ sent me a message of thanks, and everything seemed fine between them again. As angry as they could get with each other, there was always this bond.

One year earlier, Natalie was on board *Splendour* with Sarah Gregson, David Niven and Olivier's son Tarquin, but without RJ, who was taping an episode of *Switch*. After discussing the recent death of Elvis Presley, they moved to the inevitable subject of Hollywood marriages and divorces. "I've never been unfaithful to RJ," Natalie said. "I don't believe in that."

Laurence Olivier was unable to join the others because he was filming *The Betsy,* but during his stay in California the Wagners threw a party for him in the garden of 603 North Canon Drive. As usual, George Segal remembered, "They provided the glitter, and Natalie put on a real Hollywood performance for Olivier—green bikini, scarf around her waist, clicking around the pool in high heels to make sure everyone had drinks. He clearly adored her." And once again "everything seemed fine" with the Wagner marriage.

IN THE LAST week of November 1978, Natalie began filming exteriors in Cleveland, Ohio, for another TV movie. Four days later the production unit moved to California and began shooting interiors at the Veterans Hospital in West Los Angeles. In *The Cracker Factory,* which seemed to Natalie like a reward for losing *Sybil* and *I Never Promised You a Rose Garden,* she played a Cleveland housewife in severe midlife crisis: alcoholic, Catholic, with a repressive mother, three children and a husband who "understands" but can't help her.

The opening scene shows Cathy suddenly disoriented in a supermarket. Back home she attempts suicide; she is forcibly admitted to a psychiatric ward and given heavy sedation. "Don't you have anything to look forward to?" the psychiatrist (Perry King) asks at their first session. "Only menopause and senility—and with my luck they'll probably overlap," Cathy replies. The rest of the movie dramatizes her treatment, relapses alternating with progress until she's well enough to return home, and although the format is familiar, the writing and direction are exceptionally sharp, and Natalie's performance is not only one of her finest, but her bravest.

In many ways it's a "new" Natalie, not the still famously beautiful actress of *Cat* and *From Here to Eternity,* but a woman of forty who looks as if she was still very beautiful only a few years ago. "We had two things that we called 'Ugly Number One' and 'Ugly Number Two,' " Natalie remembered. "And there were certain distorted lenses when I was really supposed to look bad."

When she first read the novel by Joyce Rebeta-Burditt, Natalie unhesitatingly embraced the idea of opening her own Pandora's box, tried to option the rights, then discovered that ABC had already acquired them. And her performance embraced Cathy's wide range of moods, formidable when bitter and angry, endearing when funny,

From Here to Eternity. *William Devane as Milt,*
*Natalie as Karen, in the love scene in the ocean*

pathetic but never sentimental when helpless and childlike. The psychiatrist diagnoses Cathy as "arrested emotionally," and the director, Burt
Brinckerhoff (who had played Natalie's brother in the 1955 TV show
*Miracle at Potters Farm*), perceived "the inner child that Natalie managed
to bring with her, although she still had to deal with interior demons."

When an actor not only chooses but pursues a role, one reason is
obviously professional, but there's often an intimate personal motive as
well. In Garbo's case, Queen Christina: the bisexual sovereign who lived
alone and eventually abdicated, like the star of MGM. In Natalie's case,
*The Cracker Factory:* an autobiographical novel that became an autobiographical film for actress as well as author.

*Burt Brinckerhoff: Natalie's fear of dark water reminded me*
*of an account of Tolstoy's wife in a biography I'd recently read.*

*It described her as always about to throw herself into dark*
*water, then waiting for someone to save her.*

In March 1979, Natalie's performance in *From Here to Eternity* won a
Golden Globe award for best actress in a TV series. (Although her even
more impressive performance as Maggie the Cat had been nominated
for an Emmy two years earlier, there would be no nominations for *The
Cracker Factory.*) TV coverage of the Golden Globe event showed
Natalie's genuine astonishment when her name was read out, RJ's no less
genuinely proud reaction during her acceptance speech; and the couple
looked not only as if everything was fine between them, but always
would be.

Executives at ABC had been eager to exploit the high ratings of *From
Here to Eternity* by turning it into a weekly series, and pressured Natalie
to repeat her role. Wisely, she refused, and accepted instead an offer to
appear on the big screen in *The Last Married Couple in America.* But it
proved a case of choosing a rock over a hard place. The movie's only
interest is as a reflection of changing times, a kind of *Bob & Carol & Ted
& Alice* ten years later, sanctimonious dialogue about "the new morality"
replacing sly human observation, wretched jokes about premature ejac-
ulation and prostate problems instead of wit. Unfortunately, Natalie
convinced herself that the script was better than mediocre because she
liked the director, Gil Cates, and her co-star, George Segal, and the idea
of a romantic comedy about a storm-tossed marriage that finally made
safe harbor.

But less than midway through the shoot, she had a premonition of
failure. "After a while," she said to Segal, "it gets to be just one damn
clapper board after another."

Her final clapper board on *The Last Married Couple* was struck on
March 18, and five days later the Wagners flew to Leningrad for *Treasures
of the Hermitage,* a TV documentary on the famous art museum. Natalie
and Peter Ustinov had agreed to act as tour guides, and the American-
British co-production, with a mixed British and Russian crew, was
planned to coincide with a telecast of the Moscow Olympics. But soon
after taping was completed, the Cold War grew even colder, the USA
withdrew from the Olympics, and NBC put the documentary on ice
until April 1981.

Although the idea of visiting the homeland she'd never seen fascinated Natalie, Mud predicted a descent into hell; and it provoked a major disturbance in Fahd, who once again recalled the horrors of the revolution. But Ustinov, another Russian born in exile, was as fascinated as Natalie. He'd never met her before, was "amazed that she spoke Russian better than I did," and found her "very agreeable to be with." Unfortunately, they had little time to exchange impressions, because for reasons that he never understood, "We were kept more or less apart when we weren't taping the show."

At that time in Soviet Russia, Ustinov added, "You were very closely supervised and limited in where you could go." Natalie soon found herself too closely supervised. Although she had an agreement with the Soviet authorities that she could phone Natasha and Courtney once a day, she soon realized that the calls were being wiretapped. She insisted that an interpreter put through an urgent call to the minister of culture in Moscow, then took the phone and informed him she would leave the country, and NBC would halt production, unless the wiretaps stopped at once. They stopped.

Ustinov recalled Natalie's excitement, during their tour of the museum's treasures, at the collection of van Goghs, Gauguins and Cézannes, and his own at an authenticated Leonardo da Vinci that had never been seen outside the country: "It was known as the 'Madonna Benois' because it had been bought by my great-grandfather Benois from itinerant Italian peddlers from Astrakhan." Also included in the documentary was their visit to "a two-thousand-year-old man from Siberia, packed in powdered ice with steam rising from it. He was desiccated but preserved with more vitality than a mummy, reddish hair and eyelashes, mouth open as if about to speak, and all except two teeth still there."

Like Ustinov, every Russian that Natalie met was astonished by how well she spoke their language. "To them," she remembered, "I looked very typically American." The only American movies playing in Leningrad were *The Apartment* (1960) and *Cleopatra* (1963), so "they were quite behind and nobody recognized me in the streets." Her most vivid impression of "old Russia" occurred when she was allowed to enter a church where a christening was in progress. The sacristan came over as she watched, she spoke to him in Russian and explained that "my parents had been born in Russia and I had learned the language as a child. So he took us around and showed us more about the church, places that were not open to the public."

*RJ photographs Natalie at work on* The Cracker Factory.

The Cracker Factory. *Left to right: psychiatric patients Donald Hotton, Delia Salvi, Natalie "Ugly Number One" and Sidney Lassick*

Another memory, no doubt reflecting a personal preoccupation, was how quickly Russian women seemed to age, looking worn and tired soon after they turned thirty.

THE WAGNERS returned to Beverly Hills on April 10, three days before Nick Gurdin had a serious heart attack. He recovered, but was very diminished for the rest of his life. Vulnerable as ever to feelings of guilt where the Gurdins were concerned, Natalie connected the attack with his emotional disturbance over her trip to Russia. By then Mud and Fahd were both sixty-eight years old, and she decided to move them to a rented condominium on Goshen Avenue in Brentwood, where they would have fewer household responsibilities.

Nick's declining health also seems to have aroused thoughts of mortality in Natalie. On April 18 she instructed her lawyers to draw up two documents, "Instructions Regarding My Medical Care" to her family and physician, and a "Directive to Physician." She approved and signed both of them. From the first:

> I am not conscious of any fear of death. It is as much a part of the human scene as the beginning and the middle span of life. So, do not try to postpone the inevitable termination, for I do not believe that such is the proper goal of medical science. A departure from this world which is artificially delayed to no purpose, increasing the span of disability, discomfort and expense, is not a proper exercise of human judgment and intelligence.

The second attested that in the case of incurable injury or illness, Natalie did not wish her life to be artificially prolonged, and directed that "all life-sustaining procedures be withheld or withdrawn, and that I be permitted to die naturally."

THAT SUMMER Richard Gregson was living in Malibu with his new wife, Julia, and as Natasha recalled: "My mother, who could be fiercely protective, was very easily threatened by my blossoming relationship with Daddy Gregson and Julia, who was quite bohemian then. When I realized Natalie was jealous, I'd tell her how I enjoyed the different atmosphere. She wanted me to have a good relationship with my father, but anxieties would overtake her. Sometimes she'd ask, 'If you had to choose between us, who would it be?' And of course I'd say, 'You.' "

When the Gregsons took Natasha horseback riding, she enjoyed it so much that (with Natalie's permission) they enrolled her in riding school for a week. "When Natalie drove me there the first day, the woman who ran the school told her she couldn't call me during the week. My mother got very angry. 'I spent three weeks in Russia,' she said, 'and was allowed to call Natasha every day. Don't tell me I can't do that in Malibu.' The woman backed down and agreed she could."

LANA WOOD added a characteristic footnote to Gurdin family history that summer, as Liz Applegate discovered when she went shopping for Natalie in Beverly Hills: "At one store they asked me when Miss Wood was going to pay her bill, and it turned out that Lana had been telling the store to charge her own purchases there to Natalie." It came as the reverse of a surprise to Natalie, but enough was enough. She consulted with RJ, then told thirty-three-year-old Lana, "You have to get your act together. I'll pay for a psychiatrist." The prodigal daughter consented, then called Natalie after two sessions: "I'm cured. I don't have to see him anymore."

IN JULY, Tom Mankiewicz directed the pilot of *Hart to Hart* with RJ and Stefanie Powers as married sleuths in the tradition of Dashiell Hammett's Nick and Nora Charles; and in September RJ and Natalie went on vacation to Paris and the south of France. In Paris they met Mart Crowley, who had been living there for three months, "moving around from New York to Rome to London to Paris, depressed by the failure of my last play, and drinking my life away." Over lunch RJ mentioned that the *Hart to Hart* pilot had been sold and the series would start shooting in October, but he was very disappointed in the scripts he'd read. "Mart!" Natalie said. "You're not working, and if you were a true friend you'd come back to L.A. with us, stay at our house and rewrite those rotten scripts."

And having paid for the first six months of psychoanalysis that led Mart to concentrate on writing *The Boys in the Band,* Natalie helped him again "by finding me a second career." At first he worked as "executive story editor" of the series, and when the producer left, he took over that job as well. And after the series completed the first season of its five-year run, he moved to an apartment of his own, then started going to AA.

IN NATALIE'S next and last TV movie, *The Memory of Eva Ryker,* she played the mentally disturbed daughter of a billionaire whose mother was drowned when a German U-boat torpedoed a cruise ship in 1939. Her father hires a journalist to investigate why the liner was attacked and other survivors died later "in mysterious circumstances." And under hypnosis, Eva has a recovered memory of her mother's death.

Natalie played two parts, mother and daughter; and the story touched two exposed nerves: her interest in mental disturbance, and Maria's often repeated account of the Gypsy in Harbin who had prophesied her death by drowning. But the director (Walter Grauman) was unable to breathe life into a poorly contrived script that included a scene of Natalie's life-and-death struggle in the dark water of a studio tank. And when she saw the movie (shortly before CBS aired it on May 7, 1980, to dank reviews), she found it even harder to endure than those two hours in the tank.

By then Natalie had been offered a big-screen role in *The Mirror Crack'd,* as part of an ensemble cast that would include Angela Lansbury, Kim Novak, Rock Hudson, Tony Curtis and Geraldine Chaplin. She liked Barry Sandler's adaptation of a Miss Marple mystery by Agatha Christie, as well as the role of a movie star furiously jealous of a rival (Kim Novak), and invited Sandler to lunch at La Scala. "I was immediately captivated by Natalie," he remembered. "Unlike so many stars, she didn't want to talk about herself. In fact we hardly even talked about the script. The movie business hadn't insulated her, she was personally very curious about me, and we talked mainly about my life." This, of course, had been Arnold Schulman's experience on *Love with the Proper Stranger* and mine on *Inside Daisy Clover.* A positive relationship with a writer, director or actor was often a deciding factor for Natalie in choosing a project, and a few days later she invited Sandler to 603 North Canon: "Again we talked about many things before discussing her role, and finally she said she would do the picture. Then the doorbell rang. 'That must be Larry,' Natalie said. She took me by the hand to the hallway,

*With Peter Ustinov in Leningrad for*
Treasures of the Hermitage

where Olivier was waiting, and laughed as she introduced us: 'Larry—
Barry. Barry—Larry.' "

But a week later, Richard Goodwin (co-producer of *The Mirror
Crack'd*) called Sandler with the news that "Natalie's leaving the project.
She and [director] Guy Hamilton had a bit of a row." Goodwin gave no
details, but Sandler had already found Hamilton "very dogmatic," as
well as underendowed with humor; and as Natalie explained later, this
time the deciding factor was a negative relationship: "Barry, I'm very
sorry, but I realized I just couldn't work with Guy Hamilton."

Elizabeth Taylor replaced her.

ON JULY 16, RJ celebrated the eighth anniversary of his wedding to Natalie with a party at the Bistro. John and Linda Foreman were among the guests, and Linda remembered that "after RJ proposed a charming, elegant toast to Natalie, she turned and whispered to me: 'He always takes my breath away.'" And once again the couple looked as if everything was and always would be fine between them.

A few days later Nick Gurdin, weakened by alcoholism as well as coronary artery disease, was hospitalized after another serious heart attack. Natalie, who visited him almost every day, was particularly touched to find him reading a Russian edition of *Anna Karenina*. When it became clear that he would never recover, Nick asked to die at home, and she arranged for a hospital bed and round-the-clock nurses at the Goshen Avenue condominium. "Natasha," he said one day, "you are a good girl," and she was also touched by this belated recognition.

After Nick died on November 6, Mud begged Natalie to let her stay at 603 North Canon for a few days. The afternoon of her arrival, Liz Applegate found her lying on the bed in a guest room, "hands and feet shaking in convulsions." She informed Natalie, who was reading a book in the master bedroom. "She'll be all right in a minute," Natalie said calmly, then continued reading.

> Linda Foreman: *"What did your father die of?" I asked Natalie. "My mother, I think," Natalie said.*

But during Nick's funeral service at Westwood Village Memorial Park, there was a noticeable crack in Natalie's calm. "She was very emotional," her daughter Natasha recalled, and Natalie's eulogy was a mixture of things she truly felt, things she wished were true and the impression of a united family that she felt compelled to give in public.

She talked about Nick's wife, "who loved him and shared his life for over forty years, and was the love of his life." She recalled "the supreme pleasure of watching and listening to him play his balalaika," smoothed over his alcoholic rages as "rich, wonderful Russian explosions," remarked (truly) that "his underside was soft and gentle," and concluded by reading the lines from Wordsworth's "Intimations of Immortality" that the schoolteacher quoted in *Splendor in the Grass:*

*Though nothing can bring back the hour*
*Of splendour in the grass, of glory in the flower*
*We will grieve not, but rather find*
*Strength in what remains behind.*

The depth of Natalie's emotion makes it impossible to believe that she ever suspected Nick Gurdin was not her father. But by yet another of those recurring coincidences in the lives of everyone concerned, a remark by the Captain to Natasha Zepaloff would soon convince her that *he* was unquestionably Natalie's father. Zepaloff's second wife had also been called Natalie, and after she died, he was moved to comment: "How curious. Now there have been three Natalies in my life."

It would have been out of character for the Captain to identify the third, but the number of times he repeated the comment (in conjunction with all the other hints that both he and Maria had dropped) left no doubt in Natasha's mind. All the same, she confided in no one except her mother.

"Is your mother going to live with you now?" Linda Foreman asked Natalie, who threw up her hands in horror. "No way!" A few days later Mud had another convulsion before agreeing to return to her condo, and in early December Natalie took her daughters to a memorial service for Nick in San Francisco, where he had bought a plot for himself and Maria in the Serbian cemetery, the only Eastern Orthodox burial ground in California. Although they seldom attended services at the Protection of the Holy Virgin Church, the rituals of their homeland's religion had a nostalgic appeal for the exiled couple; and they liked the idea, as they saw it, of a return to their native earth. Nick's brothers, Vladimir and Dmitri, were present at the service, also the Liuzunies, and "Natalie was very moved by them," according to Peggy Griffin, who accompanied her. "After the service she took Natasha and Courtney to meet them, wanting them to understand where she came from—'the real world,' as she called it." Vladimir later wrote Natalie and RJ to ask for a copy of her eulogy at the service in Westwood, and wrote again to thank them for sending it, as well as "for the beautiful poinsettia plant" delivered to his house on Christmas Day.

By the time Nick died, Natalie had not only understood the roots of his alcoholism and violence. He seemed to her a profoundly Russian character, and she identified his extremes with her own. Out of a growing desire for closeness with her Russian side, she invited the Liuzunies for a visit shortly before Christmas, and Constantin recalled that "both Natalie and her husband were wonderful, and RJ took us to the set of *Hart to Hart* and gave us a studio tour."

On December 31, the last New Year's Eve at the Wagners', the guests included Paul and Betsy Mazursky, George Segal and his wife, Gil Cates, Mart Crowley and myself. It was not formality that made the Wagners request black tie, but the occasion itself, which they felt was worth dressing up for, and those parties made it a pleasure to wear a uniform that I usually resisted. "There was always a very special feeling about them," Mazursky remembered. "If you were invited, you knew you were a real friend." And from that last New Year's Eve I remember another of RJ's toasts to Natalie, and her smile, and again the feeling that everything would always be fine between them.

In the spring of 1981, Natalie's current agent, Guy McElwaine at CMA, became aware that she'd developed a habit that he found "very strange." When she left a message on his answering machine, she sometimes identified herself as Natalie, sometimes as Natalie Wood, and sometimes as Mrs. Wagner. He soon realized, of course, that "Natalie" was calling as a friend, "Natalie Wood" as his client, and "Mrs. Wagner" as RJ's wife; but the habit continued to puzzle him.

Many people have multiple selves, the private, the public, the sexual and so on; many of them are aware of it, and it's only a problem when the separate selves are unaware of each other. Jung described them as fragments of the unconscious that broke off and took possession of the conscious mind. He called the result "psychic infection" and believed it was curable "only when we know what is attacking us, and how, where and when the attack will come."

Was Natalie's occasional habit of splitting herself into Natalie, Natalie Wood and Mrs. Wagner a sign that her personality had started to fracture in the last year of her life? Other signs make it seem very likely. In the past, she'd been strongly fascinated by *Sybil* and the fractured personality of the girl in *I Never Promised You a Rose Garden*. And in the spring of 1981 she became equally fascinated with Zelda Fitzgerald after reading Nancy Milford's *Zelda*. (Coincidentally, Jung had been approached by Scott Fitzgerald to treat Zelda, but by 1938 he'd decided not to accept patients that he considered psychotic.) Natalie took an option on the book in partnership with William Storke, longtime friend of both Wagners and co-producer of *Treasures of the Hermitage;* and John Irvin, whom she chose to direct *Zelda,* found her "increasingly drawn to playing wildness and exploring the dark side. She attributed part of this to being Russian, which she was very proud of."

But "the dark side" had another source, and Natalie wasn't proud of it. Toward the end of April, she left an "emergency message" with the answering service of Jeffery Rochford, who had recently founded the holistic Rochford Clinic, asking for an appointment at the clinic on the following Saturday, when it was closed. Today the clinic offers personal counseling and various "alternative" treatments, including acupuncture and reflexology, has many clients from the movie industry and not a few troubled children of Beverly Hills families; but in 1981 its reputation had only just begun to grow. Natalie, always quick to learn about new methods of therapy, became its first "celebrity client," and as Rochford remembered: "She was very charming, and on the surface self-possessed. But I noticed that her eyes were not focused, their pupils too dilated, and I detected that 'buzz in the body' when people take drugs. When Natalie told me that she had headaches and neck pain, I asked what medications she was taking. She hesitated, then said: 'Some medications for pain. I need help to get going in the morning.' She also mentioned 'anxiety' and 'needing help to sleep.' "

As well as studying Chinese medicine, Rochford had acquired expert knowledge of the use of drugs to control pain as a hospital worker and assistant at surgical procedures. He knew that "addicts are even more expert than pharmacists," and soon realized that "Natalie knew exactly how to manipulate herself by adjusting doses so that she never got too high or too low, but achieved the state of mind she wanted to be in." He also knew that "people in Natalie's situation don't understand that the results are not quite what they imagine. Long-term use of pain medications screws up the nervous system."

Natalie returned to the clinic for four more sessions, during which she began to reveal the extent of her addictions. She said that she "needed help to sleep every night," and when Rochford asked if she'd had to increase the dosage over the years, she admitted it. "But then she shut up." Their final session was the frankest. Natalie confided that she drank wine every day, at first admitting to "just one glass," then saying

*With RJ on the swim step of* Splendour, *1980*

that "sometimes" she drank more, and "she also needed more and more adrenaline to function as an actress."

Her eyes also told Rochford that "Natalie's liver was challenged," even though he knew that "the Russian liver," with its genetic legacy of several centuries of heavy drinkers, was extraordinarily resilient and had adjusted to metabolize large quantities of alcohol: "But it seems I got too frank about drug use and addiction to alcohol. I realized I'd gone too far when Natalie's expression suddenly changed. A look of withdrawal came over her face, she didn't say anything, but she never came back."

And never told RJ that she went there.


ALSO TOWARD the end of April, when Natalie and I met for lunch, I had no idea that I would never see her again. She began by mentioning that her forty-third birthday was not far away, and asked if I thought she looked her age. ("To stay on an even keel," Tom Mankiewicz said to me later, "Natalie needed all her cards, and she was very afraid of losing her beauty card.") I told her that she looked wonderful, although a different kind of wonderful from the Natalie of *Love with the Proper Stranger*. It pleased her in one way and disappointed her in another. Did Vivien Leigh, she asked, ever consider a face-lift? Yes, I said, and decided against it, "because if you've been famous for your beauty, everyone *knows*."

Although Natalie saw the point of this, she was very aware of the fate of "older" stars in Hollywood, and very afraid of sharing it. She told me how Barbara Stanwyck, who admired her and invited her to dinner at her house, "seemed so bitter and lonely, and dismissed so many people we talked about, particularly actors and writers, as commies or fags." The experience determined Natalie "never to end up like that," and she made the same resolution after Bette Davis dined with the Wagners at North Canon Drive. The more drunken Bette became, the more ego-maniacal, and while talking about her career (well past its prime but still almost her only subject), she mentioned *The Star*. "But of course you're too young to remember it," she told Natalie. "Bette," Natalie reminded her, "I played your daughter in that picture." No hiccup of surprise, and not even a sign that the star had heard what Natalie said.

Natalie also knew that Rita Hayworth and I had been friends until Alzheimer's disease incapacitated her, and recalled my account of her desperation at the way movie producers dismissed her as an over-the-hill Gilda. All these things, and the experience of *Cat on a Hot Tin Roof*, Natalie said, had started her thinking about the theater. And she decided to talk about doing a play with Robert Fryer, a movie producer who was also on the board of the Ahmanson Theater in Los Angeles. They considered and dismissed several possibilities, and shortly before Nick Gurdin died, Fryer sent her a copy of *Anastasia,* the romanticized story of Anna Anderson, a stateless refugee whose memory was wiped out by a powerful trauma during World War II, then partly recovered in a Berlin hospital, when she believed herself to be the only Romanov who escaped execution in 1917. "It clicked," Natalie said, "with where I came from."

ROBERT FRYER HAD also agreed to produce *Zelda,* and while waiting for him to set up the movie, Natalie and RJ took advantage of his spring break from *Hart to Hart* by spending the last two weeks of May in Paris. During the second week John Foreman called her from Los Angeles with the offer of a role in his forthcoming production of *Brainstorm* at

MGM. He began by outlining its story, about two research scientists who develop a sensory device that enables all kinds of personal experiences, memories, dreams, fears, even the taste of foods, to be transferred from one subject to another. Then he hoped Natalie would agree to play the wife of one of the scientists, whose immersion in work strains their marriage until his device hooks them up to experience each other's feelings, and they become close again.

*Zelda* remained Natalie's first choice, but when she returned to L.A., Fryer reported a lack of interest in the studios he'd approached so far; and she told McElwaine that she'd accept the role in *Brainstorm*. He read the script and thought the scientist's wife "a nothing part, but Natalie wanted to work, there was nothing else on offer, so I made the deal."

She had asked for Edith Head to design her costumes, but Edith became ill at the end of June, and Foreman engaged Donfeld, who remembered that "the reunion with Natalie was joyous. She took the initiative by saying, 'Weren't we awful to each other on that Blake Edwards picture?' And right away we were friends again."

Don told her that "a fashion statement" would be out of place for Karen in *Brainstorm,* and he wanted "*less* of everything—movie-star hair, jewelry and accessories." Natalie agreed, but when he criticized a bracelet she was wearing, she refused to take it off. "I asked her why and she said, 'I can give you two reasons. One, Jimmy Dean gave it to me during *Rebel* and I've never taken it off. Two, I had a fall roller-skating when I was a little girl and fractured my wrist.' Then she smiled and asked which story I liked best. 'Well,' I said, 'I don't think you'll get much mileage out of a little girl roller-skating.' " The real reason, of course, was yet one more example of Natalie, in RJ's phrase, "sitting on" anything that would threaten the official story of her "normal" parents and "normal" childhood.

Foreman also proposed to cast Christopher Walken as Karen's husband, Michael, and asked John Irvin (who had directed Walken in his latest movie, *The Dogs of War*) to arrange a dinner for the Wagners to meet him: "Chris was a theater actor who lived in New York, and Natalie thought he was New York real, New York honest. But she had a very romantic fantasy of New York—creative, dangerous and artist-friendly as opposed to Beverly Hills with its sprinklers and endless movie talk. Chris encouraged this, was very dismissive of Hollywood, and very early on, I think, RJ sensed there might be trouble."

At first, according to John Irvin, Natalie romanticized Walken for what he represented, "a symbol of the daring, free-spirited actor," rather than for himself. She had seen him in *The Deer Hunter,* a performance that won him an Academy Award for Best Supporting Actor, was even more impressed by his talent after Foreman arranged a screening of *The Dogs of War,* and became "genuinely excited" when they discussed the script of *Brainstorm.* Walken, who was openly contemptuous of it, encouraged Natalie to be "creative" and improvise. "He'll make this film important," she told John, who recognized the signs of an intense "fixation" and likened Natalie to "someone driving a car so fast that she was in danger of losing control."

By this time it was clear to John that she found Walken personally attractive, and he felt sure that "it suited Chris's sense of fun and mischief to encourage her. He made her laugh, and he carried himself like a toreador, always prodding, probing and teasing."

"Sometimes addicts get too high," Jeffery Rochford discovered from treating them, "and then they go for danger." Natalie had previously gone for danger in the person of Nicky Hilton, when she was already seriously involved with Richard Gregson and addicted (to a lesser extent) to various medications. Ten years later, although dangerously close to "the dark side," she could still pull back and become briskly professional. At MGM, where she met Donfeld for costume fittings, she told him matter-of-factly that she'd gained a few pounds, but was going on a diet, and as usual would cut out liquor during the shoot. "By the time *Brainstorm* went into production," he recalled, "I didn't even have to use the waist suppressor we'd made for her."

As well as dieting and not drinking, Natalie employed a personal trainer; and according to Asa Maynor, she was "typically alert to the times" in following the new exercise routine called Pilates, imported from Britain, which involved holding on to a pulley while raising her legs above her head. But her confidence was temporarily jolted when she saw the costume, makeup and hair tests shot by the *Brainstorm* cinematographer, Richard Yuricich. Donfeld reassured her by insisting it wasn't her fault. He found Yuricich's work for the tests "pitifully inept," and would see no improvement during production, when he realized that the director, Douglas Trumbull, chosen for his brilliant special effects in *2001: A Space Odyssey,* was far more interested in technology than in how actors looked or performed.

ON SEPTEMBER 18, when she left for the weekend at Esalen, Natalie was unaware that an ambulance had arrived at a hacienda-style house only a few minutes away on Coldwater Canyon, to take Edith Head, eighty-three years old and suffering from a progressive blood disease, to Good Samaritan Hospital. At Esalen, Donfeld remembered, "Natalie bonded instantly with Stan and Christina Grof," but he wondered if it was a sign of things to come when she broke her rule by drinking two glasses of white wine at dinner.

September 28 was Natalie's first day of location filming in and around Raleigh, North Carolina. The schedule had been rearranged so that she'd be free the next day to fly back to Los Angeles for Natasha's birthday. And to her family, she seemed the tender, playful wife and mother they loved so much; but in mid-October, when RJ took a week-end break from filming *Hart to Hart* and flew to Raleigh, he became very uneasy about the situation with Walken. "It crossed my mind that they were having an affair, but I wasn't sure, and didn't say anything about it to Natalie." A few days later, during one of the regular phone calls she made to her family, something else disturbed him: "Some kind of change seemed to be coming over Natalie. She told me about heli-copters hovering over the hotel and dropping a net over it for a scene in the movie. But I knew there was no such scene."

For Donfeld, there were other disturbing signs. Natalie continued to break her rule and was not only drinking but drinking too much, some-times during the day. And Walken seemed determined to needle him with complaints about his costumes. "Finally, after he wanted to change the color of his shoelaces, it came to a showdown, and I told him I was fed up. He reached in his pocket, took out a key, placed it on the table, then stared at me. Natalie and I had more or less adjoining suites at the hotel, so I knew her room number. It was the number on that key, and Walken's way of telling me who was in charge."

Michael Childers, a longtime friend of the Wagners, had a special assignment as still photographer on the movie. He soon realized that Walken, usually a light drinker, had begun to keep pace with Natalie, who was drinking vodka as well as white wine. "What do you think of Chris?" she asked, the day after Childers arrived, but he'd already seen the excitement in her eyes when they were together, and knew "she had already made up her mind that he was wonderful." On a personal level, Childers found Walken "a very strange guy, with a darkness about him." Professionally, he noted "telltale signs of Natalie's white-wine-and-vodka routine on her face." Natalie herself was worried about them, and asked him to "protect" her by checking the lighting for her close-ups: "The cameraman seemed inexperienced in lighting faces, so on occasion I did suggest a few changes, which were grudgingly accepted. And when I took portrait stills of Natalie, I used just about every filter in my collection."

Like Donfeld, Childers suspected that Natalie and Walken were having an affair. "From the way she looked at him, I thought she was determined to have one great location romance in her life." Walken, without being specific, told John Irvin later that "Natalie made all the moves." Although the affair with the key could have been an example of Walken "prodding" and "teasing," she had already broken her rule about not drinking; and she gave both Donfeld and Childers the impression that she'd also broken her rule about never being unfaithful to RJ.

After Natalie's death, Walken refused to discuss what happened on board *Splendour* during the last weekend of her life, except in his statements to the police. Later, in three separate media interviews, he made a few brief, noncommittal remarks, then maintained a silence that he refused to break for this book, although he knew that the Wagner family hoped he would. But whatever finally occurred between Natalie and Walken, her emotional involvement with him, and the way he reacted, is not in question. Irvin believes that "she never got as much as she wanted from Chris, because it was part of his 'teasing' approach to life to hold back. If he actually made love to her, and maybe he did, I'm sure it didn't happen more than three or four times." Again, whether or not she was technically unfaithful to RJ, Natalie knew that she'd made him jealous. As a mother, she appeared to have inherited a few of her own mother's genes, and in her relationship with Walken she inherited another. But unlike Maria, who chose to live on the edge, Natalie was driven to it in a state of confusion that prepared the way for the final scenes with RJ and Walken on board *Splendour.*

THE CHAOTIC SHOOT of *Brainstorm* mirrored the chaos of Natalie's personal life. Douglas Trumbull, whom Walken encouraged Natalie to try and get rid of, had experience and skill in handling sci-fi effects, but not in directing actors. He was additionally handicapped by an inept screenplay and a cinematographer whose overlit visuals were unsympathetic to the human face, and even made some of the bleached-out laboratory scenes look as if they were shot on defective stock. And there was soon no producer to take charge, according to Donfeld, as "John Foreman had become infatuated with a young assistant who introduced him to the delights of heroin." After reports filtered back to MGM, in fact, Jack Grossberg was appointed "executive in charge of production," and Foreman (who produced only one more movie, *Prizzi's Honor,* before dying of AIDS in 1992) is not listed in any capacity on the credits.

In Natalie's case, the dual chaos led to a strange, uncharacteristic nonperformance, with no hint of the actress that Burt Brinckerhoff had found "at the top of her game" only two years earlier. She seems to be somewhere else, and it's hard to decide whether she was more disconnected from her role or from herself, particularly in the reaction shots, when you're not always sure who or what she's reacting to. When Jeffery Rochford saw the movie, he had the same impression, although he detected an occasional private moment of "connection" in the looks exchanged between Natalie and Walken.

But the overall effect is their lack of connection with each other, especially as their only erotic scene ended on the cutting-room floor. Among the memories of past happiness that the sensory device enables Karen and Michael to share is a night of love in a boat on a moonlit lake. For Natalie, torn between her fear of dark water and her excitement at playing the scene with Walken, it was another source of conflict. Michael Childers, who witnessed the scene, described it as "alarming. Natalie wore an almost see-through nightgown, was in a state of suppressed hysteria, and clung passionately to Walken, partly because she was so attracted to him, partly for protection."

Stan and Christina Grof, whom Natalie had asked to visit her during the location shoot, found her "in a time of great upheaval." They encouraged her "to discuss the need to find a way out of her own darkness," and although it proved to be the same kind of darkness that she'd discussed with Rochford, their final impression was of "someone not at all despairing, but determined to work her way out." In fact, according to Christina, "she was basically optimistic."

During that first visit the Grofs also supervised a session of deep-

*On the* Brainstorm *location: "Her eyes were
not focused, the pupils dilated."*

breathing exercises and meditation. "Walken attended, because she
wanted him to, and because we always liked the subject to be accompanied by a friend." During and after the experience, he appeared noncommittal; but Natalie was very open in her reactions: "grief, anger and
finally a kind of transcendence." Donfeld saw her shortly after the session, and "the look of happiness on her face, the sound of genuine peace
in her voice, was something I'll never forget, partly in itself and partly
because it was so different from the way she'd recently looked and
sounded."

ON NOVEMBER 5, the *Brainstorm* unit moved to MGM for four weeks
of studio shooting. On November 16, Natalie's daybook records that she

watched Mike Wallace's TV profile of Jean Seberg, whom she had liked and admired. It might seem to throw light (or more darkness) on the last weeks of Natalie's life that she watched a program about a deeply troubled actress who had committed suicide two years earlier; but in fact suicide was not on Natalie's mind, and as the Grofs realized, she was literally fighting for her life.

*Anastasia* was due to start rehearsals on January 4, 1982, and she was deeply involved with the choice of a director and leading actors. She had hoped that Laurence Olivier would be available to direct, but he sent apologies by Western Union:

MY DARLING GIRL PLEASE FORGIVE ME I FIND IMPOSSIBLE TO REFUSE A BIG JOB OVER THE NEW YEAR STOP WAS HALF AFRAID OF THIS FROM OUR PERSONAL POINT OF VIEW BUT ANXIOUS FOR IT TO HAPPEN FROM OTHER POINTS OF VIEW STOP PLEASE FORGIVE ME HAVE RE-READ ANASTASIA AND FIND IT VERY RESPECTABLE STILL AND NOT AS I WAS AFRAID OLDFASHIONED STOP IT STANDS UP VERY WELL STOP I AM SO SAD NOT TO HAVE THIS LOVELY EXCUSE TO SEE YOU BOTH AND HUG YOU LIKE A GREAT BIG BEAR ALWAYS YOUR DEVOTED LARRY

Although Natalie's daybook lists three other possible directors, Lindsay Anderson, José Quintero and Andrei Serban, she accepted Robert Fryer's choice of Arvin Brown, whose recent productions for the Long Wharf Theatre in New Haven had been highly praised. Her next concern was to cast the role of the Grand Duchess, Anastasia's Grand Inquisitor. Viveca Lindfors, who had played Anastasia in the original Broadway production forty years earlier, and Natalie's stepmother-to-be in *No Sad Songs for Me,* wrote to propose herself as the Grand Duchess, and hoped that "we could get together and create magic, and do the piece on television too." She also advised Natalie to get hold of the English translation of the original French play (by Marcelle Maurette), which had provided the basis for the movie with Ingrid Bergman and was far superior to the Broadway version by Guy Bolton.

Natalie took Lindfors's advice about the French play, but after considering other candidates (including Eva Le Gallienne and Lila Kedrova) for the Grand Duchess, she asked Olivier to intercede on her behalf with Wendy Hiller, and he was successful.

The daybook also contains a reading list for background information: *Thirteen Years at the Russian Court* by Pierre Gilliard, *The Woman Who Rose Again,* by Gleb Botkin, *Anastasia* by Harriet von Rathlef-Keilman, and *The Murder of the Romanovs* by Paul Bulygin and Alexander Kerensky. Another note refers to forthcoming sessions with Michael Childers, to photograph her in costume for the theater poster, and with Donfeld, to discuss his designs for her gown at the opening-night reception. She also agreed to another photo session, for a feature in *Life* magazine. The date was set for November 26, the day after Thanksgiving, and the magazine accepted Natalie's conditions: Childers as photographer, Donfeld as adviser during the session, and a case of Dom Perignon.

*John Irvin: The last week was very ominous.*

On November 20, Natalie arrived for dinner at Roddy McDowall's house. Naturally he'd invited RJ as well, but although she explained that he was away on location, she brought Christopher Walken instead, without letting Roddy know in advance. "Don't tell RJ," she said, taking Roddy aside, and he was shocked because "it seemed so out of character for Natalie to do a thing like that."

On November 21, Natalie postponed the *Life* photo session until the following week, and told Childers and Donfeld that "RJ had set his heart on a weekend of sailing."

By November 23, *Brainstorm* was four days behind schedule, and when Natalie received the new shooting schedule for her remaining scenes, she found that MGM had deleted four of them. She immediately dictated a businesslike memorandum to her new agent, Stan Kamen at the William Morris office. (By then Guy McElwaine had become a production executive at Columbia.) After itemizing every preproduction meeting, costume fitting, makeup test and rehearsal she had attended, Natalie offered to waive all payments due if MGM agreed to reinstate the deleted scenes.

The next day, November 24, Stanislav and Christina Grof paid Natalie a second visit at MGM and found her more relaxed than before. RJ, who had just returned from location in Hawaii for an episode of *Hart to Hart,* was also visiting the set that day, and when he joined the Grofs for a while in Natalie's trailer, Christina noticed two photographs

*Christopher Walken and Natalie on the set of* Brainstorm

of *Splendour* on the wall behind him. In retrospect, the conversation that followed seemed deeply ironic. "We talked about how much they enjoyed the boat. RJ said that he and Natalie had become such expert sailors that they could almost handle it without a crew."

And while they sat talking, Christina recalled, "a vote was being taken from the crew of the movie, because it was behind schedule, whether or not to work overtime through the holiday. By a majority of one, they voted to observe the holiday." Like the "eerie presence" of Christopher Walken, who came by the trailer a few minutes before Natalie was called to the set, it struck her in retrospect as "a shadow across the movie."

Another shadow: At Edith Head's wish, reports of her illness had been withheld from the media, and with RJ's consent, Donfeld kept the news from Natalie. But he arranged for his assistant, Sally Edwards, to get a regular account of Edith's condition from her supervising nurses at Good Samaritan. Edwards also regularly left messages and sent flowers "from Natalie" and sometimes "from Natalie and RJ" to Edith's room.

The day before *Brainstorm* stopped production for the holidays, Edith died, and Donfeld broke the news to Natalie in her trailer. "She was deeply upset that she hadn't been in contact with Edith in hospital. I assured her that she *had,* and explained *how.* Then she wished she'd sent flowers, and I assured her that she *did.* And the nurses had told me, I added, that Edith was particularly pleased when the message on the card was 'from Natalie.' "

Natalie had once described Edith as "kind of a surrogate mother." Now, on the verge of tears, she thanked Don, then said quietly: "I'd begun to suspect that Family Hollywood was gone forever"—as if recalling the years, as Robert Mulligan commented, "when a movie lot was a second home."

NATALIE HAD dinner alone with Delphine Mann on the evening of November 22, and suddenly confided as they said goodnight outside the restaurant: "I've never been happier or unhappier in my life." Then she drove off in her Mercedes. But to Josh Donen, who kept her company and stayed at 603 North Canon Drive for the week that RJ was away on location, "Natalie seemed terribly lost and conflicted. Once she pointed to the security iron grillwork in front of the door of the house and said, 'I feel like I'm living in a cage.' And she was taking three separate sleeping pills every night."

To Josh it seemed clear that "in spite of her love for RJ and her daughters, Natalie had been fired by Walken's talk of freedom and dedication to art." Although only five years younger than Natalie, "in her eyes he represented a new, independent generation, like Robert de Niro and Al Pacino." And she desperately wanted to be part of it. "She was looking for a way to bust out, although she knew it wouldn't be right, and her restlessness encouraged her to flirt openly with Chris Walken in RJ's presence. It made him terribly jealous, and jealousy made RJ drink too much. A very kind and thoughtful man, but his demons came out when he was drunk."

To Guy McElwaine, the situation with Natalie and RJ seemed "very bad" and reminded him of *Who's Afraid of Virginia Woolf?* John Irvin remembered Natalie arguing with RJ about the superiority of New York theater to Hollywood, and "her desire to get out of Los Angeles led to an ugly scene. She told RJ, 'You've only got five expressions as an actor,' and forced him to a 'commercial' defense that wasn't his true position. 'But they paid for this house,' he came back at her, '*and* your jewelry.' "

Another irony: As RJ recalled, "Originally there was no real conflict" about leaving Los Angeles. "When Natalie first planned to do *Anastasia*, and before she met Walken, we'd talked of buying a farm in upstate New York, and it had nothing to do with what we argued about later. We'd become very disturbed that Natasha couldn't go outside the house to mail a letter, or whatever, without a crowd of autograph seekers waiting. And we wanted to get away from all that."

But now that both of them had begun to drink heavily, their demons came out to fight each other, and cast the longest shadows of all. RJ never confronted Natalie with his jealousy of Walken until Thanksgiving weekend, when all three, literally and metaphorically at sea, had been drinking for several hours; and it struck all three with the force of a delayed explosion. In retrospect, he explained his reluctance to face the situation earlier: "By that time I'd got to know the signs of Natalie 'possessed.' The switch from her career to her marriage, then back again, and a few years later, the switch to her children. Perhaps I didn't pay enough attention, and wasn't giving her enough, too busy working when Natalie, as Howard Jeffrey used to say, stamped her foot. And there were always people around telling her, 'You're so talented, you mustn't give it up.' "

But although it wasn't only Walken who encouraged Natalie's career drive, his talk of "freedom and dedication to art" encouraged her to undervalue her role as wife and mother; and Walken's voice was obviously the most persuasive for someone disturbed, overmedicated and attracted to him. The prospect of a long weekend on stormy waters discouraged almost everyone that the Wagners invited to join them on *Splendour*—Michael Childers, Mart Crowley, Donfeld, Josh Donen, Peggy Griffin, Delphine Mann. Although some had a genuine excuse to decline the invitation, like a family commitment, others invented one. The only person to accept was Christopher Walken.

On the cold, rainy Thursday evening of November 26, Thanksgiving dinner at 603 North Canon Drive was a very muted celebration. Natalie's daybook listed the guests: Mud, Mrs. Wagner (RJ's mother), Mart Crowley, Josh Donen, Delphine Mann and Kate Wagner. RJ went to bed early, shortly after Natasha and Courtney. The other guests left early, except for Delphine. Natalie needed company until she went to sleep, and Delphine recalled that it took her until three a.m. on November 27.

"11.0. *Splendour*. Chris Walken," Natalie wrote in her daybook for November 27; and on that cold, drizzly and windy Friday the Wagners met him at Marina del Rey, where the boat was docked. During the twenty-two-mile voyage to Catalina, Walken was mildly seasick and spent most of the time in his stateroom until *Splendour* dropped anchor four hours later, offshore from Avalon, the island's tourist center. Although the Wagners were experienced sailors, Natalie had once told Sophie Irvin that she was always unnerved by the ocean when "it was turbulent, and never still"—and at this stage in her life, the last thing she needed was additional turbulence.

In 1975 Dennis Davern had brought the boat from Florida to Long Beach, where the owner had instructed him to sell it; and when RJ bought it, he retained Davern as skipper. The Wagners were his first experience of movie people, but their weekend cruises had introduced him to many others—Elia Kazan, Roddy McDowall, David Niven, Laurence Olivier. The thirty-four-year-old skipper remained starstruck, and although totally unprepared for what happened that weekend, he had been around long enough to realize it was ripe for exploitation.

Media speculation over what happened began at the press conference of Dr. Thomas T. Noguchi, the Los Angeles coroner, on the afternoon of November 30, ten hours after Natalie's body had been found. A horde of alleged close friends (former child actors, classmates from Van Nuys High, Natalie's stand-in on *Rebel*) came forward with personal confidences in various magazine and tabloid interviews, an E! channel *True Hollywood Story*, and in the recent TV miniseries partly based on *Natasha*, a "biography" of Natalie Wood published in 2001.

Many people live in the hope of living on as a memory, and one way of ensuring this is to become part of the memory of a famous dead person. The invasion of a dead person's memory is occasionally an act of total fantasy, but more often it has a shallow root in reality; and the invader has at least been friendly (without reaching the true friendship stage) with the dead person before he or she became celebrated. And if so many people chose to invade Natalie's memory, and claimed to know things that nobody else knew about her childhood, her love affairs, her fears, her death, "it's because she had a quality of paying attention," RJ believes, "that made them feel they were important to her."

But Lana Wood and Dennis Davern, the captain of *Splendour*, are more complex cases. Lana grew up in the shadow of a beautiful and talented movie-star sister, and her "memoir" is transparent with envy. Perhaps not coincidentally, in 2001 she validated the "discovery" of an extract, published in the *Globe,* from a spurious autobiography that Natalie was alleged to have begun in the mid-1960s. At one point it referred to the pride Natalie took in her "stunningly beautiful" and "talented" sister. And it seems even less of a coincidence that soon after RJ refused Lana's request for a loan, the same tabloid ran a feature about Robert Wagner refusing to pay the medical bills of his favorite niece (Lana's daughter).

Like other tabloids, the *Globe* pays for "inside information," but Lana was not the only self-appointed insider who needed money. Dennis Davern, as Liz Applegate recalled, "had a lot of debts and owed support payments to his ex-wife, who was going to sue him." In a succession of tabloid and TV interviews, several of them paid for, he gave increasingly lurid accounts of the night of November 29. And Lana not only endorsed his final "revelation" that Natalie fell overboard after a furious argument with a drunken RJ, who stood on deck and watched her drown; she agreed that Peter G. Rydyn, a British journalist who describes himself as "the International Retributor," "could be right" when he claimed in a 1994 interview with the *Globe* that Natalie was "murdered by Christopher Walken," and the crime was "contrived by Robert Wagner, backed by Jill St. John." After ten years of relentless pursuit, however, the Retributor has yet to produce any evidence.

In relating the events of that weekend, I have relied on the only verifiable firsthand sources. Police files confirm that RJ was first questioned by Deputy Kroll of the Los Angeles County Sheriff's Department's station around six a.m. on November 30, later that morning by Duane Rasure of the Sheriff's Department, and again on December 4. Walken was questioned on November 30 and December 3, and his statements, like RJ's and Rasure's, are matters of police record. Other important evidence in police files comes from Ann Laughton and Linda Winkler, respectively night clerk and day receptionist at the Pavilion Lodge motel on Catalina, and Kurt Craig of the Two Harbors patrol office.

Robert Wagner talked to me at length about that weekend, including his discussion with Doug Bombard, the owner of Doug's Harbor Reef, who first discovered Natalie's body, and Bombard confirmed RJ's account of their discussion. Equally important are the coroner's report of Thomas T. Noguchi, his subsequent memoir of the case in *Coroner,* which includes vital evidence from Paul Miller (whose boat was moored not far from *Splendour* on the night of November 29), and the joint autopsy report by Noguchi and his deputy examiner, Dr. Joseph Choi.

During the last day of her life, Natalie made three phone calls from Catalina, one to Mart Crowley, the others to Josh Donen. Like the final entries in her daybook for November 28–29, 1981, they never came to light during the police investigation.

> *Lillian Hellman: Much of what appears perfectly clear when you're drinking never appears clear again, probably because it never was.*

*Splendour* anchored offshore around three o'clock on the afternoon of November 27, and around two hours later RJ took Natalie and Walken to Avalon in the motorized dinghy. While Davern remained on board to prepare dinner, the trio inspected a few tourist boutiques and the art deco casino, then began drinking margaritas with beer chasers at the El Galleon bar. Around nine o'clock they decided to return to *Splendour*. By this time a storm had been forecast, there was a heavy ocean swell, and an argument erupted between Natalie and RJ when she refused to take the dinghy in cold, dark and turbulent water.

From this point on, mainly due to the Hellman syndrome, RJ's memory (like Walken's) is alternately clear and foggy. He recalls that he finally persuaded Natalie to change her mind about getting in the dinghy; and he agrees that his suspicion of an affair between Natalie and Walken, and Natalie's anger with him for being suspicious, fueled all their later arguments.

During dinner on board, all three began drinking again; and like the ocean swell, tension mounted. When RJ suggested moving *Splendour* to calmer waters close to the shore, Natalie gave him another argument, described by Walken as "some kind of hubbub" that he overheard as he left the saloon for his stateroom because he felt seasick again.

Evidently alcohol and emotional confusion overcame Natalie's earlier fear of dark, turbulent water. She broke off the argument with RJ by insisting that Davern take her to Avalon in the dinghy, and he was unable to dissuade her. Ann Laughton, on the night desk at the Pavilion Lodge motel when Natalie booked rooms for herself and Davern, thought they both seemed equally "intoxicated." Linda Winkler, day clerk at the motel, thought Natalie seemed "somewhat disoriented" the next morning, when she asked about transportation to the mainland. She was unsure of her room number and had forgotten that she'd paid for both rooms by credit card the previous night.

The message that Natalie left on Josh Donen's answering machine that morning confirms Winkler's statement: "Have you heard from RJ? I'm here [at the Pavilion Lodge] with Dennis. I don't know what happened. I'm lost."

Later, when she called Mart Crowley from the dock at Avalon, Natalie had regained control of herself. "I had a terrible fight with RJ last night," he recalled her saying, "and decided to leave the boat and got Dennis to take me in the dinghy to Avalon. We spent the night at the Pavilion Lodge and as I was scared to be alone, Dennis slept on the floor of my room. I'm going back to the boat now and make one more attempt to talk sense into RJ. But stay by your phone, and if it doesn't work, I'll call you again and ask you to meet me where the helicopter takes off."

Mart heard nothing more from Natalie, but she left a second message on Josh's machine: "I'm back on the boat. Everything's fine."

RJ could not recall what was actually said during the "hubbub" that Walken had overheard, only that in essence, like the even more violent dispute that would occur after Natalie returned, it was a replay of the scene when she was filming *From Here to Eternity* in Honolulu. The difference was that Natalie as well as RJ had drunk too much, and in the deepest personal crisis of her life, she was "swishing her tail" at Walken far more insistently than she'd swished it at William Devane. Only Walken, who responded in kind, knows for certain what the flirtation led to, and whether he played an Iago-like role in provoking RJ's jealousy, or whether it was justified.

His silence also makes it impossible to know why Natalie became so angry that she insisted on going ashore. Because RJ's jealousy, as in Devane's case, was unfounded? Or because it was justified, she felt guilty, and took flight? But should Walken ever break his silence, some will disbelieve him if he denies that they had an affair, and others will be equally incredulous if he admits that they did. Either way, it's clear that Natalie was at least emotionally unfaithful to RJ, and that her "everything's fine" message to Josh Donen confirms Jim Sikking's verdict on the Honolulu episode: "As angry as they could get with each other, there was always this bond."

In fact, Walken echoed Natalie when he told the police that next day "everything was fine." But not for long. After Natalie cooked a breakfast of huevos rancheros for four, RJ again suggested moving the boat to calmer waters. This time she agreed. "Cruise to isthmus. Chris Walken, RJ," her daybook noted, and by one o'clock that afternoon *Splendour* was moored offshore at Isthmus Cove, on the more isolated northern end of the island. Not surprisingly, everyone decided to nap for a while, but Natalie and Walken woke up before the others, decided to go ashore together in the dinghy, and left a note for RJ.

This was Natalie's "going for danger" personality taking over again, an act of clear provocation to RJ, and a response to Walken's "sense of mischief." (After all, he could have refused to go along.) They docked the dinghy at Two Harbors, then walked to its only bar and restaurant, Doug's Harbor Reef, and sat drinking for two hours. Around four o'clock RJ and Davern joined them, after calling for a shore boat by radio, and the drinking continued until seven, when they moved to the restaurant area for dinner.

By then Natalie's mood was distinctly "Russian." She consulted the wine list, found it unsatisfactory and sent Davern to fetch three bottles from *Splendour*. Later in the evening, according to Walken, "we proposed a toast" (to whom or what his statement didn't specify, and it's hard to imagine). They all raised their glasses, and after Walken threw his glass to the floor, Natalie followed suit, announcing that it was an old Russian custom.

Before they left the restaurant around ten o'clock, the manager phoned Kurt Craig at the Harbor Patrol office to warn him that they were all very drunk. Craig later told the police that he watched the group board the dinghy and heard Natalie "scream," but didn't know whether it was because she was drunk or "unhappy at something that happened in the restaurant." RJ has no memory of this.

Back on board *Splendour*, the drinking continued in the saloon, and according to RJ: "Walken kept encouraging Natalie to pursue her career as an actress, to follow her own desires and needs. He talked about his 'total pursuit of a career,' which was more important to him than his personal life, and said it was obvious I didn't share his point of view. It struck me as some kind of put-down, and I got really angry. I told him him to stay out of it, then picked up a wine bottle, slammed it on the table, and smashed it to pieces."

But Walken didn't stay out of it. He told RJ to "let Natalie do what she wanted to do," which had the effect of switching the focus of RJ's anger to Natalie. "I complained that doing what she wanted to do took her away from home and the kids too often." Instead of answering, Natalie got up, turned her back on both of them and left for the master stateroom. The drinking and "the circular argument" between the two men continued until Walken also left the saloon and stepped out on deck. For how long? RJ wasn't sure, but thought he came back "soon afterward," and "soon afterward" went to bed.

Police reports of Walken's two interviews suggest that the Hellman syndrome had blurred his memory as well. In the first interview, he stated that he "got into a small beef" with RJ and went outside on deck for a few minutes. When he returned, Natalie was still sitting in the saloon. She "seemed disturbed," then got up and left, and he presumed "she had gone to bed." In the second, more detailed interview, he said that "they had all been drinking," and RJ began to complain that "she [Natalie] was away from home too much." Walken defended her, saying "she was an actress, she was an important person, this was her life." Then he realized he was violating his own rule "about getting involved in an argument between a man and his wife," and stepped out "for some air." When he returned, "everybody was apologizing, particularly Robert Wagner, and everything seemed fine."

Davern's statement that he and RJ "sat up drinking until one-thirty in the morning," after Natalie and then Walken left the saloon is one of the few that RJ endorsed. But he was unable to recall exactly how long they sat up, and it's unclear from either of Walken's statements how long he stayed in the saloon with RJ before going to bed. But although a precise time frame is impossible to establish, the time frame is not the key to what happened after Walken left for his stateroom.

The position of the dinghy is far more relevant. It could be hoisted up on deck or tied up to either port or starboard side of the boat. In the past, the ropes had occasionally loosened, and when tied up to port, *Valiant* banged against the side of the master stateroom. According to Guy McElwaine, a frequent guest on the boat, "RJ was a better ship's captain than the captain he employed, and his final night duty before going to bed was to make sure that everything was secure, including the dinghy." RJ was certain that *Valiant* had been tied up to port when they returned from Two Harbors on the night of November 29, and that he hadn't checked the ropes by the time Natalie retired to the master stateroom. He also recalled that "some time after" Walken went to bed, he went down to the master stateroom "to make sure Natalie was all right," and found she wasn't there. "Then I checked the dinghy—gone. In my totally fuddled state, I wondered if she'd taken it and gone off because we'd started arguing again. Then I thought, surely not. Natalie was terrified of being alone on dark water, and besides, when you started the dinghy engine, it fired very quickly and we'd certainly have heard it from the saloon."

"She's not there, nor is the dinghy," he told Davern, who was equally fuddled; and in a daze of confusion and panic, RJ convinced himself that Natalie must have gone off in the dinghy after all. "I radioed for a shore boat to take me to the Isthmus. I searched the dock, but the dinghy wasn't there. The Harbor Patrol office was closed for the night, so I went to Doug's Harbor Reef to ask the bartender if anyone had seen Natalie, but that was closed too, so I took the shore boat back to *Splendour.*"

By then it was around one-thirty a.m., and RJ decided to radio for help on the Harbor Channel, which was monitored by all boats in the vicinity. By yet another of those coincidences that haunt the lives of RJ, Natalie and her mother, the owner of a boat moored not far from *Splendour* that night was a deputy on the staff of the Los Angeles County Medical Examiner's Office. Paul Miller had met the Wagners a few times, and when his radio picked up the call, he heard a man say, "Someone's missing in a dinghy," and after a moment recognized RJ's voice.

"Soon afterward," according to RJ, he called the Coast Guard, and by two a.m., according to Noguchi in *Coroner,* searchlights from Coast Guard helicopters, Harbor Patrol boats and private Baywatch boats were scanning the coastline around Isthmus Cove. (He was misinformed about Baywatch. They were not alerted, according to the police report, until three hours later.) "The search took a long time," RJ explained, "because around the Isthmus area the ocean shelf goes down very deep, then rises again." Around five-thirty a.m. the dinghy was found in an isolated cove beyond Blue Cavern Point, a mile away from Two Harbors. It was smothered in kelp, its gear was in neutral, its ignition key in the off position, and its oars still fastened to each side.

Evidently no one on *Splendour* had heard the engine start because Natalie never started it.

Shortly before dawn Doug Bombard joined the search in a private patrol boat, and toward seven-forty-five a.m. he spotted a red object bobbing up and down in the ocean swell. It was Natalie's parka, swollen with water. She lay facedown, and when he lifted her out of the ocean with the help of a Baywatch lifeguard whom he'd alerted by radio, her eyes were wide open.

> *George Segal: Those wonderful dark Russian eyes. Behind all the chatter that might be going on, they were sad and knowing.*

The handwriting of the two final entries in Natalie's daybook slants irregularly upward. The first begins on the page for November 28, continues across part of the page for November 29, and is factual: "The undertow is very strong today." The second, which occupies the rest of the November 29 space, is confessional: "This loneliness won't leave me alone."

It seems most likely that Natalie wrote the first entry after she returned to the boat in the dinghy with Davern, and before she left it again in the dinghy with Walken. When I told Courtney Wagner about the second entry, she identified it as a line from a Ray Charles song. Its strange, terrible urgency suggests that Natalie wrote it when she went below to the master stateroom, after the climax of RJ's final argument with Walken.

The clothing found on her body, and the autopsy report (on the alcohol and medications in her system, the bruises on her legs and arms), provide a number of clues to what happened, and didn't happen, during the short period of consciousness left to her. On the human level, all speculation seems indecent in view of the unimaginable terror she must have endured. But much of the later speculation is so indecent that some correctives are essential.

UNDERNEATH THE RED PARKA Natalie was wearing a flannel nightgown and slipper socks. There were several rings on her fingers. The autopsy report listed the alcohol level in her blood as .14 percent——.04

percent above the intoxication standard in California, equivalent in Noguchi's reckoning to seven or eight glasses of wine. But the test was performed several hours after her death, and she had drunk a good deal more during the previous night. The level would have been much higher when she retired to the master stateroom, and the amount of pain medication (Darvon) found in Natalie's system would have increased the effect of the wine.

The autopsy also revealed that she'd taken a new and powerful anti-seasickness drug called cyclizine, but found no trace of any of her regular sleep medications. Evidently she wasn't ready to go to sleep, and the state of the dinghy near Blue Cavern Point makes it equally clear that she never planned to leave *Splendour*. In the absence of a witness, it's impossible to prove why she went out to the aft deck, but the plan of the deck provides strong circumstantial support for RJ's conjecture.

In the past, when Natalie was reading or sunbathing on the aft deck during the day, she had more than once been irritated by the sound of the dinghy banging against the side, and gone to open the door to the swim-step below. The rope that secured the dinghy was tied to a brass ring beside the step, and after untying the knot, she had to pull the rope tight, then retie it.

If, as RJ believed, Natalie heard the dinghy banging against the side of the stateroom that night, she knew it would prevent her from sleeping. When it occasionally woke them both at night, RJ always got up to tighten the rope; and normally, of course, Natalie would never have gone out to the swim-step and faced the dark ocean alone. But now she was emotionally disturbed and mentally dulled by a combination of Darvon and too much wine. Although she could have returned to the saloon, and asked RJ or Davern to secure the dinghy, it seems improbable. She knew they were both drunk, the situation with Walken had created "a terrible fight" with her husband the night before, and only an hour or two earlier she had walked out when they got into a heated argument.

Even during the day you had to be careful when securing the dinghy from the teakwood swim-step, a feature of *Splendour* that Guy McElwaine always found "curious." Teakwood is exceptionally durable, and much used in shipbuilding because its essential oil resists the action of water; but when an ocean swell kept washing over the swim step, as it did that night, it always became slippery. The autopsy reported a heavy bruise on Natalie's right arm, a lesser one on her left wrist, as well as various bruises on both legs, her left knee and right ankle, and an abrasion on her left cheek. They first led Noguchi to conclude that "Natalie Wood, possibly attempting to board the dinghy, had fallen into the ocean, striking her face," and because of the absence of head wounds, "she had been conscious while in the water."

From fingernail scratches on one side of the dinghy, Noguchi also concluded that when Natalie tried to climb into it, the weight of the parka pulled her down. (She weighed around ninety-eight pounds at the time, and the parka, when waterlogged, weighed forty. Ironically, after she drowned, it kept her afloat.) But the conclusion was premature, and by announcing at his press conference that Natalie intended to go off in the dinghy by herself, Noguchi caused several journalists to wonder (hopefully) if she had been in physical danger; and the wheel of the Hollywood rumor mill began spinning overnight.

The next day, Noguchi's belief that "every death is a homicide, unless proved otherwise," decided him to instruct Paul Miller to search *Splendour* and the dinghy for signs of violence or struggle. Although Miller reported that "there weren't any signs of a struggle in the yacht or the dinghy," he would later disagree with RJ's theory that Natalie had heard the dinghy banging against the side of *Splendour*. It was made of rubber, he said, and would have created almost no sound at all. But he was evidently unaware that the dinghy had an outboard motor, and the impact of metal on wood would have been far from silent; just as Noguchi was unaware, when he first believed that Natalie had tried to leave the boat, that to board it from the swim step was notoriously dangerous in rough weather, and even when the ocean was calm, one person usually held the rope close to the step while the other climbed in.

On December 12, the police concluded that Natalie's death was accidental, and the case was officially closed. But media speculation continued, and the sleaze mongers found it "mysterious" that in the hours following Natalie's death, RJ first denied having an argument with Walken, then admitted it, and that he alternately thought she'd gone off in the dinghy by herself, then felt sure she hadn't. They also found it "mysterious" that Walken first denied, then admitted having an argument with RJ, and that the two men didn't always agree on the exact timing of events.

All this, of course, fails to take the Hellman syndrome into account, as well as the natural desire of both men to protect their own and

Natalie's privacy. It would only have been "mysterious" if a stunned, drunken RJ had managed to act immediately and precisely when he discovered that Natalie was missing, or if RJ and Walken, when questioned by the police, had immediately and precisely agreed on what happened, and when, during that disoriented alcoholic night.

Two INCIDENTAL questions remain. Paul Miller reported to Noguchi that if Natalie fell off the swim step, tried to climb into the dinghy, then managed to hang on to it, the wind would have blown both of them toward the mainland instead of Blue Cavern Point. According to RJ, equally familiar with local winds and tides, the current as well as the wind flowed toward the mainland. But as Natalie noted in her daybook for November 28, the undertow was very strong, and an undertow always flows in the opposite direction to the surface current. There was also a second, milder surface current that flowed closer offshore from Isthmus Cove, ran south toward Blue Cavern, and like the undertow would have carried Natalie and the dinghy further along the coast. According to the autopsy, she could have clung to the dinghy for at most an hour before hypothermia set in; then body and dinghy would have continued to drift with the offshore current.

Among the many pieces of trivial or publicity-seeking "evidence" in the gossip columns and police reports, one gained some attention at the time. John Payne (*not* the actor) and his fiancée, Marilyn Wayne, whose boat was moored approximately eighty feet from *Splendour,* claimed to have heard a drowning woman's cries for help that night, followed by "drunken male voices" calling from another nearby boat, "Don't worry, we're coming to get you." But neither RJ nor Walken recalled hearing any voices from another boat, and RJ said later that he was "not convinced the couple heard anything. Although we'd been drinking, we'd certainly have heard a cry for help, if it came from nearby, because water's a great conduit for sound."

On December 3, Wayne's story appeared in the *Los Angeles Times,* but the Sheriff's Department was unconvinced, and ignored it.

*THIS LONELINESS WON'T LEAVE ME ALONE.* "This" implies that Natalie's loneliness was not a sudden, momentary feeling. And it certainly started no later than the age of fourteen, when she realized that Nick and Maria's love was not the parental love celebrated in the movies she made, but dependent on the money she earned. Two years later, it was still a familiar spirit when she worked the room at parties, "looking for love." Much later, at another party, Richard Gregson glimpsed her looking "so beautiful and so alone," and her first reaction to Daisy Clover was that "at every important moment in her life, she's alone."

But if she still felt alone on November 29, 1981, perhaps time as the great healer is overrated; and once Natalie became aware of that hole in her world, she could still fall into it even when genuinely loved and loving.

> *Micky Ziffren: If Natalie had lived, I think the marriage would have survived.*

"She's gone! She's gone!" RJ's voice on the phone, "distraught and hysterical," woke Mart Crowley shortly before seven a.m. on November 30. "The police are taking Chris and me by helicopter to Santa Monica Airport. Please pick us up."

When the limousine that Mart ordered brought him to the airport, Duane Rasure had already interviewed RJ and Walken, and the helicopter had left. "I looked around, and saw two men standing, hunched, their backs to each other, alone on the airfield. When the limo drove over, they got in without a word. RJ, who was fighting back tears, wanted to stop at the house of psychiatrists Dr. Malin and his wife, to ask how to break the news to Natasha and Courtney. Walken was silent while we waited."

A crowd of "reporters, photographers and gawkers" waited outside 603 North Canon, and the living room was already full of friends, including Roddy McDowall, Josh Donen, Linda Foreman, Guy McElwaine and Tom Mankiewicz, who remembered that "it was as if the world was in color, but RJ was in black and white." Liz Applegate, whom RJ had phoned and asked to stay at the house, had already received a hysterical phone call from Georgiane Walken, "who didn't know that her husband was on the boat." RJ's doctor, Paul Rudnick, was waiting with an offer of sedation, but he refused it, "wanting to be there for the kids."

He went straight upstairs to the nursery, and shortly afterward Mart heard "a scream from Natasha. 'It's not fair! It's not fair!' " Then RJ came downstairs again and asked Mart to go to the Pierce Brothers mortuary in Westwood, where Natalie's body had been taken after the autopsy, and "arrange for Natalie to be fixed up before he let her daughters see her." If he saw her body there, RJ explained, he knew he'd break down. Then he went upstairs again.

As Howard Jeffrey had handled the funeral arrangements for Norma Crane at Westwood Memorial Park, and knew the supervisor, Mart asked him to help. They went to the mortuary together, and Bill Pierce took them to see Natalie's body, "naked under a sheet. He folded back the sheet, and she looked terrible—hair matted—she'd been in salt water all night—bruises and scratches on various parts of her body, an abrasion on her cheek." Then Mart called Sydney Guilaroff: "I asked him to fix Natalie's hair, and he promised to come right over. As BJ [Bob Jiras] was in New York, I called RJ's makeup man, Frank Westmore, to fix her face, but he begged off. 'I just couldn't,' he said. So I tried Eddie Butterworth, who did Natalie's makeup for the studio scenes on *Brainstorm,* and he agreed. Then Howard and I hurried back to Canon Drive to choose a long dress, shoes, stockings and so on, and we got her dressed at the mortuary just before Guilaroff arrived."

Immaculate as ever in a dark suit, white tie and white shirt, Guilaroff inspected Natalie's hair and said it would take two hours to fix. The supreme professional had come prepared, and brought along a fall he'd created for Ava Gardner, whose hair was almost exactly the same color. He shampooed Natalie's hair by hand, blow-dried it, then began very carefully to comb the front over Gardner's fall.

Meanwhile, Eddie Butterworth worked on Natalie's face, and at first his hand shook so much that he asked Mart: "Is it okay if I rest it on her cheek?" Mart nodded, then held Natalie's hand until Guilaroff and Butterworth finished. After Guilaroff stepped back to check the effect of Gardner's fall, he said quietly: "You'd never know."

And to Mart and Howard, "She looked beautiful. Like Natalie."

Until December 2, the day of the funeral, RJ spent most of the time in bed, numb with shock and grief. His lawyer, Paul Ziffren, made him promise not to talk to the press, but then issued his own surprisingly inaccurate and unhelpful attempt at damage control: "Since Mrs. Wagner often took the dinghy out alone, Mr. Wagner was not immediately concerned. However, when she failed to return after ten or fifteen minutes, Mr. Wagner took his small cruiser and went to look for her."

Meanwhile, telegrams of condolence arrived from President Reagan, Prime Minister Pierre Trudeau of Canada, Queen Elizabeth of England, Prince Philip and Princess Margaret; and friends gathered every day in the living room. "I'm so sorry about this," Liz Applegate told Chris Walken when he came by on December 1 and sat alone at the bar. "So am I," he replied. "So why don't you shut up about it?"

In London, Hugo Gregson had heard the news on the radio and immediately informed his father. Richard Gregson caught the next available plane to Los Angeles, arrived there on the morning of December 1 and went straight to Canon Drive: "After I had a talk with Natasha, I went upstairs to see RJ in his bedroom. He was in tears, and very concerned about my plans for Natasha. I told him that I'd already explained to her that I didn't want to break up the family, and she agreed. RJ was relieved and grateful."

Soon afterward, Natasha said that she wanted to see her mother before the body was transferred to a closed coffin. RJ, who was initially doubtful about this, called Drs. Lindon and Malin. They both approved, and he arranged for his driver to take Richard, Natasha, Courtney and Liz Applegate to the mortuary. But he didn't feel capable of going with them.

When they arrived, Natasha hesitated, as if unsure whether she could go through with it. "There's nothing to be afraid of," Liz told her, and Natasha walked slowly across the room to the open casket. Mart and Howard were already there, and Mart remembered that Natasha stared at Ava Gardner's fall. "That's not Mummy's hair," she said, then told her father that she'd written Natalie a letter and wanted to put it in her hand. As rigor mortis had made the hand difficult to lift, Richard helped her. Courtney, too young to understand that her mother was dead, decided that she must give her something as well, and the driver offered his handkerchief. She lifted the blanket, and Natasha recalled that "she threw it in sort of haphazardly." Then, according to Richard: "Natasha told me very sweetly that she wanted to be alone with her mother. So the rest of us moved to the waiting room and I stayed just inside the doorway. I could hear Natasha talking very quietly to her mother, although not what she said. Then Natasha looked up and closed the door. I glanced back at the waiting room and for a surrealist moment saw Courtney playing hopscotch on the square tiles of the floor."

After a few minutes, Natasha opened the door and said she was ready to leave. On the way back to North Canon, "She was very calm and behaved as if she'd done what had to be done and what she wanted to do." For Gregson it remained "one of the most extraordinary episodes of my life," and he would never forget how "amazingly beautiful" Natalie looked, or how she'd once told him that "she always believed she wouldn't make old bones."

During the late evening of December 1, RJ came downstairs and joined Mart Crowley, Liz, Josh Donen and Arnold Stiefel in the living room. When the doorbell rang, Willie Mae went to answer it, and a chauffeur announced that Miss Taylor would like to see Mr. Wagner. Miss Taylor, who was appearing in *The Little Foxes* at the Ahmanson Theater, had changed into postperformance clothes but still wore stage makeup. "Oh baby, baby," she said to RJ. "What happened to us, baby?"

THAT SAME EVENING, Rock Hudson phoned Donfeld. He had always been very fond of Natalie, and although just out of the hospital after heart bypass surgery and still very weak, he was determined to attend the funeral service the next day. "Hang close to me at the cemetery," he said. Then, sounding on the verge of tears: "I have no understanding of why really good people have to die so horribly."

Also that evening, the famously shy and private eighty-two-year-old Fred Astaire agreed to talk about Natalie in the presence of reporters and TV cameras. Standing in the driveway of his home, he spoke quietly and simply about Natalie as a woman, an actress and "the perfect balm" for her friends. "I wanted to keep it short," he told Donfeld later, "but once I got there and began talking about Natalie, it was difficult to stop."

BOTH RJ and Gregson agreed that the funeral ceremony at Westwood Memorial Park should be brief, with only family and friends in attendance; and as they also agreed on "no religious music," Howard Jeffrey suggested balalaika music instead. Howard was one of the pallbearers, alongside Mart Crowley, Josh and Peter Donen, John Foreman, Bob Lang (the Wagners' handyman-carpenter at Canon Drive), Guy McElwaine, Tom Mankiewicz and Paul Ziffren. The honorary pallbearers included Fred Astaire, Eddie Butterworth, Sydney Guilaroff, Rock

Hudson, John Irvin, Elia Kazan, Dr. John Lindon, Arthur Loew, David Niven, Laurence Olivier, Gregory Peck and Frank Sinatra.

After Father Stephen Fitzgerald of the Russian Orthodox Church gave the blessing, two friends made brief farewell speeches. Hope Lange: "Natalie, you put us to a very severe test today. It's difficult to feel joy and laughter when you're not here to share it." Roddy McDowall: "Natalie found a way to put life in her heart and heart into her life."

By then Natasha was in tears, but Courtney was still unable to come to terms with the situation. "She stood there, her face almost blank," Richard Gregson recalled, "swinging one leg." Meanwhile, RJ approached the pall of white gardenias laid over the coffin, picked up a handful, and offered a gardenia each to Natasha, Courtney and Kate. Then he bent over the coffin and kissed it, and the ceremony was over.

Although the news of Natalie's death had induced one of Mud's longest convulsions, she recovered her sense of drama for the funeral. "If you'd been on the boat," she said accusingly to Mart Crowley, "my daughter would still be alive." But during the wake at 603 North Canon, RJ could barely control his grief. Arnold Schulman remembered him as "totally devastated, managing to play the perfect host for a while, then unable to keep up the front any longer."

The first time RJ lost Natalie, he had also been "totally devastated," but within a year it had occurred to him (and to her) that they might find each other again. Now there was no second chance, and the thought sent him back to bed, where he stayed for three days without shaving or showering.


DURING THE SECOND DAY that RJ remained in his room, he agreed to a final interview with Duane Rasure. Still totally distraught, he could only repeat that his first reaction, when he discovered both Natalie and the dinghy missing, was to decide that she must have gone ashore, because she often took *Valiant* out by herself. He was still too dazed to remember that Natalie only took the dinghy out by herself in daylight, usually to fetch groceries from the island store; but as the pain and confusion grew less acute, "He tried over and over again to make sense of what happened, and how Natalie fell in the water," according to Mart Crowley. "He kept asking if there was any way he could have prevented it, and 'What about Chris?'"

When he finally decided that Natalie must have tried to secure the dinghy to starboard, he sounded out Doug Bombard, whose boat also had a dinghy attached. "I agreed that it was definitely the most likely supposition," Bombard told me. "Because from what I knew about Natalie, there was no way she'd have taken the dinghy out by herself at night."

On the afternoon of the third day, RJ still kept to his bed. "Tell him the children are wondering why he won't come down," Liz said to Willie Mae. "Tell him he must get up and talk to them." As she hoped, it brought RJ back to "the land of the living." He shaved and dressed, took Natasha and Courtney for a walk in the garden. "We're going to be all right," he told them. "We're staying together."

And the house that had grown so eerily silent began to stir with the kind of noise that "Natalie always took as a sign that the children were happy."

*Proverb: The afternoon knows what the morning never suspected.*

When RJ accepts an invitation from David Niven to bring his family to Gstaad for Christmas, there's no way he can anticipate the chance meeting that will occur there. He takes Liz Applegate, Mart Crowley, Delphine Mann, Josh Donen and Willie Mae as well as Natasha and Courtney on the trip, and snow lies heavy on the ground when they arrive at the spacious chalet Niven has rented for them.

Next day RJ walks alone to a nearby hotel bar and finds Ladislav Blatnik sitting there alone. He's moderately drunk and looks moderately seedy. What a tragedy about Natalie's death, he remarks to RJ, then says how much he loved her, Gstaad is where they first met, and so on. "The last things I needed to hear," as RJ will recall later, adding that he made a polite but speedy escape.

The afternoon also knows that the Shoe King's empire is about to collapse, and that within a few years Blatnik will kill himself.

ON DECEMBER 29, the Wagner family and friends leave for White-brook Farm in Wales, where Richard Gregson and his wife, Julia, live. They spend New Year's Eve there, and RJ suddenly thinks: This is my first New Year's Eve without Natalie since 1973, and there will never be another. Then he breaks down.

Today, Courtney Wagner remembers her sister as "very sad, very depressed," during and for some while after the trip. By that time, Courtney also remembers, she's begun to hold imaginary conversations with her mother, like a child playing a game of hide-and-seek. "Where have you gone? When will you be back?" And once she left her a note: "Mother, where are you?"

After Courtney was born, her mother's attention had mainly focused on Natasha, "because she needed it then. But Natalie planned to get around to me very soon." Then she died before "very soon," and Courtney always felt closer to Willie Mae. During the trip, they sleep in the same bed. In one way, as RJ explains later, "Natalie's death was harder for Natasha, because she was old enough to come to terms with it, and they'd been very close."


"I've loaned Lana so much money and never been repaid," Natalie had told RJ and Liz Applegate when she made her final will, "and I'm not leaving her any money. Just my clothes." And a few days after the Wagners return to 603 North Canon, Lana Wood calls the house. RJ is filming *Hart to Hart,* and Liz answers. "I know I'm getting Natalie's clothes and I want them now," Lana says. Although Liz explains that the will is still in probate, and she must wait for the court's approval, Lana continues to call almost daily and demand her "rights." These include Natalie's fur coats, which she knows are particularly valuable. RJ had planned to store the furs and give them to Natasha and Courtney later; and "in the hope of getting Lana off my back," he tells Liz to have the furs appraised, send her the money and "let her take everything else."

Shortly afterward, a truck pulls up outside the house and Lana gets out with her current boyfriend, Alan Feinstein. She rings the front door-bell, and Liz leads the couple upstairs to Natalie's bedroom. Natasha happens to be sitting on her mother's bed when they enter. They ignore her completely, move straight to the huge walk-in closet and seize a first armful of clothes. "Something feels very wrong here," Natasha tells herself as she watches them make a series of hurried journeys to load the truck. She remembers "the pride I felt when I saw Natalie all dressed up to go out for the night," and Liz is aware of her pain: "When Lana grabbed an old bra, Natasha asked why she wanted it. 'Because your mother wanted me to have it,' she said curtly. No concern for Natasha, only for her own need of money. As RJ had put Natalie's fur coats in storage, planning to offer them to Natasha and Courtney later, Lana also asked RJ to have them appraised and send her a check. RJ wearily okayed this too and his accountant sent Lana $11,000. Meanwhile, she sold almost all the clothes to a used-clothing store in the San Fernando Valley. Some items, including old bras and panties, were hung in the window and labeled 'Belonging to Natalie Wood.' "

THE AFTERNOON also knows that as the shock of Natalie's death wears off for Maria Gurdin, so does the obsession that's taken over much of her life. For a few weeks she wears black, then begins to revert to the colorful, exuberant Musia who first attracted Nick, and to the Maria that her friends in San Francisco remembered as a flamboyant dresser. Pendant earrings, elaborate brooches and rings festoon her again, and she particularly enjoys wearing orange or purple at her occasional visits to the Church of the Holy Virgin Mary.

Maria is well taken care of, as RJ buys the condo that Natalie rented for her and makes her a monthly allowance of $2,000 for as long as she lives there. But as she no longer likes to drive a car, and Lana still lives in the San Fernando Valley, Maria asks Natasha Zepaloff to chauffeur her around. And to a lesser extent, Natasha replaces Natalie as an obsession, the last piece of unfinished business in Maria's life.

In June 1982, when Natalie has been dead for six months, and Natasha is driving her to a "Star Mothers Luncheon" at the Sportsmen's Lodge in North Hollywood, Maria suddenly feels free to dispense with winks and nudges. "I have to tell you something," she says. "Your father and I became deeply involved with each other before I married Nick, and our relationship has continued ever since." Maria also confides that she was pregnant when she married Nick, explains why she felt certain that Zepaloff was the father and concludes: "So you see, Natalie was your sister."

Half-sister, she ought to have said; but Maria still retains her sense of drama. Soon afterward, she decides to phone the Captain while Natasha is visiting at Goshen Avenue: "They talked for about ten minutes; then she handed me the phone. My father was cordial yet cool, and I had the impression that he felt embarrassed because he knew Maria had finally told me about their affair, and that he was also Natalie's father."

In 1989, Natasha divorces her husband of twenty years and changes her name legally to Lofft (adding a *t* to the last four letters of "Zepaloff"). Soon afterward she meets Richard Benson and goes to live with him in Lake Havasu City, Arizona, where they open a health-food emporium. In 2001, after talking to her mother, Nina Jaure, I fly to Lake Havasu and am met at the airport by a woman who's taller than Natalie, but whose face startles me by suggesting how Natalie might have looked at sixty. That evening Natasha tells her story, and Richard Benson contributes his impression of Zepaloff.

Back in Los Angeles, I relate the story to the Wagner family, and RJ decides to invite Natasha Lofft to tell it again at lunch in Beverly Hills. At a secluded patio table, I listen while she describes to RJ, his daughters Natasha and Courtney, and Mart Crowley, her various meetings with Natalie over the years, the various hints thrown out by her father and Maria, the climactic scene in the car when Maria announces that Zepaloff is Natalie's biological father. At this point, she's overcome with very "Russian" emotion, and tears come to her eyes as she explains why she kept silent until I got in touch with her. "All I ever wanted," she says, "was to be *accepted*." Then she shows the pendant with an engraved medallion that Natalie gave her.

RJ is alert but quizzical throughout. He leans back in his chair while the others lean forward. The girls and Natasha exchange anecdotes of Maria and, before they say goodbye, phone numbers. Afterward, Natasha Gregson Wagner says that she's very aware of a resemblance to Natalie: "Not just the eyes. The hairline's the same." Like Courtney, she wonders whether their mother "really knew, or guessed," the connection that Natasha Lofft sensed; and if Mud actually confided in Natalie, did she believe or disbelieve the story?

"Do you believe it?" Courtney asks me. On the flight to Lake Havasu City, I say, I wondered if I was going to meet another case of Anna Anderson–Anastasia. But after spending an evening and most of the following day with Natasha Lofft, I decided that although there was no way to prove the truth of the story beyond any doubt, there was no crucial reason to disbelieve it.

Mart Crowley agrees, and it becomes the consensus. RJ has said little throughout the lunch, which he's clearly found an unsettling experience. But now he remarks, "It's really extraordinary to think about." Then he adds: "Of course, when you think about Mud, it's not so extraordinary."

By the time of that lunch, Mud had been dead for three years; and over the previous ten years, she had gradually been stripped of the various layers of her personality: Musia, Maria, Star Mother, secret inamorata.

The bad times began after Lana Wood abandoned all hope of an acting and then a writing career. A year after Natalie died, she had published *Natalie,* a remarkably untruthful "memoir" of her sister. Its sales were modest, and when she failed to sell a movie story about "two girls growing up in a peculiar town," she decided to live rent-free by moving into Mud's condo with her daughter, her daughter's boyfriend, and several cats. But even though she'd received a check for $11,000 for the furs, in addition to money from the sale of the rest of Natalie's clothes, Lana continued to write letters to RJ, claiming that her daughter was seriously ill and she couldn't pay the medical bills, that her electricity was about to be cut off, or her car about to be repossessed. RJ never answered. "I'd promised Natalie that if anything happened to her, I'd look after her mother," he recalled. "But after all the unpleasantness we'd both had with Lana, I couldn't see my way to looking after her sister."

At the condo, Mud was evicted from the master bedroom and banished to the back room. When a neighbor called Liz Applegate to complain of bad smells caused by the cats, she asked the man who was checking the security system at 603 North Canon to investigate. As well as confirming the cat smells, he reported that the whole apartment was filthy, and when Mud appeared from the back room, "the daughter's boyfriend ordered her to 'get back in there. We'll tell you when you can come out.' "

RJ settled Mud in an apartment in nearby Barrington Plaza, but a few weeks later he received a call from the building superintendent that "a small fire" had broken out in Mrs. Gurdin's apartment. Although it was not serious, and quickly extinguished, Mud's account of what happened was disturbing. "I was looking for my jewels under the bed with a lighted candle," she said. Although Mud had started to hide her jewelry in various places after Lana moved into the condo, the lighted candle was not her first aberration. In recent weeks, a series of memory lapses

*Natalie driving the dinghy*

had made RJ suspect that Mud was developing Alzheimer's, and he wanted to move her to the Motion Picture Country Home. As he'd made several large contributions to the home, the director agreed to accept her; but Lana, who'd moved back to a rented house in Thousand Oaks after RJ closed the condo, refused to give permission, even though Olga was in favor of the idea. She insisted on taking Mud to live with her; and this meant, of course, that her mother's monthly checks from RJ would be readdressed to Lana's house.

Perhaps fortunately for Mud, the symptoms of Alzheimer's soon progressed to a point where she no longer knew where she was living and had to be moved to a hospital. Simultaneously, in a northern California sanitarium, the Captain relapsed into senile dementia. Alone and apart in a deepening twilight zone of the mind, both of them lost control of the lives they'd controlled for so long on their own terms, as well as the shared memory of a "great romantic love." Zepaloff recalled nothing of his two wives and three Natalies, only fragments of his young life in China; and although Maria held on to fragmented memories of her Captain, they finally became as elusive as the other scraps of her life that drifted in and out of consciousness.

When Maria Gurdin died on January 6, 1998, a month before her eighty-sixth birthday, the Captain had become a figure who appeared very occasionally on the distant horizon of her mind's eye.

So had Natalie.

# 7

# Something Extra

*You've got that little something extra. Ellen Terry, a great actress long before you were born, said that's what star quality was—"that little something extra."*

—NORMAN MAINE (JAMES MASON) TO ESTHER BLODGETT
(JUDY GARLAND) IN *A STAR IS BORN*

*When the persona fitted the role, you couldn't do better.*

—ELIA KAZAN ON NATALIE WOOD

*Ultimately film is the director's eye. You can do your best take as an actor, and if the director doesn't want to cut to you, or doesn't want to use that moment, you're out of luck. And if you disagree with a director, you're out of luck too, because he's going to cut it the way he sees it.*

—NATALIE WOOD

By 1944, when Natalie Wood played her first screen role in *Tomorrow Is Forever* at the age of seven, eight-year-old Margaret O'Brien had made eight movies, most recently *Meet Me in St. Louis;* and twelve-year-old Elizabeth Taylor was on the verge of adolescence, playing her first leading role in *National Velvet.* In 1945 another twelve-year-old, Peggy Ann Garner, gave an exceptionally touching performance in *A Tree Grows in Brooklyn.* But she would never find another role even half as good, and like O'Brien would never make the transition to a successful adult career.

O'Brien and Garner won special Academy Awards, and Mary Astor remembered the "serious, 'dedicated' look" in Elizabeth Taylor's eyes on the set of *National Velvet;* but a year later, when Astor played her mother in *Cynthia,* "the look in her violet eyes was somewhat calculating, as though she knew exactly what she wanted and was quite sure of getting it."

In fact Elizabeth Taylor became the last of the iconic movie stars, occasionally stimulated to an impressive performance by directors (notably George Stevens and Mike Nichols) who knew what *they* wanted and were determined to get it. But in the long run she was most impressive as herself, star of a grand soap-opera life more riveting than *Dynasty,* and an eloquent, pioneering spokesperson for AIDS research at charity events. As a phenomenon, incidentally, she always fascinated Natalie Wood, less for her acting than for her resolute personal independence, unshaken even when the Vatican denounced her for "erotic vagrancy."

Did O'Brien and Garner fail to develop their early promise through bad luck, personal neurosis, or the fact that their promise ended when childhood ended? To some extent, probably, for the first two reasons, and certainly for the last. They showed little promise as adult actors. But for Taylor, whose early roles were less demanding, and whose exceptional beauty became apparent much earlier than Natalie's, her later career (like her life) was a matter of choice.

Temperamentally, these child stars were very different. O'Brien, too often wasted in shallow and maudlin roles, was a mischief maker who delighted in angering property men by changing the position of props between takes. And although her extraordinary technical assurance never depended on emotion memory to make tears stream down her face, the shrewd little minx seemed lost and bewildered as a woman. She even mythologized her childhood career to the extent of believing that when Natalie imitated a monkey in *Miracle on 34th Street,* she was imitating O'Brien doing the same thing in *Meet Me in St. Louis.* But O'Brien never imitated a monkey, not even her toy one, in that movie.

To induce Peggy Ann Garner to cry in *A Tree Grows in Brooklyn,* Kazan talked to her about her father, who was serving overseas in the air force. "Implicit in what I said," he remembered, "was the suggestion that he might not come back." The thought caused Garner to burst into tears, and a display of emotion so vital to the scene became "the real thing." According to Kazan, she was still disturbed at the end of the day, but had forgotten about it next morning, "as children do."

Maybe. Roddy McDowall told me that Garner attempted suicide twice before she died (after two failed marriages and a period of near-poverty) at the age of fifty-three. And Natalie never forgot an occasion when she was about to play an emotional scene in *Tomorrow Is Forever,* and Maria made sure she would cry by describing how she once saw a boy tear the wings off a live bird. This, of course, is the dark side of the "Let's Pretend" coin. When the adult Natalie attended a few Actors Studio classes as an observer, she found that Lee Strasberg's use of "sense memory, emotion memories, where you sit and remember textures, sounds, feelings, reliving an unhappy experience to promote tears," was very similar to the way she worked as a child. "What was called preparation, I used to call getting in the mood."

"Getting in the mood" for *Tomorrow Is Forever,* then, usually involved emotion memories by another name; and inevitably some of them were unhappy. All the movie reveals about Margret is that she's an Austrian war orphan adopted by Kessler (Orson Welles). But Natalie's imagination fills in some major cracks. Her Margret is always intently focused on Kessler, with a "daughterly" feeling almost obsessive in its neediness. Although Pichel no doubt explained the feelings of an orphan who hardly knew her father, Natalie would have needed little encouragement to draw on her feelings about Nick Gurdin, alternately too threatening and too closed off for her to respond to him as a father.

Not surprisingly, Natalie's performance has some technical rough edges: the dialogue that occasionally becomes incoherent when she cries, the Austro-German accent not uniformly sustained. But they're overshadowed by her composure and dignity, and the way (always a sign of instinctive talent) she *listens* so attentively to the other actors. Welles provides the only other anchor to reality, in both performance and makeup. He ages convincingly while Claudette Colbert acknowledges the passing of twenty-five years by adopting a more "mature" hairstyle, and George Brent by adding a dash of silver to his temples.

When Colbert finally tells Welles that she knows who he really is, he tells her to forget the past because "tomorrow is forever"—a line that cues not only the heavenly choir when he dies, but the final scene as Colbert and Brent arrive to take the now doubly orphaned Margret to live with them. "Where are we going?" she asks. "*Home,*" Colbert replies, but Margret's tomorrow in an affluent and gracious Baltimore suburb is a far cry from Natalie's in a rented bungalow, where drunken Nick Gurdin will soon be pointing a knife at his wife's swollen belly.


LIKE IRVING PICHEL, the director of Natalie's next-but-one movie had also been an actor, and although *Miracle on 34th Street* is soft-centered, George Seaton permitted Natalie (and Maureen O'Hara as her mother) some hard-edged moments. In Natalie's case they're comic: the wonderfully superior look of disbelief when Edmund Gwenn's Kris Kringle insists that he's Santa Claus; and that enthusiastic imitation of a monkey, when he introduces her to the game of "Let's Pretend." It's safe to guess that Seaton perceived and encouraged Natalie's comic talent, particularly the monkey imitation. He almost certainly improvised a moment for her in a later scene between Maureen O'Hara and John Payne. When she enters the room, again in monkey mood, they're evidently used to it, and continue their dialogue while she monkeys across to a door at the other end, then exits.

The monkey business also bears out Roddy McDowall's comment that for children, acting in front of a camera becomes "an expanded version of 'Let's Pretend.' " And in the case of *Miracle on 34th Street,* "Let's Pretend" interacted with both the movie and Natalie's life. Many years later she recalled not only that she believed Gwenn *was* Santa Claus, but that Seaton and Gwenn used to have "long discussions about comedy, how the art of comedy was overlooked and not given its due." That Natalie absorbed their discussions at the age of eight, and could recall them more than thirty years later, shows her already leading a double life, playing a game and yet aware of acting as a profession.

In the same way, if Natalie the child believed that Gwenn *was* Santa Claus, her look of disbelief in the movie had to be "acted." Then how much of her performance was instinct, how much developing craft? O'Hara remembered that "the director coached us all," also that Natalie "obviously enjoyed acting," was totally unself-conscious about it, and had a "wonderful" sense of humor. And as Seaton filmed some of her dialogue scenes in takes that lasted three minutes, Natalie had clearly begun to acquire technique and a sense of timing that didn't have to be created in the editing room.

*Stella Adler: Only craft releases talent.*

*Miracle on 34th Street* was a major studio picture with a shooting schedule of more than two months. *Driftwood,* made shortly afterward, was what *Variety* termed "a low-budgeter," shot in three weeks. But Allan Dwan was another "actor's director," who had acted in high-school productions, and had directed two movies with Shirley Temple, whom he found considerably less interesting than Natalie. And *Driftwood,* although a B movie, didn't look like one. This was due partly to its cinematographer, John Alton, and partly to Dwan himself, an indomitable veteran who began making two-reelers in 1914. His exuberance and invention enabled him to produce superior work at a studio like Republic, where "to shoot a picture in anything over twenty-five days was dangerous."

Dwan quickly sensed that Natalie's talent was strong enough to carry a movie; and a potentially cloying Little-Miss-Fix-It role in the Shirley Temple mold became a display of astonishingly pure conviction, as well as an example of the difference between a child actor who believes in the character she's playing and the child performer who believes only in herself.

Jenny, the backwoods orphan who regards "How do you do?" as a question that expects an answer, disapproves of small-town folk who treat it as a formality. "Most folks don't give a damn what you really feel," the local doctor explains. "That's civilization." Jenny's response, "I don't like civilization," is one of several moments to warn of cuteness ahead, but Natalie avoids them with a sureness that reveals a child actress already "at the top of her game."

And then, in a series of inadequate movies over the next seven years, she almost disappears. *The Green Promise* (1949) is her least pallid role, although a clone of Jenny, and important only for the traumatic episode that created her lasting fear of dark water. But *I'm a Fool* (1954), the TV show that introduced her to James Dean, suggests a "new" Natalie, anxious and romantic, ready to emerge when someone gives her the chance.

A year later, someone does. S. E. Hinton, author of *The Outsiders* and other "young adult" novels, described *Rebel Without a Cause* as the film that "gave teens the right to redefine the world." It also gave Natalie the right to redefine herself as an actress, just as she'd begun to redefine herself in life.

She has two major scenes, the first only a few minutes after the movie opens. Jenny with her pigtails (who decided that she belonged to "civilization" after all, just as Susan in *Miracle on 34th Street* was converted from skeptic to "believer") is now Judy, deeply alienated from the world of middle-class suburbia that she's supposed to belong to. Wandering the streets in the middle of the night, she's picked up by a police car and taken to juvenile hall. She wears too much makeup, like most Warner actresses of the time (and also like Natalie offscreen), and her scarlet lipstick matches her coat.

It's a very demanding scene, her interrogation by the social worker, and she's equal to all its abrupt emotional changes. In retrospect, the parallels with her own life at the time seem uncanny: the need for love and her failure to find it, the anguished confession of her fear that "I'll never get close to anybody," and finally her horrified reaction (verging on hysteria, and a foretaste of the bathtub scene in *Splendor in the Grass*) when the social worker says that her mother's coming to pick her up. "My MOTHER?!"

During her second major scene, with James Dean and Sal Mineo in the deserted mansion at night, Natalie goes through another series of emotional changes. Her comic impersonation of a selfish, uncaring mother is followed by a reversion to childhood in a game of hide-and-seek with Dean, then by sisterly concern for lonely Mineo, and finally by her declaration of love to Dean, surprisingly and effectively chaste. She begins by explaining, half to herself, that she admires Jim as "a man who can be gentle but free." Then she realizes: "All this time I've been looking for somebody to love me, and now I love somebody." Unexpectedly, it's Judy who makes the first move for a mouth-to-mouth kiss (they've only brushed cheeks before), and Dean who reciprocates in an almost passive way. But at "the age when nothing fits," something begins, very tentatively, to fit.

The movie's emotional impact derives equally and indivisibly from the actors, from Stewart Stern's script, which he based on his own experience of adolescent loneliness, and from Nick Ray. As Natalie later recalled, he felt that "it was important to know a lot personally about the actor," and he also felt that the director had to discover as much as he could about himself. When he pointed the finger at absent or inadequate fatherhood in all three families, it pointed at himself as well. He drew on his own life to understand and probe the bisexuality of Dean and Mineo, and as Natalie's lover, he knew the intensity of her need for love.

*Natalie Wood: I remember Kazan, in* Splendor in the Grass, *we talked about breaking down the part into three or four sections, so that where were the beats? Where were the turning points to get from one into the other? And I've always tried to use that when I work on a part, as a starting-off point, and just sort of create a back life. (AFI seminar)*

The Natalie of *Splendor in the Grass* wears minimal makeup, revealing the extraordinary beauty of a face stripped of its Warner Bros. WarnerColor look and (with the passing of six years since *Rebel*) of its slightly plump, adolescent prettiness. In the early scenes, she's alternately restless and languid, and her movements reflect the first erotic stirrings of an inexperienced girl in 1929 Kansas. Inge's screenplay is very skillful in the parallels it draws between two different families with similar dysfunctions. Deanie's mother, Mrs. Loomis, is a dominating, puritanical figure who insists that marriage is a social/financial transaction, and sex a duty to be endured ("A woman doesn't enjoy these things"). Her father's more understanding, but weak and browbeaten. In Bud Stamper's family, the dysfunctions are mirror images of Deanie's. His mother is sympathetic but helpless, and his father a powerful, ruthless tyrant who warns Bud against becoming sexually involved with Deanie: "If anything happened, you'd have to marry her."

The contrasts and conflicts extend to the two leading characters, passionately in love but unwillingly chaste. Deanie is openly vulnerable and uncertain, Bud self-assured on the surface, but inwardly not strong enough to stand up to his father. There's also a similar pattern in the way Audrey Christie's Mrs. Loomis is a throwback to Mrs. Morel in *Sons and Lovers,* while Pat Hingle's Stamper foreshadows the corporate greed of the 1990s. And although Kazan in his autobiography objected to the way *Rebel* made parents the villains, Deanie's mother and Bud's father are clearly the villains of *Splendor.*

When Bud yields to pressure from his father and tells Deanie that he doesn't want to see her anymore, she's at first distracted, then increasingly disoriented. In the schoolroom scene, when the teacher asks her to read a few lines from Wordsworth's "Intimations of Immortality" and explain the feelings they suggest to her, she hesitates, falters, and seems in need of physical support, as if Bud's rejection has cut the ground from under her feet. Then it becomes an almost impossible effort to read the lines, and after starting to explain that they describe the loss of youthful innocence and idealism, she walks up to the teacher, asks in a desperate whisper, "May I please be excused?" and runs out of the room.

As in *Rebel*, Natalie's performance moves from one turning point to another. In the bathtub scene, Deanie reaches the edge of breakdown when Mrs. Loomis asks, "How far have you gone with Bud?" A look of terrible bitterness crosses her face as she says, "I'm *pure*!" Then she starts to thrash about in the water. Mrs. Loomis, who secretly hopes for Deanie to marry Bud because "he'd be quite a catch," suggests getting in touch with his father, and the effect on Deanie is like an electric shock. She sits bolt upright in the tub, face close to camera, eyes dilated. "Don't you dare!" she cries, then starts to scream.

A genuinely frightening moment, followed by the suicide attempt that decides Deanie's parents to commit her to a sanitarium, where she withdraws into an almost equally frightening lethargy. And after her gradual return to life, it's a more "adjusted" but still unfulfilled Deanie who goes to see Bud at the ranch where he's worked since his father lost his money in the Depression and committed suicide.

He's now married a waitress he met at a cafe, and Deanie's about to marry a patient she met at the sanitarium, who's become a successful doctor. It was Kazan's idea for Deanie to "overdress" for the meeting, while Bud looks grimy in overalls and his wife (Zohra Lampert) is visibly pregnant under her housecoat. Natalie recalled at the AFI seminar that Kazan wanted Deanie to feel "kind of foolish" in her white dress and hat, and Zohra Lampert "to feel embarrassed" because Deanie looked so beautiful, but he also wanted them to like each other: "So he created the bond, but he gave a very active, specific direction. He didn't just say, 'Look at your dress.' He said, 'Think, Look how lovely Zohra looks, and how sweet she is.' "

In the poignantly written and acted farewell scene, when Bud walks Deanie out to her car, there's an echo of the lines from Wordsworth's poem and its intimation of emotional loss. They ask each other if they're happy, and each gives the same answer. Happiness is not something they think about very often. But although they don't say it, the looks they exchange imply that they'll always share the memory of "what remains behind." And before she gets in the car, Deanie looks at Bud for what's probably the last time. Wistful and resigned, full of hope and regret, she seems to be looking beyond him to her whole life, past as well as future.

THERE'S NOT MUCH to say about Natalie's Maria in *West Side Story*, the only movie musical whose two leading players are not professional singers or dancers, have fewer dance numbers to perform than the supporting players, and all of whose songs are dubbed. The foreground story, in fact, is a "young love" romance that seems very conventional after *Splendor in the Grass,* and Natalie has to wait until the final sequence for a genuinely dramatic scene.

In *Gypsy,* she felt, she had "one good moment, saying farewell to the boy in the railroad scene"—one of those isolated moments, she explained, when "you feel like you managed to hit a reality level." Unfortunately, her reality is undercut by the studio set, stagy but without the deliberately theatrical flair of Boris Leven's designs for *West Side Story.* Her reality level is less compromised in the "Let Me Entertain You" sequence, as she develops the "refined" style of stripping that surprised and intrigued *Gypsy*'s audience. Called to perform for the first time at short notice, Louise stares at herself in a mirror before going onstage. Her remote expression suggests that she barely recognizes herself in low-cut gown and white gloves; but during the montage that follows her first tentative performance, she becomes increasingly confident, and each time she takes off an additional item of clothing, she seems to discard a piece of her old self.

At first Natalie was as nervous as Louise before her first strip, especially with the real Gypsy Rose Lee, full-figured and five foot ten, watching from the sidelines. But instead of trying to imitate her, Natalie followed her rule of concentrating on the persona of the character she had to play. "You may be totally unlike the person, but if it's written in such a way that it strikes you and you have the response, I think that means you're right for it." She had the response, and the Gypsy she created, although unlike the original, was right on its own terms.

ONE OF THE FEW good things about *The Great Race,* Natalie commented later, was that she had to learn fencing. Other movies required her to become adept at roller-skating, football and tennis, so perhaps George Zepaloff's athletic gene served her well. "Body movement," she believed, "is very important," and in total contrast to Deanie, coltish and hesitant, Angie in *Love with the Proper Stranger* has an abrupt, impatient "out of my way" New York walk.

This movie, like *Splendor*, demonstrates that Natalie was always at her most expressive, and most beautiful, in minimal makeup and simple costumes. The simplicity, of course, is appropriate for a Macy's salesgirl, and allows her to blend perfectly with the everyday locations. In the opening scene, directed by Robert Mulligan with an energy and sharp eye for incidental detail that he sustains throughout the movie, Angie enters a crowded theater where hundreds of jazz musicians are answering calls for gigs. She tracks down one of them (Steve McQueen) to inform him that she's pregnant as a result of their one-night stand. "All I want from you is a doctor—an address, you know." Her nervous defiance unnerves Rocky, who's lived a promiscuous, provisional life and doesn't even remember her. Until the last twenty minutes, the movie's an antiromantic romantic comedy about two people, conflicted in different ways, who fall in love without wanting to or even realizing it. Angie wants to escape from her aggressively protective older brother, head of the family since their father died, but she can't face the prospect of living on her own. She finally decides to make the break, and explains that she's always been scared of independence. But now, she adds after a moment, "I'm not scared. I'm terrified!" This is wonderfully played and timed: the buildup to her confession, the anxious laugh that follows it, the hurried exit that looks more like beating a retreat—and turns out to be exactly that, as the door opens a minute later and she returns, head bowed, unwilling to look the family (or herself) in the eye.

It's as funny and true as a later scene is chilling and true. When Angie agrees to an abortion, Rocky sets up an appointment through a friend. Nothing obviously squalid or melodramatic in the setting, an office and a corridor of an anonymous building in a quiet, anonymous street. In the office at one end of the corridor, a briskly practical woman (not a qualified doctor, as it turns out) unpacks instruments from a suitcase. Angie's mounting unease is intercut with Rocky's mounting discomfort as he waits outside. When Angie's fear proves stronger than her determination, she becomes hysterical; Rocky realizes he can't let Angie go through with it and decides they have to get married instead.

His proposal (indignantly rejected) is reluctant and unloving: "I'm willing to take my medicine." But Steve McQueen, in a performance that matches Natalie's, suggests that Rocky is trying to hide what by now he really feels. Then the script changes gears and resolves the situation in a 1960s equivalent of 1930s romantic comedy. Although skillfully handled, it brings a touch of formula to a movie that's previously avoided it.

Incidental note: Several reviewers objected to the scene at the abortionist's because they felt sure the couple could have afforded a safer one. But how? Apparently it never occurred to them that a salesgirl and a frequently unemployed musician would have very limited resources, even though the movie makes clear that Angie's savings amount to only $200, and Rocky has to borrow $250 to make up the fee—a lot of money for both of them at the time.

> *George Segal: I think* Love with the Proper Stranger *was Natalie's real breakthrough. In* Rebel Without a Cause *she was very promising, but not yet completely secure. And I found her performance in* Splendor in the Grass *a bit Hollywood, maybe because I was expecting a grittier movie from Kazan.*

In the opening scene of *Inside Daisy Clover*, shot on location in fairly broad daylight, Natalie appears as a truculent teenager in torn jeans and shabby sweater. At twenty-six, it's a bit of a stretch, but she's only required to keep up the pretense for another fifteen minutes, during which more persuasive lighting, in night scenes and/or interiors, takes care of the problem.

When the movie studio makes Daisy over, body but not soul, she plays up to her cutely lovable image as "America's Little Valentine," but manages to convey, through body movement, a person alive and well behind her manufactured persona. She wears her elaborate bridal gown as if it doesn't really belong to her; dressed as a choirboy to sing Christmas carols as a publicity stunt, she gives a wonderfully eloquent shrug at her reflection in the mirror; and when she finally walks away from the life that's been superimposed on her own, the tomboy stride returns along with jeans and sweater.

Athough the decision to remove almost all of her voice-over comments, Natalie said later, "was like cutting out half the performance," the half that remains is among her finest, consistently inventive work. And in fact it's more than half. The core of her performance remains, even if some of its comic edge has been peeled away.

*Natalie, in a Romanov dream like her mother*
*almost fifty years earlier, photographed by*
*Michael Childers for the* Anastasia *poster.*
*The production was scheduled to open in March 1982.*

Two scenes, early and late in the movie, are like points of departure and arrival as Daisy travels from scrappy teenager to unwillingly successful young movie star, and from betrayed wife to studio president's mistress. When she first arrives to make a test at the studio, the teenager huddles in a director's chair on the cavernous soundstage, blinking at the spotlight aimed directly at her face. Her posture is defensive, but the way she chews gum is defiant, and as the formidable studio head fires questions at her, she gives as good as she gets.

Much later, Daisy the star enters an almost empty soundstage, like the one she first entered as Daisy the teenager (and like Natalie at six). She wears a tailored suit, appears calm and walks briskly into the sound booth to postsynch her voice in a musical number. But as the same loop of her close shot in the movie appears over and over on the screen, she finds it difficult, then impossible, to synchronize its lip movements. Permanently out of sync with her star image on the screen, the real Daisy beats on the glass wall of her cage in a hysterical attempt at escape. Then she screams.

"Nobody could lose control on the screen like Natalie," George Segal noted when he recalled this scene, Deanie's breakdown in *Splendor in the Grass,* Angie on the verge of hysteria before leaving home in *Love with the Proper Stranger* and Cathy in *The Cracker Factory.*

DURING THE 1960S, Natalie reached her first peak as an actress with four widely different yet emotionally related performances. Deanie, Angie, Daisy, and Alva in *This Property Is Condemned* are all outsiders, at odds with convention and/or their families. But as winner or loser Natalie remained vulnerable, and when she survived, it was always at a cost: one of the reasons that "she appealed across the board," in Arnold Stiefel's view, "to macho men, women, girls, and particularly, because of all her best roles, to gay men."

When Natalie listed the movie directors with whom she had a strong rapport, and for whom she believed that she did her best work, they were all (in varying degrees) "actor's directors," and some of them had been in analysis. Nick Ray, Kazan, Jerry Robbins, Robert Mulligan, Sydney Pollack and Paul Mazursky made her list. Those who did not were either "not psychologically tuned in" to an actor's needs, like Mervyn LeRoy and Blake Edwards, or technicians like Robert Wise, who once said, "That was fine, but next time hold the scissors up a little higher so we can get them in the frame."

IN *THIS PROPERTY IS CONDEMNED,* Alva Starr is a more irretrievably lost girl than Deanie Loomis, and Natalie portrays her with the same delicate yet feverish sympathy. Like *Inside Daisy Clover,* the movie was a commercial failure on its first release, and although its central love story is weakly scripted, and Robert Redford is too dispassionate an actor to convey deep passion, it has strong incidental virtues.

The setting is a backwater southern town during the Depression. The exact year is 1932, as the marquee of the local movie theater advertises Kay Francis and William Powell in *One Way Passage;* and the train station that's nearly always empty suggests somewhere close to the end of the line. James Wong Howe uses subtly desaturated colors to suggest a town with the life seeping out of it, and to point up the contrast of Alva in her defiantly gaudy costumes.

Wong Howe also creates an extraordinary close-up of Natalie (anticipating John Alcott's similar effect in *Barry Lyndon*) by using only real candlelight to frame Alva's face as she blows out the candles on her mother's birthday cake. Its soft, flickering glow makes her look suddenly very young, almost childlike—but only for a moment. Then she turns away and becomes Alva a few years past her youth, flirtatious in a way that suggests she's starting to run out of time.

As her domineering mother, Kate Reid provides another powerful antagonist for Natalie to use emotion memory to play against, and Sydney Pollack's direction is particularly strong in their confrontations, and in the scene when Alva gets drunk before she agrees, as a way of escape, to marry a man she doesn't love. "We started it in the morning," Pollack remembered, "and it didn't feel quite right. Not enough charge. So I decided to break early for lunch, and gave Natalie a glass of wine. She drank it, but said, 'You son of a bitch, are you telling me I can't play this scene without getting drunk?' Then she laughed, and as the wine started to wear off, she asked for more. She drank six glasses in all, played the scene wonderfully—and threw up after finishing it."

Reviews for *This Property Is Condemned* were generally tepid, and (not for the first or last time) one of Natalie's best performances was overlooked. As with the reviews of *Daisy Clover,* she felt "an emotional sharp pain under the heart." But it didn't last long. She knew she'd done good work, and "it didn't change anything" in the sense of making her wonder if she ought to have played the role differently.

ALVA IS the last of Natalie's lost girls; and before portraying two lost ladies, she takes a three-year sabbatical from acting and concentrates on marriage and motherhood. When she returns to movies, it's in the kind of comedy role that she's often looked for and failed to find in the past. But *Bob & Carol & Ted & Alice,* she recalled, was made by "a serious filmmaker." In the opening "group encounter" scenes, when Carol (Natalie) almost breaks down as the relationship with her husband (Robert Culp) threatens to unravel, Paul Mazursky not only encouraged both actors to improvise, but recalled his own experience at Esalen with his wife, and as he got "very involved, he started to cry." Like his love of rehearsal, it reminded Natalie of Nick Ray and Kazan.

Although the only star name in an ensemble movie, Natalie never acts like one, and her performance stands out by refusing to stand out. It's sharp and funny, but not patronizing, like the movie itself. Affectionately indulgent toward his characters' obsession with "self-realization" and "relating," Mazursky could also be ruthless, notably in his portrait of a psychiatrist oozing with self-satisfaction and superior knowledge.

The final scene, at a hotel suite in Las Vegas, where the "liberated" quartet decides "to have an orgy, then go see Tony Bennett," was not fully scripted. Mazursky and his co-writer, Larry Tucker, were uncertain what exactly was going to happen, but Mazursky closed the set and played Cheshire Cat to the cast. After encouraging the actors to expect "something very wild and sexual," he started the scene with three of the four side by side in the king-size bed, waiting for Ted (Elliott Gould) to finish brushing his teeth in the bathroom. Then Ted got in bed next to Carol, and Mazursky told his actors, "Do whatever you feel like doing." As he suspected, both couples eventually felt like putting the brakes on "sexual freedom" by not going through with the orgy. And the decisive moment was a gesture by Natalie: "Almost at once she played the aggressor with Gould, who was shy at first but got warmed up. We had to work out her movements, to avoid frontal nudity which was not permitted in 1969. Then Elliott and Bob [Culp] decided to have a brief discussion about the stock market. It was followed by a funny, awkward silence that Natalie broke by doing something beautiful. She kissed Elliott very tenderly."

When *Bob & Carol* opened in the fall of 1969, the old major studio heads were retired or dead. Conglomerates had taken over MGM, Paramount and Warner Bros., and their studios had become technical plants, with more than half their stages leased to TV companies or independently financed movies. Continuity of production, the mainstay of the old system, no longer existed; but the major TV networks created an approximate substitute with miniseries and "Movies of the Week." They successfully courted older stars like Barbara Stanwyck and Bette Davis, and at a time when Natalie had to make do with *Peeper* and *Meteor* on the big screen, the smaller one provided three of the best roles of her career.

These roles offered emotional continuity, in the form of conflicted characters with a wide range of the "turning points" she always looked for; and *Cat on a Hot Tin Roof,* its opening scene virtually a six-page monologue by Maggie with a few brief interruptions from Brick, was particularly demanding. In a voice that Tennessee Williams describes in a stage direction as "rapid and drawling," and that echoes Maggie's frequent mood swings, she's alternately fierce and disconsolate, driving and driven, "oddly funny" and "near-hysterical."

Toward the end of the scene (played to four cameras without a break), Natalie gives a brilliant display, within the space of a minute, of the angry Cat who tells Brick that his indifference has made her go through "this hideous—*transformation,* become hard! *Frantic!* I'm not— thin-skinned any more, can't afford t'be thin-skinned any more." Then, suddenly tired, she stops clawing at him, becomes "a pleading child" and confesses in a low, clenched voice: "I get—lonely. Very!"

> *Natalie Wood: I often feel it's such an odd chemistry between all of it when it goes well. But that's your reward. That's why you do it ultimately.*

In *From Here to Eternity,* Buzz Kulik introduces Karen with an exterior shot as she walks to Schofield barracks, wearing a bright yellow halter and white skirt. It's another wonderfully expressive walk: at once tired and determined, and the look on her face has the kind of hostility that disguises loneliness. During her affair with Milt Warden, Karen tries to play the aggressor, but it's a mask to conceal her vulnerability, like the sudden blank expression that crosses her face after she starts to reveal herself, then cuts off.

The desperation underlying their affair, more naked than in the original movie, leads to a breakup that's less sentimental. A few terse criticisms of the first-draft script in her exercise book show Natalie on the lookout for any sign of compromise with her character. (On Karen's first scene with Milt: "Boring. No particular tension. In original [novel] they were *adversaries*." And when the affair is almost over, she notes disapprovingly that Karen "starts to CRY. Wishy-washy!") By the end of the movie, as Karen realizes she has no future with Milt, but fears she has no future without him, Natalie's performance has come full circle. Karen is left emotionally as uncertain and inaccessible as she appeared in the opening shot.

In *The Cracker Factory,* she's even more uncompromising: no attempt to soft-pedal the character's bitter, angry, self-destructive side, or to flinch from the distorting lenses of "Ugly Number One" and "Ugly Number Two." When Natalie started reading Richard Shapiro's script, "on page four the love took place"; but as Burt Brinckerhoff recalled, she was at once deeply involved with the character and in full command of her technique. For "one very emotional scene, when she was walking along the corridor to her hospital room," he decided to use two cameras for a single take, one pulling back in front of her, one tracking her from behind. When Natalie opened the door to her room and suddenly stopped, Brinckerhoff assumed she was preparing for "an emotional moment." Instead, she turned back and said, "My slippers are in the wrong place."

Brinckerhoff also recalled "Natalie's flirtatious sense of humor" in the scene when Cathy returns to the hospital at night after getting drunk at a local bar: "She had a drunken grin on her face, but had to sneak past a nurse and wasn't sure how to play it. She was wearing a woolen hat, and I suggested that she pull it over her face. She liked the idea, and when she did that, it was like a magician's trick. After she got past the nurse, she raised the hat again—and her face was dead sober."

NATALIE'S DEATH at forty-three was not only a personal tragedy. It cut off an actress in her prime. As well as knowing that the movie industry considered iconic female stars past their prime at forty, she was aware that the growing corporate takeover of Hollywood had increased the threat to creative work. But she also knew, as she once said, that "you have to keep up." So her first reaction had been to try and make a new career for herself in the theater.

Would she have succeeded? It's very possible, but not certain. Although vocal training had extended the range and flexibility of her voice over the years, it needed to acquire more projection for the theater. She knew this as well, and planned to take an intensive course of vocal exercises. But if *Anastasia* failed, Natalie was left with two choices: to accept forgettable supporting roles in forgettable movies, or to become a producer. The first would never have satisfied her; the second might eventually have proved a solution.

Over the past thirteen years she had done her most creative work on the small screen, and during the 1980s TV still offered hope for someone as committed as herself. Years of making "obligation" movies under assembly-line conditions had not worn down her talent, or the "something extra" that so often seemed to mirror Natalie's own personality— radiant and edgy, stubborn and fragile. And the independent-film movement that gathered momentum by the end of the decade might well have decided her to become a producer and make the movies of her choice by setting up projects (like *Zelda*) that the major studios had rejected.

For the movie actor, "something extra" implies an emotional and physical transaction between the audience and an image on the screen. It's instantaneous, like love at first sight, and in Natalie's case the first shot of her in *Tomorrow Is Forever* sealed the transaction. A tiny seven-year-old walks hand in hand along a street with Orson Welles, who overshadows her physically, of course, and yet the eye is drawn to this mysteriously composed child. You want to know more about her, just as you want to know more about the adolescent at juvenile hall in *Rebel Without a Cause,* who wears too much makeup and seems as mysteriously tense as the child in *Tomorrow Is Forever* was composed. In the same way, the adult Natalie immediately catches the eye with a minimum of "acting." In the opening shots of *Love with the Proper Stranger,* when she hurries into a New York theater crowded with jazz musicians, and looks around in a way that suggests she's a stranger in that world, you wonder what brought her there and why she's so anxiously determined. And sixteen years later, when the housewife in *The Cracker Factory* pushes her shopping cart along a supermarket aisle, why does the

apparently simple act of hesitating about what to buy suggest that her confusion lies much deeper?

In an unusually reflective moment, Bette Davis gave her own definition of "something extra," which she herself had in spades. "The real actor," she said, "has a direct line to the collective heart." It explains why, when Natalie Wood died, the collective and the personal loss became one.

# NOTES ON SOURCES

*(Not acknowledged in text)*

## Chapter 1: Out of Russia

Stella Adler epigraph: *On Ibsen, Strindberg and Chekhov* (Knopf, New York, 1999). Gerhardie: Dido Davies, *William Gerhardie* (Oxford University Press, New York, 1990). Bunin quote: Foreword to *Wolves and Other Love Stories* (Capra, Santa Barbara, 1989). Russia 1918: John Lawrence, *A History of Russia* (Meridian, New York, 1957). Zudilovs in Russia and Harbin: Olga Viripaeff and Constantin Liuzunie to author; Soren Clausen and Stig Dagerson: *Harbin: The Making of a Chinese City* (Sharpe, New York, 1995). Zacharenkos in Russia and Shanghai: Olga Viripaeff and Dmitri Zacharenko to author. Lepkos in Russia and Shanghai: Irene (Lepko) Agnew to author; Stella Day: *Shanghai, The Rise and Fall of a Decadent City* (Morrow, New York, 2000). Maria Gurdin interview quotes: Georgia Holt and Phyllis Quinn, with Sue Russell, *Star Mothers* (Simon & Schuster, New York, 1988). Russians in San Francisco: Olga Viripaeff, Nina Jaure, Natasha Lofft, Constantin Liuzunie to author. Gurdins in Santa Rosa: Olga Viripaeff to author; Ed Canevari in *Santa Rosa Democrat,* June 17, 2001. Gurdins in Hollywood, Natalie's test: Olga Viripaeff to author. Maria as driver: Olga Viripaeff to author. Maria on the set: Lon McCallister to author.

## Chapter 2: Lost Childhood

Wagner epigraph: to author. Roddy McDowall on child actors: *Starring Natalie Wood* (TV) (Ellen M. Krass Productions, 1987). Welles on Pichel: Welles and Peter Bogdanovich, *This Is Orson Welles* (Da Capo, New York, 1998). Lepkos and Gurdins in Hollywood: Irene Agnew to author. Hollywood and House Un-American Activities Committee: Otto Friedrich, *City of Nets* (Harper & Row, New York, 1986). Irving Pichel: obituaries in Margaret Herrick Library. Natalie as child actress: Lon McCallister and Maureen O'Hara to author. *The Bride Wore Boots:* Ella Smith, *Starring Miss Barbara Stanwyck* (Crown, New York, 1974). Background to *Driftwood: American Film Institute Catalog of American Films, 1941–50* (University of California Press, 1999). Natalie in *Driftwood:* Mary Sale to author; Allan Dwan in Peter Bogdanovich, *Who the Devil Made It* (Knopf, New York, 1997). Michael Panaieff and Tamara Lepko: Irene Agnew, Robert Banas to author; Larry Billman: *Film Choreographers and Dance Directors* (McFarland & Co., Jefferson, North Carolina, 1997). Andrew Paris letter: Natalie Wood private archive. Edmund Gwenn on dying: Natalie Wood, American Film Institute (AFI) Seminar, 1979. *No Sad Songs for Me:* Lawrence J. Quirk, *Margaret Sullavan*

(St. Martin's Press, New York, 1986). Natalie and Nick Gurdin on *Never a Dull Moment* set: Peggy Griffin to author. Nina takes Natasha Zepaloff to meet Maria and Natalie: Nina Jaure and Natasha Lofft to author. *The Green Promise: AFI Catalog of American Films, 1941–50.* Accident on bridge: Olga Viripaeff to author. Jim Williams on himself and Natalie: Suzanne Finstad, *Natasha* (Harmony Books, New York, 2001). Olga Viripaeff's rebuttal: Olga to author.

## Chapter 3: Growing Pains

Epigraph: Donfeld to author. Natalie at Esalen: Donfeld, Stanislav and Christina Grof to author. Jack the Jabber: Mart Crowley to author. Beverly Hills Halloween: Natalie Wood to author. *Pride of the Family:* Fay Wray, *On the Other Hand* (St. Martin's Press, New York, 1989). Natalie's Warner Bros. contract: Warner Bros. file, USC Special Collections. *Rebel Without a Cause:* Richard Beymer, Dennis Hopper, Stewart Stern to author; Natalie Wood at AFI Seminar. Natalie's report card: Natalie Wood private archive; Natalie to author. Graduation: Olga Viripaeff to author. *The Searchers:* Natalie Wood at AFI Seminar. Jack Warner and 3331 Laurel Canyon Boulevard: Jack Warner file, USC. John Ford and Robert Wagner: Wagner to author. Nick Ray and Natalie's urine sample: Wagner to author. *Heidi* and death of James Dean: Jeannie Carson to author. *A Cry in the Night:* Natalie Wood, AFI Seminar. *The Burning Hills:* Warner Bros. files, USC. Natalie's wristband: Donfeld to author. Maria and Henry Willson, Natalie at parties: John Carlyle to author. Willson and "respectability": Nan Morris Robinson to author. Tab Hunter and Natalie: Hunter to author. Natalie and Hugh O'Brian: Olga Viripaeff to author. Natalie and gay men: Robert Wagner to author. Natalie on Elvis Presley: Sarah Gregson to author. Norman Brokaw, Natalie and Maria: Brokaw to author. Karl Malden and Natalie: Malden to author. Natalie and Robert Wagner's courtship: Wagner to author; Natalie Wood in *American Weekly* (5/19/58), confirmed by Wagner to author. Wagner on rumors of male lovers: Wagner to author. Natalie and Natasha Zepaloff: Natasha Lofft to author. Herman Wouk and Natalie: Wouk in *American Weekly* (5/11/58). Natalie and Claire Trevor on *Marjorie Morningstar:* Donfeld and the late Claire Trevor to author. Wagner on *Morningstar* location: Wagner to author. Natalie and *Kings Go Forth:* Norman Brokaw to author. Frank Sinatra: Tom Kuntz and Phil Kuntz, *The Sinatra Files* (Three Rivers Press, New York, 2000). Natalie as flirt: James B. Sikking to author. Natalie's journal: Natalie Wood private archive.

## Chapter 4: Love and Marriage

Epigraph quotes: Natasha Gregson Wagner and Robert Wagner to author. Bridal shower and train to Phoenix: Mary Sale to author. Jack Warner's gift: Jack Warner file, USC. Honeymoon: Natalie Wood in *American Weekly;* Robert Wagner to author. Natalie on Sinatra show: Warner Bros. files, USC. All Steve Trilling memos: Warner Bros. files, USC. Natalie and *The Devil's Disciple:* Steve Trilling memo. Suspension: Warner Bros. files. Robert Wagner on Nick Gurdin's drunken driving, and Maria's reaction to leaving 3331 Laurel Canyon Boulevard: Wagner to author. Natalie's new contract: Warner Bros. files, USC. Natalie on negotiations with Warner: Roy Plomley, *Plomley's Pick* (Weidenfeld & Nicolson, London, 1982). Hated *Cash McCall:* Mart Crowley to author. Natalie's letter to Warner on return to work: Jack Warner files, USC. Tab Hunter buys out contract: Hunter to author. 714 North Beverly Drive: Mart Crowley and Asa Maynor to author. Natalie on bathtub and marriage: Arnold Schulman to author. FBI surveillance at Atlantic City party: *The Sinatra Files.* Barbara Gould and Nick Adams: Robert Wagner to author. Natalie and Mrs. Wagner: Mart Crowley to author. Lana pushed into background: Robert Banas and Gigi Perreau to author. Olga disagrees: Olga Viripaeff to author. Natalie on Lana: Peggy Griffin to author. *Bob Hope Show:* Warner Bros. files, USC. Inge and Natalie: Robert Wagner to author. Kazan–Jack Warner correspondence: Warner Bros. files, USC. Natalie's "game" with Warner Bros.: Natalie Wood, AFI Seminar. *Splendor in the Grass,* Natalie and RJ's marriage, Natalie and Warren Beatty, "everybody on the emotional edge," suicide scene: Mart Crowley to author. Beatty's proposal: Joan Collins, *Past Imperfect* (Simon & Schuster, New York, 1984). Bathtub scene: Natalie Wood, AFI Seminar. Kazan's version of suicide scene: Elia Kazan, *A Life* (Knopf, New York, 1988). Natalie on Kazan as "trickster": Robert Wagner to author. Casting of *West Side Story:* Donfeld to author; United Artists files, USC. Jerry Robbins and Robert Wise view *Splendor* footage: Robbins in *Starring Natalie Wood. West Side Story:* Robert Banas, Richard Beymer, Mart Crowley, Donfeld, Rita Stone to author. Natalie on Robbins: AFI Seminar. Natalie and *Rome Adventure:* Mart Crowley to author. Natalie granted indefinite leave: Warner Bros. files, USC. Marriage breakup: Robert Wagner and Mart Crowley to author. The "nucleus": Asa Maynor to author.

## Chapter 5: Love and Marriage (Encore)

Epigraph quotes: to author. Warren Beatty: Leslie Caron and Guy McElwaine to author. Natalie at Chalon Road, *All Fall Down* location, St. Ives Drive after Bel-Air fire: Mart Crowley to author. RJ's note: Natalie Wood private archive. Leonard Spigelgass, Delmer Daves and Jule Styne on *Gypsy:* Warner Bros. files, USC. Karl Malden on LeRoy and Rosalind Russell: Malden to author. Natalie on LeRoy: AFI Seminar. Natalie's confrontation scene with Mama Rose: Mart Crowley to author. Nick Gurdin loses driver's license: Robert Wagner to author. Natalie and Dr. Lindon: Asa Maynor to author. Natalie's daybooks: Natalie Wood private archive. Start of Natalie's dependence on sleeping pills: Guy McElwaine to author. Natalie and President Kennedy: Robert Wagner to author. Wagner on *The Longest Day:* George Segal to author. RJ, David Niven, Marion Donen and Mart Crowley in Rome: Robert Wagner, Mart Crowley and Kate Wagner to author. Donen's detective: Robert Wagner, Mart Crowley to author. McElwaine and Schoenfeld: McElwaine to author. *Love with the Proper Stranger:* Robert Mulligan and Arnold Schulman to author. Robbins proposes marriage: Robert Wagner and Mart Crowley to author. Arthur Loew and Natalie: Stewart Stern to author. Edith Piaf project: Donfeld to author. *Cassandra at the Wedding:* Mart Crowley and Martin Manulis to author. RJ and Natalie at Arthur Loew's house: Robert Wagner to author. Maria and Natasha Zepaloff visit Natalie: Natasha Lofft to author. Natalie and Paul Ziffren: Micky Ziffren to author. Russian Easter lunch: Stewart Stern to author. Natalie on Arthur Loew: Natalie Wood to author. Natalie and RJ at La Scala: Mart Crowley to author. Natalie at Hollywood parties: Donfeld, Dominick Dunne, Asa Maynor and Richard Gregson to author. Natalie as friend: Tom Mankiewicz and Mart Crowley to author. Frances Klampt: RJ and Maureen O'Hara to author; Shirley Temple, *Child Star* (McGraw-Hill, New York, 1988). *The Great Race:* Donfeld and Jack Lemmon to author; Natalie Wood at AFI Seminar; Warner Bros. files, USC. Natalie's dislike of Tony Curtis: Robert Wagner to author. David Lange and Natalie: Lange to author. Paris nightclub tour: Donfeld to author. Natalie's suicide attempt: Mart Crowley and David Lange to author. Warren Beatty at house: Beatty, Mart Crowley to author. *Inside Daisy Clover* contract: Warner Bros. files, USC. *Daisy Clover* in production: Natalie Wood, AFI Seminar. Encounter on set with RJ: Robert Wagner to author; William Goldman, *Adventures in the Screen Trade* (Warner Books, New York, 1973). Ladislow Blatnik and Natalie: Asa Maynor and Mart Crowley to author. Natalie and *This Property Is Condemned:* Sydney Pollack to author. John Houseman and *This Property:* Houseman, *Final Dress* (Simon & Schuster, New York, 1983). Ralph Roberts letter to Natalie: Natalie Wood private archive. Richard Gregson and Natalie: Gregson to author. Henry Jaglom and Natalie: Jaglom to author. *Harvard Lampoon:* Natalie Wood in *Starring Natalie Wood.* Natalie and Gregson in London: Gregson and Delphine Mann to author. Return to Los Angeles and episode with Nicky Hilton: Richard Gregson to author. Natalie and Eugene McCarthy: Micky Ziffren to author. Natalie and Gregson back in London: Gregson to author. Natalie, Paul Mazursky and *Bob & Carol & Ted & Alice:* Mazursky to author. Marriage and honeymoon of Natalie and Gregson, Natalie pregnant, start of problems: Gregson to author.

## Chapter 6: First and Last Things

Natalie epigraph on first pregnancy: *Starring Natalie Wood.* Mankiewicz and Wagner epigraphs: to author. Foreman party: Linda Foreman and Robert Wagner to author. Natalie, "I've fallen in love": John Irvin to author. Natalie and motherhood: Leslie Caron, David Lange to author. *The Headshrinker's Test:* Richard Gregson to author. Ann Watson: Guy McElwaine and Sarah Gregson to author. Poolside barbecue, phone call and consequences: Richard Gregson and George Rondo to author. Natalie forgetting keys: Robert Wagner to author. Trip to Europe: Mart Crowley, Olga Viripaeff to author. Property settlement: Natalie Wood private archive. RJ and *Rosemary's Baby:* Mart Crowley to author. Steve McQueen call: Robert Wagner to author. Smedley's letter: Natalie Wood private archive. Lana Wood loans, visits to Wagner house: Elizabeth Applegate and Wagner to author. Maria and Natasha in Palm Springs: Robert and Natasha Gregson Wagner to author. Norma Crane and radiation treatment: Sue Barton and Mart Crowley to author. Natalie's remarks at funeral: Natalie Wood private archive. 603 North Canon Drive as "family house": Robert and Kate Wagner, Asa Maynor to author. Studio raids: Mart Crowley to author. Natalie as mother: Natasha Gregson Wagner and Richard Gregson to author. Natalie's letters to RJ: courtesy of

Robert Wagner. *Splendour:* Guy McElwaine, Delphine Mann. Natalie at San Francisco Film Festival: Arnold Stiefel, Mart Crowley to author. *Cat on a Hot Tin Roof:* Natalie Wood at AFI Seminar; Derek Granger and Robert Wagner to author; Anthony Holden, *Laurence Olivier* (Atheneum, New York, 1988). Natalie and RJ in Hawaii: Tom Mankiewicz, James B. Sikking, Mart Crowley, and Robert Wagner to author. *From Here to Eternity:* Natalie Wood, AFI Seminar. *The Cracker Factory:* Burt Brinckerhoff to author; Natalie Wood, AFI Seminar. Natalie in Moscow: Peter Ustinov and RJ to author; Natalie Wood, AFI Seminar. Nick Gurdin's heart attack: Peggy Griffin to author. Natalie's directives to physicians: Natalie Wood private archive. *The Mirror Crack'd:* Barry Sandler to author. Natalie's hospital visit to Nick Gurdin: Mart Crowley to author. Eulogy: Natalie Wood private archive. Nick and burial in Serbian cemetery: Olga Viripaeff to author. Vladimir Zacharenko's letter to Wagners: Natalie Wood private archive. Natalie and *Zelda:* John Irvin to author. Natalie at Rochford Clinic: Jeffery Rochford to author. "Never told RJ": Robert Wagner to author. Natalie's first impressions of Walken: John Irvin, Donfeld to author. Edith Head to Good Samaritan: Donfeld to author. Natalie on *Brainstorm* location: Robert Wagner, Michael Childers, Donfeld, Stan and Christina Grof to author. Olivier cable and Viveca Lindfors letter: Natalie Wood private archive. Natalie's conditions for *Life* feature: Donfeld to author. Natalie and Walken at Roddy McDowall's: Dennis Osborne to author. Memo to Stan Kamen: Natalie Wood private archive. Natalie on Edith Head: Mike Steen, *Hollywood Speaks* (Putnam, New York, 1974). Thanksgiving dinner: Delphine Mann to author. Natalie to Sophie Irvin about the ocean: John Irvin to author. Dennis Davern and boat: Robert Wagner to author. Last weekend on boat and Catalina: Robert Wagner to author. Natalie's phone calls from Catalina: Mart Crowley and Josh Donen to author. Kurt Craig, Dennis Davern, Ann Laughton, Robert Wagner, Christopher Walken, Linda Winkler statements: L.A. police records. The search: Robert Wagner and Douglas Bombard to author; Thomas T. Noguchi, with Joseph de Mana, *Coroner* (Simon & Schuster, New York, 1984). 603 North Canon before the funeral: Elizabeth Applegate, Josh Donen, Tom Mankiewicz, Guy McElwaine, Robert Wagner to author. Preparing Natalie's body: Mart Crowley to author. Telegrams: Elizabeth Applegate to author. Richard Gregson, Natasha, Courtney, and Liz Applegate at mortuary: Gregson, Natasha Gregson Wagner, and Applegate to author. Elizabeth Taylor arrival: Liz Applegate and Arnold Stiefel to author. Rock Hudson and Fred Astaire: Donfeld to author. List of pallbearers at funeral: Natalie Wood private archive. Natasha and Courtney at funeral: Richard Gregson to author. RJ's interview with Rasure: Robert Wagner to author. RJ "tried . . . to make sense of what happened": Mart Crowley to author. RJ's discussion with Doug Bombard: Bombard to author. Blatnik in Gstaad: Robert Wagner to author. Lana Wood and Natalie's clothes: Liz Applegate, Natasha Gregson Wagner and Robert Wagner to author. Maria colorful again: Natasha Lofft to author. Lana at Maria's condo, her constant requests for loans: Liz Applegate and Robert Wagner to author. RJ moves Maria to Barrington Plaza: Liz Applegate and Robert Wagner to author. Maria and Alzheimer's: Natasha Gregson Wagner, Natasha Lofft and Robert Wagner to author. Zepaloff and dementia: Natasha Lofft to author.

## Chapter 7: Something Extra

Kazan epigraph: *Starring Natalie Wood.* Natalie epigraph: AFI Seminar. Mary Astor on Elizabeth Taylor: Mary Astor, *A Life on Film* (Delacorte Press, New York, 1971). Margaret O'Brien and Natalie's monkey imitation: Suzanne Finstad, *Natasha.* Kazan and Peggy Ann Garner: Kazan, *A Life.* Natalie on Actors Studio: AFI Seminar. George Seaton and Edmund Gwenn discussing comedy: Natalie Wood, AFI Seminar. Allan Dwan on Republic: Peter Bogdanovich, *Who the Devil Made It.* Kazan and *Splendor in the Grass,* "one good moment" in *Gypsy,* "body movement is very important": Natalie Wood, AFI Seminar. All quotes from George Segal: Segal to author. Natalie's list of actor-friendly directors: AFI Seminar. Natalie in *This Property:* Sydney Pollack to author. "Orgy" scene in *Bob & Carol:* Paul Mazursky to author. Natalie in *The Cracker Factory:* Burt Brinckerhoff to author. Bette Davis quote: Robert I. Fitzhenry: *Barnes & Noble Book of Quotations* (Barnes & Noble Books, New York, 1987).

# ACKNOWLEDGMENTS

THIS BOOK owes its primary existence to Robert Wagner, who once said to me: "When you tell the truth about Natalie as you see it, I shall be at peace."

The cooperation that he offered was indispensable and in every sense unconditional. He never attempted to influence what I wrote or declared any topic off bounds; he talked very openly, and offered many valuable leads. I'm equally grateful for the same cooperation and openness to a few others who were particularly close to Natalie: Elizabeth Applegate, Mart Crowley, Donfeld, Richard Gregson, Olga Viripaeff, Courtney Wagner, Kate Wagner and Natasha Gregson Wagner.

Equal thanks, also, to others who agreed to talk about Natalie, Maria Gurdin and/or the Russian connection, in person, by phone or by e-mail: Irene Agnew, Elizabeth Ashley, Robert Banas, Sue Barton, Warren Beatty, Richard Benson, Charles Berliner, Richard Beymer, Douglas Bombard, Burt Brinckerhoff, Norman Brokaw, the late John Carlyle, Leslie Caron, Carlton Carpenter, Jeannie Carson, Michael Childers, Dick Clayton, Tom Courtenay, Trent Dolan, Josh Donen, Dominick Dunne, Linda Foreman, Derek Granger, Sarah Gregson, Peggy Griffin, Christina and Stanislav Grof, Dennis Hopper, Tab Hunter, John Irvin, Henry Jaglom, Jim Janisch, Nina Jaure, David Lange, Hope Lange, Jack Larson, the late Jack Lemmon, Constantin Liuzunie, Natasha Lofft, Karl Malden, Tom Mankiewicz, Delphine Mann, Martin Manulis, Asa Maynor, Paul Mazursky, Lon McCallister, Guy McElwaine, Juliet Mills, Robert Mulligan, Ronald Neame, Connie Nichols, Maureen O'Hara, Dennis Osborne, Gigi Perreau, Jeffery Rochford, Sydney Pollack, Richard Polo, George Rondo, Mary Sale, Barry Sandler, Arnold Schulman, George Segal, James B. Sikking, Stewart Stern, Arnold Stiefel, Rita Stone, the late Claire Trevor, Sir Peter Ustinov, Dmitri Viripaeff, Jill St. John Wagner, Marion (Donen) Wagner, Dmitri Zacharenko, Micky Ziffren.

Many thanks also to Sandra Archer and the staff of the Margaret Herrick Library, Academy of Motion Picture Arts and Sciences, for their informed help and cooperation; Michael Childers for such beautiful prints of his photographs of Natalie; Dominick Dunne for his private photographs of Natalie; Peter Fitzgerald for a VHS of his documentary *West Side Stories;* Ron Levaco for a VHS of his documentary *Round Eyes in the Middle Kingdom,* about Russian refugees in China; Dennis Osborne for a VHS of Natalie among the guests at an all-star 1965 Roddy McDowall party; Richard Shapiro for a VHS of *The Cracker Factory;* Nan Morris Robinson, former Henry Willson associate, for background information on Willson; Miles Kreuger, historian of the American musical theater, for verifying the singers who dubbed Natalie's vocals; Olga

Viripaeff, Constantin Liuzunie and Natasha Lofft for invaluable family photographs and documentation; Linda Foreman for Natalie's letter to John Foreman; Sarah Gregson for Natalie's letters to her; Noelle Carter and Ned Comstock at University of Southern California Cinema and Television Library, Special Collections, for allowing me to consult the Warner Bros., Jack Warner, Natalie Wood and United Artists files; and the Museum of Television and Radio, Beverly Hills, for arranging viewings of *Cat on a Hot Tin Roof, From Here to Eternity, I'm a Fool, Heidi, Miracle at Potters Farm,* and the *AFI Tribute to Orson Welles.*

Finally, as always, many thanks to my always creative editor, Victoria Wilson.

# INDEX